The Supreme Court in the Early Republic:

The Chief Justiceships of John Jay and Oliver Ellsworth

John Jay, in a portrait believed to have been begun by Gilbert Stuart, ca. 1793, and completed by John Trumbull, ca. 1806. Oil on canvas (NPG. 74.46, National Portrait Gallery, Smithsonian Institution).

Oliver Ellsworth. Pastel on paper attributed to James Sharples, ca. 1796 (courtesy of Independence National Historical Park, Philadelphia).

The Supreme Court in the Early Republic:

The Chief Justiceships of John Jay and Oliver Ellsworth

by William R. Casto

University of South Carolina Press

CHIEF JUSTICESHIPS OF THE
UNITED STATES SUPREME COURT

Herbert A. Johnson, General Editor

© 1995 University of South Carolina

Cloth edition published by the University of South Carolina Press, 1995
Paperback edition published in Columbia, South Carolina,
by the University of South Carolina Press, 2012

www.sc.edu/uscpress

Manufactured in the United States of America

21 20 19 18 17 16 15 14 13 12   10 9 8 7 6 5 4 3 2 1

The Library of Congress has cataloged the cloth edition as follows:

Casto, William R., 1946–
    The Supreme Court in the early republic : the chief justiceships of John Jay and
Oliver Ellsworth / by William R. Casto.
        p. cm. — (Chief justiceships of the United States Supreme Court)
        Includes bibliographical references and index.
        ISBN 1-57003-033-2
        1. United States. Supreme Court—History—18th century. 2. Political questions
    and judicial power—United States—History—18th century. 3. United States—Politics
    and government—1783–1809. 4. Jay, John, 1745–1829. 5. Ellsworth, Oliver, 1745–1807.
    I. Title. II. Series.
    KF8742.C36 1995
    347.73'2609033—dc20   94-18750
    [347.3073509033]   CIP

ISBN: 978-1-61117-147-1   (pbk)

for
Pamela Collette Casto
my beloved wife

CONTENTS

Editor's Preface   xi

Preface and Acknowledgments   xv

Repository Symbols   xvii

Short Titles and Abbreviations   xix

Introduction   1

1 Creating the Court   4
   The Federal Courts' Subject-Matter Jurisdiction   5
   Judicial Appointments   16
   Good Behavior and Compensation   18
   Judicial Review   19
   Nonjudicial Duties   23
   Looking to the Future   25

2 The Judiciary Act of 1789   27
   Drafting the Judiciary Act   27
   Opposition to the Federal Courts   29
   The Seeds of a Compromiss   31
   Limiting the Supreme Court's Jurisdiction   33
   Federal Trial Courts: Admiralty Jurisdiction   38
   Shaping the Compromise on Federal Trial Courts   41
   The Congress Accepts Ellsworth's Compromise   47
   Congressional Instrumentalism   51

3 Selecting the Justices and Initial Operations   54
   The First Nominees   56
   Assessing Washington's Nomination Criteria   65

4 A National Security Court   71
      The Nootka Sound Crisis   71
      Relations with France and Great Britain   72
      The Neutrality Proclamation   74
      The Treaty of Alliance and the Correspondence of the Justices   75
      Admiralty Jurisdiction I: *Glass v. The Sloop Betsy*   82
      The Jay Treaty I: Extrajudicial Service   87
      The Jay Treaty II: The Rutledge Fiasco   90
      Oliver Ellsworth and Samuel Chase   95
      The Jay Treaty III: Advisory Opinions   97
      The British Debt Cases   98
      The Power to Tax   101
      Admiralty Jurisdiction II: *La Vengeance*   105
      La Vengeance: Majority Opinions and Chiefly Leadership   110
      Admiralty Jurisdiction III: Restitution of Prizes   112
      The Jay Treaty IV: Sale of Prizes   115
      Bushrod Washington   117
      The Quasi-War I: The Ellsworth Mission   118
      Alfred Moore   120
      The Quasi-War II: *Bas v. Tingy*   120
      The Quasi-War III: Chief Justice Ellsworth Resigns   124

5 National Security and Federal Criminal Law   126
      Political Grand Jury Charges   126
      Common-Law Crimes   129
      Enforcing the Law of Nations   130
      Beyond the Law of Nations: The *Worrall* Case   141
      The Problem of Seditious Libel   147
      Federal Common Law and the *Williams* Case   152
      The *Williams* Case and Interstitial Federal Common Law   154
      Common-Law Crimes and Common-Law Thinking   155
      Statutory Crimes: The Whiskey Rebellion   163
      Statutory Crimes: Justice Chase on Circuit   165

6 Nonjudicial Activities   173
      Ex-Officio Duties   174
      The Invalid Pensioners Act   175
      Advisory Opinions   178
      A Pragmatic Approach to Nonjudicial Activities   180

7 The Constitution and State Sovereignty 184
   Chisholm v. Georgia 188
   The Eleventh Amendment 197
   The Scope of the Eleventh Amendment 202
   Suits by Foreign States 203
   Suits in Admiralty 204
   Enforcement of Federal Rights 205
   The Federalists and the Eleventh Amendment 211

8 The Court and the Constitution 213
   Judicial Review of Federal Actions 214
   The Sovereignty of the People 215
   Justice Chase's Doubts 220
   Interpreting the Constitution 222
   Congressional Power to Restrict Jurisdiction 239

9 An Assessment 247

Table of Cases 255

Index 259

EDITOR'S PREFACE

The volumes in this series are intended to provide readers with a convenient scholarly introduction to the work and achievements of the Supreme Court of the United States for the period of one or more chief justiceships. An effort will be made to examine the Court's personnel and administration and to summarize its contribution in constitutional law, international law, and private law.

While the periodization of the separate volumes follows the now well established historical tradition of focusing upon the chief justices, it should be emphasized that there is no intention to defend the doubtful thesis that the presiding officer of the Supreme Court is its dominant member. Custom and tradition assign certain administrative responsibilities to the chief justice, and it is these functions which distinguish his service from that of his associate justices. This institutional management role justifies our decision to divide the series into monographs delineated by chief justiceships. Leadership in the Supreme Court is predominantly a function of interpersonal relationships. The chief justice lacks authority to command obedience even in administrative matters. He must rely upon and cultivate the respect and deference that his associate justices are willing to accord him. Any scholarly attention to the role of the chief justice inevitably requires close examination of all relationships among the justices.

Professor Casto's volume draws upon his extensive study of the Supreme Court in the earliest decade of its history, and more particularly upon his biographer's knowledge of the life and career of Oliver Ellsworth, who was not only the third Chief Justice of the United States but also one of the prime architects of the Judiciary Act of 1789. It provides valuable insights into Court activities during the Federalist administrations of George Washington and John Adams. Until recently this has been a neglected period of Supreme Court history, largely eclipsed by

the great changes in administration and jurisprudential direction introduced by Chief Justice John Marshall beginning in 1801. Publication of
the manuscript collection of the Court's earliest years is now underway,
and this monograph's many citations to those original sources evidences
the great contributions being made by Dr. Maeva Marcus and her colleagues in the DOCUMENTARY HISTORY OF THE SUPREME COURT OF THE
UNITED STATES (DHSC). In addition there is a reawakening of interest in
these early years of the Supreme Court,[1] as Professor Casto's footnotes
show quite clearly. It is hoped that this survey of these two important
chief justiceships will generate even more scholarly research on this formative period.

Every historical period deserves to be studied on its own record and
not to be judged through the jaundiced eye of hindsight. The Jay-
Ellsworth Courts sought continuity with treasured English common law
and established colonial practice. However, they also were keenly aware
of the need to adapt those familiar institutions to accommodate new relationships in post-Revolutionary, and republican, America. As Professor
Casto demonstrates, virtually every member of these Courts had seen judicial and/or legislative service in colonial America or in the alternative
had practiced law in the King's courts. Prominent in the political and
professional life of their respective states, each brought localized prefer-
ences to his work on the Court. Despite their shared loyalty to the Federalist party, their views of federalism and their interpretations of the
Federal Constitution were quite divergent.

Moving forward cautiously at first the Jay-Ellsworth Courts made a
tentative start in construing the Constitution of the United States. Their
most notable contribution, in *Chisholm v. Georgia*,[2] so violated pretensions
of state sovereignty that it was overrruled by the Eleventh Amendment
within two years of its decision. By way of contrast the Court's 1796

---

1. An early monograph, emerging from the ongoing editorial work on the papers of
Chief Justice John Jay, is Richard B. Morris, JOHN JAY: THE NATION AND THE COURT (1967).
Professor Casto and Professor Wythe W. Holt, Jr., of the University of Alabama School of
Law, have contributed a substantial number of law review articles over the past decade,
most of them cited in the footnotes to this monograph. In addition Professor Stephen R.
Presser has written extensively in law reviews and elsewhere, concerning the "bad boy"
of the Ellsworth Court, Samuel Chase. His rehabilitation of Chase is set forth most
completely in THE ORIGINAL MISUNDERSTANDING: THE ENGLISH, THE AMERICANS AND THE DIALECTIC
OF FEDERALIST JURISPRUDENCE (1991). For an excellent introduction to the historiography of
this period see ORIGINS OF THE FEDERAL JUDICIARY: ESSAYS ON THE JUDICIARY ACT OF 1789 (Maeva
Marcus ed., 1992), which contains a number of Interpretive essays concerning the work
of the early Supreme Court.

2. 2 U.S. (2 Dall.) 418–78 (1793).

decision in *Ware v. Hylton*[3] marked the Court's premier position as the highest tribunal of international law within the American nation. Indeed it is in this field that the Jay-Ellsworth Courts made their major contributions. In an Atlantic world where international affairs were dominated by monarchial governments the new American republic badly needed the legitimacy that attaches to sound fiscal, commercial, and diplomatic policy. The Court's close connection to international matters gained emphasis through the diplomatic assignment of Chief Justice Jay to the 1794 British mission and the subsequent dispatch of Chief Justice Ellsworth to negotiate peace terms with France from 1799 to 1800.

It is remarkable that there is surprisingly little evidence of close friendships or political affinities between the Supreme Court judges who served during this time period. Apparently neither Jay nor Ellsworth exhibited those interpersonal skills necessary to encourage collegiality or jointly shared decision-making in the Court's conferences. This apparent social distance between them fitted well into an English tradition of rendering seriatim opinions. Their long and arduous tours of circuit duty also kept them apart and diminished their energies for comraderie or leisurely deliberations when they gathered to render decisions en banc.

Thus it becomes apparent that Professor Casto describes a Supreme Court that is markedly different from the later Court under Marshall, and yet this was a period in the Court's history that laid a foundation for future greatness. The Judiciary Act of 1789 long served as the fundamental charter for the federal judiciary, and the Ellsworth Court's system of per curiam opinions was a first step toward the adoption of the unitary opinion of the Court that became prevalent under Marshall and his successors. The Jay-Ellsworth Courts played a vital role in securing American adherence to the law of nations, and in riding their circuits the judges demonstrated the growing importance of federal law and law enforcement in the lives of all American citizens. Finally the Jay-Ellsworth Courts represent the declining years of a tradition that the judicial functions of government served and reenforced the policy decisions of the executive and legislative branches. With the 1800 election of Thomas Jefferson cooperation among the three branches of government came to an abrupt halt. This development called for a reassessment of the place of the Supreme Court in the constitutional system and gave birth to a new stage in judicial history.

---

3. 3 U.S. (3 Dall.) 197–285 (1796).

The Jay-Ellsworth Courts played a major role in establishing the federal judicial tradition, and Professor Casto has put us in his debt by demonstrating how important their contribution is to the rule of law in modern America.

—Herbert A. Johnson

PREFACE AND
ACKNOWLEDGMENTS

When Herb Johnson asked me if I would be interested in writing a book-length monograph on the early Supreme Court as part of a series on the Court's history, I was delighted. I had been studying the early Court for a number of years and had a special interest in Oliver Ellsworth, who played the foremost role in the creation of the federal judiciary and later served as the Court's third Chief Justice. In writing this introductory volume, I have not tried to provide a comprehensive study that treats every case adjudicated by the Court in its early years. For example, I pay virtually no attention to technical issues of practice and procedure except where those issues relate directly to the scope of the Court's authority. Procedural technicalities are of little intrinsic interest and are boring even to lawyers. Instead of writing a comprehensive history, I have selected representative issues, incidents, and cases that illustrate the Court's creation and initial operation. In particular, I have stressed the direct and almost pervasive relationship between the early Court and national security.

This monograph could not have been written without the aid of countless organizations and individuals. My knowledge of Oliver Ellsworth is based primarily upon primary sources gathered with the assistance of grants from the American Philosophical Society and the M.D. Anderson Foundation. In addition, I appreciate the continuing support of the Texas Tech University Law School Foundation. Like the characters in this book, I labor with pen and ink rather than a keyboard. I would therefore like to give special thanks to Lynda Levels and Gloria Smith, who typed my manuscript.

Although I have visited many archives, collections, and documentary projects, I am particularly appreciative of the assistance that I received from Maeva Marcus at the Documentary History of the Supreme Court of the United States Project and Charlene Bickford and Kenneth Bowling at the Documentary History of the First Federal Congress of the United States of America Project. In addition, Herbert Johnson carefully read manuscripts and provided many valuable insights and comments. Finally, I want to acknowledge the unstinting assistance and support of Wythe Holt, who graciously and critically reviewed every line of this book. Wythe and I view the 1790s from different philosophical perspectives, and I have profited enormously from his insights.

This book is based in significant part on public and private sources from the 1790s and contains many quotations. As a matter of editorial style, thorns and abbreviations have been expanded to modern spellings. For example, *ye* and *wh* have been changed to *the* and *which*. In addition, I have made a conscious effort to reduce the number and length of footnotes. Each paragraph of text generally has no more than one, and frequently the footnote includes multiple references pertinent to various concepts and quotations in the paragraph. I also have made extensive use of short titles, abbreviations, and repository symbols.

REPOSITORY SYMBOLS

The following list provides all repository symbols used in this book:

CtHi	Connecticut Historical Society, Hartford, Connecticut
CtHUCC	United Church of Christ Connecticut Conference, Hartford, Connecticut
CtY	Yale University, New Haven, Connecticut
DLC	United States Library of Congress, Washington, D.C.
DNA	United States National Archives and Records Services, Washington, D.C.
GU	University of Georgia, Athens, Georgia
MHi	Massachusetts Historical Society, Boston, Massachusetts
NHi	New York Historical Society, New York, New York
Nc-Ar	North Carolina State Department of Archives and History, Raleigh, North Carolina
NcD	Duke University, Durham, North Carolina
NcU	University of North Carolina, Chapel Hill, North Carolina
Nh	New Hampshire State Library, Concord, New Hampshire
NjMoHP	Morristown National Historical Park, Morristown, New Jersey
NjP	Princeton University, Princeton, New Jersey
NjR	Rutgers–The State University, New Brunswick, New Jersey
PHi	Historical Society of Pennsylvania, Philadelphia, Pennsylvania
ScU	University of South Carolina, Columbia, South Carolina

SHORT TITLES
AND ABBREVIATIONS

The following list includes all short titles and abbreviations used in this book:

ANNALS

Annals of the Congress of the United States, 42 vols. (Washington, D.C.: Gales and Seaton, 1834–56).

ASP

American State Papers: Documents, Legislative and Executive of the Congress of the United States, 38 vols. (Washington, D.C.: Gales and Seaton, 1832–1861).

BLACKSTONE

William Blackstone, *Commentaries on the Laws of England,* 4 vols. (Oxford: Clarendon Press, 1765).

BROWN

William Garrott Brown, *The Life of Oliver Ellsworth* (New York: Macmillan, 1905).

Casto, *Admiralty*

William R. Casto, "The Origins of Federal Admiralty Jurisdiction in an Age of Privateers, Smugglers, and Pirates," *American Journal of Legal History* 37 (1993): 117–57.

Casto, *Calvinism*

William R. Casto, "Oliver Ellsworth's Calvinism: A Biographical Essay on Religion and Political Psychology in the Early Republic," *Journal of Church and State* 36 (1994): 507–26.

Casto, *Congress*

William R. Casto, "The First Congress's

	Understanding of Its Authority over the Federal Courts' Jurisdiction," *Boston College Law Review* 26 (1985): 1101–41.
Casto, *Erie*	William R. Casto, "The Erie Doctrine and the Structure of Constitutional Revolutions," *Tulane Law Review* 62 (1988): 907–62.
Casto, *Iredell*	William R. Casto, "James Iredell and the Origins of Judicial Review,"*Connecticut Law Review* 27 (1995)
Casto, *Orthodox*	William R. Casto, "An Orthodox View of the Two-Tier Analysis of Congressional Control over Federal Jurisdiction," *Constitutional Commentary* 7 (1990): 89–96.
Casto, *Torts*	William R. Casto, "The Federal Courts' Protective Jurisdiction over Torts Committed in Violation of the Law of Nations," *Connecticut Law Review* 18 (1986): 467–530.
COMBS	Jerald A. Combs, *The Jay Treaty: Political Battleground of the Founding Fathers* (Berkeley: University of California Press, 1970).
COUNTER CASE	*The Counter Case of Great Britain as Laid Before the Tribunal of Arbitration, Convened at Geneva* (Washington, D.C.: Government Printing Office, 1872).
DECONDE	Alexander DeConde, *A History of American Foreign Policy*, 3rd ed., vol. 1 (New York: Charles Scribner's Sons, 1978).
DHFFC	*Documentary History of the First Federal Congress of the United States,* 9 vols. to date: vols. 1–3, ed. Linda Grant DePauw; vols. 4–6, ed. Charlene Bangs Bickford and Helen E. Veit; vol. 9, ed. Kenneth R. Bowling and Veit; vols. 10–11, ed. Bickford, Kenneth R. Bowling, and Veit

(Baltimore: Johns Hopkins University Press, 1972–1992).

DHRC

The Documentary History of the Ratification of the Constitution, 9 vols. to date: vols. 1–3, ed. Merrill Jensen; vols. 8–9 and 13–16, ed. John P. Kaminski and Gaspare J. Saladino (Madison: State Historical Society of Wisconsin, 1976–90).

DHSC

Documentary History of the Supreme Court of the United States 1789–1800, 4 vols. to date: vol. 1, ed. Maeva Marcus and James R. Perry; vols. 2–4, ed. Marcus (New York: Columbia University Press, 1985–92).

ELKINS & MCKITRICK

Stanley Elkins and Eric McKitrick, *The Age of Federalism* (New York: Oxford University Press, 1993).

ELLIOT

Jonathan Elliot, ed., *The Debates in the Several State Conventions, on the Adoption of the Federal Constitution, as Recommended by the General Convention at Philadelphia, in 1787*, 2d. ed., 5 vols. (Philadelphia: J. B. Lippincott, 1876).

FARRAND

Max Farrand, ed., *Records of the Federal Convention of 1787*, 4 vols. (1937; reprint ed. New Haven: Yale University Press, 1966); 4th supplementary vol. ed. James H. Hutson, 1987.

FEDERALIST

Jacob E. Cooke, ed., *The Federalist* (Middletown, Conn.: Wesleyan University Press, 1961).

FLANDERS

Henry Flanders, *The Lives and Times of the Chief Justices of the Supreme Court of the United States*, vol. 2 (New York: James Cockcroft, 1875).

FREEDOM'S FETTERS

James Morton Smith, *Freedom's Fetters: The Alien and Sedition Laws and American Civil Liberties* (Ithaca: Cornell University Press, 1956.)

FRIEDMAN & ISRAEL	*The Justices of the United States Supreme Court 1789–1969: Their Lives and Major Opinions,* ed. Leon Friedman and Fred L. Israel, vol. 1 (New York: Bowker, 1969).
GOEBEL	Julius Goebel, Jr., *History of the Supreme Court of the United States: Antecedents and Beginnings to 1801* (New York: Macmillan, 1971).
HAMILTON PAPERS	Harold C. Syrett, ed., *The Papers of Alexander Hamilton,* 27 vols. (New York: Columbia University Press, 1961–87).
HAMILTON'S LAW PRACTICE	*The Law Practice of Alexander Hamilton,* vols. 1–2, ed. Julius Goebel, Jr.; vols. 3–5, ed. Goebel and Joseph H. Smith (New York: Columbia University Press, 1964–81).
HART & WECHSLER	Paul M. Bator et al., *Hart and Wechsler's The Federal Courts and the Federal System,* 3rd ed. (Westbury, N.Y.: Foundation Press, 1988).
HASKINS & JOHNSON	George Lee Haskins and Herbert A. Johnson, *History of the Supreme Court: Foundations of Power: John Marshall, 1801–15* (New York: Macmillan, 1981).
HENDERSON	Dwight F. Henderson, *Courts for a New Nation* (Washington, D.C.: Public Affairs Press, 1971).
Holt	Wythe Holt, " 'To Establish Justice': Politics, the Judiciary Act of 1789, and the Invention of the Federal Courts, *Duke Law Journal* 1989 (1990) 1421–1531.
HYNEMAN	Charles S. Hyneman, *The First American Neutrality* (Urbana: University of Illinois, 1934).
IREDELL CORRESPONDENCE	Griffith John McRee, *Life and Correspondence of James Iredell,* 2 vols. (1857; reprinted in 1 vol., New York: Peter Smith, 1949).
JACOBS	Clyde E. Jacobs, *The Eleventh Amendment*

and Sovereign Immunity (Westport, Conn.: Greenwood Press, 1972).

JAY PAPERS — Henry P. Johnston, ed., *Correspondence and Public Papers of John Jay,* 4 vols. (1890; reprinted New York: Burt Franklin, 1970).

JEFFERSON PAPERS — *Papers of Thomas Jefferson,* 25 vols. to date: vols. 1–20, ed. Julian P. Boyd; vols. 21–23, ed. Charles T. Cullen; vols. 24–25, ed. John Catanzariti (Princeton: Princeton University Press, 1950–1992).

JEFFERSON PAPERS (Ford) — Paul Leicester Ford, ed., *The Works of Thomas Jefferson,* 12 vols. (New York: G. P. Putnam's Sons, 1904–5).

KING CORRESPONDENCE — Charles R. King, ed., *The Life and Correspondence of Rufus King,* 6 vols. (New York: G. P. Putnam's Sons, 1894–1900).

LEE LETTERS — James Curtis Ballagh, *The Letters of Richard Henry Lee,* 2 vols. (New York: Macmillan, 1911–14).

LOBBAN — Michael Lobban, *The Common Law and English Jurisprudence, 1760–1850* (New York: Oxford University Press, 1991).

MADISON PAPERS — *The Papers of James Madison,* 17 vols. to date: vols. 1–7, ed. William T. Hutchinson and William M. E. Rachal; vol. 8, ed. Robert A. Rutland and Rachal; vols. 9–10, ed. Rutland (Chicago: University of Chicago Press, 1962–77); vols. 11–13, ed. Rutland and Charles F. Hobson; vol. 14, ed. Rutland and Thomas A. Mason; vol. 15, ed. Mason, Rutland, and Jeanne K. Sisson; vol. 16, ed. J. C. A. Stagg, Mason, and Sisson; vol. 17, ed. David B. Mattern et al. (Charlottesville: University Press of Virginia, 1977–91).

Marcus & Wexler — Maeva Marcus and Natalie Wexler, "Suits Against States: Diversity of Opinion in the 1790s," *Journal of Supreme Court History* 1993 (1993) 73–89.

MARSHALL PAPERS

The Papers of John Marshall, 6 vols. to date: vol. 1, ed. Herbert A. Johnson; vol. 2, ed. Charles T. Cullen and Johnson; vol. 3, ed. William C. Stinchcombe and Cullen; vol. 4, ed. Cullen; vol. 5–6, ed. Charles F. Hobson (Chapel Hill: University of North Carolina Press, 1974–90).

MASON PAPERS

Robert A. Rutland, ed., *The Papers of George Mason, 1725–1792,* 3 vols. (Chapel Hill: University of North Carolina Press, 1970).

O'CONNOR

John E. O'Connor, *William Paterson: Lawyer and Statesman 1745–1806* (New Brunswick, N.J.: Rutgers University Press, 1979).

ORIGINS (Marcus)

Maeva Marcus, ed., *Origins of the Federal Judiciary: Essays on the Judiciary Act of 1789* (New York: Oxford University Press, 1992).

PRESSER

Stephen B. Presser, *The Original Misunderstanding: The English, the Americans and the Dialectic of Federalist Jurisprudence* (Durham: Carolina Academic Press, 1991).

QUASI-WAR

Alexander DeConde, *The Quasi-War: The Politics and Diplomacy of the Undeclared War with France 1797–1801* (New York: Charles Scribner's Sons, 1966).

RICHARDSON

James Daniel Richardson, ed., *A Compilation of Messages and Papers of the Presidents,* vol. 1 (Washington, D.C.: Government Printing Office, 1896).

RITCHESON

Charles R. Ritcheson, *Aftermath of Revolution: British Policy Toward the United States, 1783–1795* (Dallas: Southern Methodist University Press, 1969).

RITZ

Wilfred J. Ritz, *Rewriting the History of the Judiciary Act of 1789: Exposing Myths, Challenging Premises, and Using New Evidence,* ed. Wythe Holt and L. H. LaRue

	(Norman: University of Oklahoma Press, 1990).
SLAUGHTER	Thomas P. Slaughter, *The Whiskey Rebellion* (New York: Oxford University Press, 1986).
THOMAS	Charles Marion Thomas, *American Neutrality in 1793: A Study in Cabinet Government* (1931; reprinted New York: AMS Press, 1967).
TREATIES (Miller)	Hunter Miller, ed., *Treaties and Other International Acts of the United States of America,* 8 vols. (Washington, D.C.: Government Printing Office, 1931–48).
WARREN	Charles Warren, *The Supreme Court in United States History,* rev. ed., vol. 1 (Boston: Little, Brown, 1926).
WASHINGTON WRITINGS	John C. Fitzpatrick, ed., *The Writings of George Washington,* 39 vols. (Washington, D.C.: Government Printing Office, 1931–44).
WHARTON	Francis Wharton, ed., *State Trials of the United States during the Administrations of Washington and Adams with References Historical and Professional and Preliminary Notes on the Politics of the Times* (1849; reprinted New York: Burt Franklin, 1970).
WHEELER	Russell Wheeler, "Extrajudicial Activities of United States Supreme Court Justices: The Constitutional Period, 1790–1809" (Ph.D. diss., University of Chicago, 1970).
WOOD	Gordon S. Wood, *The Creation of the American Republic, 1776–1787* (New York: Norton, 1972).

The Supreme Court in the Early Republic:

The Chief Justiceships of
John Jay and Oliver Ellsworth

INTRODUCTION

This book is an introduction to the Supreme Court's creation and roughly its first decade of operation, up to 1801, when John Marshall became its fourth Chief Justice. The book is intended for general readers—both lawyers and nonlawyers—with a scholarly interest in the subject. Much of the book is devoted to matters that the Founding Generation deemed important. For example, consistent with the federal government's original primary purpose, chapter five's chronological survey of the Court's first decade is organized entirely around national security issues. In addition, the book covers topics like the relationship between the Court and the Constitution that have proved from a late-twentieth-century perspective to be of enduring significance.

Today the Supreme Court is a unique political institution whose immense power is supported and limited by over two hundred years of tradition. This tradition, however, was not always so well established, and we should strive not to project our current understanding of the Court back into the late eighteenth century. Some of the central tenets of the Court's formative years have faded from existence or suffered a flat rejection; some were in an embryonic form that has been subtly but significantly changed over the years. This book depicts the beginning of the experiment that was to become the Court we know today.

A student of the Court's creation must constantly bear in mind that the Court originated as part of a grand experiment. In 1790 John Jay, the first Chief Justice of the United States, reminded the nation in the first paragraph of his first grand jury charge that "Whether any People can long govern themselves in an equal uniform & orderly manner, is a Question . . . exceedingly important to the Cause of Liberty. This Question, like others whose Solution depends on Facts, can only be determined by Experience." Jay believed that "the present national Government already affords advantages," but he did not think the new

1

government was perfect. "It is a consolation," he continued, "to reflect that the good Sense of the People will be enabled by Experience to discover and correct its Imperfections."[1]

In addition to remembering the tentative nature of the Court's creation and initial operation, readers in the late twentieth century must understand the drastic differences between today's fundamental principles of jurisprudence and those of the late eighteenth century. When the Court was created, virtually all American attorneys were natural lawyers who believed that judges did not and should not resort to considerations of policy in adjudicating cases. They believed that law was a comprehensive and systematic body of principles based upon divine wisdom and the perfection of human reason. As Thomas Jefferson wrote in the Declaration of Independence, natural lawyers believed in "the Laws of Nature and of Nature's God."[2] This system of laws existed in nature independent of the state.

In contrast, legal positivism is the mainstream of American jurisprudence in the late twentieth century. Today virtually all Americans with any background in the study of law are legal positivists, at least insofar as we believe that law is an expression of political power and that the law's content is largely a function of individual human lawmakers' views of appropriate policy. Moreover, virtually all Americans in the late twentieth century believe that judges are lawmakers and therefore that judges necessarily must look to considerations of public policy in adjudicating cases. The difference between legal positivism and natural law is so vast that many of the Founding Generation's thoughts and actions cannot be understood without setting positivism aside and studying those earlier thoughts and actions in their original natural-law context.

Another significant difference between the legal landscape of the late eighteenth century and that of the present relates to the geographic orientation of the country, or at least of its ruling class. When the federal government was created, the country perched on the eastern seaboard and looked toward Europe. Only Vermont, Kentucky, and Tennessee—all admitted to the Union after the original thirteen states—did not face the Atlantic. On the other side of the Atlantic, Europe was the acknowledged cultural center of America's world in 1789, and Europe had three large and powerful nations (Great Britain, France, and Spain) that had open designs on American territory. The raison d'être of the federal gov-

1. John Jay, Charge to the New York Grand Jury (Apr. 12, 1790), *reprinted in* 1 DHSC 25–30.

2. THE DECLARATION OF INDEPENDENCE para. 1 (U.S. 1776). *Accord*, 1 BLACKSTONE 40–44.

ernment was to deal more effectively with foreign affairs and national security issues.

The Founding Generation believed that prize cases, cases related to the enforcement of revenue laws, cases in which a foreigner was involved, and cases involving the law of nations had a direct impact on foreign affairs and national security.[3] Using this definition, most (58%) of the cases from the Supreme Court's first decade had significant national security and foreign affairs implications. But as decades passed, the nation turned inward toward the vast North American continent and became absorbed in its own huge market economy. Today the Supreme Court still deals with national security and foreign affairs issues, but most of its cases relate to the regulation of internal affairs.

---

3. *See* chapter 1 at 6–9.

1

CREATING THE COURT

There was a fundamental ambivalence among the delegates who converged upon Philadelphia in the summer of 1787 to consider a new constitutional order for their loosely confederated states. Almost all of them wanted to create a more powerful general government. For example, virtually everyone at the Constitutional Convention agreed that under the Articles of Confederation, the Continental Congress lacked sufficient legal authority and fiscal stability to deal effectively with foreign affairs. Similarly, most of the delegates believed that the general government needed more power to remedy domestic problems implicating significant national interests. At the same time, however, many—probably most—of the delegates feared that a new and more powerful general government might abuse its new authority.

After the Convention, James Madison—with characteristic elegance and insight—forthrightly described the delegates' dilemma:

> If men were angels, no government would be necessary. If angels were to govern men, neither external nor internal controls or government would be necessary. In framing a government which is to be administered by men over men, the great difficulty lies in this: you must first enable the government to control the governed; and in the next place oblige it to control itself. A dependence on the people is, no doubt, the primary control on the government; but experience has taught mankind the necessity of auxiliary precautions.[1]

The delegates were especially concerned about the general government's greatly expanded legislative authority and spent most of the summer

---

1. FEDERALIST No. 51 at 349 (J. Madison).

searching for appropriate "auxiliary precautions" against the abuse of this new power. Obvious examples are the Grand Compromise, apportioning representation in the House and Senate, the provision securing the importation of slaves until 1807, and the abortive attempt to require a super majority vote for legislation regulating commerce.

When the delegates considered the new government's judicial powers, the search for auxiliary precautions intensified. Indeed, the need for precautions against judicial abuse was especially acute because the federal judges' life tenure effectively negated Madison's "primary control"—periodic election by the people. As a result, much of the Convention's deliberations on the judiciary involved a search for auxiliary precautions against judicial abuse.

THE FEDERAL COURTS' SUBJECT-MATTER JURISDICTION

The most significant issues regarding the judiciary involved the extent of the national courts' authority to adjudicate cases. In particular, there was significant disagreement among the delegates about the answer to two questions: what specific categories of judicial cases should be entrusted to federal determination, and should there be an extensive system of federal trial courts distributed throughout the nation? Everyone agreed that there should be a Supreme Court, and there was a consensus that the federal judiciary's authority should extend to certain types of cases. But a serious effort was made to prevent the creation of an extensive federal judicial system with trial courts in each state. There was also significant initial disagreement over the specific categories of cases that should be entrusted to federal determination—what twentieth-century attorneys call federal subject-matter jurisdiction.

This legal concept of jurisdiction, then and now, does not refer to the substantive rules of law that are used to regulate society and to determine who wins or loses lawsuits. Instead, jurisdiction is a technical concept concerning the courts' power to adjudicate particular categories of cases. As Alexander Hamilton explained, the word *jurisdiction* "is composed of JUS and DICTO, *juris, diction,* or a speaking or pronouncing of the law."[2] In other words, a court without jurisdiction is without authority to speak or pronounce judgment in a case. If a claim is filed in a court without jurisdiction over that particular type of claim, the litigation must be dismissed for lack of jurisdiction. Such a dismissal is not necessarily a

---

2. FEDERALIST No. 81 at 551 (A. Hamilton).

victory for the defendant; the dismissing court has simply refused to decide the case one way or another. The claim ordinarily may then be refiled in some other court that does have jurisdiction.

Although jurisdiction is an esoteric legal concept, it had enormous implications at the Philadelphia Convention because it involved the new federal government's power to act directly upon American citizens. To the extent that the federal courts lacked jurisdiction to adjudicate cases implicating a national interest, the cases would have to be determined by state courts. Therefore questions of jurisdiction directly involved the allocation of power between the state and federal governments. Any expansion of the federal courts' subject-matter jurisdiction would enhance the federal government's ability to implement federal laws. Conversely, the simple device of limiting the federal courts' jurisdiction could serve as an effective auxiliary precaution against abuse of the federal government's extensive powers.

The delegates' proposals on federal jurisdiction provide excellent clues to their collective reasons for establishing a federal judicial system. The Virginia delegation and Charles Pinckney of South Carolina each presented a plan on the Convention's first working day. After about two weeks of debate on the Virginia Plan, a loose coalition of delegates opposed to the Virginians' proposals presented the Paterson Plan. Finally Alexander Hamilton drafted his own plan but evidently did not make a formal submission. Although these plans sometimes covered different issues and were even in direct conflict, all four of them were drafted by men who eventually supported the Constitution that was finally adopted by the Convention.[3]

While there are considerable variations among the various plans' provisions for the categories of cases that could be adjudicated by federal courts, the plans evidence a firm consensus on the need for federal jurisdiction over cases that involved foreign affairs and national security. Edmund Randolph of Virginia opened the Convention by bluntly stating that the general or federal government needed adequate authority to guard against foreign invasion and that these national security powers "could not be executed without money." There may not have been a firm national consensus on this need for revenue, but there was certainly one among the delegates. Given the direct link between the fisc and national security, it comes as no surprise to discover that every plan urged the federal courts' participation in the collection of federal revenues.[4]

---

3. *See* 3 FARRAND appendices C, D, E, F at 593–630.

4. 1 FARRAND 19. The Founding Generation's understanding of the link between revenue and national security is a recurring theme in ROGER BROWN, REDEEMING THE REPUBLIC: FEDERALISTS, TAXATION, AND THE ORIGINS OF THE CONSTITUTION (1993).

In addition to revenue cases, all the plans sought to vest the federal courts with power over prize cases. This branch of admiralty law has long since disappeared, but it was important in the eighteenth century. These sui generis proceedings were usually commenced by privateers officially licensed by their country to capture commercial enemy vessels during times of war. When a privateer brought its capture to port, an admiralty court could condemn the seized property and award the privateer lawful ownership of the ship and cargo. This jurisdiction enabled admiralty courts to assist and regulate the privateering trade. The courts' ability to regulate the trade was based upon their authority to protect the rights of neutral shippers by ordering the return of illegally seized ships and cargoes.[5]

The drafters of the four plans probably viewed prize litigation as sui generis proceedings implicating unique national security concerns and therefore insisted upon vesting the federal courts with specific jurisdiction over cases of capture. But prize cases were not the only litigation directly implicating the interests of aliens and foreign countries. The drafters of all four plans understood this and therefore provided for a more general jurisdiction over cases involving aliens. The Virginia, Paterson, and Hamilton plans would have created an express alienage jurisdiction by generally extending federal judicial power to all cases involving aliens. The Pinckney Plan more narrowly confined jurisdiction concerning aliens to all maritime claims (including but not limited to prize cases) and cases involving treaties or the law of nations. Although Pinckney's categories were not expressly keyed to claims by or against aliens, maritime litigation and international-law cases usually involved the rights of aliens.

In referring to treaties and the law of nations, Pinckney undoubtedly had in mind two specific foreign affairs issues that had plagued the Confederation. The first issue involved a cause célèbre that had arisen four years earlier when the Chevalier De Longchamps, whom Thomas Jefferson described as an "obscure and worthless character," assaulted a French diplomat in the streets of Philadelphia. A scandalized Jefferson wrote that the diplomat was "obliged . . . in his own defense to box in the streets like a porter." Even worse, after De Longchamps was arrested and released on bail, he began sending the French ambassador anonymous letters containing assassination threats.[6]

---

5. *See* chapter 2 at 40–41; Casto, *Admiralty*.

6. Thomas Jefferson to James Madison (May 25, 1784), *reprinted in* 7 JEFFERSON PAPERS 289.

The De Longchamps Affair was a national sensation that attracted the concern of virtually every public figure in America. The international community was outraged and demanded that the Continental Congress take action, but under the Articles of Confederation the Congress lacked authority to deal directly with De Longchamps. Eventually he was successfully prosecuted by the state of Pennsylvania for his flagrant violation of the diplomatic immunity accorded foreign embassies under the law of nations. The Affair clearly demonstrated the Continental Congress's impotence to remedy violations of the law of nations.[7]

In addition to high-profile but isolated incidents like the de Longchamps Affair, there was an ongoing and more serious foreign policy problem that all delegates to the Convention were familiar with. The provision in Pinckney's Plan vesting the federal courts with power over cases involving treaty violations and the more general alienage provisions in the other three plans were undoubtedly drafted to enhance the enforcement of the Treaty of Paris that had concluded the Revolutionary War. In Article IV of the Treaty, the United States had pledged that British creditors "shall meet with no legal impediment to the recovery of the full value in sterling money of all bona fide debts heretofore contracted." This article was designed to rescind economic measures adopted during the Revolutionary War by the rebelling states. As part of the war effort, the states successfully encouraged American debtors to suspend their payment of debts to British merchants. British creditors were barred from suing in American courts, and statutes were enacted to confiscate British debts or authorize American debtors to discharge their British debts by paying depreciated paper money into state treasuries. Article IV was inserted in the Treaty to remedy harm to British merchants by guaranteeing them an ordinary judicial remedy free from the legal impediments that had been enacted during the war.[8]

But after the war, many American debtors—particularly in the South—continued refusing to pay their debts. Moreover, the legislatures and courts in several states ignored the Treaty and, through their construction of the law and other means, overtly cooperated with this ongoing delinquency. In some states the courts remained closed to British creditors. Another legislative strategy was to place severe limitations upon the enforcement of any judgments that a British creditor might obtain. Even without these formal impediments, juries frequently refused to return verdicts favoring British creditors. Years later, Chief Justice Marshall recalled, "The fact was notorious that it was the general opinion

---

7. *See* Casto, *Torts* 491–94.
8. *See generally* Holt.

of [Virginians] and of the juries that a British debt could not be recovered." As long as local debtors had significant control over the courts, there was no real possibility that these debts would be recovered.[9]

This ongoing delinquency had direct national security consequences. Under the Treaty of Paris, the British had agreed to evacuate their military posts that dominated the northern borders of the United States from Vermont to Detroit. The British, who wanted to retain control of the lucrative fur trade and who still smarted from their military defeat, insisted that the failure of the United States to comply with Article IV justified continued British occupation of the posts. "What a misfortune it is," wrote George Washington to John Jay, "that Britain should have so well founded a pretext for its palpable infractions!"[10]

Notwithstanding apparent agreement upon the key issues of revenue collection, prize litigation, and alienage cases, there was a serious and fundamental disagreement between the Virginia Plan and the other plans. In addition to vesting the federal judiciary with jurisdiction over these key issues, the Virginia Plan called for federal jurisdiction over cases in which "citizens of other states . . . may be interested." Finally, and as a general backstop, the Virginians sought to vest the federal courts with a general jurisdiction over "questions which may involve the national peace and harmony." These expansive proposals were clearly designed to facilitate, rather than to limit, the use of a federal judiciary to implement national laws and policies.[11]

The Virginians envisioned a federal government in which representation in the national legislature would be based entirely upon state populations, and therefore they trusted that the new government would not abuse its authority. James Madison candidly explained in private that, from the viewpoint of the large states, this proportional representation would assure that the general government would exercise its new powers in a wise and trustworthy manner. In other words, Madison viewed the large states' effective control of the national legislature as an auxiliary precaution against legislative abuse. Proportional representation, he wrote, would "obviate the principal objections of the large states to the necessary concessions of power [to the new federal government]."[12]

---

9. Dunlop v. Ball, 6 U.S. (2 Cranch) 180, 182–83 (1804). *See generally* Holt 1440–58.

10. George Washington to John Jay (Aug. 15, 1786), *reprinted in* 3 JAY PAPERS at 207–9. *See* FREDERICK MARKS, INDEPENDENCE ON TRIAL 5–15 (1973).

11. *See* 1 FARRAND 22.

12. James Madison to George Washington (Apr. 16, 1787), *reprinted in* 9 MADISON PAPERS 382–87. *See also* James Madison to Edmund Randolph (Apr. 8, 1787), *reprinted in id.* 368–71.

The assumption that the new government would be trustworthy had enormous implications for the need to limit its powers. The Virginians evidently contemplated vesting the government with broad—almost open-ended—powers. In addition to the powers previously exercised by the Continental Congress, the proposed federal legislature was to have authority "to legislate in all cases to which the separate States are incompetent or in which the harmony of the United States may be interrupted by the exercise of individual Legislation; [and] to negative all laws passed by the several States, contravening in the opinion of the National Legislature the articles of Union."[13] These general concepts of state incompetence, harmony of the Union, and a congressional right to negative all state laws are obviously ambiguous and susceptible to broad interpretations.

Consistent with this expansive approach to federal legislative authority, the Virginians similarly proposed that the new federal judiciary should be granted a broad subject-matter jurisdiction. Their proposals for a national judiciary are particularly significant because their plan effectively established the Convention's agenda. Moreover, the Convention eventually adopted virtually every significant aspect of the Virginia Plan's judicial system.

A more subtle but equally open-ended aspect of the Virginia Plan involved the number and types of federal courts that were to be created. The Virginians contemplated an extensive system of "inferior tribunals to be chosen by the National Legislature." Federal trial courts would be distributed throughout the Union to hear and determine all cases within the national judicial power. In addition, "one or more supreme tribunals" would be created with final appellate jurisdiction.[14]

The Virginia proposal for a national judiciary got off to a good start on June 4 when the Convention agreed without a single objection "that a National Judiciary be established." The Convention also voted that the judicial branch should "consist of one supreme tribunal, and of one or more inferior tribunals." These measures were passed at the end of the day with little or no debate. But within hours, the South Carolina and Connecticut delegates and probably the New Jersey delegates began having second thoughts. They agreed on the necessity of creating one supreme national tribunal but had strong reservations about an extensive system of lower federal trial courts throughout the states. The next day John Rutledge of South Carolina convinced the Convention to recon-

---

13. 1 FARRAND 21.
14. *Id.* 21.

sider the matter and then moved to strike from the Constitution the entire concept of lower federal courts. Roger Sherman of Connecticut seconded the motion, and a lively debate ensued in which the delegates considered virtually every argument that has ever been made on the need for federal trial courts.[15]

The heart of the controversy was, and still is, localism versus nationalism. Rutledge and his fellow South Carolinian Pierce Butler argued that neither the states nor the people would tolerate federal encroachments on the authority of state courts. In response, James Madison and James Wilson, from the populous states of Virginia and Pennsylvania, pressed the need for a national judiciary to implement national laws and policies. In an only slightly veiled reference to the Continental Congress's debility under the Articles of Confederation, Madison reminded the delegates that "[a] Government without a proper Executive & Judiciary would be the mere trunk of a body without arms or legs to act or move."[16]

The South Carolinians initially prevailed in this debate by offering what seemed to be a reasonable compromise. Rutledge suggested that federal cases could be tried in the existing state courts and immediately assured the Convention that national interests would not be harmed. A "right of appeal to the supreme national tribunal [would be] sufficient to secure the national rights & uniformity of Judgments." This suggestion that the Convention could have its cake and eat it too was most attractive. Using the existing state courts protected local interests and — as Roger Sherman pragmatically noted — saved money. If an occasional state court improperly sacrificed national interests, the error could be corrected through appeal to the national Supreme Court.[17]

Madison and Wilson were hard pressed to refute this practical and easily understood compromise. Madison resorted to an important but technical distinction between trying a case originally in a federal trial court instead of seeking federal appellate review of trials in state courts. He asked, "What was to be done after improper Verdicts in State tribunals obtained under the biassed directions of a dependent Judge, or the local prejudices of a undirected jury?" In theory, this problem could have been solved by having the Supreme Court itself conduct a new trial, and there was eighteenth-century precedent for this kind of de novo review. But Madison noted as a practical matter that the Supreme Court could not conduct a new trial because in most cases the witnesses would be too

---

15. *Id.* 95, 104–05, 124–25.
16. *Id.* 124.
17. *Id.* 124.

far removed from the seat of government. Therefore trials and retrials would have to be conducted in the potentially biased state trial courts. This practical necessity would have given the state courts tremendous discretion to shape and influence the adjudication of cases in ways that were not subject to effective appellate supervision by the federal Supreme Court.[18]

These arguments on technical procedure were cogent and were ably presented, but they failed to sway the Convention. Rutledge's compromise provided limited but significant protection to national interests. In response, Madison and Wilson refused to budge from their original proposal, which clearly encroached upon local interests. Perhaps they and the other proponents of an extensive lower court system thought they had enough votes to defeat Rutledge's motion. When the question was called, however, Rutledge's motion carried five states to four with two delegations divided.

Almost immediately Madison and Wilson countered Rutledge's state trials–federal appeals proposal with a compromise of their own. Instead of mandating the creation of lower federal courts, they moved "that the National Legislature be empowered to institute inferior Tribunals." In support of this counterproposal, "[t]hey observed that there was a distinction between establishing such tribunals absolutely, and giving a discretion to the Legislature to establish or not establish them."[19] This new approach had the enormous political advantage of postponing the question to some date in the distant future and was quickly accepted by a vote of seven states to three with one divided. This agreement, however, did not completely dispel all the opposition among the delegations to federal trial courts. Obviously the South Carolinians were adamantly opposed. In addition, the Connecticut and New Jersey delegations remained unpersuaded. All three voted for Rutledge's proposal, and all three voted against the subsequent Madisonian Compromise.

There is particular irony in the Connecticut and New Jersey votes because these two delegations included Oliver Ellsworth and William Paterson. Just two years later, Paterson and Ellsworth personally drafted the Judiciary Act of 1789, which created an extensive system of lower federal trial courts. Indeed, they were probably the first federal Congress's firmest and most capable advocates of federal trial courts. Ellsworth subse-

---

18. *Id.* 124. On the availability of a trial de novo in the "appellate" courts of the eighteenth century, *see* RITZ 35–46.
19. 1 FARRAND 125.

quently became the third Chief Justice of the United States, and Paterson served for thirteen years on the High Court as an associate Justice.

On June 13, just eight days after the Madisonian Compromise was forged, the Convention revisited the proposed federal judiciary to consider the types of cases that should be tried in the federal courts. Apparently there was substantial disagreement over the precise contours of federal jurisdiction, and Edmund Randolph therefore proposed that the Convention simply agree to some general principles and leave the details to be worked out by a committee of detail. The Convention unanimously agreed and resolved "that the jurisdiction of the national judiciary shall extend to all cases of national revenue, impeachment of national officers, and questions which involve the national peace or harmony." Two days later William Paterson, with the assistance of Oliver Ellsworth and others, formally launched a final and concerted effort to place severe limitations on the proposed national judicial power. This effort was part of a general assault upon the Virginia Plan's combination of proportional representation and apparently open-ended powers. The large states that would presumably control the federal government had little reason to fear a more powerful central government. This assumption of political fact, however, had unsatisfactory implications for the small states. On June 15 William Paterson proposed a new plan cobbled together by a loose coalition of small-state delegations. His plan firmly rejected proportional representation and severely limited the Virginians' proposed cession of additional powers to the federal government.[20]

Although the Paterson Plan provided for federal jurisdiction over revenue cases, cases of capture, and cases in which foreigners might be interested, no provision was made for jurisdiction over cases in which citizens of other states were interested. Nor was there to be an openended grant of federal jurisdiction over questions involving the national peace and harmony. Paterson and his confederates distrusted the Virginia Plan's expansive approach to federal jurisdiction. Instead of facilitating the exercise of federal judicial power, they sought to limit it.

Paterson's most significant limiting proposal was to resurrect and reinforce Rutledge's June 5 motion to eliminate inferior federal courts. Except for the impeachment of federal officers, there would be no federal trial courts. The federal judiciary would consist of a single supreme tribunal that would exercise appellate but not original jurisdiction. The Paterson Plan expressly required virtually all cases within the federal

---

20. *Id.* 223–24, 231, 232, 238, 244.

courts' jurisdiction to be commenced and tried in state trial courts. Federal appellate review would be available only after the trial.

The contrast between the Paterson Plan and Paterson's subsequent position in the first federal Congress is striking. Just two years later he would vehemently argue that federal trial courts were essential. Obviously his understanding of judicial procedure and the significant power of trial courts to shape litigation did not change between his firm rejection of federal trial courts in 1787 and his enthusiastic endorsement of federal trial courts in 1789. Something else changed. On July 5 the Grand Compromise of the Convention was announced. Voting in the House of Representatives was to be in proportion to population, but each state would have an equal vote in the Senate. This compromise gave the smaller states significant power to negative undesirable legislative measures. Years later Madison related, "From the day when every doubt of the right of the smaller states to an equal vote in the Senate was quieted, [Ellsworth and Paterson] exceeded all others in zeal for granting powers to general government. Ellsworth became one of its strongest pillars. Paterson was for the rest of his life a federalist of federalists."[21]

On July 18, less than two weeks after the Grand Compromise, the Connecticut and New Jersey delegations dropped their objections to the Madisonian Compromise. The Convention unanimously agreed that the national legislature should be empowered to appoint inferior tribunals and that "the jurisdiction of the national Judiciary shall extend to cases arising under laws passed by the general Legislature, and to such other questions as involve the National peace and harmony." These and other resolutions were referred to a five-person Committee of Detail consisting of John Rutledge, Nathaniel Gorham, Oliver Ellsworth, Edmund Randolph, and James Wilson. The Committee met for a little over a week and worked out a rough draft of the Constitution, including provisions for a federal judiciary. Following the Convention's specific direction, the new federal courts' subject-matter jurisdiction was extended to cases arising under Congressional legislation. Although no express mention was made of revenue cases, by definition this general jurisdiction over Congressional legislation included them. In addition, the Committee fleshed out the Convention's general direction that federal jurisdiction should extend to questions involving "the National peace and harmony." The Committee limited this peace and harmony jurisdiction to cases affecting foreign diplomats, the trial of impeachments of federal officers, admi-

---

21. *See* 4 FARRAND 88–89.

ralty cases, controversies involving citizens of different states, controversies involving aliens, and controversies to which a state was a party.[22]

The Convention basically accepted the Committee's recommendation with few changes and clarifications. In retrospect the most significant changes were to move the trial of impeachments from the judiciary to the Senate and to expand the Court's power over cases arising under federal legislation to include cases arising under treaties and the Constitution itself. The Committee of Detail also worked the Madisonian Compromise into its draft Constitution. Inferior courts could be created, but only "such inferior courts as shall, when necessary, from time to time, be constituted by the legislature of the United States." Moreover, the Committee further provided that Congress "may assign any part of the jurisdiction [of the federal courts] in the manner, and under the limitations which it shall think proper, to such Inferior Courts." Although this latter language was eventually eliminated by the Convention, there is no other evidence that the Convention intended to rescind the Madisonian Compromise. Influential and knowledgeable delegates like Edmund Randolph and Oliver Ellsworth subsequently assumed and stated that Congress had a broad discretion to limit the lower federal courts' jurisdiction. Therefore the Convention's action can be explained most plausibly as a matter of style rather than substance.[23]

In addition to codifying Madison's Compromise on lower federal court jurisdiction, the Committee of Detail decided that Congress also should be given some control over the Supreme Court's jurisdiction. In cases involving foreign diplomats and in which a state shall be a party, the Supreme Court was to have an original or trial jurisdiction. In all other cases, the Supreme Court's jurisdiction was to be "appellate, with such exceptions and under such regulations as the Legislature shall make."[24] Precisely what the members of the Committee had in mind when they added this provision is difficult to determine. "Regulations" presumably would regulate the manner in which appeals to the Supreme Court would be conducted. On the other hand, "exceptions" seems to encompass a Congressional authority to exclude cases from the Court's appellate jurisdiction. The Committee probably sought to extend the principle of the Madisonian Compromise to the Supreme Court's appellate jurisdiction.

---

22. 2 FARRAND 39, 186.
23. *Id.* 186–87, 430–31, 493. For subsequent understandings of the continuing validity of the Madisonian Compromise, *see* Casto, *Congress;* Casto, *Orthodox.*
24. 2 FARRAND 186.

JUDICIAL APPOINTMENTS

The search for "auxiliary precautions" against abuse also featured prominently in the debates over the proper method of selecting federal judges. The delegates were utterly perplexed in their attempts to assure the appointment of capable, honest, and disinterested individuals to the judiciary. At various times, the Convention rejected delegating appointments to the states, appointment by the entire Congress, appointment by the Senate, nomination by the Senate with a negative by the President, appointment by the President, and nomination by the President with a negative by the Senate.[25] The delegates simply did not fully trust any of the possible appointing authorities.

Vesting Congress with the appointment power was unacceptable because "Intrigue, partiality, and concealment were the necessary consequences" of the Congress's large size. No one would be in charge of the appointment process, and therefore no one would be personally or politically responsible. Giving the power to the smaller Senate would have been a slight improvement, but the inherent problem remained. "Public bodies feel no personal responsibility and give full play to intrigue & Cabal." Obviously the problem of direct personal responsibility could be completely solved by giving the appointment power to the President, but this expansion of presidential authority would give the appearance of "leaning too much towards Monarchy." Moreover, the President was no more trustworthy than the Senate and indeed might "be more open to caresses and intrigue than the Senate."[26]

Although some delegates worried that unqualified individuals would be appointed to judgeships, this concern does not plausibly explain the Convention's total disarray. The delegates were capable and practical individuals with extensive experience in public life. They undoubtedly understood that a limited degree of official incompetence was inherent in all forms of government. They surely did not believe that a government organized according to republican principles would be especially prone to official incompetence. The delegates' references to intrigue and cabal suggests a far more serious basis for their quandary over the appointment process. Eighteenth-century Americans had a profound and pervasive fear of conspiracies in which secret cliques of governmental officials would manipulate the government to further improper poli-

---

25. *See* Joseph Harris, The Advice and Consent of the Senate 17–24 (1953); 2 Farrand 81 (O. Ellsworth prefers nomination by Senate with presidential negative).

26. 1 Farrand 119 (J. Wilson); 2 Farrand 42 (N. Gorham); *id.* 81 (O. Ellsworth); *id.* (E. Randolph); 1 Farrand 119 (J. Rutledge).

cies.[27] The words *intrigue* and *cabal*, with their connotation of conspiratorial manipulation of governmental power, were undoubtedly used as shorthand expressions for this pervasive fear of conspiracies. The quandary over the appointment power becomes more intelligible if the delegates' primary concern was that the federal courts might be influenced by individuals or cliques bent on implementing improper policies.

This notion that the appointment power might be abused to accomplish improper ends is especially close to the surface of the July 21 debates. Gouverneur Morris argued against appointment by the Senate because he assumed that the states would use their direct control over the selection of senators to influence the disposition of litigation in which the states had a corporate or political interest. He bluntly noted, "Next to the impropriety of being Judge in one's own cause, is the appointment of the Judge." James Madison suggested that the states' equal voting rights in the Senate would give the more numerous northern states control of the Supreme Court and furnish "a perpetual ground of jealousy and discontent . . . to the Southern States."[28]

In the same debate, George Mason favored appointment by the Senate as preferable to appointment by the President. Mason embraced Morris's point that the power to select judges gives some control over the eventual adjudication of cases and applied it to the President. Mason "considered the appointment by the executive as a dangerous prerogative. It might give him an influence over the Judiciary department itself." Similarly, Alexander Hamilton subsequently noted the danger that a President might appoint judges whose "insignificance and pliancy [would] render them the obsequious instruments of his pleasure."[29]

Finally the Convention settled upon a compromise. Individual responsibility was assured by giving the President the power to nominate, but presidential abuse would be checked by requiring Senate approval. Given the general mood of distrust, the delegates must have assumed that the Senate would examine the ability and qualifications of individuals nominated for judgeships and would not always act as a rubber stamp to Presidential nominations. Alexander Hamilton subsequently explained that the Senate would provide "an excellent check upon a spirit of favoritism in the President, and would tend greatly to prevent the appointment of

---

27. *See* BERNARD BAILYN, THE IDEOLOGICAL ORIGINS OF THE AMERICAN REVOLUTION 144–59 (1967). *See also* Gordon Wood, *Conspiracy and the Paranoid Style: Casualty and Deceit in the Eighteenth Century*, 39 W. & M. Q. (3d ser.) 401 (1982).

28. 2 FARRAND 82 (G. Morris); *id.* 81 (J. Madison).

29. *Id.* 83 (G. Mason); FEDERALIST No. 76 at 513 (A. Hamilton).

unfit characters from state prejudice, from family connection, from personal attachment, or from view of popularity."[30]

At the Convention, some practical delegates direly and accurately predicted that the Senate's "right to supersede [the President's] nomination will be ideal only. A nomination under such circumstances will be equivalent to an appointment." Hamilton agreed, but he did not think the Senate would become a mere rubber stamp. He believed the Senate's theoretical power to overrule the President's choice "would have a powerful, though, in general, a silent operation." The President would have to nominate individuals with an eye toward confirmation by the Senate, and the consequent presidential self-restraint would solve the problem.[31]

GOOD BEHAVIOR AND COMPENSATION

The general theme of distrust resurfaced when the Convention turned to the issues of judicial tenure and compensation. Virtually everyone agreed that federal judges should have a more or less permanent tenure and hold their office during good behavior. Likewise there was general agreement that judicial salaries should not be subject to diminution. Alexander Hamilton succinctly explained the Convention's concerns when he later wrote that *"a power over a man's subsistence amounts to a power over his will."* The Virginia and North Carolina delegations pressed this concern to a logical extreme and even opposed salary increases to serving judges. In favor of this extreme position, James Madison contended that "whenever an increase is wished by the Judges, or may be in agitation in the legislature, an undue compliance in the former may be felt toward the latter." But a clear majority of the delegations thought salary increases should be permitted to reflect increases in the cost of living, added levels of work, and changing views regarding the proper salary of high judicial offices.[32]

In the subsequent ratification process, Alexander Hamilton offered a thorough analysis and justification of the Constitution's salary and tenure provisions. He briefly mentioned that these provisions would assure the necessary stability to attract capable and honest men. But his principal argument was based upon separation of powers and the need to as-

---

30. FEDERALIST No. 76 at 513 (A. Hamilton).

31. 2 FARRAND at 81 (O. Ellsworth); *id.* at 83 (G. Mason); FEDERALIST No. 76 at 513 (A. Hamilton).

32. FEDERALIST No. 79 at 531 (A. Hamilton) (emphasis original). For Madison and North Carolina, *see* 2 FARRAND 45. For the "clear majority," *see id.* 44–45; *see also* FEDERALIST No. 78 at 522 (A. Hamilton).

sure that the judiciary could check legislative or executive oppression. Relying upon Montesquieu, he noted that the judiciary was the least powerful branch of government because judges lack authority to appropriate money and because they neither frame nor enforce the laws. As a result of this "natural feebleness," the judicial branch "is in continual jeopardy of being overpowered, awed, or influenced by its co-ordinate branches." Hamilton was particularly concerned that in an elected government, "designing men" or special interests might improperly influence the electorate to choose a government prone to "dangerous innovations . . . and serious oppressions of the minor party in the community." An independent judiciary could check legislative and executive overreaching by fairly interpreting the laws and conscientiously administering the judicial process. But Hamilton emphasized a more straightforward check upon the political branches. "The complete independence of the courts of justice is peculiarly essential in a limited Constitution." To protect the people, the Constitution included many limitations to the federal government's power. Hamilton insisted that the ultimate interpretation of these Constitutional limitations was vested in the judiciary, not the legislature. The courts are "designed to be an intermediate body between the people and the legislature in order, among other things, to keep the latter within the limits assigned to their authority." Because judges had this special responsibility, it was essential to guarantee them lifetime tenure and a salary beyond congressional control.[33]

JUDICIAL REVIEW

Hamilton's suggestion that the federal courts would override acts of Congress was more than the idiosyncratic insight of a brilliant politician and attorney. Many of the Convention delegates assumed that the federal courts would exercise this power, which today we call judicial review. In the later ratification process, Oliver Ellsworth argued that judicial review would be a valuable check upon Congressional abuse. He explained,

> If the general legislature should at any time overleap their limits, the judicial department is a constitutional check. If the United States go beyond their powers, if they make a law which the Constitution does not authorize, it is void; and the national judges, who to secure their impartiality are to be made independent, will declare it to be void.

---

33. Federalist No. 78 at 522–30 (A. Hamilton), *citing* Montesquieu.

But others saw this power of judicial review not as a check upon abuse but rather as a font of abuse.[34]

The period's most detailed and cogent criticism of judicial review is presented in the letters of Brutus[35] that were written to defeat the Constitution's ratification in New York. Like everyone else who discussed judicial review before the Constitution was ratified, Brutus assumed that the proposed federal courts would have the authority to declare unconstitutional acts of Congress to be void. His main concern was that there was no constitutional mechanism to control Supreme Court Justices who might abuse their power of judicial review. Neither the Congress nor the President could act directly to correct an expansive and unwarranted interpretation of the Constitution. Nor were the indirect controls of removal and salary adjustment available to correct this subtle but serious potential form of abuse.

Brutus carefully and presciently detailed two significantly different approaches to Constitutional interpretation. Under the first "mode of construction,"

> the courts are to give such meaning to the constitution as comports best with the common, and generally received acceptation of the words in which it is expressed. . . . Where words are dubious, they will be explained by context. The end of the clause will be attended to, and the words will be understood, as having a view to it; and the words will not be so understood as to bear no meaning or a very absurd one.

Using this mode of construction, a judge would conscientiously seek an objective constitutional meaning and would not impress the Constitution with his particular values. In contrast to the first mode of construction, Brutus noted the existence of a second and more freewheeling interpretive tradition. In construing acts of Parliament, English courts occasionally strayed from the apparent meaning of a statute to achieve an equitable result. Brutus predicted that Supreme Court Justices would use this approach: "And in their decisions they will not confine themselves to any fixed or established rules, but will determine, according to what appears to them, the reason and spirit of the constitution." This approach may have been acceptable in England, where there was a legislative power of review over judicial decisions—that is, review by the House

---

34. *See* RAOUL BERGER, CONGRESS V. THE SUPREME COURT 337–46 (1969); Oliver Ellsworth, Speech of Jan. 7, 1788, *reprinted in* 3 DHRC 548, 553.

35. *Brutus XI–XV, reprinted in* 15 DHRC 512–17 and 16 DHRC 72–75, 120–22, 172–75, 255–58, 328–32, 431–35. *See* William Jeffrey, *The Letters of "Brutus"—A Neglected Element in the Ratification Campaign of 1787–88*, 90 U. CIN. L. REV. 644 (1971).

of Lords. But under the Constitution, the "opinions of the Supreme Court, whatever they may be, will have the force of law; because there is no power provided in the constitution, that can correct their errors, or control their adjudication."[36]

The influential English writer Sir William Blackstone warned that this equitable approach "must not be indulged too far, lest thereby we destroy all law, and leave the decision of every question in the breast of the judge." Brutus strongly suggested that in this regard the new federal judiciary would be overly indulgent. He believed the Supreme Court would push federal powers beyond the limits expressed in the letter of the Constitution. "Perhaps nothing could have been better conceived," wrote Brutus, "to facilitate the abolition of state governments than the constitution of the judicial."[37]

Almost immediately, Alexander Hamilton wrote his *Federalist* Nos. 78–81, in which he defended the proposed federal courts against Brutus's sophisticated assault. The basic problem was that Brutus was correct in pointing out the virtual absence of effective control over the judiciary's power to construe the Constitution. Here was a significant grant of power with no "auxiliary precautions" against its abuse. The judges literally did have life tenure, and their salaries were not subject to diminution. In addition, Hamilton tacitly conceded that the supposed remedy of impeachment would extend only to the most blatant forms of judicial misconduct and therefore would be nugatory. Hamilton reminded his readers, however, that the Supreme Court's power of judicial review was itself an auxiliary precaution—a valuable check to Congressional overreaching.[38] Then he sought to assure the public that Brutus's fear of an uncontrolled judiciary was overdrawn.

Instead of seeking controls that did not exist, Hamilton argued that in the special case of the judiciary there was comparatively little need for auxiliary precautions against abuse. In a famous paragraph he argued that the judiciary was "the least dangerous" branch of government. The executive wielded the government's sword, and the legislative controlled its purse. "The judiciary on the contrary has no influence over either the sword or the purse, no direction either of the strength or the wealth of the society, and can take no active resolution whatever."[39]

Moreover, Hamilton noted that the judiciary would be subject to a unique internal control based upon the nature of the judicial process. The judi-

36. *Brutus XI, reprinted in* 15 DHRC 512, 513–14.
37. *Brutus XV, reprinted in* 16 DHRC 431, 434 *quoting* 1 BLACKSTONE 62.
38. FEDERALIST No. 78 at 523 (A. Hamilton).
39. FEDERALIST No. 78 at 523 (A. Hamilton).

ciary, wrote Hamilton, "may truly be said to have neither Force nor Will, but merely judgment." In striking down a Congressional enactment, the Justices of the Supreme Court would not be imposing their political will upon the government. Instead they would be enforcing the will of the people in whose name the Constitution was framed and ratified. To be sure, the Court would have to ascertain the meaning of the Constitution, but this process would entail the exercise of mere judgment—not political will. Brutus had worried that the Justices would abuse their authority under the pretense of giving the Constitution an equitable construction. Hamilton replied that "there is not a syllable in the plan under consideration which *directly* empowers the national courts to construe the laws according to the spirit of the Constitution, or which gives them any greater latitude in this respect than may be claimed by the courts of every State."[40]

This sophisticated exchange between Brutus and Hamilton is particularly valuable evidence of a consensus regarding the proper scope of judicial review. Both men agreed that the Supreme Court would exercise a power of judicial review. Similarly, they agreed that judicial review would be improper to the extent that the judges ventured beyond the Constitution's self-evident or objective meaning. In particular, they agreed that the Justices should not impose their political will on the country under the guise of Constitutional interpretation. "It can be of no weight to say," Hamilton wrote, "that the courts on the pretense of a repugnancy, may substitute their own pleasure to the constitutional intentions of the legislature." Finally, Hamilton and apparently Brutus agreed that judicial review would be appropriate in situations in which the Court used its power to enforce clear Constitutional limitations like the provisions against bills of attainder and ex post facto laws. Their disagreement was over practice, not principle. Brutus feared that the Supreme Court would use the doctrine of equitable construction to create principles of constitutional law that were not clearly present in the written Constitution ratified by the people. In contrast, Hamilton sought to reassure the public that the Court would limit constitutional law to the written principles actually approved in the ratification process. In the short run, Hamilton's assurances were vindicated; but in the long run, Brutus's prediction has come to pass.[41]

---

40. Federalist No. 81 at 543 (A. Hamilton) (emphasis original). For a valuable discussion of the distinction between will and judicial judgment, *see* H. Jefferson Powell, *The Political Grammar of Early Constitutional Law,* 71 N.C. L. Rev. 949, 996–97, 1006–8 (1993).

41. Federalist No. 78 at 526 (A. Hamilton). *See* chapter 8 at 214–27.

NONJUDICIAL DUTIES

Judicial review and the nature of the judicial process also entered into the Convention's consideration of various proposals to vest the federal judiciary with supplemental, nonjudicial duties. The original Virginia Plan proposed the creation of a Council of Revision to consist of "the Executive and a convenient number of the National Judiciary."[42] This Council would have had a veto (subject to a congressional override) over acts of Congress. Although this proposal was eventually rejected, the various arguments for and against the Council provide rich insights into the delegates' understanding of judicial review and the nature of the judicial process.

Many delegates insisted that judges had no particular qualifications to participate in the legislative or lawmaking process. Elbridge Gerry of Massachusetts insisted, "It was quite foreign from the nature of the [judicial] office to make them judges of the policy of public measures." Similarly, Nathaniel Gorham noted, "As Judges they are not to be presumed to possess any peculiar knowledge of the mere policy of public measures." Luther Martin explained, "A knowledge of mankind, and of Legislative affairs cannot be presumed to belong in a higher degree to the Judges than to the Legislative."[43]

Even firm supporters of judicial participation in the Council of Revision apparently agreed with this analysis. Oliver Ellsworth, who was himself a judge, argued that the judges' "systematic and accurate knowledge of the Laws"—especially the laws of Nations—would be very useful to the Council. Ellsworth did not, however, contradict the opponents' contention that the judiciary had no business weighing public policy. Indeed, he probably agreed with this proposition. Nine years later, while serving as Chief Justice of the United States, he emphatically stated that "suggestions of policy and convenience cannot be considered in the judicial determination of a question of right." This firm insistence that judges—as judges—are incompetent to consider questions of policy is an obvious explication of Hamilton's insistence that the power of judicial review involved mere judgment and not political will.[44]

The delegates also had a shared belief that the power of judicial review was directly relevant to the desirability of judicial participation upon the

---

42. 1 FARRAND 21.

43. 1 FARRAND 97–98 (E. Gerry); *id.* 73 (N. Gorham); *id.* 76 (L. Martin).

44. *Id.* 73–74 (O. Ellsworth); Moodie v. The Ship Phoebe Anne, 3 U.S. (3 Dall.) 319, 319 (1796), *discussed in* chapter 4 at 114. *Accord,* Cowper v. Telfair, unreported (C.C.D. Ga. 1799) (Ellsworth, C. J.), *reprinted in* Casto, *Iredell.*

Council of Revision. During the course of the debates, many delegates expressly assumed that the judiciary would exercise this power, and there is no record of even a hint to the contrary. The delegates, however, drew quite different conclusions from their shared assumptions. Rufus King, Elbridge Gerry, and Luther Martin thought that the judges' power of judicial review made their participation on the Council of Review unnecessary. The judges, acting in their capacity as judges, "will no doubt stop the operation of such [laws] as shall appear repugnant to the constitution." But the proponents of the Council of Revision were quick to respond that the power of judicial review was limited. James Wilson clearly and concisely explained why judicial participation upon the Council would not be superfluous:

> It had been said that the Judges, as expositors of the Laws would have an opportunity of defending their constitutional rights. There was weight in this observation; but this power of the Judges did not go far enough. Laws may be unjust, may be unwise, may be dangerous, may be destructive; and yet not be so unconstitutional as to justify the Judges in refusing to give them effect. Let [the judges] have a share in the Revisionary power, and they will have an opportunity of taking notice of these characters of a law, and of counteracting, by the weight of their opinions the improper views of the Legislature.

George Mason made the same point and wrote that the power of judicial review could be exercised only when a law was "plainly contrary to the Constitution.[45]

Both of these arguments about the need for a judicial presence upon the Council of Revision made sense. The power of judicial review rendered the judicial presence superfluous—but only to a degree. Perhaps the delegates were finally persuaded by another argument. John Rutledge was against a judicial presence on the Council of Revision because "the Judges ought never to give their opinion on a law till it comes before them." Other delegates took the same position when they noted that "Judges ought to be able to expound the law as it should come before them, free from the bias of having participated in its formation."[46]

Although the Convention clearly decided that the judiciary should not

---

45. 1 Farrand 97 (E. Gerry); id. at 109 (R. King); 2 Farrand at 76–77 (L. Martin); 2 Farrand 73 (J. Wilson); id. 78 (G. Mason).

46. 2 Farrand 80 (J. Rutledge); 1 Farrand 98 (R. King); id. 108–9 (Dickerson); 2 Farrand 75 (C. Strong); id. 79 (G. Morris).

participate directly in the veto process, the possibility remained that the judiciary might be a source of legal advice for the legislative and executive branches. If so, the Constitution makes no mention of this advisory function. Certainly the federal courts' jurisdiction over the various cases and controversies listed in Article III, §2 of the constitution was not intended to comprehend extrajudicial advice. Near the end of the Convention, Madison noted that it was "generally supposed that the jurisdiction given [under Article III] was constructively limited to cases of a Judiciary nature."[47]

Some influential delegates believed that the President should at least be formally empowered to seek legal advice from the Court, and proposals to this effect were referred to the Committee of Detail that had prepared the initial draft of the Constitution. But this idea did not emerge from that committee. The only mention in the Constitution of presidential authority to seek advice is limited to requests directed to "the executive Departments."[48]

LOOKING TO THE FUTURE

As with some other issues, the framers did not write clear and express constitutional language on the propriety of judges' giving advisory opinions or performing other nonjudicial public functions. Their Constitution created only the bare bones of a federal judicial system and left many details to be fleshed out by the legislative, executive, and judicial branches. The judicial branch was to play an important role in shaping guidelines on the comparatively minor issue of whether federal judges might appropriately perform nonjudicial functions.[49] Other details, far more significant, were left to be filled in by the President and Congress.

In 1790 Attorney General Edmund Randolph explained, "The supreme court, though inherent in the Constitution, was to receive its first motion from Congress; the inferior courts must have slept forever, without the pleasure of Congress."[50] The Constitution created the Supreme Court but left open the question whether there would be inferior federal courts. Likewise, the outer limits of federal judicial power were defined by Article III's list of cases and controversies within the courts' subject-matter jurisdiction, but Congress was authorized to narrow the actual

---

47. 2 FARRAND 430 (J. Madison).
48. 2 FARRAND 340–41; U.S. Const. art. II, § 2. *See also* HART & WECHSLER 7–8.
49. *See* chapter 6.
50. Edmund Randolph, *Report on the Judiciary* (1790), *reprinted in* 4 DHSC 128, 162 n.6.

scope of the courts' jurisdiction. Finally, a procedure for appointing judicial officers was written into the Constitution, but the number of officers was left to the future.

Looking to the future, the Congress and the President would necessarily play crucial roles in giving the Supreme Court its "first motion" and awakening the inferior courts. The President would have to nominate individuals to fill judicial posts, and Congress would have to resolve some of the highly politicized issues that the Philadelphia Convention ducked.

2

THE JUDICIARY ACT OF 1789

By the spring of 1789, the Constitution had been ratified, and the new federal government was ready to commence its operations. In early April, the Senate began its legislative work by designating a Grand Committee consisting of a senator from each state to draft a bill for organizing the federal judiciary. Following eighteenth-century Parliamentary practice, Oliver Ellsworth—whose name appeared first on the Committee's roster—undoubtedly served as the Committee's chairman. More significantly, members of the Congress generally recognized Ellsworth as the judiciary measure's "leading projector." Some five months after his Committee commenced its work, the Congress formally enacted the Judiciary Act of 1789 and created a comprehensive system of federal trial and appellate courts.[1]

DRAFTING THE JUDICIARY ACT

Ellsworth's selection was fortunate and in no way coincidental. No one was better qualified to implement the Constitution's judicial article. Ellsworth had been a successful and skilled litigator and a respected state judge before he was chosen to serve in the Senate. At the time, some believed that he should be considered for the position of the first Chief Justice of the United States, and seven years later he became the nation's third Chief Justice. In addition to his extensive courtroom experience, he had served with distinction in the Connecticut General Assembly and the Continental Congress. As a Continental legislator, he

---

1. Paine Wingate to Timothy Pickering (Apr. 29, 1789), *excerpted in* 4 DHSC 381–82. The best general treatments of the Judiciary Act of 1789 are Charles Warren, *New Light on the History of the Federal Judiciary Act of 1789*, 37 Harv. L. Rev. 49 (1923); and Holt.

had drafted the ordinance that created the national appellate court under the Articles of Confederation for the review of state court prize decisions. He had also been a leading participant in the framing and ratification of the Constitution. Finally, Ellsworth was an immensely practical politician who thoroughly understood the art of political deal making.[2]

Ellsworth arrived in New York a full month before a quorum was formed in the Senate, but he did not waste his time on frivolous pursuits. He epitomized the Protestant work ethic and was a thoroughgoing Calvinist who had personally experienced his election by God for salvation. With characteristic seriousness, he wrote his wife, "I employ my time as I presume a number of others do, in looking into and preparing for the business we are soon to enter upon." His friend and roommate Abraham Baldwin reported that from the time Ellsworth first arrived in New York, he worked on the Judiciary Bill "night and day" until it was ready for the Senate's consideration in mid-June.[3]

On the Committee, Ellsworth was ably assisted by William Paterson of New Jersey and Caleb Strong of Massachusetts. Like Ellsworth, Paterson and Strong were staunch Calvinists. Ellsworth and Paterson had developed a personal friendship at the Constitutional Convention, and Ellsworth and Strong became close friends during their service in the Senate. All three wanted to create a strong federal judicial system.

Although Ellsworth worked closely with his friends Paterson and Strong, he did not snub the members of the Committee who were opposed to the system he created. Senator Paine Wingate of New Hampshire, who served on the Committee but voted against the Committee's bill, privately described Ellsworth as "a very sensible man." Aside from the triumvirate of Ellsworth, Paterson, and Strong, the most valuable member of the Committee was probably Richard Henry Lee of Virginia. Lee came to the Senate with a brief from his state to place radical restrictions on the new federal judicial system, but he did not have a closed mind on the subject. Although he finally voted against Ellsworth's bill, he was not stridently opposed to the measure. Indeed, he believed that he had "endeavored successfully in the Judiciary bill to remedy so far a law can remedy, the defects of the Constitution." Within the Committee, he probably served as a valuable source of in-

---

2. *See generally* BROWN. *See also* N.Y. JOURNAL, Apr. 16, 1789, *reprinted in* 1 DHSC 611–12 (mentioning Ellsworth as a possible Chief Justice).

3. Oliver Ellsworth to Abigail Ellsworth (Mar. 8, 1789) (CtHi); Abraham Baldwin to Joel Barlow (June 14, 1789), *quoted in* 4 DHSC 23 n.8. *See also* Casto, *Calvinism.*

sights into the nuances of the opposition to federal courts. Lee's negative input was probably especially valuable in shaping the lower federal courts' jurisdiction.[4]

In fashioning the new federal judicial system, Ellsworth's Committee had to grapple with the issues of federal judicial power that the Constitutional Convention's acceptance of the Madisonian Compromise had skillfully postponed. Would Congress restrict the judicial power of the United States to a single, relatively isolated Supreme Court in the nation's capitol, or would there be an extensive system of federal courts distributed throughout the states? Within a month, Ellsworth and his fellow Committee members had worked out a compromise proposal that was subsequently enacted by the Senate and House with little significant change.

OPPOSITION TO THE FEDERAL COURTS

Ellsworth's compromise was in response to the opposition that had first emerged at the Constitutional Convention when John Rutledge attempted to excise all mention of inferior federal courts from the Constitution. This opposition stemmed from an interlocking collection of general and specific fears about the potential abuse of federal judicial power. During the ratification process, George Mason of Virginia had warned the public in a widely circulated statement that the new federal courts would "absorb and destroy the judiciaries of the several states." In addition to this general and almost visceral objection, the opponents of federal courts were deeply disturbed by the absence of any Constitutional guaranty of the right to trial by jury.[5]

These two objections were particularly troubling in the case of small claims against relatively poor defendants. For example, Senator Lee, who undoubtedly led the opposition within Ellsworth's Committee, was particularly concerned about "the vexatious and oppressive calling of citizens from their own country . . . to be tried in a far distant court, and as it may be without a jury, whereby in a multitude of cases, the circum-

---

4. Paine Wingate to Timothy Pickering (Apr. 29, 1789), *excerpted in* 4 DHSC 381–82; and Richard Henry Lee to Patrick Henry (Sept. 14, 1789), *quoted in* 4 DHSC 511 n.1. *See also* Richard Henry Lee to Patrick Henry (May 28, 1789), *reprinted in* 2 LEE LETTERS 487.

5. GEORGE MASON, OBJECTIONS TO THE CONSTITUTION (1787), *reprinted in* 13 DHRC 40–46. For comments on jury trials, *see, e.g., Richard Henry Lee's Proposed Amendments, reprinted and discussed in* 8 DHRC 59–67.

stances of distance and expense may compel numbers to submit to the most unjust and ill-founded demand."[6]

These more or less general objections were directly implicated by one of the most serious domestic and foreign policy problems of the new republic. As we have seen, during the Revolutionary War, the rebelling states had adopted an array of legislative strategies that successfully prevented British creditors from recovering debts owed by American debtors. To remedy this problem, the negotiators of the Treaty of Paris that ended the war agreed in Article IV of the treaty that "creditors on either side shall meet with no lawful impediment to the recovery of the full value in sterling money of all bona fide debts heretofore contracted." Notwithstanding Article IV, many American debtors—particularly in the South—continued refusing to pay their British debts, and some state legislatures and courts overtly cooperated with them.[7]

To a degree, this endemic refusal to repay was probably motivated by simple dishonesty. In addition, however, Professor Wythe Holt has pointed to another aspect of the debt problem not readily apparent to late-twentieth-century minds steeped in a commercially oriented and individualistic society. Many Americans of the Founding Era viewed themselves primarily in terms of their relationship to society rather than as individuals seeking to maximize individual goods. Particularly among nonmerchants, this communitarian outlook extended to contractual relations.[8]

These communitarian Americans viewed their contracts with British creditors as just one aspect of their overall relationship with Great Britain. Another aspect was a long and costly war caused, in the opinion of many Americans, by British overreaching and oppression. Great Britain's blatant misconduct must have appeared to communitarian Americans as a hideous rent in the fabric of society. When the British contracts are seen as part of the overall relationship between America and Great Britain, the notion of honoring those contracts in the face of Britain's misdeeds becomes outrageous. Immediately after the war, people complained, "If we are now to pay the debts due to British Merchants, what have we been fighting for all this while." This combination of communitarian principle and personal greed was a potent political force, and it was enhanced by an economic depression in the 1780s. As a result, British creditors were unable to obtain a remedy in the courts of some states,

---

6. *Richard Henry Lee's Proposed Amendments, reprinted and discussed in* 8 DHRC 59–67.

7. *See* chapter 1 at 8–9.

8. *See generally* Holt.

particularly Virginia. As long as local debtors had significant control over the courts, there was no real possibility that the debts would be paid.[9]

This status quo was threatened by the Constitution's provision for federal courts. In a close and hard-fought political struggle, the Virginia ratifying convention eventually approved the proposed Constitution— but only after recommending amendments for a drastic curtailment of federal judicial power. These proposed amendments would have authorized only two kinds of federal courts. Congress could create inferior admiralty trial courts whose power would be limited to maritime cases. In addition, there would be a Supreme Court with significantly attenuated authority. In cases affecting foreign diplomats or in which a state was suing or being sued, the Supreme Court would act as a trial court. In all other cases except maritime proceedings in the inferior admiralty courts, trials would be conducted in state courts. The Supreme Court's appellate authority over state court litigation would have been restricted to cases arising under treaties, controversies in which the United States itself was a party, and litigation between parties claiming lands under grants from different states. Even within this narrow scope of federal appellate jurisdiction, the Supreme Court was to have no power to review the state trial courts' determination of facts except in cases of equity and admiralty jurisdiction, in which by tradition juries were not used. Finally—and clearly with an eye to the claims of British creditors—the Virginians proposed that no federal court should have any power over cases in which the claim originated before the ratification of the Constitution. A Connecticut friend and political ally of Oliver Ellsworth subsequently wrote that the "obvious effect of these restrictions would have been to divest the general government of *all control* not only over *many* questions arising under the *Constitution and Laws of the United States,* but over *all questions* relative to *infractions of the fourth article of the treaty of peace.*"[10]

THE SEEDS OF A COMPROMISE

Ellsworth and Paterson, who were the principal Senate proponents of an extensive system of federal courts, were immensely practical men. An insightful biographer who knew Ellsworth wrote that "he was formed by

---

9. Holt 1445–49; George Mason to Patrick Henry (May 6, 1783), *reprinted in* 2 MASON PAPERS 769.

10. OLIVER WOLCOTT, BRITISH INFLUENCE ON THE AFFAIRS OF THE UNITED STATES, PROVED AND EXPLAINED (1804) (Shaw Shoemaker No. 7793) (emphasis original). For the Virginia Convention's proposed amendments, *see* Amendments Proposed by the Virginia Convention (1788), *reprinted in* 4 DHFFC 15–19.

nature more for the discharge of active duties, than for contemplative study, or abstract science." Similarly, Paterson thought it "a grand fault of all the fine writers on government that they do not distinguish between theory and practice." In theory, the judicial power of the United States should extend to all matters within the federal government's legislative competence. If Congress could pass a law on a particular subject, a Federal court should be available to adjudicate disputes over the applicability or enforcement of the law. Moreover, Article III of the Constitution explicitly authorized this pleasing symmetry. The problem was that extending the judicial power to the limits of the Constitution would have played directly into the theoretical and practical fears of those who opposed the federal courts. Rather than commit this political gaffe, the two men adopted a restrictive approach to federal jurisdiction.[11]

Ellsworth and Paterson did not see the creation of federal courts as an ultimate objective. Instead they sought to create a judicial system as a means to achieve several discrete and important national security objectives. This concern for national security cannot explain all of the Judiciary Act's jurisdictional contours. The Act was a human endeavor involving a mishmash of conflicting, supporting, and interlocking purposes. Therefore any monolithic explanation of the Congress's legislative agenda is implausible. Nevertheless, national security clearly was a major—probably the primary—motivation of the Federalists who created the new nationwide system of federal trial courts. The bill that Ellsworth and Paterson drafted, which Congress enacted, vested the federal courts with plenary power over prize cases, suits to enforce federal revenue laws, and prosecutions for violations of federal criminal law. In exchange, the federal courts' jurisdiction over other cases was severely restricted.

During the initial month of the Committee's work, Ellsworth presumably tried to broker a compromise within his Committee. If he did, he failed because three of the ten members eventually voted against the passage of his judiciary bill. This failure to reach a consensus within the Committee complicated Ellsworth's task. Instead of directly negotiating an accord with fellow Committee members, he had to propose a unilateral compromise that he judged would be acceptable to the Congress at large.

Fortunately for Ellsworth, there was a limited but significant consensus

11. [Gulian Verplanck], *Biographical Sketch of Chief Justice Ellsworth,* 3 ANALECTIC MAGAZINE 382 (1814); *William Paterson's Address to a Conference* (Mar. 5, 1777), *reprinted in* 2 SOMERSET COUNTY HIST. Q. 1, 4 (1913).

within the Congress on the need for a federal judicial system. Everyone—even the Virginians—agreed that at the very least there should be a Supreme Court with some appellate jurisdiction. Likewise, all agreed that inferior federal admiralty courts should be established on each state's seaboard. This consensus begged the fundamental question of whether there should be a Supreme Court and a system of federal trial courts spread throughout the nation. Therefore Ellsworth's primary task was to draft acceptable statutory language that would define and establish the limits to the inferior courts' and the Supreme Court's subject-matter jurisdiction.

LIMITING THE SUPREME COURT'S JURISDICTION

The most significant aspect of the Supreme Court's jurisdiction was its appellate authority to review the decisions of state courts and inferior federal courts. The Constitution itself vested the Court with broad authority over cases involving federal law, admiralty cases, and cases of diversity and alienage jurisdiction. Within these categories there was no constitutional limitation to the Court's authority to overturn state court judgments. The Constitution also expressly provided for Supreme Court appellate review "both as to law and fact."

The potential reach of the Supreme Court's appellate authority may be illustrated by an opinion written by Ellsworth when he was a state judge in Connecticut. In *Huntington v. Chaplin*,[12] Ellsworth held that under the common law, a person interested in the payment of a debt may not testify as to the plaintiff's acceptance of the payment. But Roger Sherman, Ellsworth's good friend and political mentor, dissented. Judge Sherman thought this general common-law rule was subject to equitable exceptions. If the same issue were to arise in a British creditor case, Ellsworth's strict view of the issue would prevent an American debtor from presenting evidence of his partial payment of the debt. A state court might therefore adopt Sherman's more lenient view and—depending upon the equities of the case—allow the debtor to testify.

If a state court adopted Sherman's more lenient view in a British creditor case, the Constitution's broad grant of appellate authority authorized the Supreme Court to overrule the state court on this simple common-law issue of the admissibility of evidence. The Court's appellate authority under the Constitution extends to controversies between an alien and an American citizen and draws no distinction between obviously federal is-

---

12. 1 Kirby 166 (1786) (By the Court). The manuscript opinion in the Connecticut State Archives is in Ellsworth's hand.

sues like the meaning of a treaty and simple common-law issues like the admissibility of evidence. Under the Constitution, the Court is literally vested with appellate jurisdiction over entire cases and controversies, not merely over discrete legal issues that may arise within cases and controversies.

This notion that the Supreme Court of the United States may correct a state court's common-law decision rings strange to modern ears, but an eighteenth-century attorney would have been hard-pressed to deny the Court's constitutional jurisdiction over such issues. Today virtually all American attorneys are more or less legal positivists, but eighteenth-century Americans were natural lawyers. A closer look at the eighteenth century's predominant natural-law philosophy will help to clarify this fundamental shared understanding among Americans in the Founding Era.[13]

The most influential written example of natural-law thinking in the Founding Era was Blackstone's *Commentaries,* published in 1765. Blackstone emphatically denied that judges made law, and in the case of statutes this model of the judicial process was easily applied. Statutes were preexisting laws that judges simply read and applied in particular cases. Blackstone's model was more complicated in common-law cases because the common law was unwritten. Blackstone and virtually all eighteenth-century English-speaking lawyers believed that the common law preexisted judges and was independent from them. The metaphysical problem was, Who made the common law—where did it come from? In the case of statutes, this question was easily answered by reference to Parliament. But in the case of the common law, the answer was not so simple.

Blackstone, Ellsworth, and late-eighteenth-century common lawyers believed the common law existed independently from the state. Neither kings nor legislators nor even judges were necessary to create the common law. Instead, it was part of the law of nature. But by "nature" they did not mean a godless system organized by Darwinian striving. Nietzche's announcement of God's death was more than a century into the future. In eighteenth-century America, virtually everyone still believed that nature was God's creation and was ordered by him. This vision was especially strong in the case of Calvinists like Ellsworth who believed that God had absolutely and minutely predestined human existence.

Consistent with this vision of God's nature, Blackstone wrote that God had ordained a system of "external immutable laws of good and evil."

---

13. *See* introduction at 2. *See also* Casto, *Erie* 912–14, 931–38.

Human laws—especially the common law—"derive all their force, and all their authority" from this universal natural law and are invalid if they are contrary to it. Turning specifically to England, Blackstone defined the common law as a body of unwritten customs that receive "their binding power, and the force of laws, by long and immemorial usage, and by their universal reception throughout the kingdom."[14]

Under this theory, judges do not make laws. They are not legislators. They are, to use Blackstone's phrase. "the living oracles" of a common law that preexists in nature. Reasoning in humans was a process bestowed by God that enabled them to detect the subtleties of the preexisting natural law; judges, through their talent, experience, and wisdom, were supposed to use their reasoning to discern the law in the cases that came before them. A judge's task was thus to discover rather than create common law, and Blackstone wrote that "the principal and most authoritative evidence" of the common law is the corpus of judicial decisions.[15] Blackstone was quite conservative and firmly believed in the doctrine of stare decisis, the idea that prior judicial decisions should be followed. But he admitted an "exception, where the former determination is most evidently contrary to reason." A prior decision that is clearly contrary to reason should not be followed. In these exceptional situations, "the subsequent judges do not pretend to make a new law, but to vindicate the old one from misrepresentation." He did not think that a clearly unreasonable decision was "*bad law*" but rather insisted that it was "*not law*" at all.[16]

Under this almost Platonic vision of the common law, a particular judicial determination was proper only to the extent that it approximated natural law that had an existence outside and independent of the court. Judges, after all, are only human and occasionally err. Therefore, natural lawyers of the Founding Era viewed unreasonable judicial opinions as simply erroneous applications of the true common law. To repeat Blackstone's words, an erroneous determination of the common law was not "*bad law;*" it was "*not law*" at all.

This natural-law thinking had enormous consequences for the Supreme Court's appellate jurisdiction over state court judgments. Obviously the Court could correct an erroneous application of a federal statute, a treaty of the United States, or the federal constitution. But the Court's appellate authority over cases presumably also gave it authority

---

14. BLACKSTONE 64. *See also id.* at 45, 67, 73.

15. *Id.* 69. *See also id.* 63–64.

16. *Id.* 70 (emphasis original).

to correct erroneous applications of the common law on the basis that a state court had departed from proper common-law principles.

In practice, the Supreme Court's appellate power over the state courts' administration of the common law would have arisen in any state court litigation involving citizens of different states or aliens. But the power was also inherent in the Court's appellate jurisdiction over cases arising under federal law. In 1789 no one could predict the scope of this ambiguous "arising under" jurisdiction. The specific wording of the Constitution extended the Court's jurisdiction to "cases" rather than to discrete issues of federal law that may arise in particular cases. Therefore the constitutional language "cases . . . arising under" federal law might reasonably be interpreted to include any case that might be decided by a rule of federal law. Thus the language could clearly extend to nonfederal issues in a case. In the event, the Supreme Court under Chief Justice Marshall settled on this reasonable but expansive interpretation in 1824.[17]

Fortunately, the Constitution provided a mechanism for limiting the Supreme Court's potentially immense appellate power. The Court's appellate jurisdiction was subject to "such exceptions, and under such regulations as the Congress shall make." Ellsworth had been a member of the Committee of Detail that added this clause to the Constitution, and he fully understood the clause's potential reach. He made extensive use of this grant of legislative authority over the Court's appellate jurisdiction. Ellsworth proposed limiting the Supreme Court's jurisdiction to specific situations in which there was an obvious and direct interest in assuring a federal court review of a particular issue. Under his bill, the Court's appellate authority over state courts extended to specific issues governed by positive, written federal laws—specifically to "the constitution, treaties or laws of the United States . . . or [a federal] commission." To clarify this limitation, he expressly provided that "no other error shall be . . . regarded as a ground of reversal in any such case as aforesaid, than such as . . . immediately respects the before mentioned questions of validity or construction of the said constitution, treaties, statutes, commissions, or authorities." These words cannot reasonably be expanded to permit the review of common-law determinations of state courts.[18]

Ellsworth also limited the Court's appellate authority over the lower federal courts. Insofar as legal issues were concerned, the Court's power over litigation originating in federal courts was both broader and narrower than its authority over state courts. The Court was given no appel-

---

17. Osborn v. Bank of the United States, 22 U.S. (9 Wheat.) 738 (1824).
18. Senate Judiciary Bill §24, *reprinted in* 4 DHSC 86.

late authority over federal criminal trials. But in civil cases coming from the lower federal courts, it was given a general authority to review all legal issues regardless of whether they were controlled by written federal law, written state law, or the unwritten common law.[19]

In addition to crafting precise limitations to the Supreme Court's power to review issues of law, Ellsworth had to deal with the Court's power over issues of fact. This technical legal distinction between issues of fact and issues of law may be illustrated by the issue that sparked the disagreement between Ellsworth and Sherman in *Huntington v. Chaplin*. Whether the debtor in that case should have been allowed to testify as to his partial payment was an issue of law, and the Court did not allow the testimony. But if the debtor had prevailed on this legal issue, he would not necessarily have won. A debtor's bald assertion of a partial payment does not mean that the payment was made. There would still have been an issue of whether there was an actual transfer of money from the specific defendant to the specific plaintiff. The resolution of this kind of factual issue requires a trial in which a jury hears conflicting evidence and decides what in fact happened.

The Supreme Court's potential authority under the Constitution to review and overturn a jury's determination of factual issues had obvious implications for the general right to trial by jury and the trial of specific British creditor cases. Ellsworth resolved the potentially explosive issue of the Court's appellate review of facts by limiting its appellate power to review by "petition in error" (later changed to "writ of error"). The subtle limitation of the Court's appellate jurisdiction to writs of error effectively preserved litigants' traditional right to have factual issues determined finally by a jury. In Connecticut and all other common-law jurisdictions, "in the case of issues in fact tried by courts or juries, let the judgment be ever so erroneous [a writ of] error will not lie." A writ of error could be used only to obtain the review of a legal issue.[20]

---

19. *Id.* §21, *reprinted in* 4 DHSC 80–81.

20. *See Id., as amended.* Ellsworth's use of the phrase "petition in error" rather than "writ of error" was probably inadvertent. *But see* Holt 1500–1501. He and his committee clearly intended to preclude the Supreme Court from reviewing issues of fact. Ralph Izard to Edward Rutledge (Apr. 24, 1789), *excerpted in* 4 DHSC 377–78; Oliver Ellsworth to Richard Law (Apr. 30, 1789), *excerpted in* 4 DHSC 382. Moreover, in private correspondence, a working member of the Committee actually used the phrase "writ of error" rather than "petition in error." Caleb Strong to Nathaniel Sargeant (May 7, 1789), *reprinted in* 4 DHSC 387–88; Caleb Strong to Robert Treat Paine (May 24, 1789), *reprinted in* 4 DHSC 395–99. On the limitation of writs of error to issues of law, *see* 2 ZEPHANIAH SWIFT, A SYSTEM OF THE LAWS OF THE STATE OF CONNECTICUT 275 (1796).

Ellsworth rounded out the Court's jurisdiction by confirming the Constitution's grant of original or trial jurisdiction. The Constitution extended the Supreme Court's trial jurisdiction to "cases affecting ambassadors, other public ministers and consuls, and those in which a state shall be a party" and made no provision for exceptions or additions. Ellsworth nevertheless chose not to reenact the precise words of the Constitution. His proposed language, however, was subsequently amended in the Senate to conform the act to the Constitution.[21]

In crafting the Supreme Court's appellate jurisdiction, Ellsworth astutely used the Constitution's exceptions and regulations clause to defuse all possible objections. On legal issues he expressly and drastically limited the Court's power over state courts to a narrow range of clearly defined federal laws. On factual issues he completely eliminated the Court's power of review. This concession on the review of facts turned a major fairness issue into a nonissue, but it also made the creation of federal trial courts crucial. Cases are frequently won or lost on the basis of the fact finder's resolution of the pertinent factual issues, and Ellsworth's concession gave trial courts a virtual plenary power over the resolution of facts. If federal trial courts were not created for the trial of cases impressed with a federal interest, the cases would have to be tried in state courts.

FEDERAL TRIAL COURTS: ADMIRALTY JURISDICTION

When Ellsworth turned to federal trial courts, he was greatly assisted by another fortunate consensus. Virtually every member of the first Congress agreed on the necessity of creating federal trial courts with an admiralty jurisdiction over maritime disputes.[22] This specialized head of jurisdiction is worth exploring because admiralty courts epitomized Ellsworth's legislative agenda for the lower federal courts' general trial jurisdiction. In addition, the reason for creating federal admiralty courts has been seriously obscured by the passage of two hundred years and a radical change in the nature of admiralty cases tried by federal courts.

Today the federal courts' jurisdiction over maritime cases is dedicated almost entirely to private disputes between private litigants. But there is no evidence that the Founding Generation thought of admiralty litigation primarily in terms of private disputes. Eighteenth-century Americans understood that admiralty courts adjudicated some types of private claims, but this understanding was irrelevant to their decision to move maritime litigation from the existing state admiralty courts to federal ad-

---

21. *See* 4 DHSC 69–71 (comparing the Bill and the Act).
22. *See generally* Casto, *Admiralty*.

miralty courts. Surviving records indicate clearly that the admiralty clause was placed in the Constitution and the federal admiralty courts were subsequently created to assure complete federal jurisdiction over three specific categories of litigation: prize cases, criminal prosecutions, and cases arising under federal revenue laws. The Founding Generation's paradigm of federal admiralty jurisdiction was not private dispute resolution but maritime cases that implicated a direct sovereign interest of the United States—cases involving the regulation of maritime warfare, the collection of revenues, and the prosecution of criminals. The Founding Generation's basic concept of federal admiralty jurisdiction is best described as public, not private, litigation.

Crimes on the high seas were the least significant of the three types of cases that epitomized admiralty litigation. One reason for vesting the federal courts with special criminal jurisdiction related to the technical transfer of sovereignty from the states to the federal government. Because crimes on the high seas are committed outside of individual states' borders, there was some concern that the states lacked authority over them. In contrast, the federal government, with its general sovereign power over international transactions, clearly had authority. Moreover, crimes on the high seas—especially piracy—had traditionally been viewed as a proper subject of admiralty jurisdiction, so there was an unexamined assumption that the federal admiralty courts would try them.

In contrast to jurisdiction over crimes on the high seas, admiralty jurisdiction over revenue cases was vital. An adequate and reliable stream of revenue was essential to the federal government's operations, and virtually all of the government's revenue was expected to come from import duties upon goods brought in by sea. In fact, during the first eleven years of the federal government's operation, 87 percent of its revenue came from customs duties. In North America, the pre-Revolutionary imperial vice-admiralty courts and the subsequently created state admiralty courts, with their traditional authority to seize ships and cargoes, had always been used to enforce import and navigation laws. Most people therefore assumed that federal admiralty courts with jurisdiction over revenue cases would be a fiscal necessity for the new government. While the Judiciary Act was being drafted, a knowledgeable observer deeply interested in revenue matters insisted that "it is indispensably necessary that Courts of Admiralty be immediately instituted [because] without them no system of Revenue can be put in Execution."[23]

---

23. Otho Williams to David Humphries (May 12, 1789), *quoted in* 4 DHSC 377 n.; D. DEWEY, FINANCIAL HISTORY OF THE UNITED STATES 110 (1936).

A federal jurisdiction over prize cases was also vital to the federal government. The United States was a maritime nation separated from Europe by the Atlantic Ocean. This ocean isolated the nation from European land powers and at the same time provided a great highway for commerce. Because of the maritime nature of the United States, naval warfare was central to national security, and prize courts played a critical role in supporting the nation's ability to wage naval war. A major objective of naval warfare has always been to capture or disrupt the enemy's commercial shipping, and in the eighteenth century captured vessels—known as prizes—were sold for the benefit of the capturing vessel. The prize money served as a reward to the crews of regular navy vessels. Even more significantly, the prize system was used as a quick and inexpensive method of increasing effective naval strength. During times of war, private merchants would be commissioned as privateers and authorized to prey on enemy shipping. In return, the privateers were allowed to keep their lawful captures.

During the Revolutionary War, the vast majority of American armed vessels were privateers, and they captured some two thousand British vessels and cargoes worth an estimated eighteen million pounds sterling.[24] The resulting injury to British commercial interests is obvious. Moreover, this privateering activity required the British to commit a significant number of naval units to the protection of their merchant marine. The ability to launch a host of maritime raiders without direct financial cost and at the mere stroke of a pen was an invaluable asset to a maritime nation that could not afford the enormous expense of a significant naval establishment.

After taking a prize, the privateers would sail the captured vessel and cargo to a friendly port, where the capture would be reviewed by a prize court. If the court determined that the captured vessel was a lawful prize, the court would condemn the vessel and give the privateer lawful title. This use of prize courts to regulate captures was one of the primary characteristics that distinguished privateering from piracy, and the judicial condemnation obviously facilitated the sale of prizes. In addition, efficient and effective prize courts were a necessary inducement for encouraging privateering ventures. In 1779 James Wilson and a group of Philadelphia merchants urged the creation of efficient prize courts because, they said, "In the privateering trade in particular, the very life of

---

24. *See* JOHN MCCUSKER & RUSSELL MENARD, THE ECONOMY OF BRITISH AMERICA, 1606–1789, at 362–63 (1985). *See also* EDGAR MACLAY, A HISTORY OF AMERICAN PRIVATEERS viii–ix (1899).

which consists in the adventurers receiving the rewards of their success and bravery as soon as the cruise is over, the least delay is uncommonly destructive."[25]

Besides encouraging the privateering trade, prize courts played an essential role in regulating privateers' activities. Given that these raiders were officially commissioned by the national government to wage maritime war on the nation's enemies, that government had a compelling interest in assuring that privateers did not venture beyond the scope of their commissions into piracy. This regulation was accomplished through the determination of the key issue in all prize cases—prize or no prize? In making this determination, the prize court inevitably considered the nature of the privateers' conduct toward foreign vessels and the status of the United States' foreign relations with other countries involved in particular captures. When Alexander Hamilton urged ratification of the Constitution, he explained that admiralty cases, especially prize cases, "so generally depend on the laws of nations, and so commonly affect the rights of foreigners, that they fall within the considerations which are relative to the public place."[26] These obvious national security concerns, coupled with the need to provide for effective enforcement of revenue laws and the need to punish crimes on the high seas, made the existence of federal admiralty courts inevitable.

The consensus on admiralty jurisdiction had enormous implications for the creation of a nationwide system of federal trial courts. The daily administration of prize laws during times of war and of revenue laws during both war and peace required an admiralty court in each major seaport. The option of restricting federal judicial power to a simple and relatively inexpensive Supreme Court in the nation's capital was therefore not a realistic possibility. There was definitely going to be a system of lower federal courts, and the only issue was what sort of cases—in addition to admiralty matters—would be committed to the lower courts' jurisdiction.

SHAPING THE COMPROMISE ON FEDERAL TRIAL COURTS

To a significant degree, the lower courts' nonadmiralty jurisdiction presented the same problems that had confronted Ellsworth in working out the Supreme Court's appellate jurisdiction. When Ellsworth turned

---

25. *See* The Flad Oyen, 165 Eng. Rep. 124 (Adm. 1799) (condemnation facilitates sales); Essays on the Constitutional History of the United States at 25–26 (J. Jameson ed., 1889) (quoting the petition).

26. Federalist No. 80 at 538 (A. Hamilton).

to this nonadmiralty lower court jurisdiction, he drew heavily on the same insights that had informed his approach to the Supreme Court's appellate jurisdiction and the district courts' admiralty jurisdiction. He made no serious effort to track the jurisdictional language of the Constitution but instead limited the lower courts' jurisdiction to discrete and unambiguous categories of cases that were obviously essential. In addition, he added a few more unambiguous categories that—like admiralty cases—were both noncontroversial and impressed with an obvious national interest. The Constitution's provision for jurisdiction over cases arising under federal law was by far the most troubling issue. The problem was that this particular head of jurisdiction had no clear limits. The "arising under" language could be reasonably construed as encompassing any case whose resolution might require the application of federal law, and this broad construction was eventually placed on the Constitution's "arising under" clause.[27] Under this expansive interpretation, a case predominately governed by nonfederal law would nevertheless be deemed to arise under federal law as long as even a single substantive aspect of the dispute might be governed by federal law.

Given this potentially broad sweep, the "arising under" clause played directly into the generalized visceral fear that the federal courts were ideally suited to "absorb and destroy the judiciaries of the several states." Moreover, the Constitution's ambiguous language also directly implicated the specific fear that the federal courts would be used to effectuate Article IV of the Treaty of Paris. British creditors' suits always involved the enforcement of a debtor's promise to pay money. These promises, like most legally enforceable promises, were actionable as a matter of common law, not federal law. But some states provided American debtors with defenses based either upon misapplication of the common law or upon specific state statutes. To the extent that these defenses violated the Treaty, they could be trumped. Thus even though thousands of the legal issues in the case would not be governed by specific federal law, the case would nevertheless "arise under" a treaty of the United States. To make matters even worse, thousands of the British creditors' claims against individual debtors were for relatively small amounts. Therefore the "arising under" clause also directly implicated the fear that defendants would be unfairly and at great expense hailed to distant federal courts to defend against small claims.

Although some of Ellsworth's contemporaries, including Edmund Randolph, believed that Congress should vest the federal trial courts

---

27. Osborn v. Bank of the United States, 22 U.S. (9 Wheat.) 738 (1824).

with a general jurisdiction over all cases arising under federal law,[28] the Constitution did not require a plenary vesting of jurisdiction. The entire purpose of the Madisonian Compromise was to authorize a more flexible approach, and Ellsworth ably wielded this authority. Perhaps there were sufficient votes in Congress to pass a general grant of federal question jurisdiction, but Ellsworth evidently chose not to gamble. He made no reference whatsoever to a general jurisdiction over cases arising under federal law, and he thereby preempted the argument that the federal courts would absorb and destroy the state judiciaries.

Ellsworth's basic approach to delimiting the lower courts' trial jurisdiction is evident in an obscure but specific provision for alien tort claims. Ellsworth proposed and the Congress enacted his proposal that the lower courts would have jurisdiction over "all causes where an alien sues for a tort only in violation of the law of nations or a treaty of the United States." This provision has little intrinsic importance, but it is worth considering as a clear illustration of Ellsworth's conscious decision to draft around the political problems implicated by the British debt cases. In drafting this obscure clause, Ellsworth undoubtedly had in mind incidents like the De Longchamps Affair and the 1787 arrest of the Dutch ambassador's coachman.[29]

Of course, the primary sanction for this kind of misconduct was a criminal prosecution, and Ellsworth's bill gave the federal courts criminal jurisdiction over attacks on diplomats.[30] But these attacks also might cause property damage or personal injury. Ellsworth's alien tort claim provision empowered the federal courts to try civil actions seeking private compensation from defendants who committed torts in violation of international law.

The Alien Tort Claim provision is interesting because it is, to a significant degree, open-ended. If violations of diplomatic immunity were the sole concern, the statute could easily have been drafted to apply only to foreign embassies. But Ellsworth chose to open the federal courts to any alien who may have suffered from any tortious violation of international law. Quite possibly he also had in mind the continuing problem of American citizens' mounting private military expeditions against the Spanish territories in Florida. In addition, he may have contemplated torts by American citizens against aliens who under United States treaties

---

28. *See* Edmund Randolph to James Madison (June 30, 1789), *excerpted in* 4 DHSC 432–33. *But see* Randolph, *Report on the Judiciary* (1791), *reprinted in* 4 DHSC 127, 162 (conceding the propriety of an amount in controversy limitation).

29. Judiciary Act § 9. *See generally* Casto, *Torts. See* chapter 1 at 7–8.

30. Judiciary Act §§ 9, 11.

were entitled to the free exercise of religion or to safe passage through the country.[31]

The idea that the federal courts should be open to any alien who had suffered tortious injuries in violation of international law was similar to the national consensus on the need for federal admiralty courts. The clear national interest was so obvious that Ellsworth felt free to use broad, open-ended language to vest the courts with complete power over these cases. At the same time, however, he chose to exclude the most flagrant, significant, and ongoing breaches of international law. The British creditors, who clearly were aliens, could not use the alien tort claims act because their claims were not tort actions.

This strategy of carefully carving out discrete and clearly defined categories of federal question jurisdiction is repeated in more important portions of Ellsworth's bill. Although duties on goods imported by sea were to be the federal government's primary source of revenues, Ellsworth anticipated that taxes unrelated to maritime commerce would also be levied, and he therefore provided an open-ended jurisdiction over nonadmiralty revenue collection cases. In the eighteenth century, revenue laws were typically enforced through the seizure of property and the imposition of penalties and forfeitures. Accordingly, Ellsworth's bill also vested the federal district courts with "exclusive original cognizance of all seizures on land, or . . . waters [not otherwise subject to Admiralty jurisdiction] and of all suits for penalties and forfeitures incurred under the laws of the United States."[32]

Another clear example of a case arising under federal law was a criminal prosecution, and within this discrete category of cases Ellsworth again resorted to open-ended language. In addition to their plenary jurisdiction over admiralty cases, aliens' tort claims, and revenue cases, the federal trial courts were given "cognizance of all crimes and offenses that shall be cognizable under the Authority of the United States."

Although Ellsworth was clear that the federal trial courts should have a complete jurisdiction over any and all crimes, his bill called for the creation of two separate types of lower federal trial courts. The district courts, whose primary job was to adjudicate admiralty cases, also were authorized to try minor crimes involving moderate punishment. In the case of whipping, fines, and imprisonment, punishment could not exceed thirty stripes, one hundred dollars, and six months. In practice,

---

31. *See* Casto, *Torts* 506. *See also* HYNEMAN 133–42.
32. Judiciary Act § 9.

these ceilings proved so low that the district courts almost never tried criminal cases.[33] For punishments in excess of these limits, a case had to be prosecuted in a federal circuit court.

Federal circuit courts were a major innovation. Each district court was staffed by a federal district judge who was required to reside in the district for which he was appointed. The act called for the creation of thirteen districts that essentially followed state borders, except that separate courts were created for the districts of Maine and Kentucky that were then parts of the states of Massachusetts and Virginia. In contrast to the one-judge district courts, the circuit courts were originally envisioned as three-judge courts to consist of the resident district judge and two circuit-riding Supreme Court Justices.

The basic purpose of the circuit courts was to provide Supreme Court supervision of the federal trial courts without requiring expensive and inconvenient appeals from the local federal trial courts to the national capitol. Instead, circuit-riding Justices would in effect make Supreme Court decision making more accessible to litigants throughout the country. As Senator Paterson explained, the circuit courts would "carry Law to [the People's] Homes, Courts to their Doors."[34] The Supreme Court Justices' participation in criminal trials in the circuit courts was especially important because a criminal conviction was traditionally not subject to appellate review. Following this tradition, Ellsworth's bill did not authorize appeals in criminal cases but vested only the circuit courts with jurisdiction over major federal crimes.

The circuit courts were also given a trial jurisdiction over civil cases in which an alien is a party or in which a citizen of one state sues a citizen of another. In defense of these provisions, Ellsworth forcefully explained that the Constitutional convention

> had in view the condition of foreigners when they framed the judicial of the U. States. The Citizens were already protected by [state] Judges & Courts, but foreigners were not. The Laws of nations & Treaties were too much disregarded in the several States. Juries were too apt to be biased against them, in favor of their own citizens & acquaintances: it was therefore necessary to have general Courts

---

33. *See* HENDERSON 62, 156 n.36 (1971). *See also* Richard Peters to Timothy Pickering (Dec. 8, 1806) (explaining a glitch in the statutory language) (Pickering Papers, MHi.).

34. William Paterson, Notes for Remarks on Judiciary Bill (June 23, 1789), *reprinted in* 4 DHSC 416.

for causes in which foreigners were parties or citizens of different States.[35]

The basic problem with this alienage jurisdiction was that the British creditors' claims were the prototypical civil action in which an alien was a party, so alienage jurisdiction flew straight in the teeth of the strongest objections to federal trial courts.

Ellsworth had stated and restated in the Continental Congress and the Connecticut ratification convention that Americans' failure to repay the British created serious foreign policy problems.[36] But he also understood that his proposed alienage jurisdiction would engender powerful opposition. He therefore agreed to compromise the nation's need to provide for effective enforcement of Article IV of the peace treaty. He limited the circuit court's alienage and diversity of citizenship jurisdiction to cases in which the amount in controversy exceeded five hundred dollars.

In the late twentieth century, five hundred dollars does not seem a very significant limitation, but it was a substantial sum two hundred years ago. During the secret Senate debates on the Judiciary Bill, one Senator noted that "[t]he Farmers in the New England States [are] not worth more than 1,000 Dr. on an Average."[37] The five-hundred-dollar amount in controversy limitation effectively denied these farmers—and, more importantly, their out-of-state creditors—the protection authorized by the Constitution's diversity provision. It also effectively barred a vast number of common-law tort actions from the federal trial courts. During the closed Senate debates, the point was made that the circuit courts' jurisdiction would extend to "Money, Merchandize, Land bought and sold." Tort actions are notably absent from this list, and Ellsworth fully understood that the limitation would be a significant barrier to tort claims. He had served on the highest judicial court in Connecticut for four years and knew that tort judgments in excess of five hundred dollars were virtually nonexistent.[38]

The monetary limitation had its most significant impact upon the British debt cases. Although the total debt owed to British creditors was high, the great majority (for some firms, over 90 percent) of the individual

---

35. William Laughton Smith to Edward Rutledge (Aug. 9–10, 1789) (quoting Ellsworth), *excerpted in* 4 DHSC 496–99.

36. Madison, Notes of Debates in the Continental Congress (Jan. 16, 1783), *reprinted in* 6 MADISON PAPERS 4647; 3 DHRC 544.

37. William Paterson, Notes on Judiciary Bill Debate (June 24–27, 1789), *reprinted in* 4 DHSC 421–23.

38. *See* Casto, *Congress* 1113–14 n.93.

debts was for sums of less than five hundred dollars. Moreover, the technical legal rules that regulated the joinder of claims (common-law pleading) did not permit a plaintiff to try multiple claims in one lawsuit. Therefore, as a practical matter, the amount in controversy limitation barred the great majority of British claims from the new federal courts.[39]

Because of its impact upon the British debt cases, the five-hundred-dollar limitation was the most significant compromise in Ellsworth's bill. In theory, Supreme Court appellate review was available to correct errors in the tremendous number of British claims relegated to the mercy of the state judiciaries. In practice, however, an appeal all the way to the Supreme Court would have been prohibitively expensive in comparison to the size of the claim. Therefore the limitation must be viewed as a conscious decision to compromise a significant national security interest.

This compromise could easily be described as a raw political deal designed to acquiesce in continued violations of the peace treaty, but such a view would be too simplistic. During the ratification process, Senator Lee had forcefully and persuasively pointed out the issues of fairness in forcing a local farmer to defend against a small and possibly invalid claim in a district federal trial court, and Ellsworth agreed with this self-evident criticism. Some seven years later he noted in a different context the immense "difficulty of bringing [witnesses] from the remotest parts of the union to the seat of government." An amount in controversy limitation was thus almost inevitable on the simple basis of fairness.[40]

THE CONGRESS ACCEPTS ELLSWORTH'S COMPROMISE

When the Senate took Ellsworth's bill under consideration, the proposed compromise on the Supreme Court's appellate jurisdiction was readily accepted with some minor tinkering but no known objection. The lower courts, however, proved more controversial. The issue that had sparked significant debate at the Constitutional Convention and whose resolution was postponed by the Madisonian Compromise was finally to be resolved. On the first day of the Senate's debates, Senator Lee moved to restrict the lower courts' jurisdiction to admiralty cases.

---

39. For the common-law rules of joinder, see Williams, *Pleading Reform in Nineteenth Century America: The Joinder of Actions at Common Law and Under the Codes*, 6 J. LEGAL HIST. 299 (1985); Reed, *Compulsory Joinder of Parties in Civil Actions*, 55 MICH. L. REV. 327, 356–74 (1957). For the size of British creditors' individual claims, see Holt 1488 n.234.
40. *See* this chapter at 29–30; Wiscart v. Dauchy, 3 U.S. (3 Dall.) 321, 329 (1796) (Ellsworth, C.J.).

In the ensuing debates, Lee, his fellow Virginian William Grayson, and Pierce Butler of South Carolina bluntly explained their conviction that the creation of federal trial courts would cast a "Stigma upon State Courts [by implying] that [they would] not do what is right." More significantly, they charged that "the ultimate tendency of [the Bill was] manifestly . . . to destroy, to cut up at the Root the State Judiciaries, to annihilate their whole system of Jurisprudence and . . . finally swallow up every distinguishing mark of a distinct [state] government." These strong words were not mere political posturing for the public. The Senate debates were closed and forbidden to be published. We know the debates only from the surviving private records of individual senators.[41]

The southern objections had been more or less persuasive two years earlier at the Constitutional Convention, but in Philadelphia the federal courts' potential jurisdiction was not clearly demarked. Quite to the contrary, the proposals for subject-matter jurisdiction at the Convention were almost open-ended. Ellsworth's bill, however, almost completely reversed this situation. He was fully aware of the concern that the federal courts might swallow up the state judiciaries. All of his jurisdictional proposals were impressed with a clear and direct federal interest and, with the possible exception of admiralty jurisdiction, were subject to precise and easily recognizable limits.

In the Senate debates, Ellsworth responded to the southern senators' arguments with characteristic bluntness. He warned that "there will be attacks on the General Government that will go to the Very Vitals of it [and that state] Judges may Swerve."[42] Unfortunately, no one recorded the details of Ellsworth's argument, but he clearly saw federal trial courts as vital to the defense of the federal government. From earlier speeches that Ellsworth delivered in his successful efforts to achieve the Constitution's ratification, it is reasonable to assume that he saw federal trial courts as essential to the effective enforcement of federal criminal and revenue laws.

During the ratification process, Ellsworth had stated that the proposed Constitution was necessary to create an "energetic" government that could act directly to vindicate the national interest. In his words, "A more energetic system is necessary. The present [under the Articles of Confed-

---

41. For Lee's and Grayson's comments, *see* William Maclay, Diary Entry (June 22, 1789), *excerpted in* 4 DHSC 409; and William Paterson, Notes on Judiciary Bill Debate (June 22, 1798), *reprinted in* 4 DHSC 410. For Butler's comments, *see* Pierce Butler, Notes for Remarks on Judiciary Bill (July 17, 1789), *reprinted in* 4 DHSC 471–73.
42. Pierce Butler, Notes on Judiciary Bill Debate (June 22, 1789), *reprinted in* 4 DHSC 408.

eration] is merely advisory. It has no coercive power. Without this, government is ineffective or, rather is no government at all." He emphasized that an energetic government especially needed the power of "raising and supporting armies [to] protect the people against the violence of wicked and overgrown citizens, and invasion by the rest of the mankind." Although Ellsworth emphasized the need to raise and support armies, he was not a soldier. Reasoning from his wartime service in the Continental Congress, he equated military power with fiscal power. "Wars," he explained, "have now become rather wars of the purse, than of the sword." In fighting a war, a government without revenue "has [not] the means to enlist a man or buy an ox."[43]

An effective military establishment was necessary also to deal with domestic rebellion, but Ellsworth did not view armed force as the optimal solution to internal discord. Given that "a coercive principle [is] necessary for the Union," he reasoned, "the only question is, shall it be a coercion by arms?" The answer was obvious: "I am for coercion by law [that] singles out the guilty individual and punishes him for breaking the laws of the Union."[44] Obviously an extensive system of federal courts would contribute directly to effecting Ellsworth's coercion principle by punishing crimes and enforcing revenue laws.

In the secret Senate debates on the Judiciary Bill, William Paterson, who had also played a significant role in drafting the bill, forcefully explained the need for federal trial courts to enforce criminal laws and revenue laws. Picking up on Ellsworth's imagery of attacks on the vitals of the general government, Paterson saw criminal jurisdiction as a matter of "Self-Preservation." He asked, "If Offenses be committed against this Union, will you put it in the Power of State Judges to decide thereupon—to acquit or to condemn—I hope not—You put your Life in their Hands." The problem was that there was no appeal in criminal cases, especially where the defendant had been acquitted. To deprive the federal courts of jurisdiction to punish crimes was to present the states "with a Sword to destroy" the union. Similarly, Paterson urged the Senate not to "give up the Power of collecting your own Revenue . . . you will collect Nothing." The problem was that "State Officers will feel it their Interest to consult the Temper of the People of the State in which they live rather than that of the Union."[45]

---

43. Oliver Ellsworth, Speech of Jan. 4, 1788, *reprinted in* 3 DHRC 541, 542. *See also Landholder V, reprinted in* 3 DHRC at 480–84.

44. Oliver Ellsworth, Speech of Jan. 7, 1788, *reprinted in* 3 DHRC 548, 553.

45. William Paterson, Notes for Remarks on Judiciary Bill (June 23, 1789), *reprinted in* 4 DHSC 414, 415–16.

Paterson's and Ellsworth's arguments undoubtedly were particularly persuasive because their fellow senators knew that these two forceful men were sensitive and attentive to state interests. Today the federal government—even Congress—is frequently viewed as divorced from the individual states. The primary concerns of a member of Congress are his or her individual constituents and national interests, with the interests of state governments playing a distinctly secondary role. This comparative lack of concern for state interests, however, did not exist in the first Congress.

Ellsworth and his fellow senators were not elected by the people; they were chosen by their state legislatures. In preparing the Judiciary Bill, Ellsworth specifically sought the advice of Connecticut's Governor, Lieutenant Governor, and Chief Justice. All three of these officers approved his plan and recommended the creation of a comprehensive system of lower federal courts. In a letter to his friend the chief justice of Connecticut, Ellsworth emphasized his concern for the interests of state courts.

> Without [a system of federal trial courts], there must be many appeals or writs of error from the Supreme Courts of the States, which by placing them in a subordinate situation, and subjecting their decisions to frequent reversals, would probably more hurt their feelings and their influence, than to divide the ground with them at first, and [establish a system of federal trial courts].

These thoughts were not penned for public consumption. They were private and intended for a personal friend.[46]

Ellsworth's obvious concern for a fair balancing of national and state interests was undoubtedly apparent to his fellow senators and must have added great credence to his forceful advocacy of federal trial courts. Most significantly, by defusing the explosive issue of British debt, Ellsworth succeeded in splitting the potential southern bloc and actually gained a slight majority of southern votes. His bill passed the Senate by a vote of 14 to 6.[47]

Ellsworth's strategy was equally successful in the House of Representatives. The bill was not entirely acceptable to the southern representatives, but neither was it an anathema. For example, there was an initial belief in the House that James Madison would lead the fight against the

---

46. Governor Samuel Huntington to William Samuel Johnson and Oliver Ellsworth (Apr. 30, 1789), *excerpted in* 4 DHSC at 383; Lt. Gov. Oliver Wolcott, Sr., to Oliver Ellsworth (June 27, 1789), *excerpted in* 4 DHSC 423–24; Chief Justice Richard Law to Oliver Ellsworth (May 4, 1789), *excerpted in* 4 DHSC 386–87; Oliver Ellsworth to Richard Law (Apr. 30, 1789), *excerpted in* 4 DHSC 392.
47. 1 DHFFC 85 (Senate Legislative Journal).

judicial bill, and Madison did not especially like the measure. Nevertheless, he decided not to take an active role in opposition to it and apparently maintained a low profile in the debates. The House debates more or less paralleled the Senate's deliberations, and the bill passed the House by a comfortable majority of 37 to 16. The southern representatives—like their fellow senators—approved the measure by a slight majority.[48]

Perhaps Ellsworth should have gritted his teeth and pressed for a broader federal jurisdiction adequate to enforce the Treaty of Paris. If he had, he might have prevailed, albeit by a closer vote. He chose, however, not to gamble, and the Senate's treatment of a process bill that he drafted that same year suggests that his concessions to localist concerns in the Judiciary Act were wise. In the process bill, Ellsworth sought to establish technical procedural rules regulating the commencement of common-law actions in federal court and the enforcement of judgments. He took a nationalist view and proposed uniform rules for all the federal courts. The Congress, however, gave the back of its hand to this proposal. Instead of enacting uniform rules, Congress provided that the institution of common-law suits and the enforcement of judgments would be regulated by the local rules of the state in which the federal court was located. If Ellsworth had pressed harder in the Judiciary Act to enforce rights under the Treaty of Paris, the localist sentiment that gutted his process bill might have jeopardized the passage of the Act.[49]

Even if Ellsworth had narrowly prevailed on the enforcement of treaty rights, the victory might have been pyrrhic. He undoubtedly understood that a close and controversial vote would have detracted from the political legitimacy of the new government. As it happened, the large margins of victory in both chambers had the practical effect of assuring the public that the new federal judiciary was organized on sound and uncontroversial principles.

CONGRESSIONAL INSTRUMENTALISM

The most striking aspect of the Judiciary Act of 1789 is the Congress's rampant instrumentalism in shaping the federal courts' subject-matter jurisdiction. Today most discussions of federal jurisdiction are based

---

48. For initial concerns about Madison, see Jeremiah Wadsworth to Pierpont Edwards (July 26, 1789), *quoted in* 4 DHSC 483 n.3; Fisher Ames to John Lowell (July 28, 1789), *excerpted in* 4 DHSC 480–83; James Madison to Samuel Johnston (July 31, 1789), *excerpted in* 4 DHSC 491–92. For the House debate, see 1 ANNALS 782–85, 796–834. For the House vote, see 5 DHFFC 1171 n.29.
49. *See* 4 DHSC 108–21. *See also* GOEBEL 509–51.

upon a shared assumption that the scope of federal jurisdiction should be determined by general principles more or less unrelated to the outcome of particular cases. In contrast to this ideal of neutrality, the drafters of the Judiciary Act viewed the federal courts as a tool to effect specific substantive results. Members of the first Congress like Oliver Ellsworth, William Paterson, and Richard Henry Lee were gifted lawyer-politicians intent upon launching a new government. They were not trying to explain or understand a uniquely powerful and preexisting judicial system. Nor were they milling the gist of over five hundred volumes of United States Supreme Court decisions. To a significant degree, they shaped the federal courts' jurisdiction to assure that specific parties would prevail in specific categories of litigation.

Professor Holt has ably explained the strong visceral opposition to the creation of federal courts that would facilitate British creditors' debt-collection efforts.[50] The Congressional opponents of federal courts undoubtedly had a theoretical concern about the appropriate allocation of judicial power between state and federal courts, and they also sought to prevent distant federal courts from adjudicating small claims far from a defendant debtor's home. But the British debt controversy lent immediacy to these concerns. American debtors also may have been interested in the proper allocation of judicial power, but surely they were more interested in their personal finances. What debtors really feared was the increased likelihood of plaintiffs' judgments.

In contrast to the instrumentalist concerns of those who sought to restrict federal jurisdiction in order to influence the substantive outcome of litigation, the Congressional advocates of alienage and diversity jurisdiction were not as interested in the specific outcome of particular cases. In this context, Ellsworth was more interested in assuring the fair and orderly resolution of private disputes than in assuring the victory of particular classes of litigants. In addition to this apparently general concern, he was also undoubtedly worried about the severe diplomatic problems caused by the ongoing violations of the Treaty of Paris. Nevertheless, he evidently thought the instrumentalist opposition to an extensive jurisdiction over private civil actions was strong enough to endanger his bill's passage. Therefore, in cases valued at five hundred dollars or less, he acquiesced in continued treaty violations and sacrificed his general concern about fairness to foreigners.[51]

---

50. Holt.

51. *See* this chapter at 45–47.

To say that instrumentalism was rampant in the first Congress is not to say that more theoretical, results-neutral concerns were irrelevant. Although the amount in controversy limitation was driven in part by a desire to bar British creditors from the federal courts, the limitation was also inserted to protect small debtors from being forced to travel long distances to defend minor claims. In addition, and notwithstanding the compromises offered by Ellsworth, significant theoretical arguments based upon general principles continued to be advanced against his proposed act.

In the crucial Senate debates, the opponents of the Judiciary Act evidently regarded Pierce Butler of South Carolina as their leader; they elected him as their representative to the Committee of Conference on the measure. Butler's basic argument was that the measure's "Ultimate Tendency . . . will be to destroy, to cut up at the Root the State Judiciaries." This essentially theoretical argument was to no avail. The compromises on jurisdiction over British creditors' claims had effectively mooted the opposition's instrumentalist objections. In the Senate debates, Ellsworth and Paterson held the instrumentalist trump cards. In the all-important categories of litigation arising under federal criminal and revenue laws, Ellsworth and Paterson did not view the federal courts as disinterested forums that would mediate disputes between the government and its citizens. Undoubtedly they assumed that the courts would fairly resolve these disputes according to the law, but their driving concern was to assure the conviction of criminals and the collection of taxes. Otherwise, "Attacks on the very vitals of the General Government" would go unpunished, and in revenue cases, "you will collect nothing." Even Pierce Butler was forced to concede the necessity of jurisdiction "in whatever related to the Collection of the Revenue of the General Government." Ellsworth's and Paterson's powerful, self-evident arguments went directly to the new government's ability to function and therefore carried the day. And so the statutory structure of the federal judiciary was formed.[52]

---

52. *See* 1 DHFFC 177 (Senate Legislative Journal: selection of Conference Committee); for Paterson and Ellsworth, *see* this chapter at 48–49. For Butler, *see* Pierce Butler, Notes for Remarks on Judiciary Bill (July 17, 1789), *reprinted in* 4 DHSC 471–73.

3

SELECTING THE JUSTICES
AND INITIAL OPERATIONS

On the same day that Ellsworth's judiciary proposals were finally enacted, President Washington nominated a slate of six individuals to serve as the nation's first Supreme Court. He selected John Jay of New York for the leading post of Chief Justice. In addition, Washington nominated five associate Justices: John Rutledge of South Carolina, James Wilson of Pennsylvania, William Cushing of Massachusetts, Robert H. Harrison of Maryland, and John Blair of Virginia. Senator Izard of South Carolina enthusiastically wrote that these proposed Justices "are chosen from among the most eminent and distinguished characters in America, and I do not believe that any Judiciary in the world is better filled." His fellow senators evidently agreed and formally consented to all six nominations just two days later.[1]

Although the Court was now ready for business, there was very little business ready for the Court. The first session, which took place in February 1790, was anticlimactic. Chief Justice Jay and Justices Wilson, Cushing, and Blair were present; but Justice Rutledge and Justice Harrison, the latter of whom had recently resigned, did not attend. In any event, there was nothing to do other than admit attorneys to practice before the Court, so the Court was adjourned eight days later. A half a year later, the same four Justices, together with Justice Iredell, who filled Harrison's vacancy, met for the August term of 1790. Once more Justice Rutledge did not attend, and again the Court quickly adjourned without having heard a single case. This pattern of virtual inactivity continued for a few years. The Court's docket book, minutes, and surviving case files indicate that no cases were filed in 1790 and only two in '91. In 1792

---

1. 2 DHFFC 44–45 (Senate Executive Journal); Ralph Izard to Edward Rutledge (Sept. 26, 1789), *excerpted in* 1 DHSC 668–69.

and '93, the Court considered a few significant cases, but its overall case-load was light, with only five filings each year.[2]

During these early years, the Justices performed virtually all of their official duties while they were serving as trial judges in the circuit courts, a physically arduous task that they found irksome. While riding the southern circuit, Justice Iredell wrote his wife, "I scarcely thought there had been so much barren land in all America as I have passed through." In a letter of resignation to President Washington, Justice Johnson explained, "I cannot resolve to spend six Months in the Year of the few I may have left from my Family, on Roads at Taverns chiefly and often in Situations where the most moderate Desires are disappointed." Chief Justice Jay seriously considered leaving the Court in 1792 because "he had got quite tired of the Circuits." Throughout the 1790s the Justices frequently attempted to persuade Congress to relieve them of their circuit court duties. Their efforts, however, were largely unsuccessful, and at the end of the decade they were still riding circuit.[3]

The most interesting aspect of the Court's first few years is George Washington's apparent set of criteria for selecting his nominees. With his initial run of appointments, the President established many precedents and themes in the appointment process that have endured to the present. The Court might have become a reliquary for political hacks, but Washington's nominations firmly established a contrary tradition. He regarded "the due administration of Justice as the strongest cement of good government" and therefore "considered the first organization of the Judicial Department as essential to the happiness of our Citizens, and to the stability of our political system." Instead of seeking place-servers, Washington sought "the fittest characters to expound the laws and dispense justice."[4] This is not to say that he nominated no mediocre

---

2. Supreme Court Docket Book, *reprinted in* 1 DHSC 483–93; Supreme Court Fine Minutes, *reprinted in id.* 169–219; Supreme Court Case Files, DNA. Significant cases decided by the Court in this early period were Hayburn's Case, 2 U.S. (2 Dall.) 409 (1792), *discussed in* chapter 6 at 177–78; and Chisholm v. Georgia, 2 U.S. (2 Dall.) 419 (1793), *discussed in* chapter 7 at 188–97.

3. *See* James Iredell to Hannah Iredell (May 10, 1790), *excerpted in* 2 DHSC 65–66; Thomas Johnson to George Washington (Jan. 16, 1793), *reprinted in* 1 DHSC 80; Benjamin Bourne to William Channing (Feb. 21, 1792), *excerpted in* 1 DHSC 733; Egbert Benson to Rufus King (Dec. 18, 1793), *excerpted in* 1 DHSC 742–43. Wythe Holt, *"Federal Courts Have Enemies in All Who Fear Their Influence on State Objects": The Failure to Abolish Supreme Court Circuit-Riding in the Judiciary Acts of 1792 and 1793*, 36 BUFFALO L. REV. 301 (1988).

4. *See, e.g.,* George Washington to John Rutledge (Sept. 29, 1789), *reprinted in* 1 DHSC 20–21.

judges. He did. But his initial selections also included a number of capable individuals.

A careful student of the Supreme Court appointment process has concluded that in seeking "the fittest characters," Washington consistently required the following characteristics and experience in nominees to the Court:

(1) support and advocacy of the Constitution;
(2) distinguished service in the Revolution;
(3) active participation in the political life of state or nation;
(4) prior judicial experience on lower tribunals;
(5) either a "favorable reputation with his fellows" or personal ties with Washington himself; and
(6) geographic "suitability."[5]

Washington's initial run of nine nominations in the years 1789–1793 indicates, however, that the President did not always hew to these criteria.

THE FIRST NOMINEES

Because the Court itself had comparatively little business in its early years, President Washington's initial nine nominations may conveniently be considered as a group. These nominations provide a basis for assessing the President's selection criteria. Subsequent nominations by Washington and President Adams will be noted in the context of the Court's consideration of national security issues through the 1790s.

John Jay

John Jay was born into a wealthy New York family in 1745.[6] Following distinguished studies at Kings College (later Columbia University), where he was graduated with honors in 1764, he commenced his legal career as a law clerk for a respected New York attorney. In 1768 he was admitted to practice, and six years later he married the daughter of William Livingston, who subsequently became governor of New Jersey dur-

---

5. HENRY ABRAHAM, JUSTICES AND PRESIDENTS 72 (3d ed., 1992). The best study of early Supreme Court appointments is James Perry, *Supreme Court Appointments, 1789–1801: Criteria, Presidential Style, and the Press of Events*, 6 J. EARLY REPUBLIC 371 (1986).

6. For biographies of Chief Justice Jay, *see* HERBERT ALAN JOHNSON, JOHN JAY, 1745–1829 (1970); FRANK MONAGHAN, JOHN JAY (1935). *See also* RICHARD MORRIS, JOHN JAY: THE NATION AND THE COURT (1967). For briefer sketches, *see* Irving Dillard, *John Jay*, in FRIEDMAN & ISRAEL 3–22; *John Jay* in 1 DHSC 3–8.

ing the Revolution. With these social and political connections, Jay was virtually assured of success.

Jay quickly gravitated toward public service and gained a reputation as an intelligent and urbane man who was also an exceptionally hard worker. In the middle 1770s he served in the New York Committee of Correspondence and the New York Provisional Congress. He also helped draft his state's constitution and served briefly as chief justice of the Supreme Court of New York. Although Jay opposed the excesses of the British government, he was not an early advocate of independence. He was a cautious and conservative lawyer who, until the Declaration of Independence, consistently took a conciliatory stand toward Great Britain. After the Declaration, he became a forceful advocate for independence.

In addition to his state service, Jay was a delegate to the first and second Continental Congresses and in 1778 was elected president of the Continental Congress at the age of thirty-three. The next year he embarked for Europe as the colonies' unacknowledged commissioner to Spain and in 1781 moved on to Paris, where he, Benjamin Franklin, and John Adams served as commissioners for the negotiation of peace with Great Britain. These latter efforts culminated in the Treaty of Paris that concluded the Revolutionary War. Upon his return to America in 1784, Jay became the Continental Congress's Secretary for Foreign Affairs and served in that capacity until Thomas Jefferson took over the Department of State in 1790.

While serving as Secretary for Foreign Affairs, Jay must have been frustrated by the weakness of the national government under the Articles of Confederation and its inability to deal effectively with international relations and national security. By the end of the 1780s, he firmly believed in the necessity of creating a strong central government. He was not a delegate to the Constitutional Convention in Philadelphia, but he was a prominent and powerful advocate for the Constitution's ratification in New York. Among other contributions, he was one of the three coauthors of the Federalist Papers and contributed five essays on the conduct of foreign affairs under the proposed Constitution.

John Rutledge

Like Jay, John Rutledge came from a wealthy family.[7] He was born in 1739 and received a classical education, but he did not go to college. In-

---

7. For a biography of Justice Rutledge, *see* RICHARD HAYES BARRY, MR. RUTLEDGE OF SOUTH CAROLINA (1942). For briefer sketches, *see* Leon Friedman, *John Rutledge, in* FRIEDMAN & ISRAEL 33–49; *John Rutledge, in* 1 DHSC 15–18.

stead he served a two-year apprenticeship with a South Carolina attorney and then attended the Middle Temple in London, where he was called to the bar in 1760. On his return to South Carolina, Rutledge made a meteoric ascent in the colony's power structure. He was immediately elected to the Commons House of Assembly, and by 1763 he was refusing all but the most lucrative cases. The next year, Rutledge, then twenty-four, was appointed attorney general for the colony.

As the colonies progressed down the road toward revolution, Rutledge, like John Jay, was a moderate who was reluctant to sever ties with Great Britain. Nevertheless, he acquiesced in the movement for independence and by the mid-1770s was clearly the political leader of South Carolina. He helped draft the state's constitution and served as its president and then governor from 1776 to 1782. In addition, he was a delegate to the Continental Congress before and after his wartime service. In 1784 Rutledge was appointed chief judge of South Carolina's Court of Chancery and served on that court until he joined the federal Supreme Court.

When the Constitutional Convention was convened in Philadelphia, Rutledge was there to lead the South Carolina delegation. He was an effective and influential delegate and served on the five-person Committee of Detail that drafted the Constitution. Upon his return to South Carolina, he enthusiastically endorsed the proposed Constitution and played a leading role in the state's ratification process.

John Blair

Like Jay and Rutledge, John Blair was, in the words of an early biographer, "a gentleman of fortune, and powerful family connexions."[8] He was born in 1732 and was graduated with honors from William and Mary College in 1754. He then studied at London's Middle Temple and was called to the bar in 1757. Upon returning to his native Virginia, he entered law practice and became active in the colony's political affairs. He became a member of the House of Burgesses in 1765 and joined the conservative faction that opposed Patrick Henry's Stamp Act resolutions. By 1769, however, when the royal governor prorogued the Burgesses, he was active in establishing Virginia's boycott of imported British goods.

Blair began his judicial career in 1777, when he was named to the newly reorganized five-judge General Court. Two years later he became the court's chief justice, and by 1780 he was chancellor of the state's High

---

8. *Judge Blair, in* 8 Va. (4 Call) xvii (1833). For sketches of Justice Blair, *see* Fred Israel, *John Blair Jr., in* FRIEDMAN & ISRAEL 109–15; *John Blair, in* 1 DHSC 54–56.

Court of Chancery. By virtue of these offices, he was an ex officio member of Virginia's Court of Appeals. He continued in these judicial offices until he moved on to the United States Supreme Court. Blair was also a Virginia delegate to the Constitutional Convention and a firm advocate of the need for a stronger national government. In the subsequent ratification process, he supported ratification at the Virginia convention.

William Cushing

Although William Cushing was not born into an exceptionally wealthy family, his ancestors had played a prominent role in Massachusetts society and politics.[9] His mother was a descendent of John Cotton. His father and grandfather served on the Governor's Council and sat on the colony's highest judicial court. Born in 1732, Cushing was graduated from Harvard College in 1751. After briefly teaching school and studying theology, Cushing read law with a Boston attorney. He was admitted to practice in 1758. Cushing spent most of his early career in Maine, where he was not entirely successful. In 1771 Cushing's father resigned from the Superior Court of Judicature after reaching an agreement with the colony's Lieutenant Governor that he would be succeeded by his son. Cushing returned to Massachusetts and was appointed to the court in 1772.

During the first half of the 1770s, Cushing's relationship with the Crown's government was ambiguous. He remained silent on the locally significant issue of whether his salary should be paid by the legislature or the Crown. Finally, and under threat of impeachment, he sided with the legislature. Nevertheless, he was the only Massachusetts judge who continued to ride circuit during the tumultuous year before hostilities commenced. Notwithstanding this adherence to duty, his final position on the pay issue earned him the enmity of the royal government and the consequent friendship of the patriots. In 1775 he received a Commonwealth commission in exchange for his royal commission. He continued to sit upon Massachusetts's Superior Court until his appointment to the federal bench, serving as state chief justice from 1777 to 1789. Cushing was not a delegate to the Constitutional Convention in Philadelphia, but he supported the creation of a stronger national government. He was vice-president of Massachusetts's ratifying convention and advocated ratification.

---

9. For sketches of Justice Cushing, *see* Herbert Alan Johnson, *William Cushing, in* FRIEDMAN & ISRAEL 57–70; *William Cushing, in* 1 DHSC 24–27.

James Wilson

Unlike Jay, Rutledge, Blair, and Cushing, James Wilson came from a family that had neither social nor economic influence.[10] Wilson was born in Scotland in 1742, the eldest son of a small farmer. His parents wanted him to become a minister and scraped together sufficient funds for him to attend the University of St. Andrews. But he had to quit after four years when his father died. He soon left for America and arrived in Philadelphia in 1765.

The next year Wilson briefly read law with John Dickinson and by 1767 was a practicing attorney. In 1770 he moved to Carlisle and quickly entered patriot politics. By 1774 he headed the local Committee of Correspondence. He then served in various provincial assemblages and took a leading role in organizing the Cumberland County militia. In 1775 he was elected to the Continental Congress, and he returned to the Congress in 1783. Wilson represented Pennsylvania in the Constitutional Convention and is generally recognized as one of the two or three most influential and effective delegates. After the Convention, he was clearly the leading advocate in Pennsylvania for ratification, and he dominated the state ratification convention.

Wilson was in many ways the most capable individual George Washington nominated to the Court. He had an extensive and detailed knowledge of the law, and he also had a gift for innovative thinking. For example, in 1785, in a flash of brilliance, he argued that the Continental Congress had implicit authority outside the Articles of Confederation to charter the Bank of North America. In addition to exemplifying his gift for innovation, however, the essay in which he set forth his argument suggests a tragic and ultimately fatal flaw in Wilson's character. He was born into a humble family, and he never forgot it. At the Constitutional Convention he heroically, consistently, and admirably advocated a democratic approach to government based upon the broadest possible franchise of the people. But his early privations also created within him an insatiable desire for money. Although he espoused democratic principles, he always closely allied himself with the conservative, monied classes. This inclination was the impetus for his brilliant essay on the

---

10. For a biography of Justice Wilson, *see* CHARLES PAGE SMITH, JAMES WILSON, FOUNDING FATHER: 1724–1789 (1956). For briefer sketches, *see* Robert McCloskey, *James Wilson, in* FRIEDMAN & ISRAEL 79–96; *James Wilson, in* 1 DHSC 44–49.

Bank. He had developed a close business relationship with it and had borrowed substantial amounts of money from it.[11]

Robert Harrison

Robert Harrison was born in 1745 into a respected Maryland family.[12] His father was neither rich nor poor; he held significant but minor provincial offices. The extent of Harrison's education is unknown, but by the age of twenty he became a lawyer and moved to Fairfax County, Virginia. There he met and worked with George Washington on various committees leading up to the Revolution. When hostilities commenced, he joined a Virginia regiment but was almost immediately selected by Washington as an aide-de-camp. He served amicably with General Washington for six years and in 1781 left the army and returned to his native state of Maryland.

Back in Maryland, Harrison was appointed to the state's General Court and served as chief judge until his former commander asked him to join the national Supreme Court. Harrison did not participate in either the Constitutional Convention or the Maryland ratifying convention and seems not to have left any evidence of his thoughts on the Constitution. Although he was quickly confirmed by the Senate, he was initially inclined to decline Washington's offer of a place in the national government. But he reconsidered and set off for New York to take his place on the federal bench only to fall ill on the road. In the throes of this illness, he once more declined the position. He died within three months.

James Iredell

Washington soon nominated James Iredell of North Carolina to fill the seat vacated by Harrison.[13] Iredell was born into a Bristol merchant's family in 1751 and was thus thirty-eight at his nomination. Little is known of his schooling. He apparently never attended college, but he was a well-educated man. Although his father was not particularly successful, Iredell had a wealthy cousin who purchased a customs position for him in North Carolina when Iredell was seventeen. In 1768 the teen-

---

11. *See* Robert McCloskey, *Introduction, in* 1 THE WORKS OF JAMES WILSON 1, 21–23 (R. McCloskey ed., 1967).

12. For a sketch of Justice Harrison, *see Robert H. Harrison, in* 1 DHSC 31–33.

13. For sketches of Justice Iredell, *see* Fred Israel, *James Iredell, in* FRIEDMAN & ISRAEL 121–32; *James Iredell,* in 1 DHSC 60–63. For an excellent essay on Iredell's life through the Revolutionary War, *see* Don Higginbotham, *The Making of a Revolutionary, in* 1 THE PAPERS OF JAMES IREDELL xxxvii–xc (D. Higginbotham ed., 1976).

ager arrived in Edenton, North Carolina, without friends or relatives in North America.

This quest to the New World must have been frightening to young Iredell, but he was an engaging man who got on well with the local gentry. His entry into provincial society was undoubtedly eased by the fact that Henry McCulloh, his cousin in England, was one of North Carolina's largest landowners. Iredell quickly became a protégé of Samuel Johnston, a lawyer whose father had been royal governor of North Carolina. Iredell read law with Johnston and was admitted to the bar in 1771. In 1773 he married Johnston's sister, and by the time of the Revolution he was closely allied with the conservative merchants and planters who dominated the colony. During the Revolution he sided with some reluctance with these patriots against the country from which he had emigrated.

Iredell was recognized as a highly capable lawyer and was elected to the state's highest judicial court in 1777 at the age of twenty-six. But he detested the attendant circuit-riding duties and resigned six months later to return to private practice. He subsequently served as the state's attorney general from 1779 to 1781.

Although Iredell was not a delegate to the Constitutional Convention, he played a leading role in the North Carolina ratification process. He was not an impressive orator or (like Wilson) an imaginative and original thinker, but he was an extraordinarily thorough thinker. Before his state's ratification convention, he wrote a well-received point-by-point refutation of a pamphlet that George Mason had published against the Constitution.[14] This essay and printed versions of his well-crafted speeches at the North Carolina ratification convention won him instant fame and respect in Federalist circles throughout the United States. North Carolina initially rejected the Constitution because it lacked a Bill of Rights. But in the fall of 1789 a second convention ratified the Constitution out of fear of isolation and relief that Congress had promulgated a Bill of Rights.

Thomas Johnson

In early 1791, about a year after Iredell joined the Court, Justice Rutledge resigned to become chief justice of South Carolina, and Thomas

---

14. *See* George Mason, *Objections to the Constitution* (1787), *reprinted in* 14 DHRC 152–55; James Iredell, *Answers to George Mason's Objections to the New Constitution Recommended by the Late Convention at Philadelphia* (1788), *reprinted in* 16 DHRC 163–69, 242–48, 322–26, 379–87, 427–30.

Johnson was appointed to fill the vacancy.[15] Johnson was born in 1732 and was a member of the Maryland gentry. He was practicing law in Maryland by the late 1750s. Although Johnson was recognized as a capable and effective delegate to the first and second Continental Congresses, he dedicated most of his career to state politics. During the Revolution he was the commander of the Maryland militia and then served three terms as governor. After the war he spent most of his time in private practice and in the mercantile business, though he served briefly in the Maryland legislature. Johnson was not a delegate to the Constitutional Convention, but he actively supported ratification in Maryland. In 1790 he was appointed to succeed Robert Harrison as chief judge of the Maryland General Court.

Johnson was somewhat leery of joining the Court because he did not think that he had the physical stamina to ride circuit. In fact, he flatly stated that an assignment to the onerous "southern Circuit . . . would be an insurmountable Objection." After an agreement was reached that he would not be assigned to the southern circuit, Johnson accepted his commission and in the fall of 1791 commenced his brief and uneventful service on the Court. He quickly regretted his decision, and less than two years later he resigned his office because he found the circuit riding "excessively fatiguing."[16]

In filling the vacancy created by Johnson's resignation, Washington was somewhat inclined to pick another southerner and considered a small pool of three Marylanders, a Georgian, and William Paterson of New Jersey. At the President's request, Attorney General Edmund Randolph made enquiries and reported that the talents of three of the candidates were generally regarded as mediocre at best. This initial cut left Paterson and Senator Richard Potts of Maryland in the running.[17]

Although Randolph reported that Potts was a capable and well-regarded attorney, he urged the President to select Paterson. Randolph's overriding concern was to bolster confidence in and respect for the Court. Just two weeks earlier he had argued the highly controversial case of *Chisholm v. Georgia*;[18] and on the day that he penned his advice to

---

15. For a biography of Justice Johnson, *see* Edward Delaplaine, The Life of Thomas Johnson (1927). For briefer sketches, *see* Herbert Alan Johnson, *Thomas Johnson, in* Friedman & Israel 149–58; *Thomas Johnson, in* 1 DHSC 69–72.

16. Thomas Johnson to George Washington (July 27, 1791) and Thomas Johnson to George Washington (Jan. 16, 1793), *reprinted in* 1 DHSC 73, 80.

17. Edmund Randolph to George Washington (Feb. 18, 1793), *excerpted in* 1 DHSC 738–39.

18. 2 U.S. (2 Dall.) 419 (1793), *discussed in* chapter 7 at 188–97.

President Washington, the Court decided in *Chisholm* that states were suable in federal court without regard to their traditional sovereign immunity. Probably with *Chisholm* in mind, Randolph noted that "many decisions [of the Supreme Court] must be very grating to the states [and] that the dissatisfaction will be increased by a distrust of the abilities of some of our judges. . . . If such an idea gains ground, the state judiciaries will inevitably make a stand against the federal Bench."[19] Washington, who reposed great trust in Randolph, took his advice, and, notwithstanding the President's apparent preference for a southerner, Paterson was appointed.

William Paterson

William Paterson was born in 1745 into a Scotch-Irish family in Ireland.[20] A few years later they sailed to America, where his father eventually established a general store in Princeton, New Jersey. Paterson enrolled at the College of New Jersey (later Princeton) when he was thirteen and was graduated in 1763. He began reading law with a local attorney and was licensed to practice in 1768. Paterson had only limited social or business connections based on acquaintances from Princeton and did not meet with immediate success in the practice of law. But the Revolution changed this.

Like all of Washington's other appointments to the Court about whom we have sufficient information, Paterson was initially leery of an outright separation with Great Britain. Nevertheless, he soon joined the patriots' cause. After serving as Secretary of New Jersey's Provincial Congress, Paterson was appointed the state's first attorney general in 1776. For the next seven years he rode circuit throughout New Jersey representing the state's interests and made many invaluable contacts. By the end of the war, he was one of the state's best-regarded attorneys. He resigned his attorney generalship in 1783 and began a lucrative private practice representing creditors, including British ones. Three years later he was one of the most influential delegates at the Philadelphia Convention. In particular, he introduced the Paterson Plan and played a leading role in bringing to pass the compromise that protected small states by providing

---

19. Edmund Randolph to George Washington (Feb. 18, 1793), *excerpted in* 1 DHSC 738–39.

20. For a biography of Justice Paterson, *see* O'CONNOR. For briefer sketches, *see* Michael Kraus, *William Paterson, in* FRIEDMAN & ISRAEL 163–74; *William Paterson, in* 1 DHSC 82–87.

for their equal representation in the Senate. After this protection was assured, he became a committed Federalist.

Paterson was a respected senator in the first Congress under the Constitution and played a leading role in the Senate's deliberations and work. Upon William Livingston's death, Paterson left Congress after a year to succeed Livingston as the second governor of New Jersey. His abilities as a lawyer were highly regarded, and while serving as governor, he drafted a codification of New Jersey's statutory law and updated the procedural rules that regulated the operation of the state's chancery and law courts. As a highly respected attorney and state governor, he was ideally qualified to resolve the "many decisions that must be very grating to the states."[21]

ASSESSING WASHINGTON'S NOMINATION CRITERIA

In selecting Paterson and the earlier Justices, President Washington clearly viewed distinguished service in the Revolution as an important criterion. In retrospect, however, this qualification seems little more than a subset of the more general criterion of active participation in public life. The nominees ranged in age from fifty-seven (Cushing) to thirty-eight (Iredell), which means their ages ranged from forty-four to twenty-five in 1776. Most politically active attorneys of the eighteenth century engaged in some form of government service during this stage of their lives, so it is not surprising that all of Washington's nominees served in either civilian or military capacities in the Revolution.

Obviously the requirement of distinguished service in the Revolution excluded individuals who actively supported the Crown, but such a nomination would in any event have been inconceivable. A more interesting possibility is that Washington consciously excluded highly regarded attorneys like William Samuel Johnson of Connecticut, who sat out the Revolution in neutrality. Although there was speculation in the press that Johnson might be named Chief Justice,[22] Washington did not nominate Johnson or any other erstwhile neutral. Perhaps he feared that such an appointment would subject the new government to unnecessary criticism and therefore not contribute to the stability of the new political system. If so, however, there is no surviving evidence of such a concern other than the bare record of the nominations themselves.

Like the requirement of active participation in political life, the criterion of prior judicial experience is hardly surprising. Among Washing-

---

21. *See* this chapter at 64.
22. N.Y. JOURNAL, Apr. 16, 1789, *reprinted in* 1 DHSC 611–12.

ton's first seven nominations, Rutledge, Cushing, Harrison, and Blair had significant prior experience as judges on the highest judicial courts of their state. This kind of record was an obvious indication of professional competence. Vice-President John Adams voiced another consideration that may have influenced Washington. Adams hoped that Supreme Court appointments would be made primarily from among state chief justices. He explained, "As there is greater danger of collisions between the national and state judiciaries, if the state judges are men possessed of larger portions of the peoples' confidence than the national judges, the latter will become unpopular."[23]

Nevertheless, Washington clearly did not view significant judicial experience as an absolute prerequisite. John Jay had only a brief tenure as chief justice of New York, and there is no evidence that he actively served more than a few weeks in that capacity. Jay was a skilled lawyer and respected diplomat, but he was not a jurist. Similarly, Iredell had less than six months of prior judicial experience. Wilson's judicial experience was even more limited. He had no service whatsoever as a state judge, but he had considered about ten prize cases as an ad hoc member of the Continental Congress's Committee on Appeals.[24]

One of the two most interesting of Washington's criteria was the requirement of geographic suitability. In a private letter written in 1794, Washington indicated that geographic considerations were of immense importance in filling Supreme Court vacancies. "Whenever a [vacancy] does happen," he wrote, "it is highly probable that a geographical arrangement will have some attention paid to it." He then noted parenthetically that he also sought "the fittest characters for offices."[25]

During Washington's two terms as President and continuing throughout John Adams's term, a remarkable geographic balance was maintained on the Court. Each of the country's three regions—New England, the Mid-Atlantic states, and the South including Maryland—always had at least one Justice on the Court. Moreover, until John Marshall's appointment at the end of Adams's term, none of these three regions ever had a majority of the Justices.

In addition to a firm commitment to geographical diversity, Washington seems to have allocated at least some of the Supreme Court Justice-

---

23. John Adams to Henry Higginson (Sept. 21, 1789), *excerpted in* 1 DHSC 663.

24. For Jay, *see* GOEBEL 552 n.2; for Iredell, *see* Fred Israel, *James Iredell, in* 1 FRIEDMAN & ISRAEL 121, 124–25; for Wilson, *see* HENRY BOURGUIGNON, THE FIRST FEDERAL COURT 329 (1977).

25. George Washington to Edmund Pendleton (Mar. 17, 1794), *excerpted in* 1 DHSC 746.

John Rutledge, 1791. Oil on wood by John Trumbull (Yale University Art Gallery).

ships to specific states. For example, he seriously considered the South Carolinians John Rutledge, Edward Rutledge, and Charles Cotesworth Pinckney for a Court appointment and ultimately selected John Rutledge. When Rutledge resigned less than two years later, Washington saw the vacancy as presumptively belonging to South Carolina and offered the position to Edward Rutledge and Charles Cotesworth Pinckney. Only after these two men declined did Washington turn to Thomas Johnson of Maryland, then considered a southern state. By 1800 the inclination to fill a Supreme Court vacancy with a candidate from the same state as the erstwhile occupant was being called "the old rule of locality."[26]

At the very least Washington was consciously determined not to appoint two Justices from the same state, however. In 1794 he explained that after John Blair's appointment to the Court, a subsequent "vacancy in the supreme Judiciary . . . could not be filled from Virginia without

---

26. Ralph Izard to Edward Rutledge (Sept. 16, 1789), *excerpted in* 1 DHSC 668–69; George Washington to Charles Cotesworth Pinckney and Edward Rutledge (May 24, 1791), *reprinted in* 1 DHSC 725–27; Thomas B. Adams to Abigail Adams (Dec. 20, 1800), *excerpted in* 1 DHSC 904–5.

giving two Judges to that state, which would have excited unpleasant sensations in other states." While this passage might be read as referring to a distaste for appointing two Justices from the President's own state, Justice Paterson subsequently related that President Washington had "laid it down for a rule . . . not to select two judges from the same state." Washington's consistent use of geographic balancing also played a major role in James Iredell's appointment to the Court. The President explained in his diary that he was selecting "Mr. Iredell of No. Carolina; because, in addition to the reputation he sustains . . . he is of a state of some importance in the Union that has given *No* character to a federal office."[27]

Iredell also epitomizes the criterion of support and advocacy of the Constitution. With the exception of Robert Harrison, for which there is no surviving evidence one way or another, all of the initial nominees firmly supported the Constitution during the ratification process. Indeed, a significant number of them were leading advocates of the Constitution. The mere existence of this pattern does not necessarily mean that Washington actually used support and advocacy of the Constitution as a litmus test. Perhaps the pattern was coincidental, or perhaps it reflects a predominant tendency among politically active lawyers to support the Constitution.

Washington left no explicit statement that he required support for the Constitution. Nevertheless, a number of inferences support this litmus test theory. Restricting Supreme Court membership to friends of the Constitution was consistent with Washington's frequently stated desire to assure stability in the national government. Obviously the appointment of anti-Federalists to the Supreme Court would have created instability within the Court itself and would have diminished the Court's authority by fostering undesirable diversity of opinion among the Justices.

President Washington's treatment of Arthur Lee's candidacy for a seat on the Court provides further inferential support for the litmus test theory. A well-regarded attorney with distinguished diplomatic service, Lee had opposed ratification of the Constitution. When Lee sought a seat on the Court, Washington wrote in confidence, "I cannot bring my mind to adopt the request. The opinion entertained of him by those with whom I am most conversant is unpropitious." Although Washington did not expressly mention it, Lee's brother suggested in a letter to Patrick Henry that Washington's decision was based upon Lee's "opposition to

---

27. George Washington to Henry Lee (Aug. 26, 1794), *excerpted in* 1 DHSC 749–51; George Washington, Diary Entry (Feb. 6, 1790), *excerpted in* 1 DHSC 64; William Paterson to Jonathan Dayton (Jan. 25, 1801), *excerpted in* 1 DHSC 920–21.

the Constitution." This suggestion, however, cannot be pressed far. Washington's rejection of the Lee candidacy may have been based upon the fact that Lee was an argumentative and abrasive person who was disliked by many of his contemporaries.[28]

Washington's consideration of Patrick Henry to fill vacancies on the Supreme Court is also relevant. In the Virginia ratification process, Henry had been the Constitution's leading and most prominent opponent. It is therefore not surprising that Washington evidently rejected Henry as a replacement for Thomas Johnson when Johnson resigned his seat in early 1793. A year and a half later, Washington attempted to dispel rumors that Henry had been rejected because the President believed him to be "a factious seditious character."[29]

Apparently Washington had indeed expressed serious reservations in 1793 that Henry had "retained his enmity to the Constitution." But he recollected eighteen months later that he had learned "with very particular pleasure" that "Mr. Henry was acquiescent in his conduct, & that though he could not give up his opinion respecting the Constitution, yet, unless he should be called upon by official duty he would express no sentiment unfriendly to the exercise of the powers of a government which had been chosen by a majority of the people." Nevertheless, Washington chose not to offer a seat to Henry because he thought the nomination would place the government in a bad light. Washington believed that Henry would reject the proffered position, "[i]n which case, & supposing him to be inimical to it, the wound the government would receive by his refusal, and the charge of attempting to silence his opposition by a place, would be great." In addition, Washington noted that a Henry appointment would have placed two Virginians on the Court. A year and a half later, after Justice Blair of Virginia had resigned and it had become clear that Henry had become a firm supporter of the federal government, Washington indicated a willingness to appoint Henry to the Court.[30]

Washington's 1796 nomination of Samuel Chase presents the final piece of this puzzle. Chase, like Henry, had been a well-known opponent

---

28. George Washington to James Madison (Aug. 20–Sept. 11, 1789), *excerpted in* 1 DHSC 651–52; Richard Henry Lee to Patrick Henry (Sept. 27, 1789), *reprinted in* 2 LEE LETTERS 504–7. For a sketch of Arthur Lee's professional qualifications, *see* James Perry and James Buchanan, *Admission to the Supreme Court Bar, 1790–1800: A Case Study of Institutional Change*, 1983 YEARBOOK SUP. CT. HIST. SOC. 10, 12 (1983).
29. *See* Henry Lee to George Washington (Aug. 17, 1794), George Washington to Henry Lee (Aug. 26, 1794), *excerpted in* 1 DHSC 748–51.
30. George Washington to Henry Lee (Aug. 26, 1794), *excerpted in* 1 DHSC 749–51; George Washington to Henry Lee (Jan. 11, 1796), *reprinted in* 1 DHSC 829–30.

of the Constitution. Chase unsuccessfully sought an appointment to the Court in 1789, but seven years later Washington nominated him to fill the vacancy created by Blair's retirement. During these intervening years, Chase had become a firm proponent of the Federalist administration. To Washington, this change of heart was significant. In the fall of 1795, Washington considered appointing Chase attorney general and noted that though Chase was "opposed to the adoption of the Constitution, it is said he has been a steady friend to the general government since it has been in operation." Although Washington decided against appointing Chase to the attorney generalship, three months later he nominated him to the Supreme Court.[31]

From this meager evidence Washington appears to have considered support for the Constitution a litmus test for Supreme Court nominations. His initial appointees had supported the Constitution during the ratification process. There is evidence, moreover, that during the initial appointment process he rejected three candidates who had opposed the Constitution. He eventually changed his mind about Henry and Chase, but this change took place after these two men had themselves changed their public positions regarding the new federal government.

The Federalist/Anti-Federalist litmus test is interesting on a number of accounts. First, this criterion—like the geographic suitability criterion—highlights the political nature of Washington's understanding of the appointment process. He obviously desired to staff the Court with capable attorneys, but he had other objectives that were at least equally important. Either he believed or he thought other influential people believed that positions on the Supreme Court were political plums. In order to enhance the new government's stability, therefore, he distributed the positions evenly throughout the states so as not to "excite unpleasant sensations."[32] The Federalist/Anti-Federalist litmus test also contributed to the new government's stability.

---

31. Samuel Chase to George Washington (Sept. 3, 1789), *reprinted in* 1 DHSC 656–57; George Washington to Alexander Hamilton (Oct. 29, 1795), *excerpted in* 1 DHSC 805.
32. *See* this chapter at 68.

4

A NATIONAL SECURITY COURT

The Founders envisioned the federal courts as national security courts, and the Supreme Court's first decade is largely a story of the Justices' grappling with important issues affecting the nation's security. They devoted significant time to criminal prosecutions against Americans whom they understood to challenge federal authority directly.[1] In addition, the major recurring theme of the decade was the Justices' ongoing efforts to assist the Washington and Adams Administrations in evolving a stable relationship with the European powers—especially France and Great Britain.

THE NOOTKA SOUND CRISIS

Almost as soon as the federal government began its operations, the Washington Administration became entangled in a serious national security dispute with Great Britain. In 1789 Spanish forces attacked a British trading post on Nootka Sound, on Vancouver Island, on what what is now the Pacific coast of Canada, and the British elevated the incident to a serious international dispute by presenting Spain with an ultimatum in the late spring of 1790. The dispute was almost entirely between Spain and Britain; the United States played a minor role. Nevertheless, there was some fear in America that Britain might attack Spanish possessions in North America. President Washington wrote his cabinet that "there is no doubt in my mind" that the British would mount an overland attack from Canada upon Spanish possessions in Florida and Louisiana. Washington therefore asked his cabinet what should be done if the British requested permission to march their troops through United States terri-

---

1. *See* chapter 5.

71

tory and what should be done if the British marched without permission.[2]

That President Washington should consult his cabinet is not surprising. But the President also sought Chief Justice Jay's formal written opinion on these issues. Jay responded the next day with a lengthy and detailed analysis and recommendation. He drew upon his extensive diplomatic experience to analyze the policy considerations implicated by the crisis, but he also dedicated a major part of his opinion to advising the President on the principles of international law applicable to the issues.[3] Spain eventually acceded to the British demands, a war was averted, and nothing came of the affair. The President's actions suggest, however, that he viewed the Chief Justice as an appropriate source of both political and legal advice. Moreover, Chief Justice Jay displayed no hesitation in advising the President on the proper application of international legal principles to the diplomatic case at hand.

RELATIONS WITH FRANCE AND GREAT BRITAIN

Although Spanish Florida and Louisiana continued to be foreign policy irritants for the rest of the decade, the major international issues that confronted the Washington and Adams Administrations centered upon relations with Great Britain and France. The nation's relations with each of these European powers were seriously complicated by pervasive and destabilizing ambivalences. The United States was an English-speaking country with strong cultural ties to Great Britain, and the nation's foreign commerce was utterly dominated by British merchants. When the Constitution was ratified, about 75 percent of the country's exports were to Britain, and about 90 percent of American imports came from Britain. Given these cultural and economic realities, a close relationship with Britain was inevitable.[4]

Close relationships, however, can generate enormous friction, and British-American relations were by no means amicable. The United States had recently fought a major war against Great Britain, and the Treaty of Paris made but a promising start toward resolving the two

2. George Washington to his Cabinet and the Chief Justice (Aug. 17, 1790), *reprinted in* 17 Jefferson Papers 128–29. On the Nootka Sound Crisis, *see generally* Editorial Note, 17 Jefferson Papers 35–108; Elkins & McKitrick 212–23.

3. John Jay to George Washington (Aug. 28, 1790), *reprinted in* 17 Jefferson Papers 134–37.

4. On foreign relations in the 1790s, *see* DeConde chapter 3. On trade with Great Britain and France, *see* Elkins & McKitrick 68–74.

countries' differences. America was in flagrant violation of Article IV of the Treaty, which guaranteed the payment of debts owed to British merchants. Similarly, Great Britain ignored the provisions of Article VII that required the British to evacuate the military and trading posts in United States territory that dominated the trade routes and borders of the Northwest Territories. The British had also violated the Treaty provision forbidding them to carry off slaves and other American property. In addition, the British were actively impeding lucrative trade between the United States and the British West Indies.

American relations with France were equally complicated. On the one hand, most Americans were grateful for significant French military and financial assistance during the Revolution. In addition to providing desperately needed loans, France sent an army to fight side by side with the patriot army. And by blockading the Chesapeake Bay, the French navy had made possible the war-ending victory at Yorktown. Initially, Americans' feelings of gratitude were amplified by the French Revolution. Like the United States, France had overthrown its royal government and seemed to embrace Republican principles. On the other hand, the commencement of the French Revolution's Reign of Terror seriously complicated the American public's general attitude of amity and gratitude. For many conservative American political leaders, this bloody spectacle evoked the worst possible images of mob rule. More significantly, when the King of France was beheaded and a general European war broke out in early 1793, the United States was faced with the dilemma of whether to support Britain or France.

As France and Great Britain sporadically waged war throughout the rest of the 1790s, Franco-American relations were complicated by the 1778 Treaty of Alliance ratified at the height of the Revolutionary War. This treaty had been negotiated in the context of a major war between the United States and Great Britain and included provisions that became embarrassing ten years after the war, when most Americans wished to remain at peace with America's predominant trading partner. Among other things, the United States "forever" guaranteed French possessions in the West Indies from attack by all other powers, and French naval vessels and privateers were granted special rights during wars between France and other countries.[5]

As soon as the European war broke out, President Washington con-

---

5. Treaty of Amity and Commerce (Feb. 6, 1778), *reprinted in* 2 Treaties (Miller) 3–29. For Franco-American relations, *see* Albert Hall Bowman, The Struggle for Neutrality (1974); Elkins & McKitrick chapters VIII, IX.

sulted with his cabinet to determine the proper stance to adopt. Although the cabinet unanimously agreed that the country should follow a general course of neutrality, different members had conflicting ideas concerning what neutrality entailed. The group led by Alexander Hamilton favored a strict and impartial neutrality that would emasculate the Treaty of Alliance and favor Britain. Conversely, Jefferson wanted to give fuller scope to the Treaty and adopt a course of neutrality more favorable to France.[6]

THE NEUTRALITY PROCLAMATION

There is no evidence one way or another that President Washington consulted with either the Supreme Court or any of its Justices, but Alexander Hamilton immediately sought Chief Justice Jay's advice. In addition to discussing some technical details about the consequences of accepting an ambassador from the revolutionary government in France, Hamilton asked Jay to draft a neutrality proclamation. Two days later, on April 11, Jay replied with a "hastily drawn" proclamation.[7]

Jay's draft referred to the revolutionary French regime as a government in fact but hedged on whether it was a lawful government. He consciously avoided any discussion of the Treaty of Alliance and recommended a flat statement that "it is necessary that the United States should by a conduct perfectly inoffensive cultivate and preserve the Peace they now enjoy." Jay then proceeded to more specific recommendations. In particular, he thought the President should call for American citizens to "abstain from acting hostilely against any of the belligerent powers, under Commissions from either of them."[8]

In terms of the relationship of the judiciary to the national government, Jay's most significant recommendation was to urge the commencement of criminal prosecutions. He thought the President should proclaim that "I do also enjoin all Magistrates and others in authority to be watchful and diligent in preventing any aggressions from being committed against foreign nations and their people; and to cause all offenders to be prosecuted & punished in an Exemplary manner."[9] These were

---

6. *See* THOMAS chapter 1; BOWMAN, THE STRUGGLE FOR NEUTRALITY chapter 2 (1974).

7. Alexander Hamilton to John Jay (Apr. 9, 1793; two letters), *reprinted in* 14 HAMILTON PAPERS 297–300; John Jay to Alexander Hamilton (Apr. 11, 1793), *reprinted in* 14 HAMILTON PAPERS 307–10.

8. John Jay to Alexander Hamilton (Apr. 11, 1793), enclosing Jay, Draft Proclamation, *reprinted in* 14 HAMILTON PAPERS 307–10.

9. *Id.*

strong words from a judge who might preside over the recommended criminal prosecutions.

Whether the President and the full cabinet considered Jay's advice is not known. Eleven days later, on April 22, a proclamation drafted by Attorney General Edmund Randolph was issued. In this proclamation, President Washington formally declared that the United States would "pursue a conduct friendly and impartial towards the belligerent powers." He also directed the commencement of criminal prosecutions against persons who violated American neutrality.[10]

THE TREATY OF ALLIANCE AND
THE CORRESPONDENCE OF THE JUSTICES

The Proclamation of Neutrality finessed a difficult legal and policy issue confronting Washington's administration. Everyone agreed that the country should remain neutral, but there was fierce disagreement over whether it should adopt a policy of strict impartiality or should tilt toward the French. The existing Treaty of Alliance with France was clearly pertinent to this issue and would have supported a pro-French policy. President Washington's Proclamation, however, made no reference to the Treaty of Alliance.

Shortly after Jay finished the rough draft of his proposed proclamation, he began writing a general explanation and legal justification of the policy of neutrality that he had recommended. By April 22, when the Proclamation was issued, he had a fully developed draft. He then reworked his draft and delivered it as a grand jury charge on May 22.[11] The charge was an admirable general treatment of American neutrality. He surveyed the applicable principles of international law and a number of specific treaties in which the United States had pledged its friendship to Great Britain, France, and other European nations. Given these various pledges, he concluded, the United States was obliged to adopt a course of strict neutrality. The charge was published in newspapers, and the government sent copies to Europe as a formal explanation of its position.[12]

The course of events, however, had rapidly overtaken the Chief Justice's efforts. When Jay began drafting the charge in mid-April, Washing-

---

10. Proclamation of Neutrality (Apr. 22, 1793), *reprinted in* 11 Stat. 753 (App. 1859).

11. John Jay, Draft Grand Jury Charge (written sometime before Apr. 22, 1793), *reprinted in* 2 DHSC 359–65; John Jay, Charge to Virginia Grand Jury (May 22, 1793), *reprinted in* 2 DHSC 380–91.

12. *See* WHEATON 49 n; Thomas Jefferson to Gouverneur Morris (Aug. 16, 1793), *reprinted in* 7 JEFFERSON PAPERS (Ford) 475–507.

ton and his cabinet were concentrating upon general principles. A month later they had to deal with a series of specific actions by the French government that arguably were permitted by the Treaty of Alliance but that seriously jeopardized American neutrality. In his backward-looking charge, Jay refused to provide guidance on precisely what conduct was permissible and what conduct would violate the recently proclaimed neutrality. By the end of May, the government and its grand jurors needed far more specific advice.

Two weeks before the President's Neutrality Proclamation was issued, the new French minister arrived in Charleston, South Carolina. Citizen Edmond Genêt was a dynamo of irrepressible revolutionary action. He immediately embarked upon a number of projects, including commissioning privateers to prey upon British shipping. The privateers' commissions were signed with the stroke of a pen, but the actual maritime campaign could not be launched without converting unarmed merchant ships into armed privateers and recruiting sailors to man them. Ordinarily a neutral country could not condone these activities, but Genêt argued to the contrary. He insisted that neither the treaties nor the laws of the United States banned his recruiting activities. In addition, he argued that the Treaty of Alliance actually authorized France to fit out privateers in American ports.[13]

Genêt presented a multilayered legal argument on fitting out privateers. He pointed to Article XXII of the Treaty, which positively stated that "It shall not be lawful for any foreign privateers not belonging to [French or United States citizens] who have Commissions from any other Prince or State in enmity with either Nation to fit their Ships in the Ports of either the one or the other of the aforesaid Parties." Genêt insisted that the "not belonging to" phrase created a negative inference that the Treaty authorized French privateers to fit their ships in American ports. In addition to this general argument, Genêt and others advanced an array of technical legal arguments based upon distinctions such as whether a privateer was being fitted with American or French cannons or whether piercing a merchantman's hull for cannons but not mounting the cannons would be permissible.[14]

Genêt was an enthusiastic and personable man whose colorable legal arguments were initially accepted at face value by American supporters of France's new revolutionary government. Governor William Moultrie of South Carolina acquiesced in Genêt's plans, and a week after Genêt set foot in America, four privateers set sail. Throughout April and May,

---

13. For Genêt's activities, *see generally* HARRY AMMON, THE GENÊT MISSION (1973).
14. *See* Thomas chapter 4.

while Chief Justice Jay was preparing his exposition of general principles, the French privateers were creating a serious and immediate foreign policy crisis by preying upon British shipping. At the same time,
Citizen Genêt was parading up the East Coast commissioning privateers
and exhorting enthusiastic crowds to support France's republican government in its war against the British monarchy.

The success of Genêt's privateers created an additional issue. An effective privateering campaign required prize courts to legitimize the privateer's individual captures. Until a captured vessel and its cargo are
condemned by a prize court, the privateer's claim of ownership is open
to challenge, and the sale of the capture is problematical. But a lawful
condemnation clears up these ownership problems and makes the captured goods easily saleable. The privateers might have sailed their captures to France or a French port in the West Indies, but the distance and
the danger of recapture by British naval patrols made this theoretical option unworkable. Instead, they took their captures to American ports,
where French consuls purporting to act as legitimate prize courts condemned the captures.[15]

By May 1793 the resident British minister was bombarding the federal
government with protests regarding the fitting out of vessels, the recruitment of privateer crews, and the operation of French consular prize
courts—all on American soil. In July all of these issues coalesced around the
activities of a specific privateer, the *Little Democrat*. Just two months earlier
the vessel had been a British merchantman named the *Little Sarah*. When
she sailed from Philadelphia, then the nation's capital, she was captured by
a frigate of the regular French navy. The prize was sailed back into Philadelphia, renamed the *Little Democrat*, and fitted out as a privateer.

Because of this open affront to neutrality in the nation's capital, the
cabinet resolved to take strong formal action. All members of the
cabinet—including Jefferson, who was inclined to support France—
agreed that the fitting out of privateers, the recruitment of American
crews, and the operation of the consular courts were improper. Nevertheless, Washington, with the apparent support of his cabinet, decided to
ask the Supreme Court for an opinion on the nation's obligations under
its treaties and the customary law of nations. This request was consistent
with well-established English custom.[16]

---

15. *See id.* at 205–20.
16. Thomas Jefferson, Alexander Hamilton, and Henry Knox, Cabinet Opinion on
Vessels Arming and Arriving in United States Ports (July 12, 1793), *reprinted in* 15
HAMILTON PAPERS 87–88. On the *Little Sarah/Little Democrat, see* THOMAS 37–44. On the
English custom, *see* Stewart Jay, *Servants of Kings and Lords: The Advisory Role of Early
English Judges*, 38 Am. J. LEGAL HIST. 117 (1994).

The reasons for Washington's decision to seek a Supreme Court advisory opinion are not entirely clear. All of the cabinet officers were in agreement on the principal issues of recruitment, fitting out, and consular prize courts, so there was no real need for an advisory opinion on these subjects. Perhaps the President was more interested in creating an image of political solidarity than in obtaining the Court's legal opinion. The day before the decision was made to seek an opinion, he wrote Jefferson, "What is to be done in the case of the *Little Sarah* now at Chester. Is the Minister of the French Republic to . . . threaten the executive with an appeal to the people?"[17] If a popular appeal was to be made, an opinion from the Supreme Court would have been welcome support.

In addition to the general questions, there were myriad technical issues that needed to be resolved. For example, Jefferson, who generally agreed with the rest of the cabinet on the major issues, believed that outfitting a French vessel with cannon from another French vessel was permissible. He also thought the recruitment of French citizens rather than Americans was not a breach of neutrality.[18] Thus submitting a detailed list of interrogatories to the Court presented the cabinet an opportunity not only to resolve the major questions but also to clear up all the nagging, and even niggling, technical issues regarding the country's neutrality.

By July 18 the cabinet had agreed upon a detailed list of twenty-nine questions that Jefferson forwarded to the Court. Jefferson noted that the questions were of great importance to the peace of the nation. Moreover, he explained,

> These questions depend for their solution on the construction of our treaties, on the laws of nature and nations, and on the laws of the land, and are often presented under circumstances which do not give a cognizance of them in the tribunals of the country. Yet their decision is so little analogous to the ordinary functions of the executive, as to occasion much embarrassment and difficulty to them.

Although this formal request came from the Secretary of State rather than the President, Jefferson twice stated that he was writing on the President's behalf.[19]

---

17. George Washington to Thomas Jefferson (July 11, 1793), *reprinted in* 33 WASHINGTON WRITINGS 4.

18. *See* HARRY AMMON, THE GENÊT MISSION 92 (1973).

19. Thomas Jefferson to the Chief Justice and Justices (July 18, 1793) *reprinted in* 7 JEFFERSON PAPERS (Ford) 451–56. *See also* Draft of Questions to Be Submitted to Justices of the Supreme Court (July 18, 1793), *reprinted in* 15 HAMILTON PAPERS 110–16.

Chief Justice Jay already knew that the President was seeking the advice because Jay had been discussing the matter with Washington in private. Apparently Jay had expressed some misgivings about the propriety of the Supreme Court's advising the President on this matter, and to resolve this preliminary issue he had asked the President to send a formal written request to the Court. Washington advised Jefferson that "the Judges will have to decide whether the business which it is proposed to ask their opinion upon is, in their judgment, of such a nature as that they can comply." In accordance with this advice, Jefferson noted in his letter to the Justices that the President wished as a preliminary matter "to know, in the first place, [the Justices'] opinion, whether the public may, with propriety, be availed of their advice on these questions."[20]

Chief Justice Jay's premonition that the Court might refuse to give the President an advisory opinion proved to be accurate, and on August 8 the Justices formally rejected the President's request. As they cryptically explained,

> The Lines of Separation drawn by the Constitution between the three Departments of government—their being in certain Respects checks on each other—and our being Judges of a Court in the last Resort—are Considerations which afford strong arguments against the Propriety of our extrajudicially deciding the questions alluded to; especially as the Power given by the Constitution to the President of calling on the Heads of Departments for opinions, seems to have been *purposely* as well as expressly limited to the *executive* Departments.[21]

With this correspondence, the Justices established two precedents. The Constitution does not authorize the President to require the Court to provide legal advice, and the Court should not—as an exercise of institutional discretion—issue advisory opinions.

The Justices firmly believed that they were not obliged to answer the President's twenty-nine questions, and they clearly stated the basis for this conclusion. Their preliminary allusion to the "Lines of Separation

---

20. George Washington to Thomas Jefferson (July 18, 1793), *reprinted in* 37 WASHINGTON WRITINGS 575; Thomas Jefferson to the Chief Justice and Justices (July 18, 1793), *reprinted in* 7 JEFFERSON PAPERS (Ford) 451, 452.

21. The Justices of the Supreme Court to Thomas Jefferson (Aug. 8, 1793) (emphasis original), *excerpted in* 15 HAMILTON PAPERS 111 n.1. This full excerpt is from the letter in the National Archives that the Justices actually sent. Almost all other published versions of the letter have been based upon a slightly misedited draft that was first published in 3 JAY PAPERS 488–89.

drawn by the Constitution between the three departments of government" suggests that they thought a duty to respond would imply an unwarranted subordination of the judicial to the executive. But their clearest analysis was a negative inference drawn from the express constitutional provision that empowered the President to "require the opinion, in writing, of the principal officer in each of the executive departments." The Justices "especially" emphasized that this provision "seems to have been *purposely* as well as expressly united to the *executive* departments [that is, exclusively united]."[22]

As Genêt's controversial interpretation of the French treaty illustrates, negative inferences are not necessarily proper inferences. But the Justices' analysis on this issue went beyond a mere negative inference. Three of the Justices (Wilson, Blair, and Paterson) had been delegates to the Constitutional Convention, and they probably remembered that Charles Pinckney had specifically proposed giving the executive branch express authority "to require the opinions of the supreme Judicial Court upon important questions of Law."[23] This proposal, however, was rejected, with the result that the President's express authority to seek advice was limited to the executive departments. The Justices apparently drew upon this history when they emphasized that the President's authority seemed "to have been *purposely* . . . united to the *executive* departments."

Under this constitutional analysis, the President lacked authority to require the Court to provide advice. Nevertheless, the Justices might in the alternative have treated Jefferson's letter as a nonmandatory request that might be answered at their discretion. Given Chief Justice Jay's practice of giving advisory legal opinions on issues like the Nootka Sound Crisis and the Neutrality Proclamation, this was a plausible option. But the Court refused to address the twenty-nine questions.

One of the reasons suggested by the Court was the "separation of powers" concept that "the three departments of government [are] in certain respects checks upon each other." This argument is superficially relevant but ultimately not compelling because the request for an opinion presented the Court with a clear opportunity to provide a prior check upon the executive branch. Courts typically review government actions by adjudicating lawsuits filed after the fact of executive action. In contrast, Washington's request allowed the Court to counterbalance executive action at the planning stage.

---

22. U.S. CONST. art. II, § 2.
23. 2 FARRAND 340–41, *discussed in* chapter 1 at 25.

The Justices also stated that "our being judges of a court in the last resort [is one of the] considerations which afford strong arguments against the propriety of our extrajudicially deciding the questions alluded to." Exactly what they meant is unclear because they did not elaborate. Perhaps they were concerned that their answers might improperly bias their participation in future litigation involving the same questions. If so, their concern was more of a consideration than a firm rule. Individual Justices frequently gave advisory opinions before and after their joint correspondence with Secretary Jefferson in 1793.[24]

Jefferson had attempted to forestall this objection when he claimed that these issues were "often presented under circumstances which do not give a cognizance of them to the tribunals of the country." But the Justices knew that these issues were almost certainly going to be litigated. Questions regarding the legality of the consular prize courts were before the lower federal courts, and the Supreme Court decided the issue less than a year later in *Glass v. The Sloop Betsy*. Insofar as the recruitment of Americans was concerned, a major indictment was handed down by the Philadelphia grand jury against one Gideon Henfield while the Justices were in Philadelphia contemplating the President's questions. Similarly, at least two of the Justices delivered grand jury charges instructing that American citizens who assisted in fitting out French privateers were subject to indictment.[25]

The Justices may also have feared that answering the interrogatories would open the door for the President to routinely ask the Court for advisory opinions. If they feared the de facto establishment of such a practice, the President's request presented a perfect opportunity to scotch the practice at the outset. The Justices refused, with the knowledge that the President's questions would eventually be answered in their grand jury charges and in ongoing federal court litigation.

A final possible reason for the Justices' refusal cannot be ignored. We know that Alexander Hamilton was initially opposed to referring the matter to the Court[26] and that he disagreed with Jefferson on some of the technical legal issues. A Supreme Court decision favoring Jefferson's

---

24. *See, e.g.*, this chapter at 71–72 and 97–98.

25. 3 U.S. (3 Dall.) 6 (1794), *discussed* this chapter at 83–87. James Wilson, Charge to the Pennsylvania Grand Jury (July 22, 1793), *reprinted in* 2 DHSC 414, 420–21; James Iredell, Charge to the South Carolina Grand Jury (May 12, 1794), *reprinted in* 2 DHSC 454, 461–64. *Henfield* is *discussed in* chapter 5 at 130–35.

26. Alexander Hamilton to George Washington (May 15, 1793), *reprinted in* 14 HAMILTON PAPERS 451, 459; Alexander Hamilton, *Pacificus I* (June 29, 1793), *reprinted in* 15 HAMILTON PAPERS 33, 34.

position would effectively foreclose Hamilton. Hamilton may have privately lobbied the Court in order to assure that the whole matter would be left to the cabinet.

ADMIRALTY JURISDICTION I: *GLASS V. THE SLOOP BETSY*

While the Washington Administration was worrying over Genêt's escapades, French privateers were bringing their prizes into American ports for condemnation by French consular courts. In early May, a British ship, *The William,* was captured close to Maryland and placed under the command of an American named Gideon Henfield, who was serving with the French. Henfield then sailed the prize into Philadelphia, where it was immediately condemned by the French consul. Henfield was arrested and prosecuted in federal court for violating American neutrality, and the owners of *The William* sought to regain possession of their ship.[27]

Almost as soon as *The William* sailed into Philadelphia, the British owners sued in federal court to regain pssession, and George Hammond, the British Minister, protested the capture to Secretary of State Jefferson. Seven days later Jefferson agreed with the strategy of seeking judicial restitution and advised Hammond that it is "now supposed that the tribunals of the country will take cognizance of these cases." The owners' suit was in federal district court for Pennsylvania, presided over by District Judge Richard Peters, an experienced and sophisticated admiralty judge. Their basic contention was that the capture was made not on the high seas but within the territorial jurisdiction of the United States and therefore was unlawful under the law of nations. In response, the privateer's counsel contended that under the law of nations, the question of prize was left to the admiralty courts of the warring nations and could not be reviewed by the court of a neutral nation.[28]

Notwithstanding Jefferson's advice, Hammond was not entirely certain that an American admiralty court could review the lawfulness of a French capture, and his doubts were confirmed the day after Jefferson assured him that the federal courts "will take cognizance of these cases." Judge Peters apparently believed that the vessel was captured within American waters and that the seizure was unlawful, but he dismissed the case and a similar one for lack of jurisdiction. In writing his opinion, he

---

27. *See* chapter 5 at 130–35.
28. Findlay v. The William, 9 F. Case. 57 (D. Pa. 1793) (No. 4790); Presser 56–61 (discussing Peters); George Hammond to Thomas Jefferson (June 5, 1793), *excerpted in* 14 Hamilton Papers 548–49 n.4; Thomas Jefferson to George Hammond (June 13, 1793), *reprinted in* 7 Jefferson Papers (Ford) 382–84.

went to great length to establish that under the law of nations the fundamental question of prize or no prize (that is, the lawfulness of the capture) is reserved to the courts of the captor nation and is beyond the jurisdiction of a neutral nation's courts. Moreover, he did not believe that this well-known principle had been altered by Congressional legislation. He found the acts of Congress to be, at best, silent on the issue. Clearly the Judiciary Act vested his court with prize jurisdiction, but he wrote that to activate this jurisdiction when the "nation is at peace, appears to be a solecism in jurisprudence." Because Peters concluded that he lacked jurisdiction, he could not review either the lawfulness of the capture or the jurisdiction of the French consular court.[29]

Peters was a capable judge who understood that innovative approaches to the issue were possible. For example, his predecessor as district judge appeared as counsel in the case and urged that "though as a general principle a Court of a *Neutral Nation* will not examine the question of prize or not prize, between belligerent Powers—yet this principle must except the case of the infraction of the [territorial] Jurisdiction of the Neutral Power itself." But Peters was a conservative trial judge who was reluctant to go against the overwhelming weight of legal authority. If an exception was to be created, he believed that the decision should come from the Supreme Court rather than a single trial judge. He therefore reminded the losing ship owners that "there is an appeal, from any determination I may give, to a superior tribunal." The owners, however, elected to seek a remedy from the executive branch.[30]

Judge Peters's decision in *The William* was not an anomaly. In *Glass v. The Sloop Betsy*, William Paca, the federal district judge in Maryland, soon reached the same conclusion, and he reiterated his decision in yet another case. Justice Paterson, in his capacity as a circuit Justice, quickly affirmed the *Glass* decision and thereby facilitated an early review by the Supreme Court. But the hemorrhage of embarrassing decisions did not stop. The jurisdiction issue was also presented to Federal District Judges James Duane, John Lowell, and Thomas Bee in New York, Massachusetts, and South Carolina. Before the Supreme Court could hear the

---

29. Findlay, 9 F. Case. at 62; Moxon v. The Fanny, 17 F. Case. 942 (D. Pa. 1793) (No. 9895); George Hammond to Thomas Jefferson (June 5, 1793), *excerpted in* 14 HAMILTON PAPERS 548–49 n.4.

30. Alexander Hamilton to Rufus King (June 15, 1793) (emphasis original) (relating the argument to the court), *reprinted in* 14 HAMILTON PAPERS 547–49. *See also* Alexander Hamilton, *No Jacobin II* (Aug. 3, 1793), *reprinted in* 15 HAMILTON PAPERS 184, 186–90. Findlay, 9 F. Case. at 61. For the owners' decision, *see* George Hammond to Thomas Jefferson (June 21, 1793), *reprinted in* COUNTER CASE 530.

Glass appeal, Judge Lowell decided that his court had jurisdiction, but Judge Duane reached the same conclusion as Judges Peters and Paca. Judge Duane's decision in New York must have been particularly embarrassing because the suit was filed at the specific "instruction" of Secretary of State Jefferson. In fact, the decisions were so embarrassing that President Washington formally requested Congress to enact legislation to overturn their rationale. After this request, Judge Bee in South Carolina became the fourth federal judge to hold that his court lacked jurisdiction.[31]

Before Congress acted on President Washington's request, the Supreme Court heard argument in the *Glass* case in February 1794. Federalists on the Court and in Congress agreed that the case was "more important [than any other case before the Court], if not more famous [because it] contains principles of the utmost importance to us as a Nation in respect to Maritime Jurisdiction in our District Courts, and in respect to foreigners establishing their infamous courts in our country." The Court heard arguments for four days. Attorneys for the French privateers repeated the arguments that persuaded Judge Peters. In addition, they argued that without regard to French consular court operations, the French treaty at least guaranteed the French the right to bring prizes into an American port free from judicial interference. Finally, in a flash of misguided brilliance, they argued that the Judiciary Act of 1789 gave the federal admiralty courts no power whatsoever over any kind of prize litigation. This argument was utterly destroyed by the opposing counsel.[32]

After oral argument the Court took the case under advisement for six days and then issued a unanimous decree directing the district court to take jurisdiction and determine the merits of the plaintiff's claims. The

---

31. President Washington, Fifth Annual Address (Dec. 3, 1793), *reprinted in* RICHARDSON 138, 140. Judge Paca's elaborate and well-reasoned opinion is fully reported in MARYLAND JOURNAL AND BALTIMORE ADVERTISER, Oct. 31, 1793. *Accord,* The Roehampton, unreported (D. Md. 1793), *discussed in* George Hammond to Thomas Jefferson (Nov. 7, 1793), *reprinted in* COUNTER CASE 548–50. Justice Paterson's affirmance is *discussed in* GOEBEL 761–62. For the other decisions, *see* The Catherine (D. N.Y 1794), *reprinted in* DECREE ON THE ADMIRALTY SIDE OF THE DISTRICT COURT OF NEW YORK (1794) (Evans No. 26,915), *discussed in* George Hammond to Thomas Jefferson (June 14, 1793) (suit filed "In conformity to your instructions"), *reprinted in* COUNTER CASE 528–29; Folger v. Lecuyer, Boston Centinel, Jan. 4, 1794 (D. Mass. Dec. 6, 1793), *discussed in* MELVIN JACKSON, PRIVATEERS IN CHARLESTON,1793–1796, at 18–19 (1969); Castello v. Bouteille, 5 F. Cas. 278 (D. S.C. 1794) (No. 2504).

32. William Cushing to Increase Sumner (Feb. 24, 1794) (Robert Treat Paine Papers, MHi); Uriah Tracy to Ephraim Kirby (Feb. 24, 1794) (Ephraim Kirby Papers, NcD). Glass v. The Sloop Betsy, 3 U.S. (3 Dall.) 6, 7–15 (1794) (argument of counsel).

Court immediately and emphatically rejected the startling argument that the district courts lacked any prize jurisdiction. The Justices were "decidedly of opinion" that the federal district courts' had a complete admiralty jurisdiction.[33]

The Court then turned to the principal issue. Judge Paca, like Judges Peters, Duane, and Bee, had held on excellent authority that under the law of nations, only the capturing nation's courts were authorized to review the legality of a capture. With no explanation, the Court simply pronounced that it was "clearly of opinion, that the District Court of *Maryland* aforesaid, has jurisdiction competent to enquire, and to decide, whether, in the present case, restitution ought to be made." This brief pronouncement clearly rejected the reasoning of the lower courts and established at least an exception to the general principle that Judge Peters and his fellow district judges had so skillfully elaborated. In determining whether restitution should be granted, the Court advised that the district court should be guided by "the laws of nations and the treaties and laws of the *United States*." By this reference the Court meant the general law of nations regarding the legitimacy of captures as supplemented and perhaps modified by United States domestic law.[34]

This rejection of the settled legal doctrine upon which Judges Paca, Peters, Duane, and Bee had relied is at the same time the most interesting and the most puzzling aspect of the case. The Justices stated that they were "unanimous" and "clearly of opinion" that American courts had authority to review the legality of a French capture, but they did not explain why. In important cases, each Justice typically explained or justified his decision, but in *Glass* they did not present explanations. Perhaps they declined to give their reasons because they could not agree upon a rationale that was plausible. As Judge Peters and his fellow district judges had demonstrated, the arguments under the law of nations against a neutral country's courts' assumption of prize jurisdiction were powerful and well established. Innovative counterarguments were possible,[35] but the Justices were conservative common lawyers who were inclined to avoid innovation. Ordinarily the Justices were willing to offer differing opinions in the cases they decided, but they may have wished to present a common

---

33. 3 U.S. (3 Dall.) at 16.
34. *Id.* (emphasis original).
35. *See, e.g.,* this chapter at 83. This particular argument, however, would not have worked in Glass, where the capture was "out of the territorial jurisdiction of the United States." Glass v. The Sloop Betsy, MARYLAND JOURNAL AND BALTIMORE ADVERTISER, Oct. 1, 1793 (D. Md. 1793).

front in an important case that directly implicated the nation's ability to avoid being drawn into the European war.

Although all the Justices believed that American courts "clearly" could adjudicate the lawfulness of a belligerent country's captures, there remained one more procedural roadblock that might bar the judicial review of French captures. The problem was that the judgment of a foreign admiralty court is ordinarily binding on the courts of another nation, and the claimants seeking restitution had apparently conceded this point in the district court. In another case, the Supreme Court decreed the next year that as soon as a prize was brought into a French port for condemnation, the trial of "all questions incidental thereto, does of right, and exclusively, belong to the [French prize courts] and to no other tribunal, or tribunals, court or courts, whatsoever." Because the French consular court in Baltimore had already condemned *The Betsy*, the federal district court was possibly precluded from considering the lawfulness of the capture.[36]

Probably with this preclusion problem in mind, the Supreme Court asked counsel to discuss the legitimacy of the consular prize courts. In a puzzling lapse of advocacy skills, Peter Duponceau responded "that the parties to the appeal did not conceive themselves interested in the point; and that the French minister had given no instructions for arguing it." Accordingly, the Court announced its preconceived decision "that no foreign power can of right institute, or erect, any court of judicature of any kind." The implicit consequence of this holding was that the judgments of the French consular courts would not be given preclusive effect because they were unlawfully constituted.[37] The *Glass* case resolved a number of important legal issues but did not stop the French privateering campaign. Nine months after *Glass*, the British consul in Charleston lamented that "notwithstanding the laws of the United States are so grounded against any breach of neutrality, the French here evade them, and arm as many privateers as ever." *Glass* established that restitution was a proper judicial remedy but did not provide detailed guidance on when

---

36. For claim preclusion, *see* Glass v. The Sloop Betsy, MARYLAND JOURNAL AND BALTIMORE ADVERTISER, Oct. 1, 1793 (D. Md. 1793). *Accord,* Miller v. Miller, 2 U.S. (2 Dall.) 1, 4 (Fed. Ct. App. 1781). *See also* Rose v. Himely, 8 U.S. (4 Cranch.) 241 (1808); 5 0p. Att'y Gen. 689 (1799). For the Supreme Court's decree the next year, *see* United States v. Peters, 3 U.S. (3 Dall.) 121 (1795).

37. 3 U.S. (3 Dall.) at 15–16. *Accord,* The Flad Oyen, 16 Eng. Rep. 124 (Adm. 1799). *See generally* HYNEMAN 118–27.

restitution should be granted. The Court did not clarify the rules for restitution until a series of decisions in 1796.[38]

Nor did the Court's firm pronouncement against the consular courts' legality stop the sale of prizes. In theory, *Glass* might be read as opening the federal courts for the condemnation of prizes taken by the French, but this permissible implication would have made no sense to eighteenth-century lawyers. In 1795, Secretary of State and former Attorney General Randolph wrote the British Minister that "the very idea of such a court sitting in a neutral nation, upon the property of a belligerent party, would be irreconcilable with the condition of neutrality." Randolph also noted that the Treaty of Alliance with France barred United States courts from deciding the fundamental condemnation issue of "prize or no prize." Notwithstanding this unavailability of admiralty courts on American soil for the condemnation of French prizes, French privateers continued to sell prizes in America until 1796.[39]

With the exception of prizes that had been condemned in the French West Indies, these sales were conducted without the imprimatur of a legal condemnation. As a result, the privateers' title was suspect, and the sales prices were almost certainly discounted. This influx of inexpensive goods was a boon to the economy. "Our merchants," explained a southern newspaper editor, "finding rum, sugar, coffee and molasses, (*which they bought cheap at prize sales*) better articles of remittance than rice and indigo, derived great profits from shipping them to Europe." This lucrative trade eventually was terminated by a provision in the Jay Treaty that became effective in 1796.[40]

THE JAY TREATY I: EXTRAJUDICIAL SERVICE

While the Court was deliberating over *Glass* in February 1794, a serious war scare was brewing with Great Britain. The continued British occupation of the northwestern posts and a general belief that the British were using these posts to encourage and support Indian attacks upon frontier settlements were festering ulcers on Anglo-American relations. In addition, Britain continued to pursue policies that were openly hostile to American maritime commerce. Throughout most of 1793, Jefferson

---

38. Benjamin Moodie to Mr. Miller (Nov. 28, 1794), reprinted in COUNTER CASE 589–90. For the 1796 decision, *see* this chapter at 112–14.
39. Edmund Randolph to George Hammond (Jan. 227, 1795), *reprinted in* COUNTER CASE 599–600. *See generally* HYNEMAN 121–26.
40. RICHMOND VIRGINIA GAZETTE (June 22, 1796); *see* this chapter at 115–17.

and Madison tried to prepare the way for implementing economic sanctions against Britain that would align the United States more closely with France. These efforts were initially handicapped by the outbreak of the European war and Citizen Genêt's clumsy escapades, but by early 1794 two major assaults upon American maritime commerce had created a crisis in which war with Great Britain seemed likely.[41]

The initial assault came in the Mediterranean. Until 1793 Portugal had been more or less continuously at war with the Barbary powers, and the Portuguese navy had kept the Barbary corsairs at bay. But in the fall of 1793 Great Britain lent its good offices and outright financial support to a negotiated truce that would free up Portuguese naval units to fight the French. Freed from the Portuguese blockade, the corsairs immediately poured into the Mediterranean and Atlantic. About twenty American vessels were seized and their American crews made captive. Many Americans believed that the British had procured the truce between Portugal and the Barbary Powers specifically to encourage the ensuing onslaught on American commerce, and the supporters of France saw the episode as a chance to enact economic sanctions against Britain. A calculating Thomas Jefferson wrote, "The letting loose the Algerines on us, which has been contrived by England, has produced peculiar irritation. I think Congress will indemnify themselves by high duties on all articles of British importation. If this should produce war, tho' not wished for, it seems not to be feared."[42]

The Algerian depredations were serious enough, but neither Jefferson nor any other American knew about a secret British plan to mount a major assault on American maritime commerce in the Caribbean. In 1793 the British decided upon a campaign to conquer the French West Indies. As part of this plan, a secret Order in Council was issued in the late fall of 1793 authorizing the seizure of neutral ships trading with these French islands. American merchantmen had no forewarning of this secret Order, and while Jefferson was writing about the Algerian depredations, the British pounced. More than two hundred and fifty American vessels were captured by British cruisers, and half of the seized vessels were quickly condemned by obliging British admiralty courts.[43]

These Caribbean seizures, following closely Britain's apparently devious manipulation of the Algerian corsairs, strained American patience. In early March a small group of influential senators including Oliver Ellsworth, who

---

41. *See generally* COMBS.

42. *See generally* RITCHESON 294–96, 298. Thomas Jefferson to Martha Randolph (Dec. 22, 1793), *reprinted in* 8 JEFFERSON PAPERS (Ford) 124–25.

43. *See* RITCHESON 299–305.

favored closer relations with Great Britain, met privately and agreed "that war might and probably would be the consequence of these aggressions of England." Ellsworth then went to President Washington as the group's representative and urged the President to prepare for war and at the same time to send an envoy to England "to require satisfaction for the loss of our Property and to adjust those points which menaced a war between the two countries." The President agreed and subsequently nominated Chief Justice Jay as a special envoy to Great Britain.[44]

In the Senate, Jay's nomination was strenuously opposed by those who believed that he was pro-British and would negotiate an agreement that would draw the United States closer to Britain and away from France. In addition, the opponents of the Jay nomination believed that the nomination was contrary to the spirit of the Constitution. During the Senate debates, Aaron Burr asked the Senate to resolve that "to permit judges of the Supreme Court to hold at the same time any other office or employment emanating from and holden at the pleasure of the Executive is contrary to the spirit of the Constitution, and, as tending to expose them to the influence of the Executive, is mischievous and impolitic." But Burr's resolution was defeated 17 to 10, and the Senate consented to Jay's nomination by a vote of 18 to 8.[45]

From the scant private records of the Senate's secret deliberations, it seems that two reasons were advanced in support of Burr's resolution. Virginia's John Taylor worried that the "appointment would destroy the independence of the Judiciary by teaching them to look for lucrative employment from and dependent on the pleasure of the Executive." The senators from North Carolina strongly believed that the nomination was "unconstitutional, and consequently improper." They thought that, "As Treaties are to be the supreme Law of the land, the judge in this business on their [the North Carolina senators'] opinion should a new Treaty be made will become a legislator, and on his return will assume the judicial Chair, and be the Expositor and Judge of his own legislation."[46]

These objections to Jay's nomination may have been pretextual arguments by senators who opposed the mission itself, or they could be

---

44. Rufus King, Notes (Mar. 10–Apr. 21, 1794), *reprinted in* 1 KING CORRESPONDENCE 517–23. *See generally* COMBS.

45. 1 JOURNAL OF THE EXECUTIVE PROCEEDINGS OF THE SENATE OF THE UNITED STATES OF AMERICA 151–52 (1828); Rufus King, Notes of Senate Debate (Apr. 17–20, 1794), *reprinted in* 1 KING CORRESPONDENCE 521–23.

46. Rufus King, Notes of Senate Debate (Apr. 17, 1794), *reprinted in* 1 KING CORRESPONDENCE 521–22; Alexander Martin to Richard Spaight (June 9, 1794) (Nc-Ar). *See also* DONALD STEWART, THE OPPOSITION PRESS OF THE FEDERALIST PERIOD 188–90 (1969).

viewed as statements of general principle. Unfortunately, the Senate's rejection of Burr's resolution cannot be read as a general evaluation of the constitutional objections, because during the Senate's deliberations, a proponent of the nomination evidently suggested that "a resignation of [Jay's] Judicial character might . . . follow his acceptance of the Executive's trust."[47]

From this meager record it is difficult to believe that many people thought there should be an absolute bar to dual office holding by Supreme Court Justices. Certainly Burr did not take this extreme position in his resolution. Obviously President Washington and Chief Justice Jay saw no absolute bar, and Jay sailed for England in the spring of 1794.

THE JAY TREATY II: THE RUTLEDGE FIASCO

When the Chief Justice returned a year later from his mission to Great Britain, he resigned his position to assume the office of governor of New York, to which he had recently been elected. President Washington immediately offered the position to John Rutledge, to whom this appointment must have been very satisfying. He had personally petitioned the President for the appointment when he had learned of Jay's pending resignation. Moreover, his friends believed that he rather than Jay should have been named the country's first Chief Justice. The appointment should have been the cap to Rutledge's distinguished career, but instead the matter ended in deep personal depression and Rutledge's attempted suicide.[48]

A month after Rutledge petitioned for his appointment and two weeks after Washington offered the appointment in a letter, Rutledge committed a fatal political gaffe. Much of the country and most southerners emphatically disliked the new treaty that Chief Justice Jay had negotiated with Great Britain. When the news reached South Carolina in July that the Senate had approved the Treaty, mobs rioted in Charleston for two days. In a lengthy letter William Read described the events to his brother, Jacob, who was in the Senate and had voted to approve the Treaty. John Jay was burned in effigy. The mob threatened to burn Senator Read's

---

47. James Madison to Thomas Jefferson (Apr. 28, 1794), *reprinted in* 15 MADISON PAPERS 315–16. For a more detailed discussion, *see* WHEELER 212–16.

48. George Washington to John Rutledge (July 1, 1795), *reprinted in* 1 DHSC 96–97; John Rutledge to George Washington (June 12, 1795), *reprinted in* 1 DHSC 94–95. For the belief that Rutledge should have been selected as the first Chief Justice, *see id. Accord*, Ralph Izard to Edward Rutledge (Sept. 26, 1789), *excerpted in* 1 DHSC at 668–69.

house and "chopt the door & beat at it with sticks." Rumors were spread that Senator Read "recd £900 value in Plate from the Merchants of London for [his] services." People who spoke in favor of the treaty were physically attacked. "All was uproar & confusion," related Read's brother; "they Pumpt one Berry almost to death & chased others . . . they attack'd ["Beau Jackson's"] House & pursued him thro the Town with vengeance."[49] On the third day of the disturbances, a public meeting was held in which John Rutledge vehemently attacked the Treaty and Jay. Unfortunately for Rutledge, a detailed account of his speech was published in at least thirteen newspapers in nine different states. Going through the Treaty section by section, he ferociously attacked it as "a perversion of terms," a "puerile production," a "prostituti[on of] the dearest rights of freemen," containing "tricks, easy to be discovered in every article and clause," "a deception," "a trick adding insult to injury," and "ridiculous and inadmissible." He concluded his speech with the remarkable wish that "he had rather, [George Washington] should die, dearly as he loves him, than he should sign that treaty."[50]

Those who opposed the Treaty approved Rutledge's attack, but most Federalists around the nation were stunned. South Carolina Federalists wrote of Rutledge's "mad frolics" and indicated that he was "deranged in his mind." In Philadelphia, Secretary of Treasury Wolcott and Secretary of War (soon to be Secretary of State) Pickering thought the speech "to be a proof of the imputation of insanity." A number of Washington's advisers urged him to withdraw his promise of appointment, but the President had promised the position to Rutledge, and Rutledge had resigned a high state office in reliance upon the President's offer. Secretary Wolcott explained that "the President was pledged in such a degree, that the Commission could not be denied." So when Rutledge arrived in the capitol less than a month after his speech, he was duly commissioned the second Chief Justice of the United States.[51]

Ordinarily federal judges and other important federal officers are not commissioned until after the Senate consents to their appointment. But

---

49. William Read to Jacob Read (July 21, 1795) (ScU). Pumping was "a piece of discipline administered to a pickpocket caught in the fact, when there was no pond at hand." LEXICON BALATRONICUM: A DICTIONARY OF BUCKISH SLANG, UNIVERSITY WIT, AND PICKPOCKET ELOQUENCE, Pump (Capt. Grose ed., 1811).
50. SOUTH CAROLINA STATE GAZETTE, July 17, 1795, *reprinted in* 1 DHSC 765–70. For a listing of the various newspapers that reprinted the speech, *see id.* 767–68 n.
51. William Read to Jacob Read (July 27, 1795) (ScU); Edmund Randolph to George Washington (July 29, 1795), (relating views of the Secretaries of the Treasury and War), *excerpted in* 1 DHSC 773; Oliver Wolcott, Jr., to Oliver Wolcott, Sr. (Aug. 17, 1795), *excerpted in* 1 DHSC 782.

the Senate was not in session when Rutledge arrived, and the Constitution permits the President "to fill up all vacancies that may happen during the recess of the Senate, by granting commissions, which shall expire at the end of their next session." Rutledge was fully authorized to commence his service on the Court immediately, and he did. This recess appointment, however, was temporary, and President Washington's assurances to Rutledge were not binding upon the Senate. As Secretary Wolcott assured his father, "the Senate will have to determine, when a permanent appointment is made, whether Mr. R. shall be the man." When the President nominated Rutledge for permanent appointment in December 1795, the nomination was dead on arrival. The Senate rejected Rutledge by a vote of 14 to 10.[52]

The Rutledge negative firmly established the principle that the Senate would not always rubber-stamp the President's decisions in filling Supreme Court vacancies. The Senate's decision also established the principle that the Senate may go beyond a judicial nominee's competence and cast a negative based primarily upon the nominee's politics.

Although charges of insanity and bankruptcy were leveled against Rutledge, the available evidence indicates that these allegations were essentially pretextual and that the true basis for the negative was Rutledge's strident and public opposition to the Jay Treaty. Many Federalists were outraged by Rutledge's speech and claimed that he must be insane, but there is no credible evidence that the senators actually believed that he was mentally incompetent when they voted to reject him. At the time of the recess appointment, Oliver Ellsworth, who was the de facto majority leader of the Federalist senators, was strongly opposed to the appointment. Nevertheless, he explained that "it certainly was difficult after [Rutledge] had come not to commission him. If the evil is without remedy, we must as in other cases, make the best of it."[53] But if Rutledge really was insane, his commission surely would have been withheld as a matter of course.

James Iredell, who would have to work with Rutledge on the Court, was actually enthusiastic about Rutledge's appointment. Shortly after Rutledge had joined the Court, Iredell wrote in a private letter to his wife that, "Tho' I very much lament his intemperate expressions in regard to the Treaty, yet altogether no man likely for the appointment would have been personally more agreeable to me." Iredell was a friend of Rutledge, but—like Ellsworth—he was a solid Federalist. If Iredell placed any stock

---

52. U.S. Const. art II, § 2. Oliver Wolcott, Jr., to Oliver Wolcott, Sr. (Aug. 17, 1795), *excerpted in* 1 DHSC 782. For the Senate's vote, *see* 1 DHSC 98–99.

53. Oliver Ellsworth to Oliver Wolcott, Jr. (Aug. 20, 1795), *excerpted in* 1 DHSC 784.

in the loose charges of insanity, his enthusiasm is difficult to understand. More significantly, the fact remains that Washington did in fact commission Rutledge. If Rutledge actually was insane, how could Washington have done such a thing? As a contemporary newspaper editor vividly charged, those who claimed that the new Chief Justice "was actually insane . . . must be guilty of a vile calumny, or the President is more crazy than the Judge."[54]

Notwithstanding the evident judgment of Federalists like Ellsworth, Iredell, and Washington, High Federalists like Alexander Hamilton and Oliver Wolcott continued to state in private that Rutledge was "sottish . . . or deranged" and that he was "a driveller & fool." Perhaps they actually believed that Rutledge had become mentally incompetent, but their charges also may have been simple ad hominem attacks designed more to register their outrage at Rutledge's opposition to the Treaty them to comment on his sanity. Some five years later, Rutledge's successor, Chief Justice Ellsworth, negotiated a treaty that displeased the High Federalists, and they were again outraged. Theodore Sedgwick charged that "the mind as well as body of Mr. Ellsworth are rendered feeble by disease." Other "good federalists sa[id] Ellsworth had the gout in his head, and in fact [was] crazy." Perhaps the High Federalists viewed the mere disagreement with their policies as a symptom of mental illness.[55]

The most detailed account of the actual Senate deliberations comes from Senator Read of South Carolina. Because Rutledge was a leader of the state's small ruling clique, tremendous pressure was placed upon Read to secure the Senate's consent. Before the Senate debate, Read urged his friends to spread the word that "my efforts in Mr. R's favour have not been wanting." After he failed to secure Rutledge's nomination, he wrote a detailed letter describing his efforts. Writing almost in a panic, Read insisted that "had [Rutledge] been my Father I could not have done more for him." Read was quite blunt in explaining the Senate's action by saying that "the ill effect of rewarding a man with the first Honours & offices who had advised a system & headed a tumultuous assembly which

---

54. James Iredell to Hannah Iredell (Aug. 13, 1795), *excerpted in* 1 DHSC 780. BOSTON INDEPENDENT CHRONICLE, Aug. 17, 1795, *reprinted in* 1 DHSC 783.

55. Alexander Hamilton to Rufus King (Dec. 14, 1795), *excerpted in* 1 DHSC 811–12; Oliver Wolcott, Jr., to Alexander Hamilton (July 30, 1795), *excerpted in* 1 DHSC 774. Theodore Sedgwick to Alexander Hamilton (Dec. 17, 1800), *excerpted in* 1 DHSC 902. The views of other "good Federalists" are related in Abraham Baldwin to Joel Barlow (Dec. 19, 1800) (CtY); Richard D. Spaight to John Blount (Dec. 22, 1800), *reprinted in* 3 THE JOHN GRAY BLOUNT PAPERS 464–65 (W. Masterson ed., 1965). For the Ellsworth mission, *see* this chapter at 124.

if repeated could not fail to unhinge all order & destroy our Government was the true & real objection & in this the friends of order were immovable." The South Carolina Senator related that "very full reports of [Rutledge's] pecuniary embarrassments were also circulated but these formed a very inferior objection." Although the charges of insanity would have been a natural scapegoat for Read's failure to secure Rutledge's confirmation, Read did not even hint that this consideration entered into the Senate's decision.[56]

The actual vote in the Senate is consistent with Senator Read's eyewitness account. Fourteen senators voted against the Rutledge nomination, but ten—primarily from the South—voted to confirm the nomination. If Rutledge actually was deemed mentally incompetent, why did the senators vote to elevate him to the nation's highest judicial office? The most plausible explanation is that the vote split along the line between senatorial support for and opposition to the Jay Treaty. One newspaper sarcastically noted the "remarkable" coincidence "that the minority of members on the Treaty were the minority on this nomination."[57]

On December 16, the day after the Senate's decision, John Adams, who as Vice-President presided over the debates, wrote his wife that the vote was a reaction to Rutledge's speech that had "excite[d] opposition to the legal Acts of Constitutional Authority." In another letter to his wife, written on December 17, Adams reiterated his analysis and noted that the "Disarrangement of [Rutledge's] affairs the Reports of his Eccentrictics &c had not so much impression upon me." But revisionist history soon set in. Sometime between December 17 and December 21, Senator Walton joined the Senate from Georgia and quickly began spreading tales that Rutledge's "Disarrangement of Intellect certainly exists and has been more decisive lately than formerly." Vice-President Adams immediately saw the political value of this news. In a third letter to his wife, dated December 21, he wrote, "These Things being so we shall hear of no very sharp Rebukes Upon the Senate, for the Vote they have passed and the President will have avoided giving any offence to particular Friends."[58]

This post hoc entanglement of the insanity issue with the Senate's negative also appears in the correspondence of Virginia's Senator Tazewell. In his first letter after the vote, he merely suggested to James Mon-

---

56. Jacob Read to Ralph Izard (Dec. 8, 1795), *reprinted in* 1 DHSC 810–11; Jacob Read to Ralph Izard (Dec. 19, 1795), *excerpted in* 1 DHSC 814–15.

57. PHILADELPHIA AURORA, Jan. 2, 1796, *reprinted in* 1 DHSC at 823.

58. John Adams to Abigail Adams (Dec. 16, 1795), *excerpted in* 1 DHSC 812; John Adams to Abigail Adams (Dec. 17, 1795), *excerpted in* 1 DHSC 813–14. John Adams to Abigail Adams (Dec. 21, 1795), *excerpted in* 1 DHSC 816–17.

roe that the rejection was a reaction to Rutledge's speech against the Treaty. In subsequent letters, however, he was ambivalent in explaining the Senate's vote: "Some say it was because he is insane. Others say it was because he made a speech agnst the Treaty."[59]

The final act in this sad episode occurred on December 28, thirteen days after Rutledge's rejection. On that early Sunday morning, he "left his House by stealth" and tried to drown himself. When bystanders rescued him, he was upset and protested that "he had long been a Judge & he knew no Law that forbid a man to take away his own life." Whether Rutledge knew of the Senate's action when he attempted to end his life is not known. The next day he was "reasonable & calm" and wrote Washington a dignified letter resigning his temporary recess appointment as Chief Justice. He did not mention his attempted suicide in his letter to the President but wrote instead that he was "convinced by Experience, that it requires a Constitution less broken than mine, to discharge with Punctuality & Satisfaction, the Duties of so important an office."[60]

OLIVER ELLSWORTH AND SAMUEL CHASE

In filling the vacancy caused by Rutledge's resignation, President Washington's initial thoughts were to offer the Chief Justiceship to Patrick Henry, but Henry evidently declined. Then Washington nominated Justice Cushing, who was immediate confirmed by the Senate. Cushing, however, declined the promotion because of poor health, and he never took the oath of office. Finally, in early March 1796, the President nominated Oliver Ellsworth, who had been the de facto leader of the Federalists in the Senate since the first session of the first Congress. Ellsworth was born in 1745 into a prosperous (though not wealthy) Connecticut farming family, and his parents intended him for the ministry. He attended Yale College and was graduated from the College of New Jersey (now Princeton) in 1766. After postgraduate theological studies in Connecticut, he decided against the ministry and became a lawyer instead.[61]

---

59. Henry Tazewell to James Monroe (Dec. 26, 1795), *excerpted in* 1 DHSC 819; Henry Tazewell to [John Ambler?] (Jan. 24, 1796), *excerpted in* 1 DHSC 831–32; Henry Tazewell to Richard Cooke (Jan. 30, 1796), *excerpted in* 1 DHSC 833–34.
60. William Read to Jacob Read (Dec. 29, 1795), *excerpted in* 1 DHSC 820–21; John Rutledge to George Washington (Dec. 28, 1795), *reprinted in* 1 DHSC 100.
61. For Washington's consideration of Henry, *see* George Washington to Henry Lee (Jan. 11, 1796), *reprinted in* 1 DHSC 829–30. For Cushing, *see* 1 DHSC 101–4. For a biography of Chief Justice Ellsworth, *see* BROWN. For brief sketches, *see* Michael Kraus, *Oliver Ellsworth, in* FRIEDMAN & ISRAEL 223–35; *Oliver Ellsworth, in* 1 DHSC 115–19. *See also* Casto, *Calvinism.*

Ellsworth was admitted to the bar in 1771 and married the daughter of a prominent Connecticut family the next year. He quickly developed a lucrative law practice and entered politics. From 1773 to 1789, he was a state legislator and then a judge on the superior court, which was the state's highest judicial court. He was also an active and influential delegate to the Continental Congress from 1778 to 1783 and to the Constitutional Convention in Philadelphia. Ellsworth was a vigorous participant in the Convention's deliberations and was a member of the five-person Committee of Detail that wrote the first draft of the Constitution. During the subsequent ratification process, he was an effective advocate for ratification in his *Letters of a Landholder.* At the Connecticut ratification convention, he was the Constitution's most forceful advocate. After ratification he resigned his position in the state judiciary and served in the Unites States Senate from 1789 until he became Chief Justice.

Ellsworth was a gifted politician and was remarkably self-disciplined. One of his colleagues wrote that he "has a head of iron—just iron—that works with the precision of a mill, without its quickness and giddy manner. I profoundly admire the neatness and accuracy of his mind."[62] As his work on the Judiciary Act demonstrates, Ellsworth thoroughly understood the art and utility of political compromise.

Ellsworth was not the only new addition to the Court. In the fall of 1795 Justice John Blair resigned, and in January 1796 Samuel Chase was nominated for and confirmed to the vacancy.[63] Chase was born in 1741 into the family of an Episcopal clergyman and was educated in the classics by his father. After reading law, he was admitted to practice in 1761. He soon gravitated to provincial politics and was first elected to the Maryland General Assembly in 1764. Chase was an active and vociferous opponent of the Crown government during the Stamp Act crisis, and in 1774 he became a member of the Maryland Committee of Correspondence. Later the same year he was elected to the first Continental Congress. He continued in the Congress until 1778. By all accounts he was a hardworking and capable delegate. In 1783 he represented Maryland in a mission to England and in 1788 was named a judge in a Baltimore criminal trial court. Three years later he became chief judge of the General Court of Maryland. Chase firmly

---

62. William Vans Murray to John Quincy Adams (Nov. 7, 1800), *reprinted in Letters of William Vans Murray to John Quincy Adams, 1797–1803* (W.C. Ford ed.), *in* AMERICAN HISTORICAL ASSOCIATION, REPORT FOR 1912, at 358.

63. For biographies of Justice Chase, *see* JAMES HAW ET AL., STORMY PATRIOT: THE LIFE OF SAMUEL CHASE (1980); JANE ELSMERE, JUSTICE SAMUEL CHASE (1980). For brief sketches, *see* Irving Dilliard, *Samuel Chase, in* FRIEDMAN & ISRAEL 185–98; *Samuel Chase, in* 1 DHSC 105–10.

opposed the ratification of the Constitution, but by the mid-1790s he had become an equally firm supporter of the Federalist government under the Constitution. President Washington nominated him for a position on the Supreme Court only after being assured that Chase's "political or other errors . . . exist no longer."[64]

From this account it seems that Chase should have been an exemplary appointment of the Court. He was an industrious patriot with a distinguished record of service. In addition, he was clearly a brilliant attorney with a knack for innovative thinking. Unfortunately, however, he was plagued by one controversy after another throughout his career. He was an incredibly rude man who consistently engendered anger in and vitriolic attacks from his enemies and who regularly responded in kind. As early as the Stamp Act controversy, he was being attacked in public as "a foul mouth'd and inflaming son of Discord and Faction," to which he responded by labeling his accusers "despicable Pimps."[65]

The truth was that Chase actually was "a foul mouth'd and inflaming" man. He was a brilliant and abrasive person who seemed to disdain social norms and the rights of others. His pervasive contempt extended to financial affairs. In the Continental Congress he was caught apparently using confidential information to corner the market on flour in anticipation of provisioning the French fleet. Chase was equally irresponsible in his personal finances and in 1789 was forced to petition the state legislature to declare him bankrupt. On learning of his prospective appointment to the Court, Chase wrote that "the President shall never have reason to regret the nomination."[66] But notwithstanding Chase's obvious brilliance, his was one of the most regrettable nominations in the Court's history.

THE JAY TREATY III: ADVISORY OPINIONS

Almost as soon as Ellsworth took his oath as Chief Justice, he—like Chief Justices Jay and Rutledge before him—became entangled in a political facet of Jay's Treaty. The Senate had consented to the Treaty, but it could not be implemented without an appropriation of funds, and this technicality gave its opponents one last chance to defeat it. The Republican leaders in the House maintained that they had the right to judge the wisdom of the Treaty and to refuse to appropriate the necessary funds if

---

64. James McHenry to George Washington (June 14, 1795), *excerpted in* 1 DHSC 757–59.

65. *See Samuel Chase, in* 1 DHSC at 105.

66. James McHenry to George Washington (Jan. 24, 1796) (quoting Chase), *excerpted in* 1 DHSC 110–11.

they deemed it unacceptable. To assist the House in its consideration, Congressman Edward Livingston of New York called for the President to provide copies of all papers relevant to the Treaty's negotiation.[67]

Five days after Ellsworth became Chief Justice, he wrote an extensive advisory opinion on these developments. Although the opinion is in the form of a nine-page letter to Senator Jonathan Trumbull of Connecticut, it wound up in George Washington's files docketed under the subject "treaty making power." Whether Ellsworth wrote the letter in response to an indirect request from the President is not known, but the Chief Justice clearly intended his letter to be a formal legal opinion. His basic analysis was that, under the Constitution, the treaty-making power is vested solely in the President and the Senate. Once a treaty was approved by the Senate and ratified by the President, it became "a law of the land" binding upon the House. The fact that the Treaty coincidentally required an appropriation to carry it into effect was "an accidental circumstance [that did] not give the house any more right to examine the expediency of the Treaty, or control its operation, than they would have without this circumstance." The House was therefore bound to appropriate the funds "as it is to appropriate for the President's salary, or that of the Judges." The President subsequently refused to provide the requested papers, and the Federalists in Congress mustered barely enough votes to appropriate the funds necessary to implement the Treaty.[68]

THE BRITISH DEBT CASES

In 1796 British debt litigation finally reached the Supreme Court in the form of an appeal in *Ware v. Hylton*.[69] The British debt problem had been a major domestic and foreign relations issue for over ten years, and widespread southern opposition to the collection of British debts had played a major role in persuading the Congress to place a five-hundred-dollar amount in controversy limitation on the circuit courts' jurisdiction. This limitation by and large relegated British creditors to the state courts, but it did not bar all claims from federal adjudication. As soon as the circuit courts were opened for business, creditors with large individ-

---

67. See COMBS 174–77.
68. Oliver Ellsworth to Jonathan Trumbull (Mar. 13, 1796), *in* George Washington Papers (Microfilm ed., Series 4, Reel 108); George Washington, Message to the House of Representatives (Mar. 30, 1796), *reprinted in* RICHARDSON 186–88.
69. 3 U.S. (3 Dall.) 199 (1796). *See* Editorial Note, *in* 3 MARSHALL PAPERS 4–7; GOEBEL 748–56.

ual claims filed suit. Throughout the early 1790s these British debt cases percolated through the federal trial courts at a leisurely rate.

Ware v. Hylton involved a promise made in 1774 by Hylton to pay William Jones, a British merchant, the sum of approximately three thousand pounds. Three years later, as part of the war effort, Virginia passed a sequestration statute allowing Virginians who owed debts to British subjects to pay all or a portion of the debt to the state government and to receive a certificate discharging the debt in the amount paid. Pursuant to this statute, Hylton made a partial payment in depreciated American dollars to the state government and subsequently refused to pay a substantial part of his debt to Jones. Because Virginia's courts were effectively closed to British creditors, Jones delayed filing suit until 1790, when a federal trial court became available. As was the case in most of the debt litigation, considerable time elapsed before the case came to trial. The claim was finally tried in 1794, and the defendant prevailed. Jones then took the case to the Supreme Court, but he died before the Court considered it. John Ware, the administrator of Jones's estate, was then substituted as the party in interest, and the Court heard the case in February 1796.

Although the case involved a number of side issues, the appeal to the Supreme Court centered upon the effect of the Virginia sequestration statute. At first glance, Hylton would seem to have been entitled to relief as a matter of fundamental fairness. Having paid the debt once to the government of Virginia, he should not have been compelled to pay a second time to the plaintiff. Payments under the sequestration statute, however, were typically accomplished with grossly inflated paper currency rather than the pounds sterling originally contracted for by the parties to the debt. As Justice Paterson graphically noted, the paper "money being cried down and dead, is no better than waste paper."[70] This practice significantly attenuated the problem of requiring debtors to pay twice.

Justice Iredell had been one of the judges in the lower circuit court and therefore did not participate in the Supreme Court's decision. Nevertheless, he felt strongly about the case and, with the consent of his fellow judges, read the reasons that he had previously given in support of the judgment below. In his view, the payments under the statute should offset a debtor's liability. His argument was that the states were at war with Great Britain and that Virginia had authority to confiscate enemy property as part of the war effect. Therefore the enactment of the statute, coupled with Hylton's pay-

---

70. 3 U.S. (3 Dall.) at 250.

ments to the state, extinguished the debt. Iredell argued that, at best, this extinguishment created a claim under the law of nations on the part of Great Britain against the American government for the wrongful treatment of British citizens. Iredell agreed that the Supremacy Clause of the new federal constitution provided that past and future treaties of the United States could override otherwise valid state laws like the Virginia statute. But he thought the payment to the state created something very close to a preexisting private property right and that, absent clear and specific language, a treaty should not be construed as extinguishing such a right. Because he believed the Treaty's language was insufficiently specific, he saw no conflict with the state statute.[71]

Like Iredell, the other Justices believed that the Constitution's Supremacy Clause meant what it said. All direct conflicts between a treaty of the United States and state law are resolved by overriding the otherwise applicable state law. Unlike Iredell, the other Justices were convinced that there was a direct conflict with state law. Justice Chase wrote an elaborate opinion concluding that Article IV's intention was to override sequestration legislation like the Virginia statute.[72]

Chief Justice Ellsworth did not deliver an opinion in *Ware*, but three months later he addressed the issue in *Hamilton v. Eaton* while presiding over the circuit court in North Carolina. In a characteristic Ellsworth analysis that emphasized the economic aspects of modern warfare, the Chief Justice commenced by reaffirming that confiscation statutes are legitimate acts of war because the private "transfer of the treasure from [one warring] country to [another] would diminish the ability of the former, and increase that of the latter, to prosecute the war." But the Treaty of Paris, coupled with the Constitution's Supremacy Clause, established a new rule of decision. He brushed aside the defendant's argument that this new rule was in effect a taking of the defendant's private property. "It is," the Chief Justice wrote, "justifiable and frequent, in the adjustments of national differences, to concede for the safety of the state, the rights of individuals."[73]

In *Ware* the Court gave its uncompromising support to the enforcement of the national government's treaty obligations and established the important precedent that the Constitution's Supremacy Clause would be enforced even in highly charged political controversies like the British debt problem. The immediate practical impact of the Court's decision is

---

71. *Id.* at 256–81.
72. *Id.* at 220–45.
73. Hamilton v. Eaton, 11 F. Case. 336 (C.C.D. N.C. 1796) (No. 5980).

less clear. Many claims were settled, and cases that met the federal courts' amount in controversy requirement were tried according to the principles established in *Ware*.[74]

Nevertheless, British creditors continued to encounter problems. In the circuit courts, recalcitrant juries sometimes refused to follow the federal judges' instructions, and as late as 1805 British creditors were still complaining that many state "courts do not in practice respect the decisions of the circuit court and the Supreme Court of the United States." Eventually the United States' treaty obligation regarding the British creditors had to be settled by the Convention of 1802, in which the United States agreed to pay Great Britain a lump sum to remedy noncompliance with Article IV of the Treaty of Paris.[75]

THE POWER TO TAX

On the same day that Ellsworth was sworn into office as Chief Justice, the Court decided *Hylton v. United States,* an important case on the issue of Congress's authority to levy taxes. The case involved a carriage tax enacted by Congress in 1794, at the height of the war scare that launched Jay's mission to Great Britain. At the same time that Jay was dispatched, Congress voted to enhance the nation's self-defense by fortifying harbors, strengthening the army, and creating a navy. To finance a portion of these new expenses, Congress levied a tax upon carriages for the conveyance of persons. The new act established annual tax rates ranging from two dollars for small carriages to ten dollars for chariots, which were the largest carriages.[76]

The tax was vehemently but unsuccessfully opposed by the southern members of Congress, especially the Virginians. Because the use of carriages was more widespread in the South, the effect of the tax was to impose a geographically disproportionate burden. Not only was the tax disproportionate, but the Southerners charged that it was unconstitutional. Although these objections were overridden by majority votes in the House and the Senate, the mere passage of the Act did not silence the claims of unconsti-

---

74. *See* HENDERSON 81–82, 115.

75. *See* James Iredell to Oliver Ellsworth (Apr. 10, 1797) (commenting on federal jurors), *reprinted in* 3 DHSC 160–61; *Report on the Application for Extending the Jurisdiction of the Circuit Courts in Favor of Aliens* (Jan. 31, 1805) (state courts' continued noncompliance), *reprinted in* 1 ASP, Misc. 419–21; Convention Regarding Articles 6 and 7 of the Jay Treaty and Article 4 of the Definitive Treaty of Peace (1802), *reprinted in* 2 TREATIES (Miller) 488–91, *discussed in* BRADFORD PERKINS, THE FIRST RE-APPROACHMENT 138–43 (1955).

76. 3 U.S. (3 Dall.) 171 (1796). *See generally* 4 HAMILTON'S LAW PRACTICE 297–355.

tutionality. A number of prominent Southerners refused to pay the tax, and elaborate arguments against its constitutionality were published. The Washington Administration resolved to file a collection case against one of the protesters to test the tax's constitutionality.[77]

Unfortunately, the government could not file a suit to collect unpaid taxes in the Supreme Court itself because the Constitution limited the Court's original or trial jurisdiction to a narrow range of cases. Therefore the test case would have to be considered by the Supreme Court under its appellate jurisdiction, and the case would have to be filed originally with a state or federal trial court. Litigation in a state court system would have been fraught with uncertainty and delay, so the test case was filed against Daniel Hylton in the federal circuit court for Virginia.

At first glance Mr. Hylton seems to have been a bizarre character. He waived a trial by jury and stipulated that he had not paid taxes on "125 chariots for the conveyance of persons, and . . . that the chariots were kept exclusively for [his] own private use." In reality, however, everyone knew that the case against Hylton was feigned, that he actually owned only one chariot, and that the taxes and penalties due were only sixteen dollars. The problem was that the Supreme Court's appellate authority over the circuit courts was limited by statute to cases in which the amount in controversy exceeded two thousand dollars. Thus a suit for the actual amount due would not have been appealable to the Supreme Court. To avoid this technical problem, an informal committee consisting of Alexander Hamilton, the Attorney General, and the Commissioner of Revenue came up with the idea of claiming for the purposes of litigation that Hylton had 125 chariots, which brought the amount in controversy to two thousand dollars. Mr. Hylton also wanted a Supreme Court determination of the issue, so he agreed, with suitable protection against actually having to pay the two thousand dollars, to stipulate to his ownership of a gigantic fleet of phantom chariots.[78]

In the circuit court the case was decided by Justice Wilson and Cyrus Griffin, the federal district judge for Virginia. After extensive arguments that were subsequently published throughout the nation in pamphlet form, the court divided on the statute's constitutionality: Justice Wilson found the statute to be constitutional, and Judge Griffin did not. At this point, Hylton's attorneys apparently concluded that an evenly divided

77. *See id.*
78. 3 U.S. (3 Dall.) at 171. *See* 4 HAMILTON'S LAW PRACTICE 311–14.

court was the best they could expect, so they withdrew from the case.[79] This withdrawal was embarrassing, but it did not prevent an appeal to the Supreme Court. The government hired two capable and respected attorneys to represent Hylton in the Supreme Court, and the case of the carriage tax was finally heard there.

The *Hylton* case came to the Supreme Court with one of the strangest and most problematic procedural backgrounds in the Court's history. The case was an obvious sham involving sixteen dollars, not two thousand dollars. Moreover, this transparent legal fiction was defective on its own terms. The parties had stipulated an amount in controversy of exactly two thousand dollars, but the Judiciary Act specified that the Supreme Court could consider an appeal from a circuit court only "where the matter in dispute *exceeds* the sum or value of two thousand dollars."[80] The Court could have rejected the appeal on these grounds or the independent ground that the government's financing of both sides prevented the appeal from being a real case or controversy. Instead the Court winked at all these problems and gave the government the functional equivalent of an advisory opinion.

The fundamental issue of substantive constitutional law confronting the Court was whether the carriage tax was a direct tax. Under the Constitution, "No Capitation, or other direct, Tax shall be laid, unless in Proportion to the Census"—that is, in proportion to each state's population. If the carriage tax was a direct tax, it was obviously unconstitutional because it was being levied in proportion to the number of carriages in each state instead of the number of people. The counterargument was that the appropriate rule for allocating this tax burden was found in another part of the Constitution that authorized Congress to "lay and collect Taxes, Duties, Imports and Excise . . . but [further provided that] all Duties, Imports and Excises shall be uniform throughout the United States." Under this provision, the tax was constitutional because each particular type of carriage was subject to the same rate throughout the nation.[81]

After hearing detailed oral arguments on the issue, Justices Chase, Paterson, and Iredell delivered their opinions that the tax was constitutional. Justice Wilson decided not to give his opinion because he had been a judge in the circuit court. He did note, however, that "my sentiments, in favor of the constitutionality of the tax in question, have not

---

79. *See* William Bradford to Alexander Hamilton (Aug. 4, 1795), *reprinted in* 19 HAMILTON PAPERS 86–87.
80. Judiciary Act of 1789, § 22, 1 Stat. 73, 84 (emphasis added).
81. *Compare* U.S. CONST. art I, § 9 *with id.* § 8.

been changed." Neither Chief Justice Ellsworth, who had just assumed his office, nor Justice Cushing, who had been ill, had heard all the oral arguments, so they did not give opinions.[82]

Aside from the issue of judicial review and the way the Justices went about construing the Constitution, which will be discussed in a later chapter, the most interesting aspect of the Justices' opinions is their clear understanding that the government's practical ability to raise revenue was at issue. All three Justices noted and emphasized that, as a practical matter, Congress simply could not apportion taxes upon specific articles like carriages on the basis of state populations. Therefore they concluded that the Constitution's apportionment rule for direct taxes was not applicable. Justice Iredell succinctly stated the operative assumption: "As all direct taxes must be *apportioned,* it is evident that the Constitution contemplated none as direct but such *as could be apportioned.*"[83] This analysis was "evident" to those who assumed that the Constitution gave the federal government a comparatively broad taxing power, but it was not so evident to those who placed great emphasis upon states' rights. Opponents argued that the apportionment rule for direct taxes applied regardless of the practical difficulties the rule might cause. They viewed the apportionment rule as a significant practical limitation on the federal government's taxing authority.

Justice Iredell did not explain the basis for his pivotal assumption, but Justices Chase and Paterson provided a powerful justification. Paterson emphasized that "Congress could not, under the old confederation, raise money by taxes, be the public exigencies ever so pressing and great," and that the Constitution was drafted to remedy this serious defect. Chase agreed that the "great object of the Constitution was, to give Congress a power to lay taxes, adequate to the exigencies of government." The carriage tax had been enacted in response to the pressing exigency of the 1794 war scare, and the Justices emphatically endorsed its constitutionality.[84]

Chase and Iredell more or less conceded that their decision drastically curtailed the Constitution's direct tax provision.[85] They could not think of a direct tax other than a head tax or a land tax. But this concern was evidently insignificant in comparison to the government's overriding need for a flexible and pragmatic authority to raise revenues.

---

82. *See* 3 U.S. (3 Dall.) at 183–84 (Wilson); *id.* at 172 n. (Ellsworth); *id.* at 184 (Cushing).

83. 3 U.S. (3 Dall.) at 181 (emphasis original).

84. *Id.* at 178 (Paterson, J.); *id.* at 173 (Chase, J.).

85. *Id.* at 175 (Chase, J.); *id.* at 183 (Iredell, J.).

The immediate impact of the carriage tax decision upon the federal fisc was almost insignificant. The Court recognized a broad and flexible authority to impose national excise taxes, but throughout the 1790s, the federal government's actual reliance upon excise taxes was slight. When a significant amount of money had to be raised in 1798 to finance the Quasi-War with France, Congress chose to enact a direct tax apportioned among the states rather than an unapportioned excise tax.[86]

Hylton, however, involved more than the government's power to tax. There is a similarity in the Whiskey Rebellion, Fries's Rebellion, and the opposition to the carriage tax. In the first two movements, unsophisticated commoners protested federal taxes with armed force, and the federal judges saw the protests as treasonous challenges to the government's ability to govern. In the case of the carriage tax, a more affluent group opposed Congressional policy with legal arguments rather than armed force. This opposition could not be condemned as treason, but in the Federalists' eyes it was nevertheless a mischievous affront to federal authority. When U.S. Attorney General William Bradford learned of plans to publish a sophisticated constitutional challenge to the carriage tax, he wrote Alexander Hamilton that the issue was "the greatest one that ever came before that Court; & it is of the last importance not only that the act should be supported, but supported by the unanimous opinion of the Judges and on grounds that will bear the public inspection." The Justices were undoubtedly aware of these considerations and lent their unanimous and public support.[87]

ADMIRALTY JURISDICTION II: *LA VENGEANCE*

The extent of federal admiralty jurisdiction came before the Court once more in the summer of 1796. During the preceding summer, a French privateer, *La Vengeance,* had taken a Spanish vessel as a prize, and the two ships had then sailed into New York harbor. The owner sought restitution on the ground that *La Vengeance* had been fitted out in an American port in violation of American neutrality. In addition, the U.S. Attorney filed a suit seeking forfeiture of the privateer. In this suit against *La Vengeance,* the government contended that the French privateer was subject to forfeiture for having exported arms and munitions in

---

86. *See* DAVIS DEWEY, FINANCIAL HISTORY OF THE UNITED STATES 105–10 (12th ed., 1934); PAUL STUDENSKI & HERMANN KROOS, FINANCIAL HISTORY OF THE UNITED STATES 50–51 (2d ed., 1963).
87. William Bradford to Alexander Hamilton (July 2, 1795), *reprinted in* 18 HAMILTON PAPERS 393–97. For the Whiskey Rebellion and Fries's Rebellion, *see* chapter 4 at 163–65 & 169–71.

violation of a federal embargo act. Although the claim for restitution by the Spanish owner and the government's suit to forfeit the privateer were entirely separate suits, the two cases became entangled in practice. In both cases, Peter Duponceau was the lead counsel for the French interests. Richard Harison, the U.S. Attorney, assisted in the suit for restitution as a private attorney for the Spanish owner.[88]

The district court determined that *La Vengeance* had not been fitted out in the United States and therefore dismissed the suit for restitution of the prize. But the court determined that the privateer had illegally exported arms and munitions and therefore ordered the forfeiture of *La Vengeance* to the United States. Both cases were then appealed to the circuit court, where Justice Chase affirmed the dismissal of the restitution suit. In the forfeiture suit, Chase admitted additional evidence and entered judgment reversing the court below and holding that *La Vengeance* had not illegally exported arms.

On the basis of Justice Chase's decision, the French privateers had won both cases, but it was a hollow victory insofar as the suit for forfeiture was concerned. The litigation had been prolonged by the complexity of the case and an outbreak of yellow fever in New York, and all the while *La Vengeance* lay idle under the control of the federal court. To remedy this problem, counsel had agreed to sell the privateer and pay the proceeds into the custody of the court's clerk. But the resulting distress sale apparently netted "less than a tenth part of the cost of her armament." Although the forfeiture case now involved only a small amount of money, the U.S. Attorney sought an appeal to the Supreme Court ostensibly to obtain a clarifying interpretation of the embargo act. In the companion case of the prize, the Spanish owner's counsel had advised that there was "little or no probability of ultimate success," but the owner nevertheless insisted upon an appeal to the Supreme Court. Thus the two cases came to the Supreme Court, where the lower court's decision to deny restitution of the prize was quickly affirmed. But the resolution of the forfeiture case against *La Vengeance* was not so routine. Rather than rely upon the issues considered by the courts below, Attorney General Charles Lee took an entirely new approach to the case. In the district court the case was treated as a suit in admiralty for forfeiture and therefore, consistent with admiralty tradition, was tried without a jury. Attorney General Lee

---

88. For general background on this litigation, *see* four letters from the French Ambassador, the U.S. Attorney, and the clerk of the federal district court of New York in 1 ASP, Foreign Relations 585, 626–29 (1832). *See also* 2 HAMILTON'S LAW PRACTICE 792–808.

argued, to the contrary, that a jury was required and that both the district and circuit court decisions should therefore be reversed.[89]

This new objection was based upon section 9 of the Judiciary Act, which required that "the trial of issues in fact, in the district courts, in all causes except civil causes of admiralty and maritime jurisdiction, shall be by jury." The Attorney General began his analysis with the assumption that "principles regulating Admiralty and Maritime jurisdiction in this country, must be such as were consistent with the common law of *England*, at the period of the revolution." He then argued with the respectable support of Blackstone that admiralty jurisdiction was restricted to causes "arising *wholly* upon the sea." He concluded that the activity of exporting munitions is "done part on land, and part on sea [and therefore] the admiralty cannot claim the jurisdiction."[90]

This argument seems a bit technical, but it made a good deal of sense to eighteenth-century admiralty lawyers. Just five months earlier, the Supreme Court followed settled English precedent in holding that admiralty jurisdiction under the Judiciary Act did not extend to enforcing a contract for the construction of a ship. Moreover, Peter Duponceau, the opposing counsel, was convinced that the Attorney General's analysis of the activity of exportation was correct—so correct that Duponceau planned to "make no opposition." This capitulation was not based solely upon Duponceau's personal judgment. Before the case was argued, he wrote his co-counsel, "The general sense of the Court & Bar is in favor of the Jury trial."[91]

Duponceau could not have been more mistaken. Two days later, when argument in the case commenced, the Court peremptorily announced that the case was within the federal court's admiralty jurisdiction. Nevertheless, the Court allowed the Attorney General to present a detailed argument on the issue. The case was then taken under advisement overnight, and the next morning Chief Justice Ellsworth announced that "the court did not feel any reason to change the opinion, which they had formed upon opening the case." Dallas's report of the case does not in-

89. P. A. Adet to Timothy Pickering (Nov. 15, 1796), *excerpted in* 1 ASP, Foreign Relations 579, 585; Robert Troup to Timothy Pickering (Dec. 5, 1796), *reprinted in id.* 627. United States v. La Vengeance, 3 U.S. (3 Dall.) 297, 299–301 (1796) (Attorney General's argument).

90. 3 U.S. (3 Dall.) at 299–301 (emphasis original).

91. United States v. Judge of the District Court of the United States for the District Court of Virginia, unreported (U.S. 1796), *discussed in* Casto, Admiralty 154–55 n.191. Peter Duponceau to Brockholst Livingston (Aug. 8, 1796) (Edward Livingston Papers, NjP).

dicate that Ellsworth gave an explanation of this decision other than to assert that "exportation is entirely a water transaction."[92]

The Court's seemingly summary treatment of the Attorney General's argument is puzzling in view of Duponceau's report a few days earlier that the "general sense of the Court & Bar is in favor of the Jury trial." Another puzzling aspect of the case is Justice Chase's treatment of the appeal. He had written the decision in the circuit court, and the Supreme Court's rejection of the Attorney General's argument resulted in the affirmance of Chase's decision. Yet strangely enough, Duponceau, who was present when the Court announced its decision, wrote on the same day that the decision on admiralty jurisdiction was by a vote of 5 to 1, with "Justice Chase only dissenting."[93]

Some twelve years later, the Court's decision in *La Vengeance* was the subject of a heated exchange between Justice Chase and former Attorney General Lee in another suit involving the right to a jury trial in a forfeiture case. In response to Chief Justice Marshall's citation of *La Vengeance* against Lee's client, Lee responded, "I argued the case of the *Vengeance*, and I know it was not so fully argued as it might have been; and some of the judges may recollect that it was rather a sudden decision." Justice Chase snidely retorted, "I recollect that the argument was no great thing, but the *Court* took time and *considered the case well.*" Chase then explained, "The reason of the legislature for putting seizures of this kind on the admiralty side of the court was the great danger to the revenue if such cases should be left to the caprice of juries."[94]

With this reminiscence, some educated guesses may be made about the Court's internal decision-making process in *La Vengeance*. When Duponceau wrote before argument that the "general sense of the Court . . . is in favor of the Jury trial," he evidently based this conclusion on informal discussions with individual Justices. The jury trial issue had not been raised below, and therefore the problem may not have occurred to Justice Chase when he entered his judgment in the circuit court. But when the issue was raised by the Attorney General, Chase—like most of the other attorneys who considered the issue—was probably persuaded that the Attorney General was right. Under this analysis, Chase's subsequent vote to overrule his own decision below is not so puzzling.

---

92. 3 U.S. (3 Dall.) at 301.

93. Peter Duponceau to Edward Livingston (Aug. 11, 1796) (Edward Livingston Papers, NjP).

94. United States v. The Schooner Betsy, 8 U.S. (4 Cranch) 443, 446 n. (1808) (emphasis original).

Perhaps other members of the Court were also initially persuaded by the Attorney General's analysis of admiralty jurisdiction, but at least two of the Justices were not. If Chase's subsequent recollection that the Court's decision was based upon a legislative intent to protect revenue collection from "the caprice of juries" is accurate, the rationale of legislative intent undoubtedly came from Chief Justice Ellsworth and Justice Paterson. As senators, they had personally drafted the statutory language in question, and they were especially interested in establishing an adequate and dependable stream of federal revenue.

In drafting the statutory language vesting the federal district courts with an admiralty jurisdiction to enforce revenue laws, Ellsworth had expressly expanded the Court's admiralty jurisdiction well beyond the traditional common-law limits. *La Vengeance* was not a suit to enforce revenue laws, but the statutory language at issue also governed forfeitures under revenue laws. Therefore, a Supreme Court decision following the Attorney General's analysis would almost inevitably have expanded the right to a trial by jury in revenue cases. When the Judiciary Act was being debated in the Senate, Justice Paterson had successfully argued that revenue collection should not be left to state courts because "state officers will feel it their Interest to consult the Temper of the People of the State in which they live rather than of the Union." If Justice Chase's recollection was correct, Paterson and Ellsworth used a similar argument in *La Vengeance* to exclude juries—who represented the local temper of the people—from the federal courts' enforcement of revenue laws. Of course, the rationale was applicable only to revenue laws bearing upon maritime commerce, but in the 1790s such laws accounted for almost 90 percent of federal revenues.[95]

The Court's expansive approach to federal admiralty jurisdiction in *La Vengeance* is similar to the earlier decision in *Glass v. The Sloop Betsy*. In both cases the expansion of federal judicial power was at the expense of settled rules of admiralty jurisdiction. Moreover, both decisions were evidently motivated by national security concerns. In *Glass*, the Court was confronted with an ongoing crisis caused by the depredations of French privateers. In *La Vengeance*, it facilitated revenue collection necessary to finance the federal government, including its military establishment. In each case the Court was willing to issue a fiat overturning settled admiralty law with little or no explanation. In contrast, when national security was not at issue, the Court followed settled admiralty law without a qualm.[96]

---

95. *See* chapter 1 at 49.
96. *See* this chapter at 107.

LA VENGEANCE: MAJORITY OPINIONS
AND CHIEFLY LEADERSHIP

La Vengeance was the first opinion delivered by Chief Justice Ellsworth, and he used the occasion to establish a significant new trend in the structure of the Court's opinions. Before he became Chief Justice, the Court frequently had followed the English common-law practice in which, beginning with the Court's junior member, each Justice would deliver his individual opinion and justification of how the case before the Court should be decided. In *La Vengeance,* however, this tradition of delivering seriatim opinions was not followed. Nor did the Court issue a per curiam decision. Instead, Chief Justice Ellsworth delivered a consolidated majority opinion from which Justice Chase dissented.

In eschewing seriatim opinions, Ellsworth was simply following the practice to which he had become accustomed when he served upon the Connecticut Superior Court from 1784 to 1789. The year that he became a state judge, the Connecticut legislature passed a statute requiring that in cases turning upon an issue of law, "each one [of the Superior Judges must] give his opinion *seriatim* with the Reasons thereof, and the same reduce to Writing." The purpose of this statute was to facilitate appeals from the Superior Court and to lay "a foundation . . . for a more perfect and permanent System of Common Law in this State." Although the statute called for written seriatim opinions, the Superior Court adopted an almost uniform practice of writing majority and dissenting opinions. Perhaps the judges adopted this approach to save the judicial labor involved in having every judge write a formal opinion in every case.[97]

Before Ellsworth became Chief Justice, the Court had not developed a firm tradition regarding the use of either seriatim or majority opinions. In some cases it delivered seriatim opinions, and in others it might deliver a simple majority opinion coupled with a dissenting opinion. In one case the Court delivered seriatim opinions on one aspect of the case and a majority opinion on another aspect. In 1795 an attorney reported that the Court delivered seriatim opinions when "a difference in opinion exists on the Bench," but his statement cannot be taken literally. The Court subsequently used seriatim opinions to announce unanimous decisions

---

97. *See* An Act Establishing the Wages of the Judges of the Superior Court (1784), 5 THE PUBLIC RECORDS OF THE STATE OF CONNECTICUT 324–25 (L. Labaree ed., 1943). *See also* Preface, 1 Kirby iii–iv. The original handwritten "Reasons of Court" are scattered throughout the Superior Court files in the Connecticut Archives, and many are reported in *Kirby's Reports.*

in *Talbot v. Jansen* and *Hylton v. United States* and a majority opinion to announce a split decision in *United States v. Peters*.[98]

After Ellsworth became Chief Justice, a clear pattern emerged in which he would personally deliver short opinions of the Court, infrequently supplemented by dissenting or concurring opinions. From Dallas's Reports it appears that the Court delivered seriatim opinions only once when Ellsworth participated in the decision. When Ellsworth was not participating, the Court might deliver seriatim opinions, or the senior associate Justice might deliver a majority opinion. By 1800 the practice was so well established that Justice Chase was surprised when the Court delivered seriatim opinions in *Bas v. Tingy* while Chief Justice Ellsworth was in Europe. "The Judges agreeing unanimously in their opinion, I presumed," said Chase, "that the sense of the Court would have been delivered by the president."[99]

This custom of using majority rather than seriatim opinions became entrenched during Chief Justice Marshall's tenure and has endured to the present. Majority opinions have played a subtle but significant role in establishing the Supreme Court's hegemony over the Constitution's interpretation. A contrary tradition of seriatim opinions would have splintered many of the Court's opinions into the relatively isolated and more or less different views of the various Justices. In contrast, a single majority opinion makes it easier for the Court to speak with a single authoritative voice.

Although Chief Justice Ellsworth played an important leadership role in fostering the use of majority opinions, neither he nor Chief Justice Jay was a personable leader in the mold of John Marshall or Earl Warren. Unlike Warren and Marshall, Jay was a somewhat cold individual who

---

98. *See, e.g.*, Chisholm v. Georgia, 2 U.S. (2 Dall.) 419 (1793) (seriatim opinions); Georgia v. Brailsford, 2 U.S. (2 Dall.) 415 (1793) (majority opinion); Bingham v. Cabbot, 3 U.S. (3 Dall.) 19 (1795) (combination). Jeremiah Smith to William Plumer (Feb. 24, 1795) (William Plumer Papers, Nh); Talbot v. Jansen, 3 U.S. (3 Dall.) 133 (1795), *discussed* this chapter at 113; Hylton v. United States, 3 U.S. (3 Dall.) 171 (1796), *discussed* this chapter at 101–05; United States v. Peters, 3 U.S. (3 Dall.) 121 (1795).

99. 4 U.S. (4 Dall.) 37, 43 (1800) (Chase, J.), *discussed in* chapter 8 at 120–24. For opinions of the Court accompanied by concurring or dissenting opinions, *see, e.g.*, Sims Lessee v. Irvine, 3 U.S. (3 Dall.) 425 (1799); Turner v. The Bank of North America, 4 U.S. (4 Dall.) 8 (1799), *discussed in* chapter 8 at 243–46. For the seriatim opinion with Ellsworth participating, *see* Fenemore v. United States, 3 U.S. (3 Dall.) 357 (1797). For cases in which Ellsworth did not participate, *see* Calder v. Bull, 3 U.S. (3 Dall.) 386 (1798) (seriatim opinions), discussed in chapter 8 at 227–30; Fowler v. Lindsey, 3 U.S. (3 Dall.) 411 (1799) (seriatim opinions); Brown v. Van Braam, 3 U.S. (3 Dall.) 344 (1797) (majority opinion by Wilson, J., concurring opinion by Chase, J.).

was quite formal in his personal relations. Ellsworth also had an austere personality. Unless he was talking with real friends—especially fellow New England Calvinists—his approach to personal relations was a mixture of serious, forceful engagement with public matters and studied reserve on nonpublic matters. Except for Justice Iredell's letters and Chief Justice Ellsworth's letters to Justice Cushing of Massachusetts, there is scant evidence of friendly discussions in any of the early Justices' correspondence with each other. Jay actually tried to discourage informal exchanges of opinions on issues that were percolating through the lower courts. In early 1792 Justice Johnson apparently asked Jay about an issue in the British debt cases pending in Virginia. Jay sternly replied, "As that Case will probably be brought up to the Sup. Court by Writ of Error, I think it would be best that the other Judges should in the mean Time forbear giving any opinion respecting it."[100] In addition to the austere characters of Chief Justices Jay and Ellsworth, the Justices seldom saw each other. Except for a few weeks each year in February and August, they were dispersed throughout the nation at their homes or were riding circuit.

ADMIRALTY JURISDICTION III: RESTITUTION OF PRIZES

United States v. La Vengeance was one of many admiralty cases that were appealed to the Court in 1796. In twelve other cases the Court considered disputes over prizes sailed by French privateers into Charleston, South Carolina. In each suit a representative (usually Benjamin Moodie, the British Vice-Consul) of the owners of the captured vessel asked the federal court to declare the capture unlawful and return the ship to its rightful owner.[101] These cases built on the Supreme Court's 1794 decision in *Glass v. The Sloop Betsy*, which authorized district courts to order the restitution of unlawful captures. In the subsequent cases, the Court dealt with the issue of whether restitution was appropriate under various specific circumstances.

In the summer of 1794, the Congress confused the situation by enacting legislation giving the federal courts jurisdiction over "complaints . . . in cases of captures made within the waters of the United States." Unfortunately, the statute was silent concerning captures on the high seas. Furthermore, although the statute provided criminal sanctions for fitting out and manning privateers in American ports, no specific provision was

---

100. John Jay to Thomas Jefferson (Mar. 12, 1792), *reprinted in* 2 DHSC 244–45.
101. *See* GOEBEL 776 n.47.

made for the judicial restitution of prizes seized by privateers that were operating in violation of the 1794 Act.[102]

The need for further guidance from the Supreme Court is evident in an opinion letter written by Peter Duponceau in early 1795. Duponceau noted that the Court had held only that the federal courts could *consider* granting restitution of prizes. The Court *"did* not decide the point whether restitution *would* be made." Likewise he noted that the Act of Congress did not extend to captures on the high seas and did not expressly call for the judicial restitution of prizes. Returning to the *Glass* case, he believed that *Glass* "at most extends [jurisdiction over captures on the high seas] to the case of American & other neutral claimants." In particular, Duponceau believed that Article XVII of the French Treaty of Alliance controlled the capture of British vessels. He noted that the Treaty was "the Supreme Law of the land" and that it expressly "prohibits [the restitution] of captures made *from Enemies* by French armed vessels *duly commissioned."*[103]

A few months later Duponceau presented these arguments to the Supreme Court in *Talbot v. Jansen,* a case involving a French privateer's capture of a Dutch vessel. The Netherlands was at war with France, and the French privateer had been built and fitted out in the United States and was owned and captained by Americans. When the Dutch prize was sailed into Charleston, the owner of the captured vessel sought and was granted restitution. Notwithstanding the Treaty of Alliance, the Supreme Court affirmed the district court's order of restitution. The Court brushed aside the negative implication of the Act of Congress and the positive rights established by the French treaty. Having been armed in the United States, the privateer was acting in violation of American neutrality; therefore, under the general law of nations, restitution was appropriate.[104]

The Court, however, did not automatically order the restitution of prizes taken by French privateers. The existing Treaty with France clearly allowed the French to sail their prizes into American ports, and if the prizes were not tainted by a breach of American neutrality, the Court would not order restitution. In *Moodie v. The Ship Alfred,* the Court dealt with a prize taken by a French vessel that was built in the United States as a privateer. The ship, however, had been constructed in anticipation of a war between the United States and Great Britain. After war was averted, the ship was sold to a

---

102. Act of June 5, 1794, ch. 50, §6, 1 Stat. 381–84.

103. Peter Duponceau to Martin Jorris (Apr. 8, 1795) (emphasis original) (PHi, Duponceau Letterbook B 1792–1797, 58–64); Treaty of Amity and Commerce (Feb. 6, 1778), *reprinted in* 2 TREATIES (Miller) 3–29.

104. *See* Talbot v. Jansen, 3 U.S. (3 Dall.) 133 (1795), *discussed in* GOEBEL 770–76.

French citizen who sailed it to a French island where the vessel was "completely armed and equipped." Under these circumstances the Court saw no breach of neutrality and refused to order restitution of a British ship captured by the American-built French privateer.[105]

The most interesting of the later restitution cases is *Moodie v. The Ship Phoebe Anne,* in which a British vessel was captured by a French privateer and sailed into Charleston. Apparently the French privateer had been armed and commissioned outside the United States but had sailed into Charleston for extensive repairs that had not significantly augmented the privateer's force. The attorney for the British owner argued "the impolicy and inconveniency of suffering privateers to equip in our ports." Chief Justice Ellsworth firmly rejected this analysis. "Suggestions of policy and conveniency cannot be considered," he said, "in the judicial determination of a question of right: the Treaty with *France,* whatever that is, must have its effect." He then refused restitution on the basis of a Treaty provision giving French ships the right to effect repairs in American ports.[106]

By and large the Court's decisions in these restitution cases—especially the 1796 decisions—were disappointing to the British. Dallas's Reports provide scant information about the litigation and the Court's decisions, but Benjamin Moodie, the plaintiff of record in most of the cases, reported that the Court decided the 1796 cases "indiscriminately against me." His understanding was that

> nothing but the ownership [of privateers] being in American citizens will cause a restoration of prizes, and that the law of the 5th June, 1794, passed in Congress, as well as the general laws of nations, so far as respects the arming, equipping, augmenting, or altering the ships of war or privateers of any power in neutral ports, are entirely set aside in the courts of this country.

Even worse, Moodie noted that the Supreme Court decisions released the judicial attachments on the various prizes and cargoes involved in the cases. Therefore "those concerned in privateering will have the proceeds of the different cargoes come into their hands, and no doubt, with the favorable divisions [decisions?] they have received encourage them to adventure anew in the depredatory plans."[107]

---

105. 3 U.S. (3 Dall.) 307 (1796).
106. 3 U.S. (3 Dall.) 319 (1796) (emphasis original); Treaty of Amity and Commerce, art. 19 (Feb. 6, 1778), *reprinted in* 2 TREATIES (Miller) 3–29.
107. Benjamin Moodie to Vice-Admiral Murray (Apr. 6, 1796), *reprinted in* COUNTER CASE 604; Benjamin Moodie to Mr. Miller (Apr. 27, 1796), *excerpted in* COUNTER CASE 606–07.

THE JAY TREATY: SALE OF PRIZES

These feared "depredatory plans," however, did not come to pass. After participating in the restitution cases in early 1796, Chief Justice Ellsworth rode the Southern Circuit where his resolution of an ambiguity in the Jay Treaty effectively halted the sale of prizes captured from the British. Article XXIV of the Treaty specifically forbade the sale in America of prizes taken from the British. The French argued, however, that their Treaty of Alliance gave them a right to sell prizes in the United States and that another article of the Jay Treaty preserved this right by providing that "nothing in this Treaty contained shall however be construed or operate contrary to former and existing Public Treaties with other Sovereigns or States."[108]

Before Ellsworth reached Charleston, a French privateer, *The Leo,* brought a captured British vessel into port where it was quickly condemned by the French Consul in defiance of *Glass* v. *The Betsy.* In response, the British Consul commenced a suit in admiralty for restitution of the prize or at least to enjoin its sale. The British had little confidence in Federal District judge Thomas Bee, because his decisions were generally sympathetic to French privateers. Bee almost immediately dismissed the suit. Restitution, he explained, was not available because *The Leo* was not "fitted, or her force increased within the *United States* contrary to the laws of neutrality[, and] the prize was [not] captured within the jurisdictional limits of the *United States.*" Nor would Judge Bee enforce Article XXIV of the Jay Treaty. In the first place, there was some doubt whether an admiralty court had authority ever to issue an injunction, but Bee did not address this remedial issue. Instead he held that he lacked jurisdiction. The sale, itself, was "on land" and therefore not within admiralty jurisdiction. To be sure the sale was a "consequence" of a capture at sea, but the Treaty of Alliance barred jurisdiction over captures that did not involve violations of American neutrality, and Bee held that this bar precluded a consequential or ancillary jurisdiction over the sale.[109]

As soon as Ellsworth arrived in Charleston, the British Consul renewed his petition to enjoin the sale, and the Chief Justice immediately heard the case "at his chambers." The French believed that Ellsworth—unlike Bee—was "completely devoted to the English," and his handling

---

108. The Jay Treaty, Art. XXIV, XXV, *reprinted in* 2 Treaties (Miller) 245, 262. *See* Hyneman 123–25.

109. Moodie v. The Amity, 17 F. Cas. 650 (D.S.C. 1796) (No. 9741) (emphasis original); Stanley Morrison, *The Remedial Powers of the Admiralty,* 43 Yale L.J. 1 (1933); Benjamin Moodie to Mr. Bond (April 28, 1795)("I have nothing to expect of" Judge Bee), *excerpted in* Counter Case 600–03.

of the petition was consistent with this belief. Ellsworth apparently considered the petition under authority of an obscure statute that he had drafted in the Senate three years earlier. This statute authorized "any Judge of the Supreme Court" to grant injunctions "in cases where they might be granted by the Supreme or a Circuit Court." In other words, his authority was keyed to the Circuit Courts' alienage jurisdiction rather than the District Courts' admiralty jurisdiction, and he therefore was not subject to the technical limitations to admiralty jurisdiction. Ellsworth immediately held that the sale was barred by the Jay Treaty and granted an injunction pending a further hearing in the Circuit Court to be held three days later in Columbia. In subsequent correspondence, the French Minister noted that Ellsworth's decision was confirmed by the circuit court of Carolina."[110]

The Chief Justice's quick and innovative disposition of the petition exemplifies the early Justices' determination to support the Federalist Administrations' foreign policy. A more interesting aspect of this episode, however, is a letter penned by Secretary of State Pickering that evidences a close working relationship between the Secretary and Chief Justice Ellsworth. After completing the Southern Circuit, Ellsworth stopped in Philadelphia (then the nation's capital) where he briefly described his Charleston decision to Pickering. A few days later, after Ellsworth had continued to his home in Connecticut, Pickering learned that another French privateer was attempting to sell prizes in Boston. Pickering immediately wrote Ellsworth seeking his advice on the Boston prizes.[111]

In particular Pickering wanted to know "the mode of proceeding to prevent the sales." He knew that Ellsworth had stayed the sales in Charleston and asked, "may Judge Cushing do the same at Boston, with regard to the prizes lately carried in there? Can the District Judge do the same?" Evidently Pickering assumed that Ellsworth was an appropriate source of advice in coordinating the Administration's use of the federal courts to effect important foreign policy initiatives. As for Ellsworth, his advice a few months earlier during the House's consideration of the Jay Treaty and his private correspondence with Pickering two years later on the constitutionality of the Sedition Act indicate a willingness to serve as an adviser on these matters. Whether he responded to Pickering's letter is unknown. The letter was written on June 30, and Ellsworth may have

---

110. *See* 3 DHSC 89–91; The Judiciary Act of 1793, ch. 22, § 5, 1 Stat. 333, 334–35 (1793); 4 DHSC 408; CHARLESTON CITY GAZETTE & DAILY ADVERTISER (May 10, 1796); P. A. Adet to Timothy Pickering (Oct. 12, 1796), *reprinted in* 1 ASP, Foreign Relations 654–55.
111. Timothy Pickering to Oliver Ellsworth (June 30, 1796) (Pickering Paper, MHi).

received it in Connecticut when he was preparing to return to Philadelphia for the Supreme Court term that began on August 1.[112]

BUSHROD WASHINGTON

After the restitution cases of 1796, no significant national security cases were appealed to the Supreme Court until 1800. During this three-year interlude Justice Wilson died under tragic circumstances. As the decade of the 1790s progressed, Wilson's personal finances became more and more mired in speculations and unwise investments. Finally, in 1797, he was forced to flee his creditors but was eventually hunted down and jailed in New Jersey for nonpayment of debts. After his release, he fled again — this time to North Carolina, where he spent his last weeks with his wife in a small, uncomfortable tavern room. In August 1798 he died a financially, mentally, and physically broken man.[113]

President Adams quickly nominated Bushrod Washington, the nephew of George Washington.[114] Justice Washington was born in 1762 and entered the College of William and Mary thirteen years later. He was graduated in 1778 and commenced his law studies in the early 1780s. Washington was elected to the Virginia House of Delegates in 1787 and was a delegate to the Virginia ratification convention, where he supported the proposed Constitution.

In 1788 Washington moved to Richmond and commenced a highly successful practice of law. Between 1792 and 1796, he represented one side or the other in almost a quarter of all cases heard by the Virginia Court of Appeals. He was a highly respected attorney, and as early as 1796 he and John Marshall were considered the two Virginia Federalists most qualified to serve on the Supreme Court.[115] Justice Washington was nominated by President Adams, but he fit the criteria that President Washington had used in picking Justices. In particular, Justice Washington was a staunch Federalist and was geographically suitable.

When Justice Wilson died, there was some suggestion that the vacancy should be filled with another Pennsylvanian. President Adams conceded "that some regard to states ought to be always remembered. But Pennsylva-

---

112. *Id.*, *see* this chapter at 97–98 and chapter 5 at 149.
113. *See* CHARLES PAGE SMITH, JAMES WILSON: FOUNDING FATHER, 1742–1798, chapter 25 (1956).
114. For brief sketches of Justice Washington, *see* Albert Blaustein & Roy Mersky, *Bushrod Washington, in* 1 FRIEDMAN & ISRAEL 243–57; *Bushrod Washington, in* 1 DHSC at 124–26.
115. Cyrus Griffin to George Washington (May 23, 1796), *excerpted in* 1 DHSC 848–52.

nia has always had a Judge. Virginia has had none, since the Resignation of Mr. Blair. As far as states can have reasonable pretensions therefore, those of Virginia are at least equal to those of Pennsylvania."[116] Accordingly, President Adams narrowed his list to Bushrod Washington and John Marshall. After Marshall declined the position, Adams nominated Washington, who was immediately confirmed by the Senate.

THE QUASI-WAR I: THE ELLSWORTH MISSION

The major foreign affairs issue of the late 1790s was the severe deterioration of relations with France. Around the time of Citizen Genêt's escapades, Justice Paterson was still including the "Republic of France" in his annual Fourth of July toasts, but by 1798 his toast to France was "May the American Eagle Never Crouch to the Gallic Cock." This reference was to the undeclared naval war that had commenced with France and that was fought primarily among the islands of the Caribbean. This Quasi-War was a major bone of contention between the Federalists and Jefferson's Republican coalition. Congress passed a number of statutes authorizing limited maritime hostilities, and there was constant pressure for a full, declared war. But President Adams never sought a formal declaration of war from Congress. In early 1799 Adams became convinced that an acceptable peace could be negotiated and resolved to nominate William Vans Murray, the American minister at The Hague, as a minister plenipotentiary to France for the negotiations.[117]

Because most of Adams's cabinet members were High Federalists who had no enthusiasm for negotiating a peace, Adams submitted his nomination to the Senate without prior cabinet consultation. The Federalists in the Senate were astonished, and a select committee was quickly formed to deal with the nomination. The prospect of peace, however, was so popular that the committee decided to recommend the appointment of two additional envoys to serve as a check upon Murray, whom they did not trust. When they proposed this idea to President Adams in a private meeting, the meeting quickly degenerated to a shouting match between the senators and the President. The senators then decided to reject the Murray nomination.[118]

Although Chief Justice Ellsworth apparently was not an active participant in these preliminary discussions, he was aware of them and was dismayed by the planned rejection of the President's nomination. At this

---

116. John Adams to Timothy Pickering (Sept. 26, 1798), *reprinted in* 1 DHSC 130–31.
117. *See generally* QUASI-WAR; *William Paterson's Toasts for the Fourth of July* (ca. 1792–1796, 1798) (Paterson Collection, NjP).
118. *See* QUASI-WAR 185.

point he took it upon himself to speak with the President and managed to convince Adams to accept the idea of appointing three ministers. The President decided to name Ellsworth and Patrick Henry as the two additional nominees, and Ellsworth was in no position to refuse. Patrick Henry, however, declined the proffered position, and the President subsequently had a number of conversations with Ellsworth in which Adams mentioned Governor William R. Davie of North Carolina as a replacement. When Ellsworth rode the southern circuit that spring, he consulted with Davie and recommended his appointment, and the President formally nominated Davie.[119]

Ellsworth's nomination as minister to France implicated the same concerns about dual office holding that had been voiced against the Jay nomination in 1794, but there was surprisingly little objection. Those who favored peace negotiations probably hesitated to impede the mission, and the Federalists could hardly oppose Ellsworth. A member of the House of Representatives candidly observed,

> In appointing Mr. Ellsworth many Senators will make a sacrifice of their most settled opinions: the bench they regard as a barrier between the people & the government & appointments from the bench they regard as destroying the independence of the Judiciary inasmuch as it makes the Judges dependent upon the Executive for additional honors & favors.

The Senate subsequently approved the Ellsworth nomination by a vote of 23 to 6, and apparently the "6 Negatives [were] on account of his being Chief Justice." After a summer and fall of political maneuvering and machination among the Federalists, Ellsworth and Davie finally sailed for Europe in November 1799.[120]

---

119. See id. 185; Oliver Ellsworth to Timothy Pickering (Mar. 21, 1799) (William R. Davie Papers, Nc-Ar); John Adams to Timothy Pickering (May 8, 1799), reprinted in 8 WORKS OF JOHN ADAMS 641 (C. F. Adams ed. 1856).

120. See WHEELER 220–23; 4 DHSC 245–46. JOURNAL OF THE EXECUTIVE PROCEEDINGS OF THE SENATE OF THE UNITED STATES OF AMERICA 318–19 (1828); John Rutledge, Jr., to unknown addressee (Feb. 27, 1799) (John Rutledge Papers, NcU); James Iredell to Samuel Johnston (Feb. 28, 1799), excerpted in 3 DHSC 324. For the political maneuvering, see QUASI-WAR 187–222.

ALFRED MOORE

Two weeks before Chief Justice Ellsworth sailed for Europe, Justice Iredell died, and President Adams filled the vacancy by nominating Alfred Moore, a relatively unknown North Carolina judge.[121] Adams's reasons for selecting Moore are unknown, but Moore was regarded as a capable attorney, and he clearly met the requirement of geographic suitability. With the presidential election in the offing, Adams was probably especially sensitive to the issue of geographic suitability. A knowledgeable insider reported that one candidate from South Carolina, three from Pennsylvania, and "a number from the Eastward [New England] have been mentioned."[122] An appointment from any of these states would have upset the others, but the appointment from North Carolina to fill Iredell's seat maintained the status quo.

Moore was born in 1755 into the family of one of North Carolina's three colonial judges. He was educated in Boston but did not attend college. Instead he read law with his father and was admitted to the North Carolina bar in 1775. He almost immediately joined the revolutionary army and fought for a year and a half. By 1777 his brother, father, and uncle had died in military service, and Moore resigned his commission. In 1782 he was elected to the state legislature and almost immediately resigned to succeed James Iredell as the state's attorney general. Moore served as attorney general until 1791, when he resigned to enter private practice. He was a Federalist who actively supported the ratification of the Constitution. In 1792 he was again elected to the state legislature and in 1795 missed becoming a United States senator by one vote of his fellow legislators. Three years later he was elected to the North Carolina Superior Court.

THE QUASI-WAR II: *BAS V. TINGY*

While the Chief Justice was in Paris negotiating a conclusion to the undeclared war with France, some of the war's legal ramifications were considered by the Court in *Bas v. Tingy*. In 1799 an American merchantman was taken by a French privateer and recaptured by the *Ganges*, an American naval vessel. When the recaptured merchantman reached port, Cap-

---

121. For brief sketches of Justice Moore, *see* Leon Friedman, *Alfred Moore, in* 1 FRIEDMAN & ISRAEL 269–79; *Alfred Moore, in* 1 DHSC 137–39.
122. John Steele to John Haywood (Nov. 13, 1799), *excerpted in* 1 DHSC 880–81. *See also* PHILADELPHIA AURORA, Dec. 3, 1799 (mentioning candidates from five different states), *excerpted in* 1 DHSC 883–84.

tain Tingy of the *Ganges* filed an action for salvage on behalf of himself and his crew, seeking compensation for his services in restoring the re-captured merchantman. This otherwise ordinary suit was complicated by the fact that two different acts of Congress provided two different rules for assessing the amount of salvage for recaptures. A 1798 statute pro-vided a general rule of one-eighth the value of the recaptured vessel, but a 1799 statute gave recapturors one-half the value of a vessel "re-taken from the enemy." Thus the Court in *Bas* had to determine whether France was an "enemy" of the United States.[123]

Although Captain Tingy's claim turned in part on technical legal rules governing the interpretation of conflicting statutes, the case also raised a sensitive political and foreign policy issue. Thomas Adams, who attended the oral argument, wrote his father, the President, that the "question of war or no war as it respects the relative situations of the United States and the French Republic was brought fully into view."[124] Attorneys for the recaptured merchantman argued that the United States was not tech-nically at war and that France was therefore not an enemy. In support of this analysis, they evidently emphasized that Congress had never for-mally declared war against France. Captain Tingy's attorneys responded that a formal congressional declaration was unnecessary.

In Chief Justice Ellsworth's absence, the Court reverted to the practice of delivering seriatim opinions. This reversion surprised Justice Chase, who remarked, "The Judges agreeing unanimously in their opinion, I presumed that the sense of the Court would have been delivered by the president; and therefore, I have not prepared a formal argument on the occasion."[125] Nevertheless, he was not at a loss for words.

Like Justices Washington and Paterson, Chase drew a distinction be-tween two types of war. He had "never entertained a doubt [that] Con-gress is empowered to declare a general war, or congress may wage a limited war; limited in place, in objects, and in time." Turning to the Franco-American relationship at issue in *Bas,* Chase—along with Wash-ington and Paterson—pronounced that the country was engaged in "a limited, partial, war. Congress has not declared war in general terms; but congress has authorized hostilities on the high seas by certain persons in certain cases." Therefore France was an enemy, and salvage in the

---

123. 4 U.S. (4 Dall.) 37 (1800); Act of June 28, 1798, ch. 62, § 2, 1 Stat. 574; Act of Mar. 2, 1799, ch. 24, § 7, 1 Stat. 709.
124. Thomas Adams to John Adams (Aug. 18, 1800) (Adams Papers, Microfilm ed., Reel 398).
125. 4 U.S. (4 Dall.) at 43.

amount of one-half the value of the recaptured merchantman should be awarded.[126]

Perhaps because Chase was speaking off-the-cuff, he added a note of jocularity to the proceedings.

> I remember said the judge, about the time Congress was passing these laws, authorizing reprisals I met with a man who was what some people call a democrat. Well, says he, what are you about now, you federalists? What is it now? I don't know, said the judge, what do you think about it? Why, I think it is war, only you are afraid to say so.[127]

Justice Moore also expressed his views in the only opinion he is known to have delivered as a member of the Court or on circuit. Moore seems to have had a reputation as a capable lawyer, but he was no Iredell. Even his grand jury charges were cursory. In a brief, simplistic opinion he solved the legal issue of war or no war by simply begging the question. "[H]ow," he asked, "can the characters of the parties engaged in hostility or war, be otherwise described than by the denomination of *enemies?*" An unsympathetic biographer has concluded that Moore's most significant contribution as a Justice was his nonparticipation (which was due to absence) in two important cases decided during Chief Justice Marshall's tenure. Moore's opinion in *Bas* lends support to this ironic gibe.[128]

The *Bas* decision did not please opponents of the Adams Administration. The *Philadelphia Aurora,* one of the leading opposition newspapers, stridently proclaimed that the decision was "most important and momentous to the country, and in our opinion every Judge who asserted we were in a state of war, contrary to the rights of Congress to declare it, ought to be impeached."[129] Perhaps this allusion to congressional authority over war powers was simply a matter of overwrought polemics, but the accusation raised an issue of constitutional law that has endured to the present. In *Bas,* the Court clearly endorsed the national government's constitutional authority to wage undeclared war. Moreover, indi-

---

126. *Id.* at 43–45.

127. Thomas Adams to John Adams (Aug. 18, 1800) (Adams Papers, Microfilm ed., Reel 398).

128. *See* Raleigh Register, June 10, 1800, *reprinted in* 3 DHSC 440 (Moore, Grand Jury Charges); 4 U.S. (4 Dall.) at 39 (Moore, J.) (emphasis original). Leon Friedman, *Alfred Moore, in* Friedman & Israel 269, 276–78 (referring to United States v. Schooner Peggy and Marbury v. Madison).

129. Philadelphia Aurora, Aug. 22, 23, 25, 1800, *quoted in* Warren 157.

vidual Justices indicated that the conduct of an undeclared war was ultimately subject to congressional rather than executive control.

The war with France had been fraught with domestic and international problems. Obviously the nation did not want to become a full-fledged belligerent in the European wars following the French Revolution. In addition, so many American citizens remained sympathetic to France that an outright declaration of absolute war would not have been politically feasible. Justice Chase candidly explained:

> Considering our national prepossessions in favour of the *French* republic, congress had an arduous task to perform, even in preparing for necessary defense, and just retaliation. As the temper of the people rose, however, in resentment of accumulated wrongs, the language and the measures of the government became more and more energetic and indignant.[130]

This idea of a graduated response to threats from abroad was inconsistent with a formal declaration of absolute war. In contrast, by reading the far more flexible concept of limited war into the Constitution, the Court in *Bas* approved a more pragmatic approach to resolving disputes with foreign counties.

The opposition press charged the Court with surpassing congressional authority, but the Justices' opinions indicate that they assumed that Congress had comprehensive and even final authority over undeclared wars. Justice Chase carefully noted that America's conduct of this limited war was confined to the narrow range of specific maritime hostilities authorized by positive acts of Congress. From this, he drew the express negative inference that

> [t]here is no authority given to commit hostilities on land; to capture unarmed *French* vessels, nor even to capture *French* armed vessels lying in a *French* port; and the authority is not given, indiscriminately, to every citizen of *America*, against every citizen of *France;* but only to citizens appointed by commissions, or exposed to immediate outrage and violence.

Justice Paterson was of much the same mind when he stated, "As far as congress tolerated and authorized the war on our part, so far may we proceed in hostile operations."[131]

---

130. 4 U.S. (4 Dall.) at 45 (emphasis original).

131. *Id.* at 43 (emphasis original) (Chase, J.); *id.* at 45 (Paterson, J.).

The *Bas* decision is difficult to read as anything other than the endorsement of a flexible and pragmatic approach to congressional participation in the projection of American military power overseas in outright hostilities against foreign countries. The Justices clearly believed that Congress was authorized by the Constitution to commence a war without a formal declaration of war. The Justices also obviously thought that Congress had constitutional authority to micromanage the way in which a limited war was to be fought. Four years later, the Court expressly held what Justices Paterson and Chase implied in *Bas*. In *Little v. Barreme*, Chief Justice Marshall announced a unanimous opinion that the Constitution did not permit the executive branch to seize ships sailing from French ports when the applicable act of Congress authorized the seizures of ships sailing to French ports.[132]

THE QUASI-WAR III: CHIEF JUSTICE ELLSWORTH RESIGNS

While the Court in *Bas* was considering how the Quasi-War began, Chief Justice Ellsworth was in Paris negotiating a conclusion to it. Finally, after seven months of work, the parties reached a compromise and signed the Treaty of Mortefontaine (also called the Convention of 1800), which was subsequently approved by the Senate and ratified by the President. Ellsworth was free to come home, but the negotiations had been trying, and he had developed a painful kidney ailment. In addition, the decade of struggle between the Federalists and Jefferson's opposing coalition had gradually eroded his faith in the national government. Before he left for France, he was telling people in private "that there is in a government like ours a natural antipathy to system of every kind." His growing pessimism, coupled with his illness, led him to resign his office. Having completed his mission, Ellsworth wrote President Adams, "Constantly afflicted with the gravel, and the gout in my kidneys . . . I must therefore pray you, Sir, to accept this my resignation of the office of Chief Justice of the United States."[133]

To replace Ellsworth, President Adams initially planned to appoint John Jay and, if Jay refused, to "follow the Line of Judges most probably." Jay did refuse, but Adams could not bring himself to follow his contingency plan. Justice Cushing was first in line, but Cushing had al-

---

132. 6 U.S. (2 Cranch) 170 (1804).

133. *See* QUASI-WAR chapters 7–8; ELKINS & McKITRICK 662–90; Oliver Ellsworth to John Adams (Oct. 16, 1800), *reprinted in* 1 DHSC 123; Alexander Hamilton to James McHenry (Feb. 18, 1800) (quoting Ellsworth), *in* 24 HAMILTON PAPERS 237–38; Casto, *Calvinism.*

ready refused the Chief Justiceship once and was in any event deemed too old. Justice Paterson was next in seniority, but Adams turned instead to Secretary of State John Marshall. Years later Marshall related that the President was adamantly opposed to appointing Paterson. Marshall suggested that the President's opposition was due to Paterson's ties with Adams's political enemy Alexander Hamilton. In addition, legislation then pending in Congress would have prospectively reduced the number of Supreme Court Justices from six to five. By quickly filling the vacancy before the legislation could be enacted, Adams avoided the bill's stricture and delayed the time when Jefferson, soon to be president, would be able to appoint new Justices to the Bench.[134]

---

134. *See* James Perry, *Supreme Court Appointments, 1789–1801: Criteria, Presidential Style, and the Press of Events*, 6 J. EARLY REPUBLIC 371 (1986). John Adams to Thomas B. Adams (Dec. 23, 1800), *excerpted in* 1 DHSC 906–7; John Marshall to Joseph Story (1827), *excerpted in* 1 DHSC 928–29. For John Jay, *see* 1 DHSC 144–47. For Justice Cushing, *see* 1 DHSC at 101–4; Thomas B. Adams to Abigail Adams (Dec. 20, 1800), *excerpted in* 1 DHSC 904–5.

5

NATIONAL SECURITY AND FEDERAL CRIMINAL LAW

In the Senate debates on the proposed Judiciary Act, Senator Oliver Ellsworth had warned that federal courts were necessary to assure the unswerving enforcement of criminal law against individuals who would mount "Attacks on the General Government that will go to the Very Vitals of it."[1] His prediction that criminal law would play a significant role in bolstering national security proved to be accurate. The Justices of the Supreme Court consciously administered federal criminal law to support Federalist policies. Indeed, in retrospect, their handling of criminal prosecutions with political implications appears distinctly partisan.

Although the Justices on circuit played a major and even notorious role in the enforcement of criminal law, the Supreme Court itself made no contributions whatsoever to criminal jurisprudence. Under the Judiciary Act, the Court had no appellate jurisdiction over criminal cases that had been tried in the federal courts. The Act authorized criminal appeals from the state courts, but no state criminal prosecution was ever appealed to the Court during Jay's and Ellsworth's Chief Justiceships.[2] All of the justices' contributions to the enforcement of criminal law were made in their capacity as trial judges in the circuit courts.

POLITICAL GRAND JURY CHARGES

In the late eighteenth century, the convening of a criminal court was an occasion for pomp and ceremony that might include a procession of court officers and notable citizens. At least in New England, a clergyman attended and gave a prayer. After the presiding judges were seated, the grand juries for investigating criminal activities and the petit juries for

---

1. *See* chapter 2 at 48.
2. GOEBEL 804.

126

trying specific cases were impaneled. The senior judge would then instruct the grand jurors on their duties and the applicable criminal law. Eighteenth-century judges in America and England also used their grand jury charges to address a broad range of political and legal issues. These political charges were delivered with the knowledge that they would be published in leading newspapers.[3]

Although the practice has long since faded into disuse, eighteenth-century judges might devote over half of a grand jury charge to essentially political matters. In 1778, when Judge Iredell was a state judge, he delivered a charge in which 80 percent of his message was devoted to justifying the ongoing rebellion against Great Britain. He did this "in compliance with a custom which has long obtained, and is probably founded on very good reasons." After delivering this extensive essay in justification of the revolution, Iredell provided the jury with little specific information on the criminal law relevant to their inquest. He merely told them that "in all cases where you are in doubt you will apply to the court for information."[4]

Twelve years later, when the federal Justices began riding circuit, nothing could be more natural than that they should take up the custom of delivering political charges. Chief Justice Jay's first grand jury charge followed the same broad outline that Iredell had used in his earlier address to a state grand jury. The first half and more of Jay's charge was devoted to justifying and explaining the nature of the recently created federal government. He reminded the jurors that the United States was an almost unique experiment in which the people were attempting to "govern themselves." He emphasized that "wise and virtuous Men" had agreed that the doctrine of separation of powers was the "best guard against Abuse and Frustration." In addition, Jay charged the grand jury that the firm but fair enforcement of federal criminal laws was "essential to the welfare of Society."[5]

---

3. *See generally* 2 DHSC 4–6. *See also* Richard Law to John Jay (Feb. 14, 1790), *in id.* 11; John Jay to Richard Law (Mar. 10, 1790), *in id.* 13. For an excellent article documenting this widespread use of political grand jury charges and noting the practice's dramatic decline in the early nineteenth century, *see* Ralph Lerner, *The Supreme Court as Republican Schoolmaster,* 1967 Sup. Ct. Rev. 127 (1967). *See also* John Cushing, *The Judiciary and Public Opinion in Revolutionary Massachusetts, in* Law & Authority in Colonial America 168–86 (C. Billias ed., 1965). For the English practice, *see* J.M. Beattie, Crime and the Courts in England, 1660–1800 at 331–33 (1986).

4. James Iredell, Charge to the Edenton Grand Jury (May 1, 1778), *reprinted in* 1 Iredell Correspondence 382–89.

5. John Jay, Charge to the New York Grand Jury (Apr. 12, 1790), *reprinted in* 2 DHSC 25–30.

After providing the grand jury with these political insights, Jay turned to a brief summary of the applicable federal criminal laws. Even here, however, his charge was more political than substantive. For example, he explained to the jury that the "penal Statutes of the United States are few, and principally respect the Revenue." But he did not tell the jury what specific conduct was outlawed. Instead, he emphasized the political importance of vigorously enforcing the national revenue laws. With this charge, Jay and his fellow Justices embarked upon a decade in which they consciously used federal criminal law to bolster the new national government's stability.

In addition to the general political theme of bolstering the government's stability, the Justices frequently used their grand jury charges to address specific politically sensitive legal issues that had attracted their attention. Their ability to write formal judicial opinions on important questions was limited by the somewhat random sequence in which appropriate cases actually came before them. Although Justices gave private informal advisory opinions, they renounced a general authority to give formal advisory opinions in their correspondence with Secretary of State Jefferson during the Neutrality Crisis of 1793. Nevertheless, individual Justices obviously felt the need to deliver public advisory opinions, and they used grand jury charges for this purpose. Although the Justices maintained personal and plenary control over the content of their charges, they were receptive to private executive branch advice on the political need to address particular issues.[6]

For the entire decade, the Justices used grand jury charges to instruct the nation on proper political virtue. An 1800 charge by Justice Paterson is representative. According to a newspaper account,

> *Politicks* were set in their true light, by holding up the Jacobins, as the disorganizers of our happy Country, and the only instruments of introducing discontent and dissatisfaction among the well-meaning part of the Community: — *Religion & Morality* were pleasingly inculcated and enforced, as being necessary to good government, good order and good laws, for "when the righteous are in authority, the people rejoice."[7]

This inclination to use the bench as a platform for political oratory func-

---

6. For the Neutrality Crisis, *see* chapter 4 at 72–87. For executive branch advice, *see, e.g.,* Alexander Hamilton to John Jay (Sept. 3, 1792), *reprinted in* 17 Hamilton Papers 316–17; John Jay to Alexander Hamilton (Sept. 8, 1792), *reprinted in* 17 Hamilton Papers 334–35.

7. Portsmouth United States Oracle, May 24, 1800 (emphasis original), *reprinted in* 3 DHSC 436.

tioned reasonably well during the 1790s, when there was a loose harmony of Federalist spirit among the three branches of government. It was not to continue.

By the end of the decade, Thomas Jefferson and his political allies had developed an intense dislike for the Justices' lectures, but they lacked the power to stop them. All this changed in 1801 when Jefferson became President and his supporters gained control of the Congress. The staunchly Federalist judiciary was disinclined to expand upon the virtues of this new regime. If anything, the Justices became inclined to criticize government, and in 1803 Justice Chase did precisely this in a particularly intemperate grand jury charge. Jefferson's party responded by impeaching Chase and nearly removing him from office.[8] These proceedings effectively closed the era of political grand jury charges. The Federalist Justices were no longer inclined to support the political branches, and they probably feared the consequences of criticizing a hostile Jeffersonian government. Discretion had become the better part of valor.

COMMON-LAW CRIMES

Another of the Justices' controversial practices was their espousal of a system of common-law crimes triable in federal court. In terms of cases actually tried—even the number of federal criminal cases—common-law crimes were virtually insignificant during the 1790s. But federal common-law prosecutions eventually assumed a particularly high profile in the political arena and were widely covered in the press. By the end of the decade, these famous—or infamous—prosecutions had come to epitomize the Jeffersonian Republicans' firm belief that the Federal government was bent on an undesirable and unconstitutional aggrandizement of power. Thomas Jefferson was complaining that all the other Federalist outrages were "solitary, inconsequential timid things in comparison with the audacious, barefaced and sweeping pretension to a system of law for the U.S. without the adoption of their legislature, and so infinitely beyond their power to adopt."[9]

The Justices did not initially address the issue of nonstatutory crimes because the early cases that came before them did not require a resort to

---

8. *See* HASKINS & JOHNSON 215–34, 238–45. Chase's complete charge is *reprinted in* 14 ANNALS 673–76.

9. Thomas Jefferson to Edmund Randolph (Aug. 18, 1799), *reprinted in* 9 JEFFERSON PAPERS (Ford) 73–77. For excellent discussions of the doctrine of federal common-law crimes, *see* PRESSER chapter 6; Stewart Jay, *Origins of Federal Common Law*, 133 U. PA. L. REV. 1003–115, 1231–333 (1985); Kathryn Preyer, *Jurisdiction to Punish: Federal Authority, Federalism and the Common Law of Crimes in the Early Republic*, 4 L. & HIST. REV. 223–65 (1986).

unwritten law. The Congress's failure to pass a crimes act in its first session could have forced an early grappling with the issue. On April 4, 1790, the day before opening his first circuit court in New York City, Justice Cushing was urging the enactment of a federal crimes bill. He did "not know in what predicament our Courts will be as to carrying into Execution punishment for pyracies & felonies on the high Seas & some other matters." Nevertheless, some ten days later, two men were indicted, tried, and convicted before Cushing, Chief Justice Jay, and District Judge James Duane for conspiracy to destroy a ship and murder the captain. The federal crimes act, however, had yet to be passed, so these convictions were necessarily premised upon a nonstatutory maritime law of crimes. Evidently the issue of the federal courts' authority to enforce nonstatutory criminal laws was not raised, and neither Justice Cushing nor the other members of the court addressed it. The two miscreants were sentenced without comment to the pillory, a public whipping, and six months in jail.[10]

ENFORCING THE LAW OF NATIONS

Three years later, in *Henfield*, capable defense attorneys challenged the federal courts' authority to punish activities that were not outlawed by any federal criminal statute.[11] Henfield had sailed from Charleston on one of the first privateers commissioned by Citizen Genêt, and in early May, he brought a French prize into Philadelphia. He was then arrested and prosecuted for violating American neutrality. This prosecution briefly became a focal point for the ongoing dispute over the country's proper stance toward the warring European powers. In addition, the case squarely raised for the first time the important issue of whether federal courts had authority to enforce nonstatutory criminal laws.

Every federal officer who addressed this issue agreed that Henfield could be prosecuted notwithstanding the absence of a federal statute criminalizing his conduct. Within the executive branch, the issue was referred to Attorney General Randolph, who briefly and without explanation advised that Henfield was "punishable, because treaties are the supreme law of the land; and by treaties with three of the Powers at war

---

10. William Cushing to John Lowell (Apr. 4, 1790), *reprinted in* 2 DHSC 21–22; United States v. Hopkins, unreported (C.C.D. N.Y. Apr. 13–14, 1790), *discussed in* Wythe Holt, *The First Meeting of the Federal Circuit Court in New York: A Federal Common Law of Crimes?, in* SECOND CIRCUIT REDBOOK 1990–1991 SUPPLEMENT 119 (V. Alexander ed., 1990).

11. 11 F. Cas. 1099, Wharton's State Trials 49 (C.C.D. Pa. 1793) (No. 6360).

with France, it is stipulated, that there shall be peace between their subjects and the citizens of the United States." In addition and as a separate
basis for the prosecution, Randolph believed that Henfield was "indictable at the common law, because his conduct comes within the description of disturbing the peace of the United States."[12]

Randolph's opinion was soon confirmed in grand jury charges delivered by Chief Justice Jay and Justice Wilson. They did not mention the
pure common-law concept of "disturbing the peace of the United
States," but they clearly stated that citizens who violated the law of nations were subject to criminal prosecution in federal court. Although
these charges were ostensibly delivered to instruct the grand jury on the
elements of criminal law related to violations of neutrality, the Justices
devoted very little attention to this issue. Instead, they devoted most of
their charges to analyzing general principles of international law and the
various United States treaties relevant to the warring European powers.
After a detailed justification of the country's neutrality, each Justice
noted in a conclusory fashion that the law of nations was part of the common law and that someone like Henfield was therefore subject to a common-law prosecution in federal court. The government used these
charges as foreign policy white papers and sent them to Europe as a formal explanation of the United States' neutrality.[13]

When Henfield's case finally came to trial, his attorneys argued that
the indictment "did not include an offense at common law." They also
urged that "as there was no statute giving jurisdiction, the Court could
take no cognizance of the offense." Justice Iredell, who was one of the
presiding judges at Henfield's trial, later confessed that when he first
heard these arguments, he had "considerable doubts" whether a defendant could be prosecuted in federal court for anything other than a
statutory crime.[14]

But Justice Wilson, who sat with Iredell in *Henfield*, had no doubts. He
had seen this problem before and knew the common-law solution. In
1784 Wilson had served as a special prosecutor when the Chevalier de
Longchamps was prosecuted in state court for his attack on a French dip-

---

12. Edmund Randolph, Opinion (May 30, 1793), *reprinted in* 1 ASP, Foreign
Relations, 152.

13. John Jay, Charge to the Virginia Grand Jury (May 22, 1793), *reprinted in* 2 DHSC
380–91; James Wilson, Charge to the Pennsylvania Grand Jury (July 22, 1793),
reprinted in 2 DHSC 414–23. *See* Wharton's State Trials 49 n; Thomas Jefferson to
Gouverneur Morris (Aug. 16, 1793), *reprinted in* 7 JEFFERSON PAPERS (Ford) 475–507.

14. 11 Fed. Cas. at 1119, Wharton's State Trials at 83; James Iredell, Charge to the
South Carolina Grand Jury (May 12, 1794), *reprinted in* 2 DHSC 454, 467.

lomat. De Longchamps's attack could have been treated as an ordinary common-law assault and battery, but such a mundane approach would not have recognized the gravamen of the offense. He had attacked a foreign diplomat in flagrant violation of customary international law. Because there was no Pennsylvania statute that provided criminal sanctions for violations of the law of nations, Wilson had to resort to the common law. He found the common-law solution to his problem in a 1764 opinion by Lord Mansfield in the case of *Triquet v. Bath*.[15]

For the prosecutors in the *de Longchamps* case, *Triquet* was a common lawyer's dream come true. The case involved a claim by the servant of the Bavarian minister to Great Britain against individuals who had caused him to be arrested in violation of the privilege accorded diplomats and their servants under the law of nations. Lord Mansfield, quoting an earlier judge, declared that "the law of nations, in its full extent was part of the law of England." Therefore the arrest was in violation of English domestic law. The arrest also violated an act of Parliament that codified the diplomatic privileges in the law of nations, but Mansfield explained in a brief and fascinating history of the statute's origin that it was irrelevant to the court's decision. The statute was merely "declaratory" of the existing English common law. Parliament's action "was not occasioned by any doubt 'whether the law of nations ... was ... part of the law of England.'" Rather the statute was enacted as a diplomatic device to placate the Russian Czar's anger over a specific affront to his ambassador.[16]

In *De Longchamps*, Wilson and the attorney general of Pennsylvania cited Lord Mansfield's opinion in support of their argument that De Longchamps was subject to a common-law prosecution. The *De Longchamps* court completely agreed and, following the jury's verdict of guilty, sentenced the defendant to two years in prison and a heavy fine.

When *Henfield* was tried in the same city less than ten years later, Wilson remembered the De Longchamps Affair—or, if he did not, William Rawle, the U.S. Attorney, reminded him in oral argument by citing both *Triquet* and *De Longchamps*.[17] Although these cases involved the treatment of foreign diplomats, a common lawyer could easily read them as evidence of a broader principle that the law of nations was generally incorporated into the common law.

---

15. *See* chapters 1 and 2 at 7–8 & 43 discussing the incident; Republica v. De Longchamps, 1 U.S. (1 Dall.) 111, 113 (Pa. 1784) (noting Wilson's assistance and citing Triquet v. Bath, 97 Eng. Rep. 936, 3 Burr. 1480 [K.B. 1764]).

16. 97 Eng. Rep. at 937–38.

17. 11 F. Cas. at 1117, Wharton's State Trials at 80.

Justice Iredell, who began the *Henfield* trial with "considerable doubts," was convinced by Mansfield's opinion in *Triquet v. Bath*. About half a year later, he penned a grand jury charge, addressing the "very important enquiry, whether a right of prosecution exists [for violations of the law of nations] in cases where the Legislature of the United States has made no special provision." He first restated Mansfield's general exposition of the English common law, including the analysis that Mansfield used to distinguish the "act of Parliament passed on the complaint of the Czar of Muscovy." He then noted that this same common-law doctrine was fully applicable in America before the Revolution. In colonial times, an "offense against the Law of Nations might have been equally injurious to the public welfare and to individuals, if committed by an inhabitant of this country as if committed in England; and therefore there was the same reason for the application of the Common Law principle to it."[18]

The Revolution did not change this common-law principle. "The change in the government could not do away the Common Law in this particular . . . except in cases where its operation was absolutely inconsistent with the change in our situation."[19] In an admirably but almost tediously methodical analysis, Iredell then considered whether the Articles of Confederation or the federal Constitution affected the continuing common-law doctrine evidenced by Mansfield's opinion in *Triquet*. He concluded that neither the Articles nor the Constitution was intended to change principles of the law of nations that were incorporated in the common law.

In particular, Iredell pointed out that the Constitution merely empowered the federal courts to try particular types of cases and authorized the Congress to make laws. Clearly Congress had not directly legislated against the common-law doctrine of *Triquet v. Bath*. There were many crimes defined by Acts of Congress, but no federal statute addressed breaches of neutrality. Iredell finally concluded that "where [acts of Congress] are silent, for the reasons I have stated, the common law which existed before (so far as it is applicable to our present situation) must still operate. . . . [T]he common law therefore as to [violations of the Law of Nations] is still in force.[20]

Although the judges of the Circuit Court that tried Henfield were convinced that he was guilty of a common-law crime, the jury—to the applause of Francophiles throughout the nation—returned a verdict of not

---

18. James Iredell, Charge to the South Carolina Grand Jury (May 12, 1794), *reprinted in* 2 DHSC 454, 467–69.

19. *Id.* 468.

20. *Id.* 469.

guilty. As one newspaper reported, "The toast of the day in all republican circles in Boston is, 'the virtuous and independent jury of Pennsylvanian who acquitted Henfield.' " The reasons for the acquittal are not entirely clear. Perhaps the jurors were pro-French; perhaps they took into account the fact that Henfield joined the French without notice of the President's Neutrality Proclamation; or perhaps they did not believe in the doctrine of common-law crimes espoused by the federal judges. In any event, at its next session, Congress enacted a set of criminal laws to enforce the nation's neutrality.[21]

In retrospect, some two hundred years later, the most puzzling aspect of *Henfield* is the defense attorneys' argument that "independently of [all their other defenses], as there was no statute giving jurisdiction, the Court would take no cognizance of the offense."[22] In the late twentieth century, a "statute giving jurisdiction" is a self-evident reference to a court's subject-matter jurisdiction to try a specific category of cases. If the defense attorneys intended this modern meaning, the failure of U.S. Attorney Rawle, Justice Wilson, and Justice Iredell to address this issue in their elaborate discussions of the case is strange. Instead, all three men limited their discussions to identifying and explaining in detail the existence of substantive rules that outlawed the defendant's breach of neutrality.

Perhaps when Henfield's defense attorneys complained that there "was no statute giving jurisdiction," they were not referring to what we think of today as subject-matter jurisdiction. Perhaps they meant to argue that there was no act of Congress that outlawed breaches of neutrality. If so, when they advanced this contention "independently" of their separate argument that Henfield's activities were not indictable at common law, they meant that Henfield joined the French without notice of any written, positive, and identifiable act of Congress forbidding his conduct. Justice Wilson possibly had this understanding of the objection. Soon after Henfield's attorneys completed their argument, Wilson delivered his charge to the petty jury, noting in it that

> It has been asked by his counsel, in their address to you, against what law has he offended? The answer is, against many and binding laws. As a citizen of the United States, he was bound to . . . keep the peace in regard to all nations with whom we are at peace. This is the law of nations; not an *ex post facto* law, but a law in existence long before Gideon Henfield existed.

---

21. NATIONAL GAZETTE, Aug. 17, 1793, *quoted in* WARREN 114 n.2. *See* PRESSER 73–75 (1991). Act of June 5, 1794, ch. 50, 1 Stat. 381.
22. 11 F. Cas. at 1119, Wharton's State Trials at 83.

Wilson went on to emphasize that the "notoriety [of the country's treaties with Great Britain and other nations] may, indeed, be said to have been greater than that of the general Acts of Congress."[23]

Consitutional Underpinnings

To the late-twentieth-century mind, the most striking aspect of *Henfield* is the paucity of serious challenges to the court's jurisdiction over common-law crimes. After the trial one anti-Federalist newspaper editorialist argued that the jury verdict foreclosed future common-law prosecutions for violations of the law of nations, but no one took this suggestion seriously. Henfield's attorneys—Duponceau, Ingersoll, and Sergeant—evidently challenged the court's jurisdiction, but their challenge may have been based more on zealous advocacy than sober reflection or fundamental disagreement. For the rest of his life, Duponceau believed that common-law prosecutions in federal court for violations of the law of nations were proper.[24]

In addition, men like Edmund Randolph and Thomas Jefferson, who subsequently became virulent critics of the doctrine of federal common-law crimes, had no objection to prosecuting Henfield for violating the law of nations. In 1800 John Marshall was incredulous at the suggestion that the federal courts might not have jurisdiction to punish the non-statutory crime of violating a treaty of the United States. "I believe it is not controverted," he wrote, that this crime is "clearly punishable in the federal courts." Randolph, who had become a firm opponent of the general doctrine of federal common-law crimes, agreed.[25]

---

23. 11 F. Cas. at 1120, Wharton's State Trials at 85.

24. 11 F. Cas. at 1119, Wharton's State Trials at 83. National Gazette, Aug. 3, 1793, *quoted and discussed in* PRESSER 73–74 (1991). For another common-law prosecution for violation of American neutrality that also resulted in a not-guilty verdict, *see* United States v. Rivers, unreported (C.C.D. Ga. 1793), *discussed in* DUNLAP AND CLAYPOOLE'S AMERICAN DAILY ADVERTISER, Dec. 11, 1793. *See* PETER DUPONCEAU, A DISSERTATION ON THE NATURE AND EXTENT OF THE JURISDICTION OF THE COURTS OF THE UNITED STATES 3–4 n* (1824). *See also* Jared Ingersoll, John Coxe, and Peter Duponceau, Opinion on the British Treaty (July 26, 1796) (Duponceau Papers, Letter Board B, pp. 168–171, PHi) (violations of the Jay Treaty subject to common-law prosecution); Peter Duponceau and Joseph Thomas to Edmond Genêt (Dec. 23, 1793) (Genêt Papers, DLC), *discussed in* this chapter at 138–39.

25. For Randolph, *see* Edmund Randolph, Notes on the Common Law (ca. Sept. 1799), *reprinted in* 17 MADISON PAPERS 259–69; Edmund Randolph, *Memorandum* (ca. Dec. 1799), *reprinted in* 17 MADISON PAPERS 283–85. *See also* this chapter at 130–31. For Jefferson, *see* Thomas Jefferson to Gouverneur Morris (Aug. 16, 1793), *reprinted in* 7 JEFFERSON PAPERS (Ford) 475–507. For Marshall, *see* John Marshall to St. George Tucker (Nov. 27, 1800), *reprinted in* 6 MARSHALL PAPERS 23–25.

Notwithstanding this general agreement on the validity of common-law prosecutions for violations of the law of nations, there remained a technical problem of constitutional interpretation. Under the Constitution, the federal government is a government of limited powers. All of the government's authority—including authority to institute common-law prosecutions in federal court—had to be traced to the Constitution. The problem was to explain how common-law prosecutions fit into the Constitution.

Shortly after *Henfield* was decided, Justices Iredell and Paterson devised similar solutions to this problem. Each Justice viewed the common law as a natural law system that had been brought by the colonists from England to America. Paterson noted,

> The common law attached to the people, whether they met partially as of a state, or generally as of the United States. . . . All the parts, separately, are entitled to the common law as a common right, but when all these parts unite, this common law is [by the argument of the opponents] instantly destroyed or lost. Was this the intention of the people, when they adopted the constitution? Is this the sound construction of the instrument itself? Just the reverse I take to be true position.

When the federal government was created by the ratification of the Constitution, the portions of the common law relevant to the federal government became part of the national laws. In particular, Paterson believed that the "principle of self defense and preservation, which pervades nations, as well as individuals, render the punishment of offenses an indispensable requisite in every government." Therefore common-law prosecutions were within the federal court's jurisdiction because they were cases "arising under the Constitution."[26]

Subsequent Developments

Henfield was not an anomaly. At the very least its principle extended to all breaches of neutrality. For example, a recurring foreign policy irritant of the 1790s was a tendency of southerners to mount raids against neighboring European colonies. Four years after *Henfield,* the case's principle was again invoked against a private raid into Florida. Attorney General Lee concluded that the raid was "an offense against the law of nations," and because "Congress had passed no act yet upon the subject, [the raid-

---

26. William Paterson, Draft Opinion (ca. 1793–94), *reprinted in* Casto, *Torts* 525–30. Iredell's opinion is *discussed in* this chapter at 133.

ers] are only liable to be prosecuted in our courts at common law for the misdemeanor." That same year Lee also thought that William Blount's planned attacks on Florida and Louisiana constituted a "misdemeanor . . . and . . . an enterprise unlawful by common law."[27]

Nor were these nonstatutory offenses confined to breaches of neutrality. The principle had originated in cases like *Triquet v. Bath* and *De Longchamps* as a device to punish attacks on foreign diplomats, and throughout the 1790s attorneys and judges assumed that verbal attacks on foreign diplomats were subject to prosecution in federal court as common law misdemeanors. In 1797 a New York newspaper editor was indicted and convicted for libeling the British Consul General. Similarly Attorneys General Bradford and Lee each opined that the publication of a statement defaming an ambassador was a violation of the law of nations subject to federal common law prosecution.[28]

The most fascinating application of the *Henfield* principle was an attempt to prosecute Chief Justice Jay for allegedly lying about Edmond Genêt, the French minister. In the summer of 1793 at the height of the neutrality crisis, Genêt reportedly said that if President Washington decided to impede the French privateering campaign, he would appeal the President's decision to the people. Rumors of this threat percolated through the capital, and in the fall, Chief Justice Jay and Senator Rufus King published a formal statement that Genêt had indeed made this threat. As a result the public was forced to choose between Genêt and President Washington, and the choice was obvious. Although Genêt denied making the threat, his denial was not entirely successful, and his reputation and effectiveness as a diplomat were adversely affected.[29]

After some preliminary discussions, Genêt formally requested the government to institute criminal proceedings against Jay and King, and Secretary of State Jefferson referred the matter to Attorney General Randolph. Jefferson related that President Washington had considered the request and, in effect, wished to remain neutral. Consistent with this neutrality, Jefferson directed Randolph "to proceed in this case according to the duties of your office, the laws of the land, and the privileges of the parties concerned." After considering the matter, Randolph refused

---

27. 1 Op. Att'y Gen.68 (1797); *id.* 75 (1797). *See generally* HYNEMAN at 133–42. *See also* 1 Op.Att'y Gen. 57 (1795)(Att'y Gen. Bradford)(raid on Sierra Leone), *discussed in* Casto, *Torts* 502–04.

28. United States v. Greenleaf, unreported (C.C.D. N.Y. 1797), *noted in* GOEBEL 629; 1 Op. Att'y Gen. 52 (1794); *id.* 71 (1797).

29. *See* ALEXANDER DECONDE, ENTANGLING ALLIANCE 218, 283–96 (1958); *Introductory Note, in* 15 HAMILTON PAPERS 233–39. For the neutrality crisis, *see* chapter 4 at 72–87.

to prosecute, and explained, "I do not hold myself bound, nor do I conceive that I ought, to proceed against any man in opposition to my decided judgment." He did not, however, completely foreclose the possibility of a criminal prosecution. In a concluding sentence, he advised Genêt "that any other gentleman of the profession, who may approve and advise the attempt, will be at no loss to point out a mode which does not require my intervention."[30]

At first glance, there might be a tendency to believe that the fix was in — that there was to be a formal exchange of correspondence officially answering Genêt's request in terms of measured neutrality but subject to a clear private understanding that the Chief Justice and Senator King were not to be prosecuted. Other evidence indicates, however, that there was no such private understanding. When Jay and King learned of the neutral referral to the Attorney General and his suggestion of a private prosecution, they wrote an angry letter to President Washington. Although all copies of this letter were subsequently destroyed, King wrote in a private memorandum that Randolph and Jefferson were "treated with much severity in it" and that the letter included a "charge of injustice" against President Washington. Genêt's insistence upon a criminal prosecution obviously was a political hot potato.[31]

In this political context if Randolph had any doubts about the validity of federal common law prosecutions for violations of the law of nations, he would have been sorely tempted to dodge Genêt's request on the basis that Congress's failure to outlaw libels against diplomats left him powerless to act. But Randolph — like Attorneys General Bradford and Lee after him — had no doubts. He had formally embraced the federal common law of crimes in *Henfield* and reiterated his opinion six years later at the height of the political controversy over common law crimes. Therefore he could not deny the validity of federal common law crimes in his answer to Genêt's request.[32]

As for Genêt, he took Randolph's advice and immediately consulted Peter Duponceau and Joseph Thomas, two Philadelphia lawyers who were sympathetic to France. Although less than a year had passed since Duponceau's successful representation of Gideon Henfield, Duponceau

---

30. Thomas Jefferson to Edmund Randolph (Dec. 18, 1793), *reprinted in* 6 JEFFERSON PAPERS (Ford) 484–85; Edmund Randolph to Edmond Genêt (Dec. 18, 1793), *reprinted in* 10 HISTORICAL MAG. 342–43 (1866).

31. Rufus King, Memorandum of Feb. 1794, *reprinted in* 1 KING CORRESPONDENCE 476–80.

32. *See* this chapter at 130–31 & 135.

was "decidedly of opinion that [Jay and King] have committed an offense not only against the local law of this Country, but against the Law of Nations, for which they may be indicted and punished." He was undecided where "the prosecution ought to be instituted" but was inclined to think that "the Supreme Court has original jurisdiction." Acting on this advice, Genêt immediately arranged for Brockholst Livingston, a New York lawyer, to have witnesses brought from New York to Philadelphia for proceedings in the Supreme Court.[33]

Whether this bizarre prosecution against the Chief Justice of the United States in his own court was formally commenced is unknown, but the case apparently could have been filed there. As Duponceau noted in his opinion, the Constitution vests the Supreme Court with original jurisdiction over "all cases affecting ambassadors." Nor did Genêt need the government's permission to institute a criminal action. There was a well-established common law mode of prosecution called an appeal that authorized private persons to commence and prosecute criminal actions. The course of events, however, rapidly overtook and foreclosed Genêt's plan.[34]

In February 1794 less than two months after Genêt's lawyers began planning the prosecution, Jean Fauchet arrived in Philadelphia with orders from the French government to replace Genêt and ship him home to be guillotined. When President Washington magnanimously refused to permit this deadly repatriation, Fauchet reminded Genêt that under French law his mother and sisters were subject to execution if he persisted in embarrassing the French government with his planned prosecution. And so the matter was concluded.[35]

The *Ravara* Case

In the same month that Henfield was indicted, a Philadelphia grand jury also indicted Joseph Ravara, the Consul General of the Republic of Genoa. Evidently Mr. Ravara attempted to extort money from the British ambassador and a private citizen by sending them threatening letters.

---

33. Peter Duponceau and Joseph Thomas to Edmond Genêt (Dec. 23, 1793)(Genêt Papers, DLC); Brockholst Livingston to Edmond Genê (Dec. 27, 1793)(Genêt Papers, DLC).

34. Peter Duponceau and Joseph Thomas to Edmond Genêt (Dec. 23, 1793)(Genêt Papers, DLC), *citing* U.S. CONST., Art. III, § 2; 4 BLACKSTONE 308–12 (discussing appeals). *See also* Federal District Judge Richard Peters to William Vans Murray (Feb. 26, 1793) (NjMoHP) (noting that a criminal case may be prosecuted by "a private person . . . as well for himself as the U.S.").

35. *Correspondence of the French Ministers to the United States, 1791-1797* (F. J. Turner ed.), *in* 2 AMERICAN HISTORICAL ASSOCIATION, REPORT FOR 1903, at 279 n.a.

The indictment for threatening the British ambassador was quite similar to the *Triquet* and *De Longchamps* prosecutions. Notwithstanding the existence of a federal statute outlawing attacks on foreign ambassadors, U.S. Attorney Rawle viewed the case as a common-law prosecution. The relevant federal criminal statute had been consciously modeled after the act of Parliament discussed by Lord Mansfield in *Triquet*. Perhaps Rawle, like Mansfield, believed that the statute merely restated the common law, or perhaps he relied upon the common law because he feared that the statute was too narrow. In any event, because of the death of a crucial witness, the indictment of the British ambassador was dropped before the trial. The case then proceeded on the basis of Ravara's threatening letter to a Philadelphia merchant, and Ravara was convicted.[36]

This type of prosecution would ordinarily be left to state courts, but Rawle argued with apparent success that the case should be tried in federal court because the defendant was coincidentally a foreign consul.[37] The precise basis of the prosecution is obscure. There was no statute outlawing the extortion of money by sending threatening letters, so the case had to be a common-law prosecution. Nor was there any principle in the law of nations that purported to regulate the conduct of consuls toward private citizens, so the case had to be tried under a general common-law theory.

In retrospect, the fact that *Ravara* must have been a general common-law prosecution creates a difficult theoretical problem. The English and the state courts routinely exercised a general authority to punish wrongs without regard to criminal statutes, but the federal judges never claimed the full extent of this common-law power. When the indictment involving threats against the British ambassador was dropped, the case may have been continued without any thought about the federal court's general common-law jurisdiction. The only evidence regarding this technical legal issue comes from Peter Duponceau, who represented Ravara and who wrote years later that the case was tried under "the common law of the State of Pennsylvania."[38] This gloss may be a post hoc rationalization, but Duponceau was a sophisticated participant in the events and clearly

---

36. Act of Apr. 30, 1790, ch. 9, §§ 25–28, 1 Stat. 112, *discussed in* 1 Op. Att'y. Gen. 406 (1820) (Wirt); United States v. Ravara, 2 U.S. (2 Dall.) 297, Wharton's State Trials 189 (C.C.D. Pa. 1793). For a detailed discussion of Ravara, see John Gordan, *United States v. Ravara: "Presumptuous Evidence," "Too Many Lawyers," and a Federal Common Law, in* Origins (Marcus) 106–72.

37. 2 U.S. (2 Dall.) at 299 n, Wharton's State Trials at 91.

38. Peter Duponceau, A Dissertation on the Nature and Extent of the Jurisdiction of the Courts of the United States 36 (1824).

stated that the case as it was eventually tried did not involve the doctrine of federal common-law crimes.

BEYOND THE LAW OF NATIONS: THE *WORRALL* CASE

In 1798, some five years after the *Ravara* and *Henfield* indictments, the circuit court for Pennsylvania once more considered its authority to punish common-law crimes. In *United States v. Worrall*, the defendant was indicted for trying to obtain a government contract by attempting to bribe Tench Coxe, the federal Commissioner of Revenue. Shortly after receiving Worrall's offer, Commissioner Coxe consulted Justice Paterson, who advised that there was no statute covering the matter. Although Congress had outlawed bribery in the case of a judge, customs officer, or excise officer, there was no criminal statute forbidding Worrall's attempted bribe. Paterson concluded that if the act was "an offense, it must be so on common law principles."[39]

Worrall was significantly different from cases like *Henfield,* in which individuals violated treaties or well-established customary principles of the law of nations. In these earlier international law cases, Lord Mansfield's opinion in *Triquet* and the American precedent in *De Longchamps* provided a neat and elegant solution to the problem. But Mr. Worrall clearly had not violated the law of nations; the impeccable precedents of *Triquet* and *De Longchamps* were therefore inapplicable. The judges would have to look elsewhere to sustain a common-law indictment against Worrall.

When Justice Paterson suggested the possibility of a common-law prosecution, he undoubtedly had in mind the traditional power of common-law courts to punish any conduct harmful to the peace and public order. Five years earlier, during the Neutrality Crisis of 1793, Attorney General Randolph had alluded to this common-law power when he suggested that Henfield was "indictable at the common law, because his conduct comes within the description of disturbing the peace of the United States." In 1795 Zephaniah Swift published a lucid contemporary description of the doctrine in his treatise on the laws of Connecticut. He explained that

as it has been considered to be impossible to designate every action, that deserves punishment, *courts of law have assumed a discretionary power of punishing those acts which they deem criminal, (tho warranted by*

---

39. 28 F. Cas. 774, Wharton's State Trials 188 (C.C.D. Pa. 1798) (No. 16,766); William Paterson to Trench Coxe (Oct. 16, 1797), *quoted in* 3 DHSC 322 n.29.

no express law) as misdemeanors at common law. It has therefore been adopted as a general maxim, that all kinds of crimes of a public nature, all disturbances of the peace, and all other misdemeanors of notoriously evil example, may be prosecuted as public offenses—but injuries of a private nature, which do not concern the public, cannot be punished as misdemeanors.

By citations to Hawkins's *Pleas of the Crown* and Blackstone's *Commentaries,* Swift made it clear that he was talking about a general common-law doctrine rather than a Connecticut aberration.[40]

Although Swift described this well-established doctrine of common-law crimes as a discretionary power, it was not a grant of unlimited power. For example, because the doctrine was limited to misdemeanors, the defendant was not subject to the punishments of hanging, corruption of blood, and general loss of property. Nor were the courts vested with a free-roving commission to punish any type of conduct. Their authority was limited to crimes of a public nature, disturbances of the peace, and other conduct of a notoriously evil example. Swift, however, did not like the doctrine. He urged that the courts should "exercise such power with great circumspection, and caution." His primary concern was the potential lack of notice to individuals who might be prosecuted. He warned that "to punish a man, when he could not know that the act was the subject of criminal jurisprudence, cannot be deemed consistent with reason or justice." He also noted the potential for abuse "in times of convulsions, when the spirit of party runs high."[41]

Worrall's indictment was based upon the discretionary common-law authority that Swift described in his treatise. Hawkins, Blackstone, and Swift all spoke of the power as extending to misdemeanors that were "evil examples," and the indictment in *Worrall* repeated this formulaic language by describing his crime as being "To the evil example of others in the like case offending, and against the peace and dignity of the said United States."[42] At the trial, the evidence of Worrall's guilt was so clear that his defense counsel, Alexander Dallas, made no effort to argue Worrall's innocence. After the expected verdict of guilty, Dallas argued that the case should be dismissed because under the Constitution the federal courts had no jurisdiction over common crimes.

---

40. *See* this chapter at 130–31. 2 Z. Swift, A System of the Laws of the State of Connecticut 365 (1795–96) (emphasis added).

41. 2 Z. Swift, A System of the Laws of the State of Connecticut 365 (1795–96).

42. 28 F. Cas. at 775, Wharton's State Trials at 191.

Dallas's argument was powerful, sophisticated, and easy to understand. He obviously could not deny the well-established doctrine of common-law crimes, so he argued that the federal courts lacked a common-law criminal jurisdiction. His argument was that the federal government's powers were limited to the specific grants of authority listed in the Constitution. Specifically, he noted that the federal court's criminal jurisdiction was limited to cases arising under the Constitution, the laws of the United States, and treaties of the United States. He reasoned that a "case arising under a law, must mean a case depending on the exposition of a law, in respect to something which the law prohibits, or enjoins."[43] Dallas undoubtedly would have conceded that Worrall's attempted bribe was punishable as a common-law crime. His point, however, was that the common law was an unwritten law, and under the Constitution, federal judicial power extended only to cases arising under positive federal law.

This analysis is not so broad as it appears at first glance. If it is taken literally, Dallas was arguing that under the Constitution's provision for criminal jurisdiction the federal courts could try a criminal-law case as long as it depended upon "the exposition of a [written federal] law" that "prohibits or enjoins" the defendant's conduct. In other words, he recognized a hybrid kind of federal common-law jurisdiction in which a positive federal law might prohibit certain activities but make no specific provision for criminal sanctions. In such a case, the federal court could punish the prohibited activities as a crime. Dallas took precisely this position when he addressed *Henfield*. "The indictment against Henfield," he said, "expressly charged the defendant with a violation of the treaties [of the United States] which is a matter cognizable under the Federal authority by the very words of the Constitution."[44]

William Rawle, the United States attorney, saw that the linchpin of Dallas's argument was his narrow interpretation of the Constitution's provision for jurisdiction over cases arising under federal law. Rawle argued for a broader interpretation. Under Rawle's analysis, the case arose under the act of Congress that created Tench Coxe's office because Worrall had offered Coxe a bribe to influence Coxe's official conduct. If Congress had not invested Coxe with his official duties, "no attempt to corrupt [him] could have been made." [45]

Dallas had anticipated Rawle's broad interpretation when he stated some-

---

43. 28 F. Cas. at 777, Wharton's State Trials at 194.
44. 28 F. Cas. at 778, Wharton's State Trials at 195.
45. 28 F. Cas. at 778, Wharton's State Trials at 196.

what more elegantly that "it may be suggested, that the office being established by a law of the United States, it is an incident naturally attached to the authority of the United States, to guard the officer against the approaches of corruption, in the execution of his public trust." In anticipation, Dallas placed the prosecution on a slippery slope. Under this broad interpretation, he warned that any case in which "a Federal officer is concerned" would arise under federal law, and "a source of jurisdiction is opened, which must inevitably overflow and destroy all the barriers between the judicial authorities of the state and the general government."[46]

At the conclusion of Rawle's initial argument, Justice Chase asked him if the prosecution was based solely on the common law and without waiting for Rawle's answer announced that a "common law . . . indictment cannot be maintained in this Court." When Rawle responded that the prosecution was indeed based solely on the common law, Chase peremptorily stopped all further argument and delivered a lengthy opinion that he had obviously prepared in advance.[47]

Chase would have nothing of Rawle's expansive argument. He agreed with Dallas that the Constitution had created a government of limited powers, but he focused upon Congress's legislative powers under Article I of the Constitution and ignored Article III's provisions for judicial power. According to Chase, Article I established two fundamental rules regarding federal criminal law. First, the Constitution obviously (albeit implicitly) empowered the Congress to enact criminal laws. Second, this positive grant of authority preempted the possibility of nonstatutory federal crimes. Under Chase's theory of exclusive authority, federal criminal laws could come only from Congress.

The logic of this analysis based upon exclusive legislative authority would have barred the prosecution even in *Henfield*, and Chase was evidently willing to bar prosecutions based upon violations of positive federal law. He flatly stated that "if Congress had ever declared and defined the offense, without prescribing a punishment, I should still have thought it improper to exercise a [judicial] discretion upon that part of the subject."[48]

In addition to this logical—though not necessarily persuasive—constitutional analysis, Chase argued that in any event there could be no common-law prosecution in a federal court. He explained that "the United States, as a Federal government, have no common law; and, consequently, no indictment can be maintained in their courts, for offenses

---

46. 28 F. Cas. at 777, Wharton's State Trials at 194.
47. 28 F. Cas. at 778, Wharton's State Trials at 196.
48. 28 F. Cas. at 779, Wharton's State Trials at 198.

merely at the common law."[49] His idea was that the common law did not exist independently from the states that administered it. There was a common law of England and a common law of each state, but Chase implicitly denied the existence of a general common law that existed independently of these various states. Neither the Constitution nor any act of Congress expressly adopted the common law. Moreover, even if the federal government were to adopt the common law, Chase was not certain which common law would be adopted.

This analysis has fascinated modern scholars but is out of the mainstream of eighteenth-century natural-law thinking. Chase's concerns vanish if the common law is seen as existing in nature independent of human government. What could be more reasonable and therefore more natural than concluding that bribing a government official is illegal? And surely the common law principles that forbid bribing federal officials should be administered by the federal government rather than by the state governments.

Chase himself would not have been persuaded by this traditional natural-law analysis because he evidently had grave doubts about the validity of any theory that posited the existence of legal principles that existed outside of, and independent from, human government. In an 1803 Baltimore grand jury charge that was controversial for other reasons, Chase explained,

> I do not believe that any number of men ever existed together in a state of nature without some head, leader, or chief [that is, government], whose advice they followed, and whose precepts they obeyed. I readily consider a state of nature as a creature of the imagination only, although great names give a sanction to a contrary opinion. ... From hence I conclude that liberty and rights (and also property) must be forever subject to the modification of particular governments. I hold the position clear and safe, that all the rights of man can be derived only from the *conventions* of society, and may with propriety be called social rights.

Although Chase was speaking of natural rights rather than natural law, his analysis seems to preclude the existence of a natural law. Certainly his opinion in *Worrall* indicates that he believed that the common law did not exist independent of a government.[50]

---

49. 28 F. Cas. at 779, Wharton's State Trials at 197.
50. *See* this chapter at 144–45. Samuel Chase, Charge to the Baltimore Grand Jury (1803) (emphasis original), *reprinted in* 14 ANNALS 673, 676.

Neither Chase's nor Dallas's position persuaded District Judge Richard Peters, whose opinion is briefly reported in two paragraphs at the end of Dallas's report of the case.[51] The brevity and denseness of these two paragraphs suggest that they are merely a drastically pared down summary of Peters's actual analysis. Perhaps Dallas, who both argued the case and reported it, made an editorial decision to emphasize Chase's opinion and de-emphasize the opinion of the judge who ruled against him.

According to Dallas, Peters began his opinion by emphasizing that as part of establishing a government, "a power to preserve itself, was a necessary and an inseparable concomitant." Chase clearly agreed with, and had anticipated, this point when he conceded that the absence of a federal common-law jurisdiction "may be a defect in our political institutions [and] may be an inconvenience in the administration of justice." He believed, however, that "judges cannot remedy political imperfections, nor supply any legislative omission." Chase specifically noted that if Congress desired, it could enact sanctions for the kind of bribery charged in the *Worrall* case.[52]

In the second and last paragraph of Peters's opinion, as reported, he stated without explanation that the federal judiciary could exercise the traditional "common law . . . power to punish misdemeanors":

> Whenever an offense aims at the subversion of any Federal institution, or at the corruption of its public officers, it is an offense against the well-being of the United States; from its very nature, it is cognizable under their authority; and, consequently, it is within the jurisdiction of the court, by virtue of the 11th section of the judicial act.

Apparently Peters believed—consistent with natural-law thinking—that Worrall's attempted bribe violated a common-law principle that existed without the need for implementing legislation. Worrall's crime therefore fitted the Judiciary Act's provision giving the circuit courts "cognizance of all crimes and offenses cognizable under the authority of the United States."[53]

Judge Peters's disagreement with Justice Chase presented a difficult theoretical problem. A two-judge court may not adjudge a defendant guilty by a 1 to 1 vote. Nevertheless, "after a short consultation," the court entered a judgment of conviction, and Worrall was given a rela-

---

51. 28 F. Cas. at 779, Wharton's State Trials at 198.

52. *Compare* 28 F. Cas. at 779, Wharton's State Trials at 198 (Peters, J.) *with* 28 F. Cas. at 779, Wharton's State Trials at 198 (Chase, J.).

53. 28 F. Cas. at 780, Wharton's State Trials at 198.

tively light punishment that "was mitigated in consideration of [his] circumstances."[54] This puzzling result suggests a volte-face on Chase's part.

Many theories have been spun as to why Chase might have changed his mind. Years later, however, Peters wittily explained what happened during his short consultation with Chase:

> While [Chase] was pondering, after Conviction by the Jury, I practiced a pious maneuver & he joined in pronouncing a very just, but mild sentence. He never cordially forgave me. The gentle Punishment I Professed, deluded him; and he did not see, 'till too late, that he had pronounced judgment with a divided Court. I thought any punishment was better than none. I laughed him out of his judicial Pet.

Although Chase agreed to pronounce a judgment in the *Worrall* case, he continued for the rest of his career to reject the federal courts' authority to try criminal prosecutions based upon the common law.[55]

THE PROBLEM OF SEDITIOUS LIBEL

Notwithstanding the public disagreement between Justice Chase and Judge Peters, the *Worrall* case was not controversial in itself. Perhaps no one really cared about the fate of an unimportant businessman caught trying to bribe a government official. Chase's opinion, however, had significant implications for a number of immensely controversial prosecutions that loomed on the political horizon.

The years 1797 and 1798 were tumultuous for the federal government. The final approval of the Jay Treaty in 1796 had caused a deep rift in Franco-American relations, and the French government made a concerted effort to foster the defeat of John Adams and the success of Thomas Jefferson in the presidential election of that year. After this effort failed, French naval forces and privateers began seizing American merchant vessels that carried even the smallest cargo of British goods. In

---

54. 28 F. Cas. at 780, Wharton's State Trials at 199.

55. Richard Peters to Timothy Pickering (Mar. 30, 1816), *quoted in* Kathryn Preyer, *Jurisdiction to Punish: Federal Authority, Federalism and the Common Law of Crimes in the Early Republic*, 4 L. & Hist. Rev. 223, 235 (1986). For Chase's continuing refusal to change his mind, *see* Richard Peters to Timothy Pickering (Dec. 5, 1807) (Pickering Papers, MHi); Richard Peters to Timothy Pickering (Dec. 8, 1807) (Pickering Papers, MHi).

response, the Congress enacted statutes that amounted to an undeclared defensive naval war against France.[56]

At the same time, a diplomatic mission was despatched to France in an effort to negotiate a peaceful resolution of the ongoing crisis. The French, however, were clumsy and demanded bribes from the Americans as a condition to opening formal negotiations. When the Americans refused, the mission fell through. Back in America, the correspondence — including the French demands for bribes — was published in early 1798 with the names of the three French intermediaries changed to Misters X, Y, and Z. The XYZ Affair was a national sensation that dramatically solidified popular support for President Adams's administration. It also catapulted into national fame a Virginia attorney, John Marshall, who was one of the ministers who scorned the French request.

The Federalists began preparing for a major war with France and, as part of this effort, resolved to punish American citizens who tried to weaken the government by publishing what the Federalists considered to be scandalous and malicious criticisms of public officials and policies. Representative Robert Goodloe Harper explained that the country was "now on the point of being driven into a war with a nation which openly boasts of its party among us, and its 'diplomatic skill,' as the most effectual means of paralyzing our efforts, and bringing us to its own terms." Traditionally seditious political speech was punished by common-law prosecutions, but Chase's opinion in *Worrall* had cast some doubt on the legitimacy of federal common-law prosecutions. Just a month after *Worrall* was decided and the XYZ Correspondence was published, a congressional committee began drafting a bill to make seditious libel a statutory crime. This legislation was motivated in part by Chase's unsettling opinion.[57]

When the sedition bill was debated in the House, its opponents vehemently attacked the proposal as unconstitutional. In reply, the Federalists asserted that the measure was a proper use of the Constitution's "necessary and proper" clause to protect the federal government. In addition, they invoked the common law. For example, in a rambling speech, Representative Harrison Otis frequently alluded to the fact that seditious libel was a well-recognized common-law crime. The obvious implication

---

56. *See* DeConde 61–67. For a discussion of the legal aspects of the undeclared naval war, *see* Abraham Sofaer, War, Foreign Affairs and Constitutional Power chapter 3 (1976).

57. 8 Annals 2164–65 (Harper). The best treatment of the enactment and enforcement of the Sedition Act remains Freedom's Fetters. For the influence of Chase's opinion in Worrall, *see* 8 Annals 2113 (Mr. Kittera). *Accord,* 10 Annals 414–15 (Mr. Harper).

was that if the federal courts already had a common-law jurisdiction encompassing seditious libel, the proposed Sedition Act could not be unconstitutional. To counter this line of argument, the Republicans had to deny the federal courts' authority to punish common-law crimes. Their arguments against the bill, however, were unavailing. Congress, acting under the influence of the XYZ Affair and fearing war was imminent, passed the Sedition Act in the summer of 1798.[58]

At this time, Cabinet responsibility for supervising the various U.S. Attorneys was allocated to the Secretary of State rather than the Attorney General, and Secretary of State Timothy Pickering evidently expressed some concerns about the Act to Chief Justice Ellsworth. Notwithstanding the fact that Ellsworth expected to preside over criminal prosecutions under the Act, he had no qualms about giving Pickering an advisory opinion on the subject. Having followed the Congressional debate on the Sedition Act, Ellsworth understood the controversial relationship between the doctrine of common-law crimes and the Act's constitutionality. In December 1798, five months after the Act's passage, Ellsworth wrote Pickering that the Act presented no "constitutional difficulty" because the federal courts were already authorized to punish seditious libel as a common-law crime.[59]

Ellsworth also noted that the Sedition Act provided defendants with a number of procedural safeguards not available in a common-law prosecution. For example, contrary to common law, truth was a defense under the Act. Ellsworth wryly concluded that if the Act were to be repealed, the repealer should read, "Whereas, the increasing danger and depravity of the present time require that the law against seditions practices *should be restored to its former rigor,* therefore, &c."[60]

Two months later a House of Representatives Select Committee issued a lengthy report on the Alien and Sedition Acts that repeated the arguments that Ellsworth had advanced in his letter to Secretary Pickering. In response, Representative Wilson Cary Nicholas reiterated the Republican

---

58. The Sedition Act, ch. 75, 1 Stat. 596 (1798). 8 ANNALS 2145–51 (Mr. Otis). For the Republicans' counterargument, *see id.* 2141–42 (Mr. Nicholas), *id.* 2137, 2156–57 (Mr. Gallatin). Gallatin claimed that "every gentleman who had spoken in favor of this bill had explicitly declared, as his opinion, that the Federal Courts had no jurisdiction whatever over offenses at common law." *Id.* 2157. Given the predominant opinion to the contrary among the federal judges, this claim is difficult to accept at face value.

59. *See* GOEBEL 545, 632–33; Oliver Ellsworth to Timothy Pickering (Dec. 12, 1798) (Pickering Papers, MHi), *excerpted in* FLANDERS 193–94.

60. Oliver Ellsworth to Timothy Pickering (Dec. 12, 1798) (Pickering Papers, MHi), *excerpted in* FLANDERS 193–94.

arguments from the Sedition Act debates and added a new objection to federal common law. He argued that the federal courts' pretension to a common-law jurisdiction was a dangerous arrogation of authority without apparent limit. Nicholas warned,

> The nature of the [common] law of England makes it impossible that it should have been adopted in the lump into such a Government as this is; because it was a complete system for the management of all the affairs of a country. It regulated estate, punished all crimes, and, in short, went to all things for which laws are necessary.

Nicholas's argument that the common law was "a complete system" that regulated all human relations was to become a key part of the Republicans' objections to federal common law. If the federal courts had a complete common-law jurisdiction over all human conduct, then Congress's legislative authority must be equally comprehensive. The result would be to work a consolidation of virtually all state authority into the federal government.[61]

A year later, James Madison noted in his Report on the Virginia Resolutions that Congress's authority was coextensive with federal judicial authority. He then warned that the doctrine of a federal common law was dangerous because it meant that the "Congress would therefore be no longer under the limitations, marked out in the constitution. They would be authorized to legislate in all cases whatsoever."[62]

Chief Justice Ellsworth recognized the seriousness of the Republicans' new argument and correctly anticipated that they would make this fear of plenary federal power a key part of their campaign against the federal common law and the Sedition Act. About the time that Nicholas advanced the new argument, Ellsworth started working on a grand jury charge designed to present a complete explanation and justification of the doctrine of federal common-law crimes. Three months later, in May 1799, he delivered his charge to the grand jury in South Carolina, and the charge was reprinted in newspapers throughout the nation. Ellsworth agreed that offenses against the United States are "*chiefly* defined in the statutes," but he reaffirmed the existence of two categories of nonstatutory crimes. The first category consisted of "acts contravening the law of nations," but he did not elaborate on this category because they are "rarely met with." Instead, he concentrated

---

61. 9 Annals 2985, 2989 (Select Committee Report); *Id.* 3012 (Mr. Nicholas).
62. 17 Madison Papers 332. For an elaboration of this idea, *see* G. Edward White, *Recovering Coterminous Power Theory: The Last Dimension of Marshall Court Sovereignty Cases, in* Origins (Marcus) 66–105.

upon the second category of nonstatutory crimes, which outlawed "acts manifestly subversive of the national government, or some of its powers specified in the constitution."[63]

Ellsworth took great pains to refute the assertion that the doctrine of federal common-law crimes entailed a complete system of laws with no limits. First, the doctrine extended only to acts "manifestly subversive of the national government," and Ellsworth emphasized that he said "*manifestly* subversive, to exclude acts of doubtful tendency, and confine criminality to clearness and certainty." To Ellsworth it was not "necessary to particularize the acts falling within this description, because they are readily perceived, and are ascertained by known and established rules; I mean the maxims and principles of the common law of our land." Ellsworth also noted in passing that he was talking about a doctrine of "misdemeanors."[64]

In addition to explaining the substantive limits of this unwritten criminal law, Ellsworth saw the grand jury process itself as a limit to common-law prosecutions. He cautioned the grand jurors that "[a]lthough an indictment is but an accusation . . . yet it affects too nearly [the indicted person's] fame and his liberty, to be founded on *suspicion;* and much less on prepossession." He warned the jurors that they were "a shield from oppression [and not] the *instruments* of it." He concluded by emphasizing that grand jurors should not investigate "the *opinions* of men, but their *actions*; and weigh them, not in the scales of *passion,* or of *party,* but in a *legal* balance—a balance that is undeceptive—which vibrates not with popular opinion; and which flatters not the pride of birth, or encroachments of power." These words resonated with such a scrupulous sense of fairness that even Ellsworth's harshest critics conceded that the charge did him "the utmost honor as a judge, and as a man."[65]

In addition to indicating the limits of the federal common law of crimes, Ellsworth restated the origins of the federal common law. He clearly viewed the common law as a system of natural-law principles and had said as much in judicial opinions that he had written as a state judge in the 1780s. In his 1799 grand jury charge in South Carolina, he reminded his audience that the common law was "a known law, matured by the reason of ages." It was "brought from the country of our ancestors, with here and there an accommodating exception, in nature of local cus-

---

63. Oliver Ellsworth, Charge to the South Carolina Grand Jury (May 7, 1799) (emphasis original), *reprinted in* 3 DHSC 357–59.

64. *Id.* 357–58 (emphasis original).

65. *Id.* 358 (emphasis original); "Citizen" to Oliver Ellsworth, Virginia Argus (Richmond), Aug. 9, 1799, *reprinted in* 3 DHSC 375, 376.

toms, [and] was the law of every part of the union at the formation of the national compact."[66]

Under Ellsworth's natural-law analysis, there was no need for either the states or the federal government to enact a formal adoption of the common law. It already pervaded the nation without the need for implementing legislation. Ellsworth believed that as soon as the Constitution was ratified and the federal government was created, the common law "did, of course, *attach* upon or apply to it [the federal government], for the purposes of exposition and enforcement." Thus Ellsworth repeated the analysis espoused some six years earlier by Justices Iredell and Paterson.[67]

FEDERAL COMMON LAW AND THE *WILLIAMS* CASE

Four months after Ellsworth's charge in South Carolina, he was in Connecticut presiding over the last controversial common-law prosecution that took place before Jefferson became president. In *United States v. Williams*, Isaac Williams was tried for and convicted of joining the French navy and participating in the war against Great Britain, "which is against the peace and dignity of the said United States and contrary to . . . the Treaty of Amity Commerce and Navigation . . . between . . . Great Britain, and the said United States." During the trial, Ellsworth rendered an opinion that infuriated the Republican press.[68]

In *Williams*, the defendant admitted joining the French navy and sailing against the British. In addition, there was evidence that he had served against the British on French privateers. Williams argued, however, that he had become an expatriate by renouncing his American citizenship in 1792 and becoming a duly naturalized citizen of France. If Williams was a French citizen and not an American citizen, his service with the French was obviously not in violation of the neutrality of the United States. The prosecution argued, however, that despite Williams's attempted renunciation, he remained an American citizen and had violated the Jay Treaty.

---

66. *See, e.g.,* Adams v. Kellogg, Kirby 438 (1786) (Ellsworth, J.); Wilford v. Grant, Kirby 114 (1786) (per curium). The manuscript opinion in Wilford is in the Connecticut State Archives and is in Ellsworth's hand. Oliver Ellsworth, Charge to the South Carolina Grand Jury (May 7, 1799), *reprinted in* 3 DHSC 357, 358.
67. *Id.* For Iredell and Paterson, *see* this chapter at 133 & 136.
68. 29 F. Cas. 1330, Wharton's State Trials 652 (C.C.D. Conn. 1799) (No. 17, 708). Sentence of Isaac Williams (Oct. 17, 1799) (Petitions for Pardons, DNA, RG59). *See* Warren 159–62. *See also* Philadelphia Aurora, Nov. 7, 1799 (reprinting an essay from the Newark Centennial); Aristogiton I & II, American Daily Advertiser (Baltimore), Oct. 15, 19, 1799; Mutius II, Virginia Argus (Richmond), Oct. 25, 1799.

Chief Justice Jay and Justice Iredell had viewed the doctrine of expatriation as a "ridiculous . . . absurdity," and Ellsworth agreed. In addressing the issue, Ellsworth commenced his opinion with the inflammatory statement that "[t]he common law of this country remains the same as it was before the Revolution." He then flatly stated that an American citizen could not renounce his citizenship unless the government consented to the renunciation and that in Williams's case the federal government had not so consented. Ellsworth's analysis was based upon the idea of government as a social contract in which "all the members of civil community are bound to each other by compact." Given this bilateral relationship, it "necessarily results, that the members cannot dissolve this compact, without the consent or default of the community."[69]

The opposition press's reaction to this analysis verged upon hysteria. As one editorialist put it, "By the Chief Justice's opinion, we are still the subjects of Great Britain; we are so by this principle, her common law." Ellsworth would have replied that the Declaration of Independence lawfully severed our relationship with Great Britain. The rebelling colonies did not need to seek Britain's permission, because—to use the language of Ellsworth's opinion in *Williams*—Britain had "defaulted" on its obligations under the compact. Nor did he believe that the English common law had to be enforced in the United States without any alteration. As early as 1786, he had stated that the principles of the common law of England were not applicable in America if they "appear contrary to reason or unadapted to our local circumstance, the policy of our law, or simplicity of our practice." He had reiterated this point in the first Congress and in his 1799 grand jury charge. In *Williams* he did not blindly follow the English common law. Rather he adduced considerations unique to the United States that warranted an adoption of the English principles. Consistent with this analysis, John Marshall assumed that Ellsworth meant "the common law, not of England, but of our own country."[70]

---

69. 29 F. Cas. at 1331, Wharton's State Trials at 653; John Jay, Draft Grand Jury Charge, *reprinted in* 2 DHSC 359, 363; James Iredell, Charge to the South Carolina Grand Jury (May 12, 1794), *reprinted in* 2 DHSC 454, 464–65. *See* G. EDWARD WHITE, THE MARSHALL COURT AND SOCIAL CHANGE, 1815–35, at 898–904 (1988).

70. BEE (New London, Conn.), Oct. 30, 1799, *quoted in* WARREN at 161. Wilford v. Grant, *discussed in* this chapter at 152. For Ellsworth's earlier iterations, *see* this chapter at 151–52 and chapter 2 at 9 DHFFC 454. 29 F. Cas. at 1331, Wharton's State Trials at 654 (C.C.D. Conn. 1799). John Marshall to St. George Tucker (Nov. 17, 1800), *reprinted in* 6 MARSHALL PAPERS 23–25.

THE *WILLIAMS* CASE AND
INTERSTITIAL FEDERAL COMMON LAW

Although *Williams* was obviously controversial, the controversy was not really over the fact that the case was a common-law prosecution. Virtually all of the strident polemics against Ellsworth's opinion concentrated on the relatively narrow issue of whether Williams could unilaterally renounce his citizenship. This specific issue, however, was only coincidentally related to the fact that *Williams* was a common-law prosecution for violating the law of nations. If Congress had legislated criminal sanctions for violations of the Jay Treaty, Ellsworth would have been confronted with precisely the same issue and would have resolved it in precisely the same manner.

The common-law issue in *Williams* was significantly different from the common-law issues in cases like *Henfield* and *Worrall*. In these earlier cases, the major issue was whether the federal courts were authorized to punish conduct that Congress had not criminalized. In *Williams* the issue was not so fundamental. Even in the case of statutory crimes for which the courts have clearly been authorized to punish malefactors, issues may arise for which there is no statutory answer. In these situations the courts must find an answer, and Ellsworth indicated in *Williams* that the courts should look to the common law for answers to specific issues that may arise. Today this kind of common law is sometimes called an interstitial common law because the basic framework of the court's authority to punish has already been established. In *Williams* Ellsworth resorted to common law to fill the interstices of the case.

This concept of an interstitial common law was used by Justice Paterson in the Whiskey Rebellion trials.[71] In those cases the defendants were charged with violating the act of Congress outlawing treason, thus the cases were statutory, not common-law, prosecutions. As a preliminary issue, Paterson had to consider how many prospective jurors should be called to form the pool that would provide the jury panels for the individual prosecutions. Because Congress had not enacted a legislative answer to this question, the defendants argued for the application of a restrictive state rule that would have increased the percentage of jurors from the western counties where the rebellion had taken place.

Justice Paterson rejected this argument. He held that because "the act of Congress does not itself fix the number of jurors, nor expressly adopt any State rule for the purpose, it is a necessary consequence, that the

---

71. Trial of the Western Insurgents, Wharton's State Trials 102 (C.C.D. Pa. 1795).

subject must depend on the common law; and by the common law, the Court may direct any number of jurors to be summoned."[72] Regardless of the basis for the underlying prosecution, the issues of citizenship in *Williams* and the number of prospective jurors in the Whiskey Rebellion cases had to be resolved by the federal court. Because Congress had not supplied a federal statutory rule of decision, Paterson and Ellsworth turned to the common law.

This distinction between an interstitial common law and the more fundamental question of the federal courts' common-law jurisdiction to punish nonstatutory crimes is not anachronistic. Albert Gallatin, who was a vigorous foe of the doctrine of federal common-law crimes, conceded that the federal courts should be guided by the common law in cases otherwise within their jurisdiction. Similarly, John Marshall explained in private correspondence that in Ellsworth's *Williams* opinion, the Chief Justice did not rely on "the common law . . . as giving the court jurisdiction." Instead, the citizenship issue "came in incidentally as part of the law of a case of which the court had complete & exclusive possession."[73]

Viewed in this light, Ellsworth's decision in *Williams* that the issue of citizenship should be decided by resort to a federal common law is utterly unobjectionable. Once Williams raised the defense of unilateral renunciation of citizenship, Ellsworth had to address the issue. He could not say that he lacked jurisdiction to consider a defense proffered by the defendant. He could have resorted to state law, but had he done so, an individual's status as a United States citizen might vary from state to state as a result.

COMMON-LAW CRIMES AND COMMON-LAW THINKING

Although the dispute over common-law crimes was frequently argued as a matter of legal theory, the impetus for the controversy was political, and the debate was therefore confusingly inconsistent. Despite the vigorous theoretical objections to common-law crimes, there was scant political opposition to any of the specific common-law prosecutions in which the federal courts actually exercised their jurisdiction. Aside from Isaac Williams and Gideon Henfield, the defendants who were actually brought to trial were mainly a scurrilous collection of extortionists, counterfeiters, and corrupt would-be government contractors who richly deserved the punishment they received. Even in the case of Gideon

---

72. *Id.* at 171. *Accord,* Impeachment of William Blount, Wharton's State Trials 200, 209 (U.S. Sen. 1797) (Mr. Harper).
73. 10 ANNALS 421–22 (Mr. Gallatin); John Marshall to St. George Tucker (Nov. 17, 1800), *reprinted in* 6 MARSHALL PAPERS 23–25. *See also* 8 ANNALS 2157 (Mr. Gallatin).

Henfield there was no serious political objection to federal courts' common-law jurisdiction to punish violations of the law of nations. Thomas Jefferson supported Henfield's prosecution, and at the height of the political controversy over common-law crimes, Edmund Randolph reaffirmed the validity of Henfield's prosecution.

In fact, opponents of the doctrine of common-law crimes did not really object to the federal courts' judicial jurisdiction to try criminal cases. Their real objection was to expanding the federal government's legislative jurisdiction to make laws. Opposition to federal common-law crimes did not mount to a fever pitch until the well-established common-law crime of seditious libel was used by the Federalists to justify Congress's enactment of the Sedition Act. If the federal courts already had a common-law criminal jurisdiction, Congress obviously had authority under the Constitution's "necessary and proper" clause to codify the common law of seditious libel. This powerful justification of a broad Congressional authority could be countered only by denying that the federal courts had a common-law jurisdiction. The fundamental objection, however, was to the federal government's general legislative authority.

Although the debate over federal common-law crimes was usually couched in terms of federal court jurisdiction, the central political concern was the federal judges' administration of substantive common-law rules for the regulation of society. Today the doctrine of federal common-law crimes would be viewed as judicial lawmaking in which the judges themselves made the legislative decision to criminalize certain kinds of conduct. But eighteenth-century lawyers did not have a generally accepted philosophy or even a legal vocabulary that enabled them to attack the common law of crimes as judicial lawmaking. Virtually all lawyers agreed that judges did not make the common law; they merely administered the common law that already existed in nature. Given this widespread understanding, critics of the doctrine of federal common-law crimes had to couch their arguments in jurisdictional terms. A direct accusation of judicial lawmaking simply would not have been credible.

The closest anyone ever came to a critical analysis based upon a charge of judicial lawmaking was James Madison's Report of 1800, written as a comprehensive attack on the Alien and Sedition Acts. Because the doctrine of federal common-law crimes virtually established Congress's legislative authority, Madison was compelled to deny the doctrine's legitimacy. After parsing the Constitution, he stated a number of political and theoretical objections. In keeping with the purpose of his report, his principal objection was that the doctrine would radically expand the government's legislative authority. Because the common law was "vast and multifarious," a federal adoption of the entire system would "by one constructive operation new model the whole political fabric of the country." In addition, he argued that a national common law "would confer on the judicial department a discretion little short of legislative power." In particular, Madison was concerned that the federal judiciary would necessarily have "to decide what parts of the common law would, and what would not, be properly applicable to the circumstances of the United States." The need to assess the extension of English precedents to America meant "that the power of the judges over the law would, in fact, erect them into legislators; and that for a long time, it would be impossible for the citizens to conjecture, either what was, or would be law."[74]

Although Madison's analysis is cogent to twentieth-century lawyers steeped in legal positivism, in the eighteenth century his objection went squarely against the mainstream of natural-law thinking. In particular, Madison's objection called into question the legitimacy of every judicial system in North America. The state judges clearly exercised a common-law jurisdiction far broader than what the federal judges claimed. State common-law jurisdiction extended generally to all civil and criminal cases. If Madison's objection were taken seriously, all the state and federal judges in the United States had "erected" themselves into legislators.

Available evidence indicates that the federal judges did not take criticism like Madison's seriously. Nor is it plausible to believe that they schemed to erect themselves into legislators. The Justices wanted to defend the federal government from attacks and were happy to take full advantage of the well-established doctrine of common-law misdemeanors. Aside from Justice Chase's solitary opinion to the contrary, there was never any serious dispute among the early federal judges regarding their jurisdiction over common-law crimes. In 1800 Representative James Bayard noted that, except for Chase, all the judges were united in the opinion that a federal common law of crimes existed under the Constitution, and the existence of this early unanimity was reaffirmed in 1806 and 1816 by Judge Peters and Justice Story. Given Chase's apparent rejection of natural-law thinking and his status as a lone dissenter, his opinion should be dismissed as an anomaly—at least within the judicial community.[75]

In contrast to Chase, the other judges were not particularly concerned about how the common law of crimes fit into the new Constitution. They

---

74. James Madison, Report on the Virginia Resolutions (Jan. 7, 1800), *reprinted in* 17 MADISON PAPERS 303, 329–33.

75. 10 ANNALS 411 (Mr. Bayard); Letter from Richard Peters to Timothy Pickering (Dec. 5, 1807) (Pickering Papers, MHi 28:99); THE LIFE AND LETTERS OF JOSEPH STORY 299 (W. Story ed., 1851). *Accord,* WHARTON'S STATE TRIALS 87 n. For Chase, *see* this chapter at 141–47.

knew that the common law was a freestanding body of legal principles that naturally pervaded human society. They assumed therefore that the portions of the common law pertinent to the federal government naturally attached to the new government when it was created by the Constitution. Rather than worrying about the constitutional basis for a federal common law, they concentrated most of their efforts on exploring the substantive content of the doctrine of common-law crimes. Some two hundred years later their explorations provide valuable insights into the nature of the common law and the method of common-law reasoning.

The common law in the late eighteenth century was fundamentally at war with itself. It had a natural-law foundation and was considered to be the expression of divine wisdom and the perfection of human reason. In theory, the common law was a complete, systematic, and cohesive body of principles. But in practice, common lawyers exalted shared community experience and placed immense trust in tradition and local customs. Although humans are capable of imagining the existence of a systematic and cohesive body of principles for regulating society, no large community has ever achieved the practical implementation of such a perfect code. Therefore the common lawyers' extreme reliance upon tradition inherently conflicted with their natural-law vision. In theory, common law thinking was systematic, but in practice it was eclectic.

In retrospect, the common-law thinking of the Founding Generation seems an unstable mix of legal positivism and natural law. Blackstone is routinely criticized for mixing a positivist concept of legislative supremacy with his natural-law model, but there was a more subtle and fundamental inconsistency. Common lawyers professed to be natural lawyers, but their immense reliance upon tradition had the practical effect of leading them to define law by reference to the received customs or traditions of a particular human community. The practice of placing immense emphasis upon custom and tradition is closer to legal positivism than to natural law. A definition of law keyed to human tradition provides a procedural rather than a substantive definition of law. The key issue is the existence of the tradition, not the substantive content of the rule. In contrast, the prevailing natural-law theory defined law by reference to its substantive content. Under natural-law thinking, the key issue was whether a putative legal principle was the embodiment of reason.[76]

---

76. *See* LOBBAN 27–33 (criticizing Blackstone). *See also* David LIEBERMAN, THE PROVINCE OF LEGISLATION DETERMINED chapter 1 (1989). In LOBBAN, the author ably details the conflict between custom and natural law in the English common law of the late eighteenth century but seeks to explain the conflict as a dichotomy between theorists and practitioners.

Most common lawyers of the Founding Era, however, did not see a significant conflict between human custom and the perfectly reasonable natural law. For example, William Blackstone explained that "whenever a standing rule of [common] law, of which the reason perhaps could not be remembered or discerned, hath been wantonly broken in upon by statutes or new resolutions, the wisdom of the rule hath in the end appeared from the inconveniences that have followed the innovation."[77] Lawyers like Blackstone did not exalt custom over reason; they equated the two.

Their emphasis upon custom and tradition inclined common lawyers to compartmentalized thinking. A common lawyer or judge confronted with a specific problem wanted to know what the traditional common-law rule was and was relatively unconcerned with whether the rule was reasonable or how it compared with other rules applicable to other types of problems. These lawyers and judges were, and remain today, predominantly problem solvers. As judges, they were relatively unconcerned with elaborating a general and consistent framework of interlocking rules. Such elaboration did not contribute to the resolution of specific problems and was in any event unnecessary because a general standing body of principles already existed in nature.

To be sure, the common law's natural-law underpinnings provided a theory for rejecting an apparently unreasonable rule. The doctrine of stare decisis told lawyers to follow prior precedent, but the doctrine was not absolute. Even a strong advocate of stare decisis like Blackstone admitted an "exception, where the former determination is most evidently contrary to reason." But given common lawyers' immense conservatism, there was in fact only a slight likelihood that an established common-law rule would be overturned as unreasonable.[78]

The emphasis upon specific custom is evident in the federal judges' elaboration of the doctrine of common-law crimes. By the end of the eighteenth century, they had identified a comprehensive standing body of nonstatutory crimes. But they commenced their exploration of the topic with a compartmentalized analysis based almost entirely upon a single well-established but narrow common-law rule.

Common-law prosecutions first arose as a significant issue during the Neutrality Crisis of 1793. The Justices fully understood the political and international consequence of failing to punish American citizens' blatant depredations upon British commerce, and they undoubtedly wanted to

---

77. 1 BLACKSTONE 70. *Accord, id.* 70–71.

78. *Id.* 69. *See* LOBBAN 83–87 (detailing English jurists' conservative approach to departures from precedent).

support the Washington Administration's efforts to deal with the Crisis. The *Triquet* and *De Longchamps* cases firmly established the common-law principle that violations of the law of nations were subject to criminal sanctions. Therefore the Justices had a neat, clear, and politically pleasing solution to the specific problem at hand. No effort was made to propound a general theory of federal common-law prosecutions, because a general theory was unnecessary. The prosecution of Americans like Gideon Henfield fit precisely into a pre-existing legal compartment confined to violations of the law of nations.

Henfield's prosecution was an easy case for the Justices because the applicable common-law precedent was clearly impressed with a direct and obvious federal interest. The federal government had been specifically created to deal effectively with foreign affairs problems. Therefore all of the common law pertinent to the enforcement of the law of nations naturally attached to the federal government upon its creation.

In contrast to *Henfield,* the *Worrall* case presented a more difficult issue. The law of nations precedents simply were not directly applicable. William Rawle, the U.S. Attorney, understood this and therefore cited *Henfield* as but one specific application of a general overarching principle that any and all violations of the common law of the United States could be prosecuted in federal court. This natural-law argument was systematic and based upon general reason. Alexander Dallas, for the defense, did not question the legitimacy of *Henfield's Case* but sought instead to compartmentalize the decision by limiting it to situations in which an American citizen violated a treaty of the United States.[79]

According to Dallas's report of the case, neither Judge Peters nor Justice Chase addressed *Henfield* in their opinions. Chase's analysis was idiosyncratic, but the surviving summary of Peters's analysis is pure common-law thinking. Peters was quite unconcerned with cases like *Triquet, De Longchamps,* and *Henfield* because he viewed the *Worrall* case as fitting into an entirely different and unrelated common-law category. "The power to punish misdemeanors is originally and strictly a common law power; of which," wrote Peters, "the United States are constitutionally possessed."[80]

Peters's basic point that common-law judges had a general authority to punish misdemeanors committed in violation of the unwritten common law was irrefutable. This doctrine was at least as well established as the

---

79. United States v. Worrall, 28 F. Cas. at 778, Wharton's State Trials at 195.
80. 28 F. Cas. at 779, Wharton's State Trials at 198.

common-law power to punish infractions of the law of nations. The problem was to determine the extent of the federal courts' common-law jurisdiction over misdemeanors. Peters, in his *Worrall* opinion, and subsequently Chief Justice Ellsworth, in his charge to the South Carolina grand jury, indicated that the federal courts would enforce those portions of the common law that outlawed conduct directly affecting an important federal interest.

Although this limitation left much to the federal judges' discretion, there is scant evidence that they ever abused their discretion. The prosecutions for violations of the law of nations were fully consistent with the well-settled common-law doctrine exemplified by *Triquet v. Bath*. Similarly, almost all of the prosecutions under the more general and nebulous—though well-settled—common-law doctrine of disturbing the peace were for activities that had a direct impact upon the federal government and were presumptively criminal. In *Worrall*, the crime was bribing a federal official. In another case, *United States v. Smith*, it was counterfeiting bills of the Bank of the United States. Some might argue that two common-law prosecutions for seditious libel that were initiated shortly before the Sedition Act became law were an abuse of discretion. These prosecutions, however, were consistent with the well-settled common-law doctrine of seditious libel.[81]

The most dubious common-law prosecutions arose out of the tax protest that came to be known as the Whiskey Rebellion. As early as 1792, two tax protestors were indicted and tried in federal court for the crime of common-law riot but found not guilty. The indictment was predicated on threats made to an individual who had allowed his house to be used as a tax office. In the 1794 Rebellion, numerous individuals were indicted by a federal grand jury for various misdemeanors including "[liberty] pole raising" and sedition for saying "any man who supports the Excise is a dammed rascal." To modern eyes these convictions seem flagrant violations of the defendants' constitutionally guaranteed freedom of expression, but there is no evidence that contemporary observers, including anti-Federalists, were outraged. The truth is that these obscure common-law prosecutions went virtually unmentioned at the time. Perhaps they were found unobjectionable because the comparatively minor charge of misdemeanor provided a flexible and fair approach for punishing unlawful activities without invok-

---

81. United States v. Smith, 27 F. Cas. 1147 (C.C.D. Mass. 179[7]) (No. 16,323). For the common-law prosecutions for seditious libel, *see* FREEDOM'S FETTERS chapter 10.

ing the constitutional and statutory crime of treason with its attendant mandatory death penalty.[82]

Notwithstanding the sound legal arguments supporting the doctrine of federal common-law crimes and the Justices' restraint in enunciating and giving heed to the doctrine's limitations, the federal courts' authority to punish nonstatutory crimes did not survive. Jefferson's coalition had made such a political issue of common-law crimes that nonstatutory prosecutions were effectively precluded once he came to power. Almost as soon as Jefferson took office, his attorney general refused to prosecute "an aggravated violation of the law of nations" involving the tearing down of the [Spanish] national flag, and other acts of insult" against Spain and the Spanish minister. He explained that he "doubt[ed] the competency of the federal courts, there being no statute recognizing the offense." Later in 1812, the Court formally held that the federal courts lacked authority to punish nonstatutory crimes. With no explanation, the Court briefly noted that this lack of authority had "been long since settled in public opinion." Given the strength of the legal arguments in support of common-law crimes, this statement should be read literally. The party of Jefferson and Madison vigorously opposed the doctrine of federal common-law crimes, and their opposition had in a sense been ratified by numerous presidential and congressional elections. By 1812 the Court was willing to acquiesce in this "settled . . . public opinion."[83]

The brief life of federal common-law crimes contrasts sharply with the federal courts' related practice in civil cases. In these latter cases, which were exemplified by the Supreme Court's 1842 decision in *Swift v. Tyson*, the federal judges viewed civil common-law principles the same way they had viewed principles of criminal law. The judges did not legislate principles; they merely found them preexisting in nature. Throughout the nineteenth century, the federal courts routinely used this natural-law analysis to reject state court precedent in cases otherwise governed by state law. By the beginning of the twentieth century, the *Swift* doctrine had been expanded to encompass a broad spectrum of issues including contracts, agency, negotiable instruments, insurance, and torts. Notwithstanding this arrogation of

---

82. *See* Richard Ifft, *Treason in the Early Republic: The Federal Courts, Popular Protest, and Federalism During the Whiskey Insurrection, in* THE WHISKEY REBELLION 165, 168, 176–77, App. B at 199–201 (S. Boyd ed., 1985).

83. United States v. Hudson & Goodwin, 11 U.S. (7 Cranch) 32 (1812). *See* Gary Rowe, *The Sound of Silence: United States v. Hudson & Goodwin, the Jeffersonian Ascendancy, and the Abolition of Federal Common Law Crimes*, 101 YALE L. J. 919 (1992). For the Jefferson Administration, *see* 5 Op. Att'y Gen. 691 (1802); HASKINS & JOHNSON 355; LEONARD LEVY, JEFFERSON AND CIVIL LIBERTIES: THE DARKER SIDE 60–66 (1963).

federal judicial power, the *Swift* doctrine was not nearly as controversial as the related but short-lived doctrine of federal common-law crimes. This comparative lack of controversy is probably due to the fact that the *Swift* doctrine was never engulfed by a political firestorm like the enactment of the Sedition Act. The *Swift* doctrine was eventually abandoned in the twentieth century, but not until natural-law thinking had been supplanted by a new faith in legal positivism.[84]

STATUTORY CRIMES: THE WHISKEY REBELLION

Although the issue of common-law crimes assumed a remarkably high political profile at the end of the 1790s, common-law prosecutions had only a slight impact upon the circuit courts' criminal dockets. The vast majority of federal criminal indictments were for statutory crimes, and the vast majority of these statutory prosecutions arose from maritime matters.[85] The most interesting statutory prosecutions, however, were directed at land-based activities like Fries's Rebellion, the various incidents of seditious libel at the end of the decade, and the Whiskey Rebellion, which took place in 1794.

The Whiskey Rebellion seems insignificant today—especially in comparison to the Civil War.[86] But it was viewed with genuine consternation at the time, and in the fall of 1794 President Washington led an army of over ten thousand nationalized militia into western Pennsylvania to quell the unrest. A number of the tax protestors were hauled back to Philadelphia, where ten were tried for treason. Two of the defendants—Philip Vigol and John Mitchell—were convicted, and Justice Paterson sentenced them to the statutorily mandated penalty of death by hanging.

Paterson's conduct in the Whiskey Rebellion cases has been criticized as unduly political, and his charge to the grand jury investigating the Rebellion was far more than a bare recitation of the law of treason:

> If persons assemble to act with force in opposition to a law, and hope thereby to get it repealed; or if they endeavor in great numbers and force to work or bring about a reformation, without pursuing the methods prescribed by the constitution and laws it will be a levying of war and of course treason. . . . Ah licentiousness! thou

---

84. Swift v. Tyson, 41 U.S. (16 Pet.) 1 (1842). *See* Casto, *Erie;* William LaPiana, *Swift v. Tyson and the Brooding Omni-presence in the Sky: An Investigation of the Idea of Law in Antebellum America,* 20 SUFFOLK U. L. REV. 771 (1986).

85. *See* HENDERSON, chapter 7.

86. *See* SLAUGHTER; THE WHISKEY REBELLION (S. Boyd. ed., 1985).

bane of republics, more to be dreaded than hosts of external foes. The truth is, that civil liberty and order consist in and depend upon submission to the laws.

At least one other Justice similarly railed against the Pennsylvania protestors as "licentious abusers, of liberty." These statements, however, are fairly typical of the political exhortation that was customary in late-eighteenth-century Federalist Justices' grand jury charges.[87]

When the cases came to trial, Paterson virtually directed the jury to find the defendants guilty in the two cases that resulted in convictions. In the prosecution of Mitchell, Paterson ended his jury charge by flatly concluding that "the prisoner must be pronounced guilty," and he was equally adamant in his instructions to the jury in the Vigol case. Evidently Mitchell's and Vigol's attorneys called no witnesses in defense of their clients and made no effort to challenge the prosecution's testimony. Given this unusual trial strategy, Paterson's one-sided commentary was simply an accurate description of the state of the evidence. He undoubtedly believed that he was simply restating and summarizing what the jury already knew. In the late twentieth century no judge would ever consider giving a jury such a one-sided charge in a criminal case, but Paterson was not a twentieth-century judge and should not be judged by twentieth-century customs. Rather he should be judged by the customs of his own times. He knew no others.[88]

While Paterson was presiding over the trials of the various protestors, Albert Gallatin was sitting in the audience observing his performance. Gallatin was no friend of the Federalists. A year and a half earlier, they had expelled him from the Senate on the grounds of a technicality related to his citizenship. Moreover, Gallatin was sympathetic to the goals if not the methods of the protestors. Like Paterson, Gallatin concluded that "there is no doubt of [Vigol's] being guilty." More significantly, Gallatin observed all the trials, and his private opinion was that Paterson was an "excellent Judge, a sound lawyer and as impartial as could be expected." Gallatin was a discriminating observer. He was far less impressed by Judge Peters, who sat with Paterson in the Whiskey Rebellion cases. Ac-

---

87. *See* Trial of the Western Insurgents, Wharton's State Trials 102 (C.C.D. Pa. 1795). William Paterson, Charge to the Pennsylvania Grand Jury (May 4, 1795), *reprinted in* 3 DHSC 40, 41–42. John Blair, Charge to the Georgia Grand Jury (Apr. 27, 1795), *reprinted in* 3 DHSC 31–37 (Blair, J.). For criticism of Paterson, *see* O'CONNOR 233–36; SLAUGHTER 220.

88. United States v. Mitchell, Wharton's State Trials 176, 183 (C.C.D. Pa. 1795); United States v. Vigol, Wharton's State Trials 175 (C.C.D. Pa. 1795). *See* O'CONNOR at 234 (defense attorney's trial strategy).

cording to Gallatin, Peters "behaved during the whole course of the trials not as a Judge but as a Prosecutor."[89]

Gallatin was an intelligent and discriminating observer who sympathized with the tax protestors and whose political sympathy was against Federalists like Paterson. Gallatin probably knew that in commenting on the defendant's guilt, Paterson was following well-established English practice. Whether American judges routinely followed this English practice is not entirely clear. Nevertheless, Paterson's charge and Gallatin's comments support the unremarkable conclusion that there was no widespread objection in America to the settled English practice. From this eighteenth-century perspective, the modern criticism of Paterson's conduct in the Whiskey Rebellion trials is unfair.[90]

STATUTORY CRIMES: JUSTICE CHASE ON CIRCUIT

Justice Paterson's conduct in the Whiskey Rebellion trials did not engender public controversy, but the same cannot be said of Justice Chase's activities at the end of the decade. After the Sedition Act was passed in 1798, the Justices consistently supported the Act's vigorous enforcement.[91] Two years later, during Jefferson's successful struggle to unseat President Adams, an avalanche of political invective fell upon the nation. Further vigorous enforcement of the Act was to be expected during this presidential election year, and that year many of the Justices presided over sedition trials. Justice Chase, however, exceeded all others in his enthusiasm for searching out and punishing the President's critics.

Chase was such an enthusiastic supporter of Adams's reelection that he took time off from his judicial duties to stump for the President. A disgusted writer in the opposition press ironically complained, "[W]hat a becoming spectacle to see *Chase* mounted on a stump, with a face like a full moon, vociferating in favor of the present President." Given the tradition of political grand jury changes, it is not surprising that Chase was not particularly careful to distinguish between the political hustings and the judicial bench. In his 1800 charge to the Pennsylvania grand jury, he

---

89. *See* John Miller, The Federalist Era 163 (1960) (Gallatin's expulsion); Selected Writings of Albert Gallatin 18–30 (E. James Ferguson ed. 1967)(Gallatin's sympathy). Albert Gallatin to his wife, Hannah Gallatin (May 25, 1795), *excerpted in* Henry Adams, The Life of Albert Gallatin 149 (1879). Gallatin to his wife (June 1, 1795), *excerpted in* 3 DHSC 52–54.

90. For the English practice, *see* J.M. Beattie, Crime and the Courts in England 1660–1800, at 406–10 (1986). For the American practice, *see* 1 Jack Weinstein & Margaret Berger, Weinstein's Evidence ¶ 107 [01] (1993).

91. *See* Freedom's Fetters chapters 11–17.

went out of his way to compliment "our illustrious patriotic and beloved President . . . the determined foe of Vice, the uniform friend of Religion and piety, morality and Virtue." At the same time, he attacked Jefferson by innuendo and made veiled references to Jefferson's alleged atheism.[92]

In addition to stumping for the President from the bench, Chase took a special interest in the Sedition Act during that election year. He firmly believed that "a licentious press is the bane of freedom, and the Peril of Society" and rode his circuit with a vengeance against the President's critics. In Philadelphia, at the trial of Thomas Cooper, he frankly told the petit jury that he was outraged by Cooper's attack upon the President. "I cannot suppress my feelings," said Chase, "at this gross attack upon the President. . . . [The defendant] has published an untruth, knowing it to be an untruth." In Delaware the grand jury asked to be discharged without handing down an indictment, but Chase refused and specifically directed the jurors' attention to a "most seditious printer" in Wilmington. In Baltimore he unsuccessfully attempted to persuade the grand jury to indict the editor of the *Baltimore American,* which he described as "one of the most *licentious* presses in the United States."[93]

But Chase's most extreme conduct came during the trial of James Callender in Virginia. Before Chase went to Virginia, a friend gave him a copy of Callender's book, *The Prospect Before Us,* and Chase reportedly said that "if [Virginia] were not too depraved to furnish a jury of good and respectable men, he would certainly punish Callender." True to his word, Chase proceeded to Virginia, where a grand jury acting under his guidance indicted Callender for seditious libel. At the trial one of the most significant of Callender's seditious statements was a claim that

---

92. PHILADELPHIA AURORA, Aug. 9, 1800 (emphasis original), *reprinted in* 1 DHSC 895; Chase, Charge to the Pennsylvania Grand Jury (Apr. 12, 1800), *reprinted in* 3 DHSC 408, 416; James Monroe to Thomas Jefferson (May 25, 1800) *reprinted in* 3 DHSC 436–37.

93. For Chase's views on "a licentious press," *see* Samuel Chase to James McHenry (Dec. 4, 1796), *quoted in* 3 DHSC 403. *Accord,* United States v. Cooper, 25 F. Cas. 631, 639, Wharton's State Trials 659, 670–71 (C.C.D. Pa. 1800) (No. 14,865) (Chase, Petit Jury Charge). For Chases's comments at the Cooper trial, *see* United States v. Cooper, 25 F. Cas. at 640, Wharton's State Trials at 672–73 (C.C.D. Pa. 1800) (No. 14,865). For partisan and contradictory analyses of Chase's conduct at the Cooper trial, *see* Letter to Meriwether Jones (May 7, 1800) in PHILADELPHIA AURORA, June 10, 1800, *reprinted in* 3 DHSC 424–31; "Citizen," MASSACHUSETTS MERCURY (Boston), May 20, 1800, *reprinted in* 3 DHSC 433–35. For the Delaware grand jury, *see* 3 DHSC 406. For the Baltimore grand jury, *see* BALTIMORE CITY GAZETTE, June 4, 1800 (emphasis original), *reprinted in* 3 DHSC 439. The editor of the AMERICAN responded to Chase's unsuccessful attempt with suitable invective. *See* BALTIMORE AMERICAN, July 1, 1800, *quoted in* 3 DHSC 439 n.1.

"John Adams was a professed aristocrat; he had proved faithful and serviceable to the British interest." The grand jury culled nineteen other passages from Callender's book. For example, he was also indicted for writing that Adams was a "hoary headed incendiary" who persisted "in making his utmost efforts for provoking a French war."[94]

The trial was a local and national sensation in which Callender's counsel later admitted that they sought to "render a service, not to the man, but to the cause."[95] As part of this strategy, they actively confronted Chase at every opportunity. After the government had presented its evidence in support of the indictment, the defense called Col. John Taylor to establish the truth of Callender's charge that President Adams was a "professed aristocrat" who was "faithful and serviceable to the British interest." Apparently Taylor would have testified that he had personally heard Adams express opinions favorable to aristocracy and that, as Vice-President, Adams had favored the British interest when he had cast the deciding vote on two occasions when the Senate was equally divided. After a lengthy interchange between Chase and the defense counsel, Chase refused to allow Taylor to testify to the truth of Callender's statements about Adams's aristocratic inclination and his service to the British interest.

This ruling is difficult to square with the Sedition Act's provision that truth shall be a defense. Chase explained that at best Taylor's testimony would establish the truthfulness of a portion of Callender's seditious statements, but not all of them. Chase may have had in mind the nineteen other statements for which Callender was indicted, or he may have believed that the gravamen of the passage regarding aristocracy and the British interest was an implicit charge that Adams had betrayed American interests. Under either analysis, Taylor's testimony would not have established the complete truth of the seditious statements and therefore would not have established Callender's legal defense. Accordingly, Chase refused to allow Taylor to testify because a partial proof of truthfulness "would deceive and mislead the jury."[96]

Having lost on this issue, the defendant's lawyers gave up on trying to

---

94. United States v. Callender, 25 F. Cas. at 239, Wharton's State Trials at 688 (C.C.D. Va. 1800) *See* FREEDOM'S FETTERS chapter 15; Kathryn Preyer, *United States v. Callender: Judge and Jury in a Republican Society, in* ORIGINS (Marcus) at 173–95. For Chase's pretrial comment, *see* 3 DHSC 405. United States v. Callender, 25 F. Cas. at 240, Wharton's State Trials at 689 (C.C.D. Va. 1800) (quoted in grand jury indictment).

95. TRIAL OF SAMUEL CHASE, AN ASSOCIATE JUSTICE OF THE SUPREME COURT OF THE UNITED STATES 169 (S. Smith & T. Lloyd ed., 1805).

96. *See* PRESSER 134–36. 25 F. Cas. at 251, Wharton's State Trials at 707.

present evidence on the facts and attempted to argue to the jury that the Sedition Act was unconstitutional. Under this strategy, which apparently had some support in Virginia law, the jury was expected to determine the law as well as the facts of the case. If the jury determined that the law was unconstitutional, Callender's lawyers argued that a verdict of guilty "would violate [the jurors'] oaths." A few months earlier, the Virginia legislature had approved a report written by James Madison that condemned the Sedition Act as unconstitutional. Apparently the defense counsel hoped to persuade the jury to endorse Madison's argument.[97]

But Chase would have nothing of this ploy. "I tell you," he said, "that this is irregular and inadmissible." He had evidently anticipated that an attempt would be made to present this issue to the jury and had "therefore, deliberately considered the subject" and formed an "opinion [based on] mature reflection." Chase agreed that an act of Congress passed in violation of the Constitution was void and that courts should exercise a power of judicial review. But he insisted that this power was lodged exclusively with the judiciary and could not be exercised by a jury.[98]

Chase believed that the Constitution had a set meaning fixed by the people, that juries would inevitably err in interpreting the Constitution, and that "the opinions of petit juries will very probably be different in different states." He also did not trust all juries to be free from prejudice and error. In contrast, the ultimate decision of judges, he thought, would "not be influenced by political and local principles, and prejudices." Of course, even judges occasionally err. Chase noted, however, that "if inferior courts commit error, it may be rectified [by an appeal]; but if juries made mistakes, there can be no revision or control over their verdicts, and therefore, there can be no mode to obtain uniformity in their decisions." The inability to provide any effective control over juries' interpretations of the Constitution was doubly troubling because, as Chase emphasized, federal judges were sworn to uphold the Constitution. Given this "solemn obligation of religion" to uphold the Constitution, the judges could not abdicate their responsibility to uncontrollable and predictably error-prone juries.[99]

Although judges are probably somewhat better suited by training to interpret the Constitution, Chase's assumption that a judge is superior to a jury smacks of self-serving arrogance. His structural argument, how-

---

97. 25 F. Cas. at 253, Wharton's State Trials at 709. *See* James Madison, Report on the Virginia Resolutions (Jan. 7, 1800), *reprinted in* 17 MADISON PAPERS 303–51.

98. 25 F. Cas. at 253, Wharton's State Trials at 710.

99. 25 F. Cas. at 257, Wharton's State Trials at 717. *Accord,* United States v. Lyon, 15 F. Cas. 1183, 1185, Wharton's State Trials 222, 226 (C.C.D. Vt. 1798) (Paterson, J.).

ever, is not so easily dismissed. As he noted, a jury's erroneous interpretation of the Constitution was, as a practical matter, beyond "revision or control." In contrast, the tradition of appellate review provided an effective check to a trial judge's erroneous interpretation. This tradition of appellate review included the possibility that a majority of the Supreme Court might mistake or ignore the people's meaning in the Constitution, but Chase was evidently not willing to elaborate a system of judicial review based upon an assumption that a majority of the Court's Justices might be incompetent or act in bad faith.

Although Chase's analysis made a good deal of sense, it was the last straw for Callender's defense team. Throughout the proceedings, Callender's lawyers had been constantly at odds with Chase, and Chase had frequently interrupted their attempts to defend their client. After Chase rejected their attempt to argue constitutional law to the jury, they withdrew from the case. Callender was then quickly convicted and sentenced to a two-hundred-dollar fine and nine months in jail.[100]

The withdrawal of Callender's lawyers was unusual but not unheard of in cases tried by Justice Chase. The same thing had happened about a month earlier in a case arising from Fries's Rebellion.[101] During extensive protests in Pennsylvania against a federal direct tax enacted in the aftermath of the XYZ Affair, John Fries rescued some protestors from the federal marshal's custody. As a result, he was indicted in 1799 for treason and found guilty. Justice Iredell, however, decided that one of the jurors was improperly prejudiced against Fries and convinced his fellow trial judge that the case should be retried.

In 1800 Justice Chase rode the middle circuit, which included Pennsylvania. When he got to Philadelphia, he encountered problems created by Fries's first trial. That trial had lasted "9 or 10 toilsome & irksome days" with the result that a number of civil cases had been postponed. According to Judge Peters, Chase thought the first trial should have lasted no more than three or four days. If the second trial were conducted more efficiently, Chase believed, the court could "get through all the business which had accumulated on the civil side."[102] In addition to clearing out the civil backlog, Chase undoubtedly wanted to use some of

---

100. 25 F. Cas. at 258, Wharton's State Trials at 718.

101. *See* Dwight Henderson, *Treason, Sedition, and Fries' Rebellion*, 14 Am. J. Leg. Hist. 308–17 (1970); ELKINS & McKITRICK 690–700.

102. Richard Peters to Timothy Pickering (Jan. 24, 1804) (Peters Papers, PHi) (a lengthy and informative letter describing the *Fries* case). For an excellent discussion of Fries's second trial that is sympathetic to Justice Chase, *see* PRESSER 108–18 (1991).

his time in Philadelphia to ferret out seditious libel. After all, it was an election year.

In particular, Chase was concerned that Fries's attorneys would waste the court's time with "irrelevant authorities & unnecessary discussions" related to the law of treason. The Constitution and the pertinent act of Congress defined treason as "levying war against" the United States, and Fries's attorneys claimed that their client's actions may have been criminal but hardly amounted to levying war against the United States. The federal judges in the Whiskey Rebellion cases and in Fries's first trial had taken an expansive view of treason. They concluded that it "is treason to oppose or prevent by force, numbers or intimidation, a public and general law of the United States, with intent to prevent its operation or compel its repeal." Fries's attorneys devoted a good deal of the first trial to arguing that this broad definition was prone to abuse. As Judge Peters later recollected, "All the abominable and reported cases on constructive treason in England were suffered to be read [to the jury]."[103]

At the second trial Justice Chase was determined to preempt a repeat of all this wrangling over the definition of treason. Before the retrial began, he drafted a formal opinion consistent with Peters's position in the first trial, and Chase showed the opinion to Peters, who approved it. Peters later commented that Chase "had expressed what I had before delivered as my opinion better than I had done it myself."[104]

After the trial began, but before the prosecution started to present its case to the jury, Chase announced that the court had already "made up their minds as to the law of treason." He then had copies of the opinion distributed to the prosecutor, the defense attorneys, and the jury. This overt prejudging of the key issue in the case so angered the defense counsel that they announced that they would withdraw from the case. Chase tried to convince them to continue their representation, but he refused to reconsider his judgment on the issue of treason. According to Judge Peters, Chase insisted that, "if he could not make up an Opinion without Argument on the general Principles of Law, he was not fit to Sit there. All Judges of law did this."[105]

This kind of pronouncement from the bench did little to assuage the defense counsel's anger. They consulted with their client and apparently told him that given the court's broad definition of treason, there was no

---

103. Richard Peters to Timothy Pickering (Jan. 24, 1804) (Peters Papers, PHi). United States v. Fries, 9 F. Cas. 826, 908, Wharton's State Trials 584 (C.C.D. Pa. 1799) (No. 5126).
104. Richard Peters to Timothy Pickering (Jan. 24, 1804) (Peters Papers, PHi).
105. *Id.*

significant chance of an acquittal. This meant that Fries's only chance was to obtain a presidential pardon, and his lawyers believed that the absence of defense counsel at the trial would enhance the likelihood of a pardon.[106] Therefore, with the consent of their client, they formally withdrew from the case.

When Chase learned that the case would proceed without defense counsel, he told Fries in open court that "by the blessing of God, the court will be your counsel, and will do you as much justice as those who were your counsel."[107] The trial proceeded, and Fries was duly convicted and sentenced to death by hanging, as required by statute. In the end, however, President Adams pardoned Fries, as his defense team had hoped he would.

Chase was an intelligent man, an exceptionally capable lawyer, and an original thinker, but he was not fit to be a judge. His basic problem was that he had a massive ego and virtually no capacity for self-restraint. In public and private relationships he was willfully arrogant. His conduct in the trial of politically sensitive cases was probably symptomatic of an extremely narcissistic personality. He did not want to politicize judicial proceedings; he wanted to have his way. He had an obstinate inability to understand how his actions might be perceived by others. Some of the hallmarks of Chase's career were a failure to accept social norms, a disdain for the rights of others, irritability and aggressiveness, and a failure to honor financial obligations.[108] If these traits were inherent in his personality—and they appear to have been—his erratic and obnoxious behavior as a judge was a result of his personality rather than his politics.

For example, Chase's prejudging of the treason issue in *Fries* was not a departure from his practice in nonpolitical cases. He did almost the same thing in the earlier *Worrall* case when a common cheat was being prosecuted.[109] Although the earlier case was not political, Chase's preconceived opinion had obvious implications for the federal government's power to use the common law to punish political crimes. Moreover, unlike his thinking in *Fries*, Chase's preconceived opinion in *Worrall* went directly against the government. These two cases involved circuit court trials in which Chase was the senior and presiding judge in a two-judge court, but Chase occasionally displayed the same extreme behavior when he was not the senior judge. On at least one occasion, he was so obnoxious in stating a preconceived opinion

---

106. 9 F. Cas. at 941 (testimony of Fries's counsel).
107. 9 F. Cas. at 942, WHARTON'S STATE TRIALS 624 n.
108. *See* chapter 4 at 96–97.
109. *See* this chapter at 144.

and peremptorily foreclosing argument of counsel that Chief Justice Ellsworth rebuked him in open court.[110]

Eventually Chase's arrogant willfulness caught up with him. After Thomas Jefferson and his supporters gained complete control of the executive and legislative branches of the federal government in 1800, most of the federalist judges exercised self-restraint in their public political pronouncements—but not Chase. In a vituperative charge to the Baltimore grand jury, he vigorously attacked state and federal laws that conflicted with his personal political philosophy. This disdainful charge led directly to his impeachment.[111]

At Chase's subsequent trial in the Senate, the voting senators viewed his antics in Baltimore as his most reprehensible conduct. Chase was also impeached for his obnoxious conduct during the 1800 presidential election year at the *Fries* and *Callender* trials and the Delaware grand jury. Although more than two-thirds of the senators were Republicans who more or less supported Jefferson and opposed the Federalists, Chase's prosecutors were unable to muster the two-thirds vote that the Constitution requires for conviction and removal from office. The most plausible explanation is that, though a substantial number of senators believed that Chase had stretched the limits of proper judicial conduct, they did not consider his apparent politicization of the judicial process entirely outside the bounds of proper conduct.

---

110. FLANDERS 187–88 (recounting an anecdote from Uriah Tracy, who was an eyewitness).

111. *See generally* HASKINS & JOHNSON 215–34, 238–45; RICHARD ELLIS, THE JEFFERSONIAN CRISIS 76–107 (1971).

6

Nonjudicial Activities

Throughout the 1790s, the Justices engaged in a wide range of non-judicial activities, and many of the most significant incidents related to national security. The diplomatic missions of Chief Justices Jay and Ellsworth to Great Britain and France are obvious examples.[1] Jay and Ellsworth also gave legal advice to the executive branch on international and domestic law. But the Court refused to render a formal advisory opinion during the Neutrality Crisis of 1793. The Justices' abiding concerns regarding nonjudicial activities were to maintain separation of powers, to preserve federal judicial independence, and to support the new government. They were not guided by inflexible rules; their actions are better described as the pragmatic application of general principles to specific situations.

In his first grand jury charge, Chief Justice Jay provided the most valuable and insightful commentary on the fundamental principle of separation of powers. Jay emphasized that all "wise and virtuous Men" agreed that a government's

> Powers should be divided into three, distinct, independent Departments—The Executive legislative and judicial. But how to constitute and balance them in such a Manner as best to guard against Abuse and Fluctuation, & preserve the Constitution from Encroachments, are Points on which there continues to be a great Diversity of opinions, and on which we have all as yet much to learn. . . . If the most discerning and enlightened Minds may be mistaken relative to Theories unconfirmed by Practice—if on such difficult Questions men may differ in opinion and yet be Patriots,

---

1. *See* chapter 4 at 87–90 & 118–19.

. . . let us patiently abide the Tryal, and unite our Endeavors to render it a fair and an impartial one.[2]

Thus Jay saw both separation of powers and judicial independence as concepts in evolution. The Court was embarking upon a "Tryal" of "Theories [outlined in the Constitution but] unconfirmed by Practice." As the decade progressed, the Justices had to apply the general principle of separation of powers to various extrajudicial activities.

EX-OFFICIO DUTIES

The early Congresses passed many statutes assigning essentially administrative and executive duties to the federal judges. For example, in 1790 the Sinking Fund Commission, consisting of the Chief Justice, the Vice-President, and three cabinet members, was created to use surplus revenues to liquidate outstanding debts of the United States. Similarly, when the United States Mint was established two years later, Congress created a blue-ribbon panel to inspect the Mint's assaying operations and assure the nation that the coins had the proper content of gold or silver. The panel included the Chief Justice and appropriate cabinet officers.[3]

Chief Justices Jay and Ellsworth were willing to use the dignity of their office to bolster public confidence in these two sensitive fiscal operations. Whether anyone ever questioned the propriety of these nonjudicial services is not known. In 1792 a conflict arose between Jay's circuit-riding duties and a meeting of the Sinking Fund Commission. In Jay's absence, the Commission was evenly divided on whether the proposed repurchase price of some government debt exceeded the ceiling established by the Commission's organic statute. Jay declined a request to attend the meeting because he viewed his "Duty to attend the Courts as being in point of legal obligation primary, and to attend the [meeting of the Sinking Fund] Trustees as secondary." He did, however, break the deadlock by sending a formal written opinion construing the statutory language in question.[4]

---

2. John Jay, Charge to the New York Grand Jury (Apr. 12, 1790), *reprinted in* 2 DHSC 25–30.

3. For brief summaries of seventeen different early Acts of Congress assigning administrative duties to the federal judges, *see* 4 DHSC, App. A at 723–29. For the Sinking Fund Commission and the United States Mint, *see* Russell Wheeler, *Extrajudicial Activities of the Early Supreme Court*, 1793 Sup. Ct. Rev. 123, 139–44 (1973).

4. John Jay to Alexander Hamilton (Mar. 23, 1792), *reprinted in* 11 Hamilton Papers 172–73. Jay's written opinion is in 1 ASP, Finance 236.

THE INVALID PENSIONERS ACT

In the spring of 1792, Congress established a pension program for disabled Revolutionary War veterans. Under this program, a veteran was to submit his application for pension to the federal circuit court in his state. This court would examine the applicant's proofs and determine the nature and extent of his wounds and whether they were service-related. The court would then give the Secretary of War a written opinion certifying that the applicant should be added to the pension list. If the Secretary had "cause to suspect imposition or mistake," he was authorized to withhold the applicant's pension and report the withholding to Congress.[5]

This Act was obviously a commendable measure. Nevertheless, every Justice and four district judges almost immediately registered their opinions that the Constitution did not authorize the circuit courts to assume the duties assigned to them by the Act. They thought the Act was unconstitutional. The Justices recognized that Congress had extensive authority over the lower federal courts, but they firmly stated that Congress could not assign nonjudicial duties to the courts. Because the business assigned to the circuit courts was nonjudicial, the Justices concluded that they were forbidden by the Constitution to process the veterans' applications.[6]

The actual processing of applications looked more like what we would call today an administrative claims procedure than a traditional judicial case or controversy between a plaintiff and a defendant, and the Justices were inclined to believe that this aspect of the Act was unconstitutional. But their major objection was to the power of the Secretary of War and the Congress to review the courts' decisions. In New York, Chief Justice Jay and Justice Cushing explained that "by the constitution, neither the Secretary of War, nor any other executive officer, nor even the Legislature, are authorized to sit as a court of errors on the judicial acts or opinions of this court." In North Carolina, Justice Iredell elaborated on this point by noting that Congress had authority to establish appellate courts

---

5. Act of Mar. 23, 1792, ch. 11, 1 Stat. 243 (1792). *See* Maeva Marcus & Robert Teir, *Hayburn's Case: A Misinterpretation of Precedent,* 1988 Wis. L. Rev. 527 (1988).

6. For Justices Jay and Cushing, *see* Opinion of John Jay, William Cushing, and James Duane (Apr. 5, 1792), *reprinted in* 1 ASP, Miscellaneous 49–50 and 2 U.S. (2 Dall.) 410 n. For Justices Wilson and Blair, *see* James Wilson, John Blair, and Richard Peters to George Washington (Apr. 18, 1792), *reprinted in* 1 ASP, Miscellaneous 51 and 2 U.S. (2 Dall.) 411 n. For Justice Iredell, *see* James Iredell and John Sitgreaves to George Washington (June 8, 1792), *reprinted in* 1 ASP, Miscellaneous 52–53; and 2 U.S. (2 Dall.) 412–14 n. For Justice Johnson and presumably District Judge Thomas Bee of South Carolina, *see* GOEBEL 561 n.37.

other than the Supreme Court but that the judges of those courts would have to have the constitutional protection of an undiminishable salary and tenure during good behavior. These prerequisites obviously disqualified Congress and the executive branch from serving as an appellate court.[7]

The Justices' analyses may have been somewhat sterile, but their opinions were clearly keyed to the express words of the Constitution. The fact was that under the Act, the Secretary of War exercised a kind of appellate review over the Circuit Courts, and the Constitution made no provision for nonjudicial appellate review of the federal courts. Therefore, the Invalid Pensioners Act seemed to be clearly (albeit technically) in violation of the Constitution. In addition to this textual analysis, Chief Justice Jay and Justice Cushing raised a major policy consideration that informed their interpretation of the Constitution's language. They wrote that the federal government "is divided into *three* distinct and independent branches; and it is the duty of each to abstain from and to oppose encroachments on either."[8]

Although Justices Jay, Cushing, and Iredell were adamant in their conclusion that the Invalid Pensioners Act was unconstitutional, they became pragmatic when they decided how to act on this conclusion. They understood that the Act was popular, and they personally believed that it was "founded on the purest principles of humanity." They also understood that if they failed to perform their duties, many disabled veterans would have their benefits seriously delayed, and some might even die before Congress could rectify the problem. For these reasons, they settled upon a wildly implausible construction of the Act's language that avoided the constitutional problem and permitted the judges to process applications.[9]

Chief Justice Jay and Justice Cushing came up with a clever legal fiction. Instead of assigning duties to the circuit courts, they said, the Act should "be considered as appointing commissioners for the purposes mentioned in it by *official* instead of *personal* descriptions"—that is, by mere reference to the circuit courts rather than by naming the individu-

---

7. *See* Opinion of John Jay, William Cushing, and James Duane, *cited in supra* note 4; James Iredell and John Sitgreaves to George Washington (June 8, 1792), *cited in supra* note 6.

8. *See* Opinion of John Jay, William Cushing, and James Duane (emphasis original), *cited in supra* note 6.

9. *See* Opinion of John Jay, William Cushing, and James Duane, *cited in supra* note 6; James Iredell and John Sitgreaves to George Washington (June 8, 1792), *cited in supra* note 6.

als. Under this strained construction, the Act merely offered the judges a nonjudicial office, and the judges were therefore "at liberty to accept or to decline that office." In North Carolina, Justice Iredell reluctantly agreed to this stopgap solution.[10]

Justices Wilson and Blair in Pennsylvania and possibly Justice Johnson in South Carolina took a different tack. Wilson and Blair agreed that the Act was an unconstitutional imposition of nonjudicial duties on the Circuit Courts. They also agreed and emphasized that the Act's provision for nonjudicial "revision and control [was] radically inconsistent with the independence of that judicial power which is vested in the courts." But Wilson was unwilling to go through the charade of processing veterans' applications in a nonjudicial capacity as a commissioner. Instead, he simply refused to hear any petitions. In response to this action, the Attorney General determined to bring a test case in the Supreme Court to resolve the manner in which pensioners' petitions were to be processed. In *Hayburn* the Attorney General asked the Court to issue a writ of mandamus directing the circuit court in Pennsylvania to process the petition of William Hayburn.[11]

Notwithstanding the Attorney General's efforts, the Supreme Court did not reach the merits of Hayburn's petition. After some initial sparring over whether the Attorney General needed express permission from the President to seek a writ of mandamus, the Court heard arguments on the merits. But instead of deciding whether to grant the Attorney General's motion for a writ, the Court "observed, that they would hold the motion under advisement, until the next term." This delay, which would have lasted from August 1792 until February 1793, was not acceptable to Congress. Before the Court commenced the February term, new legislation was enacted to remove the circuit courts from the pension process. As a result, the Court apparently never decided the constitutional issue addressed by the individual Justices in their advisory opinions. It did, however, subsequently hold in *United States v. Yale Todd* that the Justices were not authorized to serve as commissioners. The *Todd* decision is unreported, so we do not know whether the Court's decision

---

10. *See* Opinion of John Jay, William Cushing, and James Duane (emphasis original), *cited in supra* note 6; James Iredell and John Sitgreaves to George Washington (June 8, 1792), *cited in supra* note 6.

11. James Wilson, John Blair, and Richard Peters to George Washington (Apr. 18, 1792), *cited in supra* note 4. *See also* GOEBEL 561 n.37 (discussing Justice Johnson); James Iredell to Hannah Iredell (Sept. 30, 1792), *excerpted in* 2 DHSC 301–2 (Wilson's refusal); Hayburn's Case, 2 U.S. (2 Dall.) 409 (1792).

was based upon the Constitution, a construction of the Invalid Pensioners Act, or some other analysis.[12]

ADVISORY OPINIONS

The Justices were flexible in their willingness to provide advisory opinions. Today the Court's 1793 refusal to answer questions about American
neutrality is usually viewed as establishing the impropriety of advisory
opinions, but this current understanding is at odds with the Justices' actual practice. Before and after the 1793 refusal, individual Justices wrote
formal advisory opinions. Soon after taking office, Chief Justice Jay provided President Washington with a lengthy advisory opinion on international law during the Nootka Sound Crisis and later saw no problem in
penning an advisory opinion for the Sinking Fund Commission on a
mundane issue of statutory construction. Similarly, Chief Justice
Ellsworth was willing to write an elaborate advisory opinion on the President's obligation to surrender papers related to the Jay Treaty, and Secretary of State Pickering felt no qualms in seeking Ellsworth's advice on
halting the sale of prizes. Associate Justices also gave advice. Justice
Chase wrote an advisory opinion on the President's authority to appoint
a public printer.[13]

The most interesting and troubling of the Justices' advisory opinions
dealt with criminal prosecutions. The Justices routinely used their grand
jury charges as a medium for delivering advisory opinions, and they also
occasionally gave private advisory opinions on significant issues of criminal law. When Robert Worrall tried to bribe the Commissioner of Revenue, the Commissioner sought and received advice from Justice
Paterson. More significantly, Chief Justices Jay and Ellsworth gave more
formal general advisory opinions on issues of criminal law that they
knew might come before them in cases they would try. During the Neutrality Crisis of 1793, Jay drafted a presidential proclamation calling for
the prosecution of Americans who violated the country's neutrality. In so

---

12. *See* United States v. Yale Todd, unreported (1794), *noted in* 54 U.S. (13 How.)
52–53; Maeva Marcus & Robert Teir, *Hayburn's Case: A Misinterpretation of Precedent*,
1988 WIS. L. REV. 527, 534–41 (1988); Susan Bloch & Maeva Marcus, *John Marshall's
Selective Use of History in Marbury v. Madison*, 1986 WIS. L. REV. 301, 308–10 (1986).
13. *See generally* Russell Wheeler, *Extrajudicial Activities of the Early Supreme Court*, 1973
SUP. CT. REV. 123, 144–58 (1973). For Nootka Sound and the Sinking Fund, *see*
chapter 4 at 71–72 and this chapter at 174. For Chief Justice Ellsworth, *see* chapter 4
at 149. For Justice Chase, *see* 1 BERNARD STEINER, THE LIFE AND CORRESPONDENCE OF JAMES
MCHENRY 431 n.3 (1907) (reprinting Chase's opinion).

doing, he prejudged the propriety of common-law prosecutions. Similarly, when Secretary of State Timothy Pickering asked Ellsworth about the constitutionality of the Sedition Act, Ellsworth responded on the merits. This Ellsworth-Pickering correspondence was not a casual exchange of ideas among friends. In the 1790s, the Secretary of State was the national coordinator of federal criminal prosecutions. Ellsworth knew this and also must have assumed that he would soon be trying cases under the Sedition Act.[14]

The early Justices also provided Congress with direct and indirect advice on the proper legislative organization and regulation of the federal judiciary. They frequently communicated with Congress, usually through the President, in a sustained effort to ameliorate the hardships of circuit riding. In addition, when individual Justices noticed glitches in federal statutes, they felt no compunction in informally proposing solutions to members of Congress. On occasion, the Justices actually drafted legislation or commented on pending legislation.[15]

A final form of advisory opinion was the writing of pseudonymous newspaper articles by Justice Paterson and others. In particular, Paterson was a prolific newspaper essayist while he served on the Court. Beginning in 1793, after he had been asked by President Washington to join the Court, Paterson wrote a series of at least forty-six newspaper essays. In these essays Paterson addressed a wide range of local and national political issues, and he incorporated some of the essays into the political portions of his grand jury charges. He did not, however, publish essays about legal issues that were before the Court. In one series of essays written in 1795, he vehemently defended the Jay Treaty. In other essays he called for the construction of better roads and for the reform of state election laws.[16]

---

14. For Justice Paterson, *see* chapter 5 at 141. For Chief Justice Jay, *see* chapter 4 at 74–75. For Chief Justice Ellsworth, *see* chapter 5 at 149.

15. *See* Maeva Marcus & Emily Van Tassel, *Judges and Legislators in the New Federal System, 1789–1800, in* JUDGES AND LEGISLATORS: TOWARD INSTITUTIONAL COMITY 31, 43–52 (R. Katzman ed., 1988).

16. *See* IREDELL CORRESPONDENCE 307–20 (discussing, inter alia, the Funding System's constitutionality); O'CONNOR 197, 225–26, 229, 239–41, 272; Richard McCormick, *Political Essays of William Paterson*, 18 RUTGERS U. LIB. J. 48 (1955) (reprinting Paterson's first five essays). For parallels between Paterson's essays and his grand jury charges, *see* 3 DHSC 13 n. & 459 n.

A PRAGMATIC APPROACH TO NONJUDICIAL ACTIVITIES

In retrospect, it is apparent that clear and absolute rules were not used for gauging the propriety of judicial participation in nonjudicial activities. Chief Justice Jay began his first grand jury charge by reminding America that there was serious doubt "[w]hether any People can long govern themselves in an equal uniform & orderly manner," and he went on to warn against relying upon "Theories unconfirmed by Practice."[17] As the decade progressed, practice was always emphasized over theory. Rather than follow fixed rules, the Justices resolved particular issues by an almost ad hoc weighing and balancing of a number considerations against the utility of the specific activity being considered. Some of the significant considerations were the problem of prejudging, the need to protect the judicial branch from encroachments by the legislative and executive branches, and whether the nonjudicial activity involved the Court as an institution or the Justices in their individual capacities. In each instance, however, the primary (though not necessarily overriding) concern was to support the new government and thereby contribute to the people's effort to "govern themselves."

Insofar as advisory opinions are concerned, a distinction might be drawn between private opinions offered by individual Justices and formal opinions issued by the Court as an institution. The Justices, however, never explicitly drew this distinction. They refused to provide an institutional advisory opinion when the President asked for one, but the precise reasons for their refusal are obscure. In contrast to their delphic response to the President's 1793 request, they had few qualms about rendering apparently institutional advisory opinions regarding the constitutionality of the Invalid Pensioners Act. Some of the Justices offered their opinions in letters written to the President, but Chief Justice Jay, Justice Cushing, and Judge Duane, who constituted the circuit court for New York, seem to have opted for an institutional advisory opinion. Like their fellow Justices, they believed the Act was unconstitutional and sent a copy of their opinion to the President. Although their opinion was issued as an abstract consideration of the Act rather than a determination of a specific application before the court, they also formally recorded their opinion in the minutes of the circuit court. This seemingly innocuous procedural step suggests that their opinion was the formal opinion of the circuit court itself rather than their collective private views. Sophisticated contemporary observers viewed the opinion as a de-

---

17. *See* introduction at 1 and this chapter at 173–74.

cision of the court, and later that year Justice Cushing indicated sensitivity to the implication of entering nonjudicial decisions in the circuit court minutes. Although he served as a commissioner for petitions under the Act, he took care that his decisions were made "without making any entry in the book about it."[18]

The Justices were also concerned about encroachments upon the judicial branch that would jeopardize their independence. When Congress passed the Invalid Pensioners Act, the Justices united in agreeing that Congress lacked constitutional authority to impose mandatory nonjudicial duties on the judiciary. Similarly, in their response to the President's formal request for advice on American neutrality, the Justices clearly rejected the idea that the President could require them to provide legal advice. But even in the case of mandatory nonjudicial duties, they displayed a pragmatic flexibility. The first few Congresses assigned an astonishing number of nonjudicial administrative duties to the federal judges, and except in the case of the Invalid Pensioners Act, the Justices acquiesced. Chief Justices Jay and Ellsworth probably viewed their services at the Mint and on the Sinking Fund Commission as a *de minimis* encroachment that had no significant impact upon the performance of their primary judicial obligations. Therefore they probably never considered the possibility that these minor activities might have been improper.

The clearest examples of the Justices' flexibility were the Invalid Pensioners Act and their 1793 refusal to answer the President's questions about neutrality. In the former case, they firmly rejected congressional authority to impose mandatory nonjudicial duties on the courts and then engrafted a transparent legal fiction on the statute to authorize them to perform their assigned duties as commissioners rather than judges. In the latter case, they refused the President's formal request for advice and yet answered the most important questions in grand jury charges and by expediting the appeal in *Glass v. The Sloop Betsy.*

When Chief Justices Jay and Ellsworth were appointed to diplomatic missions in Europe, there were objections that the availability of these salaried positions would encroach upon the judiciary's independence by "teaching them to look for lucrative employment from . . . the Executive." This concern, however, did not prevent the Senate from confirming the appointments. The same concern was registered in early 1800,

---

18. James Kent, *An Introductory Lecture to a Course of Law Lectures* (1794), *reprinted in* 2 AMERICAN POLITICAL WRITING DURING THE FOUNDING ERA 936, 943 † Charles Hyneman & Donald Lutz ed., 1983). William Cushing to John Jay (Oct. 23, 1792), *reprinted in* 2 DHSC 319–20.

when efforts were made to bar federal judges from dual office holding. These efforts were unsuccessful.[19]

Some of the Justices' most prominent nonjudicial activities implicated the problem of prejudging. When Chief Justice Jay was sent to Europe, North Carolina's senators objected that, as a treaty negotiator, he would "become a legislator, and on his return will assume the judicial Chair, and he the Expositor and Judge of his own legislation." Similarly, advisory opinions frequently required the Justices to judge legal issues in advance of actual litigation. In 1793 the Justices explained that "our being judges of a court in the last resort" was a consideration that afforded a strong argument against providing the President with an advisory opinion.[20]

Justice Iredell and District Judge John Sitgreaves of North Carolina provided a clear statement of this consideration in a 1792 letter to President Washington. "[W]e have some doubts," they wrote,

> as to the propriety of giving an opinion in a case which has not yet come regularly and judicially before us. None can be more sensible than we are of the necessity of judges being, in general, extremely cautious in not intimating an opinion in any case extra-judicially, because we well know how liable the best minds are, notwithstanding their utmost care, to a bias which may arise from a preconceived opinion, even unjudicially, much more deliberately given.[21]

This cogent statement of the problem of prejudging is especially valuable because it was written in the context of a pure advisory opinion on the Invalid Pensioners Act. Iredell and Sitgreaves clearly did not view the problem of prejudging as requiring an absolute bar to extrajudicial activities. They saw it rather as warranting a "general rule" and felt free to carve out an "exception" based upon "humanity and justice." They also refused to believe that they personally would be irretrievably biased by a premature extrajudicial consideration of the issue. "[I]f we can be convinced that this opinion is a wrong one, we shall not hesitate to act accordingly," they wrote.[22] This same pragmatic approach undoubtedly informed the judgments of Chief Justices Jay and Ellsworth. Both men

---

19. Rufus King, Notes of Senate Debate (Apr. 17, 1794), *reprinted in* 1 KING CORRESPONDENCE 521–22 (1894). *See* WHEELER 223–24, discussing legislative activities in 10 ANNALS 41, 67, 97–102, 147, 150, 523. For the Jay and Ellsworth missions, *see* chapter 4 at 87–90 & 118–19.

20. *See* chapter 4 at 79.

21. *See* James Iredell and John Stigreaves to George Washington (June 8, 1792), *cited in supra* note 6.

22. *Id.*

were willing to give advisory opinions on issues of criminal law that they knew would come before them in criminal prosecutions they would try.

The Justices' willingness to provide advisory opinions was facilitated by the eighteenth century's predominant theories of natural law and the judicial process. In that century people did not believe that judges were lawmakers but rather that they decided cases according to preexisting principles that they found in statutes, written constitutions, or the natural law. In light of this sincerely held belief, an advisory opinion was not radically different from a judicial opinion written to decide an actual case. Both were the judge's personal opinion of what the law was. Neither a private advisory opinion nor a formal judicial opinion had the status of being a law.

7

The Constitution
and State Sovereignty

Perhaps the most difficult and important task in implementing the new Constitution was to work out the appropriate relationship between the federal and state governments. Under the Constitution, each government was sovereign within its respective sphere. The problem was to determine the limits of those spheres and to devise appropriate allocations of authority where the spheres overlapped. No problem has plagued the nation's constitutional history more. Over the course of two centuries, this inherent intergovernmental conflict has been managed principally by the legislative and executive branches, but the judicial branch has played a significant supporting role.

The Supreme Court's power to review and overturn the judgments of state courts is an obvious source of intergovernmental friction, but no one seriously challenged this particular authority to trump state sovereignty until the Supreme Court exercised the power in a controversial decision in 1813. During the first decade of the Supreme Court's operation, only seven appeals were taken from state court judgments, and none was controversial. In fact, only two of the appeals seem to have involved a significant federal interest. *Olney v. Arnold* and *Olney v. Dexter* involved state tort actions against a federal revenue officer, but nothing came of these cases. The Supreme Court agreed with the state courts and affirmed their judgments.[1]

This *de minimis* volume of appeals from the state courts was not coincidental. It resulted from Oliver Ellsworth's drafting decision to minimize the necessity of federal appellate review of state courts by authorizing important federal cases to be filed initially in federal trial courts. The success of this conscious legislative strategy is illustrated by

---

1. *See* Goebel 802; Olney v. Arnold, 3 U.S. (3 Dall.) 308 (1796); Olney v. Dexter, unreported (U.S. 1796), *briefly described in* Goebel 674 n.35.

the administration of the federal revenue laws. The 1790s witnessed a tremendous amount of litigation over the federal revenue laws that would have been a major irritant to intergovernmental relations if the cases had been tried in state court. But they were not, and as a result, important Supreme Court appellate decisions like *United States v. La Vengeance* and *Hylton v. United States* did not have to carry the added baggage of involving a conflict between the federal and state judiciaries.[2]

Ellsworth's Judiciary Act also preempted possible conflicts with state courts by significantly limiting the federal courts' authority to issue writs of habeas corpus. As twentieth-century experience amply demonstrates, this particular common-law writ can be a fertile source of conflict between the federal and state judiciaries, and at least one senator in the first Congress was aware of the inevitable relationship between "Habeas Corpus & Sovereignty of the State." Whether a federal judge in the early Republic would actually have used the writ as a basis for reviewing the legality of state criminal proceedings is unclear. In any event, the potential problem was mooted by the Judiciary Act's provision forbidding the use of federal habeas corpus relief to free prisoners held under authority of state law.[3]

The Judiciary Act also averted many potential clashes with the state judiciaries by limiting the Supreme Court's appellate jurisdiction over state courts to specific issues controlled by the Constitution, acts of Congress, and treaties. This limitation lent immensely significant practical and theoretical support to the Supreme Court's appellate authority over state courts. At a theoretical level, it assured that every time the authority was exercised, the Court was functioning as the ultimate interpreter of a uniform and supreme federal law. At a practical level, the Judiciary Act allocated state and federal jurisdiction in such a way that state courts decided comparatively few federal issues that were worth appealing to the Supreme Court. By and large, the most significant issues of federal law adjudicated by courts in the early Republic involved criminal laws, revenue laws, admiralty law, and treaties of the United States. With the notable exception of the protections afforded British creditors under Article IV of the Treaty of Paris, the Judiciary Act was intentionally drafted to allocate virtually all of these issues to federal trial courts.[4]

Although the Judiciary Act's five-hundred-dollar limitation on claims protected by the Treaty was a significant exception to this drafting prin-

---

2. *See* chapter 4 at 101–09 (discussing La Vengeance and Hylton).
3. William Paterson, Notes on Judiciary Bill Debate (June 24–27, 1789), *reprinted in* 4 DHSC 421; Judiciary Act, § 14.
4. *See* chapter 2 at 38–47.

ciple, the exception did not have much practical impact upon the Supreme Court's appellate jurisdiction over the thousands of disputes relegated to the state courts. Given the notorious bias of the state courts, all British creditors with claims of over five hundred dollars filed their suits in the federal trial courts. As a result, the Supreme Court never had to exercise its appellate jurisdiction over state courts in the context of a suit by a British creditor for a significant amount of money. In theory, the smaller claims that had to be tried in state court might have been appealed to the national Supreme Court insofar as the claims turned upon the application of the Treaty. This theoretical right, however, had no attraction to creditors who by definition were motivated by financial considerations. The game was not worth the candle. Why spend a few hundred dollars to appeal a case that was worth only a few hundred dollars?

Even an utterly pragmatic creditor could see the theoretical value of obtaining a Supreme Court adjudication that could be used as precedent in many other small claims. But as a practical matter, there was no need to appeal a small claim from a state court to obtain a valuable Supreme Court precedent. The more economical strategy was to appeal a large claim from one of the federal trial courts, and this is what happened in *Ware v. Hylton*.[5]

Such practical dynamics, however, did not reach a major dispute over three hundred thousand acres in northern Virginia that were confiscated from Lord Fairfax during the Revolution. Beginning in the 1790s, the state and federal courts strove to resolve the title to this land in a complex series of interrelated suits that considered, among other things, the effect of the Treaty of Paris and the Jay Treaty upon the dispute. When the Supreme Court eventually overruled the Virginia Court of Appeals in 1813, the state court denied the federal court's constitutional authority to review state court judgments.[6]

In 1816 Justice Story's opinion in *Martin v. Hunter's Lessee* provided persuasive justification for the Supreme Court's appellate authority over the state courts. Although the Constitution did not expressly mention this authority, Story emphasized as "an historical fact" that the framers, ratifiers, and members of the First Congress had assumed that the Supreme Court had the authority. This analysis would have been equally persuasive in the 1790s, but the Judiciary Act's careful allocation of ju-

---

5. *See* chapter 4 at 98–101.

6. *See* Fairfax's Devisee v. Hunter's Lessee, 7 Cranch 603 (1813) and Martin v. Hunter's Lessee, 1 Wheat. 304 (1816), *discussed in* HASKINS & JOHNSON 357–65. *See also Editorial Note on Fairfax Lands, in* 2 MARSHALL PAPERS 140–49.

risdiction had purchased the Court some two decades of breathing space. Justice Story commented,

> It is an historical fact, that the supreme court of the United States have, from time to time, sustained this appellate jurisdiction in a great variety of cases brought from the tribunals of many of the most important states in the union, and that no state tribunal has ever breathed a judicial doubt on the subject, or declined to obey the mandate of the supreme court, until the present occasion.

And so the issue was settled with the partial assistance of a legacy from Ellsworth's Judiciary Act.[7]

In addition to the inevitable friction caused by the Supreme Court's appellate review of state court judgments, clashes between state legislation and federal law were inevitable. Fortunately, the Constitution's supremacy clause provided an unmistakable rule for resolving such conflicts: "This Constitution, and the Laws of the United States which shall be made in Pursuance thereof; and all Treaties made, or which shall be made, under the Authority of the United States, shall be the supreme Law of the Land." As early as *Ware v. Hylton* the Justices unanimously agreed that this language means what it says. Acting under authority of this explicit constitutional rule of decision, the Court in *Ware* exercised its power of judicial review and declared the state statute at issue to be unconstitutional.[8]

The *Ware* case actually involved two issues of constitutional law, as do all instances of judicial review. In addition to determining whether the legislation in question was contrary to the Constitution, the Court implicitly held that it had constitutional authority to declare a statute void. Although the Justices in *Ware* did not address the fundamental question of judicial review, they undoubtedly would have justified judicial review of state legislation on the same theory on which they justified judicial review of federal legislation. The Court did not view judicial review as a discretionary power but rather as the simple ministerial implementation of the people's sovereign will. A judicial declaration that a statute was unconstitutionally void presented no constitutional dilemma as long as the Court was merely giving force to the sovereign will of the people as clearly expressed in the Constitution. In this regard, the state and federal governments were equally subordinate to the people. Subsequently, in *Calder v. Bull,* Justice Iredell explained judicial review of state legislation in terms

---

7. 1 Wheat. at 351–52.
8. U.S. Const. art. VI; *see* chapter 4 at 98–101.

of the people's sovereign constitutional will. Similarly, in *Chisholm v. Georgia*, Chief Justice Jay and Justice Wilson each based federal jurisdiction over suits against states on the people's sovereign authority to override state sovereign immunity.[9]

CHISHOLM V. GEORGIA

In 1791, almost as soon as the federal circuit court in Georgia opened for business, Alexander Chisholm commenced a lawsuit in the federal courts that culminated two years later in the Supreme Court's most controversial decision of the 1790s. Mr. Chisholm was the executor of Robert Farquhar, a deceased South Carolina merchant who had sold the state of Georgia goods in the value of some sixty-four thousand pounds sterling during the Revolution. The state evidently had never paid, and Chisholm was suing for principal, interest, and damages in the amount of a hundred thousand pounds sterling.[10]

In response, the state contended that the circuit court lacked jurisdiction to try a suit against a state and asked that the case be dismissed. In a lengthy unpublished opinion, Justice Iredell, who was the circuit Justice in the case, concluded that the court indeed lacked jurisdiction, and the case was dismissed. Iredell advanced two separate analyses in support of his conclusion. First, he presented the exclusive jurisdiction analysis that he later used without success in *Ravara*. Just as the Supreme Court's original trial jurisdiction over cases involving consuls excluded all other federal courts' jurisdiction, so too did the Supreme Court's original jurisdiction over cases in which a state is a party. He went on to argue that, in any event, when Congress enacted the Judiciary Act, it chose not to vest the circuit courts with authority to try suits against states.[11]

Because the Judiciary Act's express grant of original jurisdiction to the circuit courts clearly did not extend to suits against states, the plaintiff's attorneys evidently relied upon section 13 of the Judiciary Act, which vested the Supreme Court with "exclusive jurisdiction of all controversies of a civil nature when a state is a party, except between a state and its citizens; and *except* also between a state and citizens of other states, or

---

9. Calder v. Bull, 3 U.S. (3 Dall.) 386, 398 (1796). For Jay and Wilson, *see* this chapter at 192–96. For the judicial review of legislation, *see* chapter 8 at 214–22.

10. *See* Chisholm v. Georgia, 2 U.S. (2 Dall.) 419 (1793). For good discussions of this litigation, *see* Mathis, *Chisholm v. Georgia: Background and Settlement*, 54 J. Am. Hist. 19 (1967); and Marcus & Wexler 78–80.

11. Iredell, Opinion in Farquhar v. Georgia (C.C.D. Ga. 1791), *reprinted in* 5 DHSC 148–55. For Ravara, *see* chapter 5 at 139–41 and chapter 8 at 222–25.

aliens, in which latter case it shall have original but not exclusive jurisdiction."[12] The argument was that the second "except" clause in this provision clearly envisioned a concurrent jurisdiction in some other court
and therefore implicitly vested the federal Circuit Court with a concurrent jurisdiction over a suit between "a state and citizens of other states."

Iredell's response was simple, straightforward, and persuasive. The
reference to concurrent jurisdiction "ought to be construed as implying a
permission for such jurisdiction to continue as before in the state courts."
Iredell continued, "[C]ertainly it cannot reasonably be maintained that
when the powers of this [circuit] court are expressly & particularly defined we should assume additional jurisdiction from an implication
merely arising out of an ambiguous exception (if it be such) to the definition of the powers of another Court."[13]

Chisholm was undaunted by the dismissal of his suit. Justice Iredell
had indicated that the Supreme Court was the only federal court competent to try the case, so Chisholm immediately refiled his suit in the Supreme Court. To give further weight to the suit, Chisholm retained
Attorney General Randolph to try the case as a private attorney. Randolph quickly filed a motion that forced the Supreme Court to grapple
with the issue of whether the states were suable in federal court.

This suit threatened to alter the traditional relationship between the
states and their creditors. The states had traditionally claimed that their
sovereign status rendered them immune to suit, but this claim of immunity should not be read as evidence that the states systematically refused
to comply with their contractual obligations. If they had, no one would
have dealt with them. They would not have been able to borrow money
or to purchase goods on credit. Sovereign immunity simply narrowed
creditors' remedial options to negotiation and reliance upon a state's
good faith. At least in large commercial transactions and state borrow-
ings, this narrowing of remedies presumably resulted in states' having to
pay a higher price for goods or loans. Therefore a decision that the states
were freely suable in federal court would result in a creditors' windfall.

Making the states suable in federal court would have been a federal
encroachment upon state sovereignty. Standing alone, this theoretical
objection probably would not have been enough to create a significant
political crisis as long as the contemplated suits were not otherwise significant. But some of the suits filed before and after the Supreme Court's

---

12. Judiciary Act § 13 (emphasis added).
13. Iredell, Opinion in Farquhar v. Georgia (C.C.D. Ga. 1791), *reprinted in* 5 DHSC
148–55.

decision in *Chisholm* were significant and involved substantial sums of money. Chisholm's claim for a hundred thousand pounds sterling (which by federal law equaled five hundred thousand dollars) was not atypical. In *Van Stophorst v. Maryland,* an earlier case filed in the Supreme Court but settled out of court, two Dutch financiers sought to recover a little over two hundred thousand dollars on loans to the state. *Hollingsworth v. Virginia* involved a claim in excess of a million dollars. In *Hollingsworth,* a group of Pennsylvanians who were shareholders in the Indiana Company sued over a land transaction that had taken place before the Revolutionary War. In 1768 some Indian tribes had conveyed about three million acres of land to the Pennsylvanians in reparation for a substantial amount of property that the Indians had seized. The Virginian legislature, however, refused to approve the conveyance, with the result that the Pennsylvanians did not obtain lawful title to the land.[14]

In deciding *Chisholm,* four of the Justices were more or less in agreement that the Constitution abrogated the states' sovereign immunity and subjected them to suit in the Supreme Court. Justices Cushing and Blair based their opinions almost entirely upon a simple parsing of the Constitution. Article III, §2 provided that the federal judicial power "shall extend to . . . Controversies . . . between a State and Citizens of another state [and that] in all cases . . . in which a State shall be a Party, the supreme Court shall have original Jurisdiction." This language determined the case in Cushing's and Blair's opinions. Jay and Wilson placed the same interpretation on the Constitution's words but wrote far more elaborate opinions. Only Justice Iredell thought Georgia was not suable.

Justice Iredell presented a superficially comprehensive analysis, in which he first considered the Constitution and then turned to relevant acts of Congress. His opinion is particularly interesting, however, for the glaring gaps in each step of his analysis. These gaps are so serious that his entire opinion may be plausibly explained as a determination to hold the states immune without regard to the apparent meaning of the applicable constitutional and statutory provisions.

Iredell dealt first with the constitutional language clearly stating that the Court "shall" have original jurisdiction of cases in which "a State shall be a Party." In a virtual ipse dixit he begged the question by announcing, "I conceive, that all the Courts of the United States must receive, not

14. Van Stophorst, 2 U.S. (2 Dall.) 401 (1791), is *discussed in* 5 DHSC 7–56. For the Indiana Company litigation, *see* Hollingsworth v. Virginia, 3 U.S. (3 Dall.) 378 (1798) (filed in 1793), *discussed in* 5 DHSC 274–351. *See generally* GEORGE LEWIS, THE INDIANA COMPANY 1763–1798 (1941). The litigation is also styled Grayson v. Virginia, 3 U.S. (3 Dall.) 320 (1796).

merely their *organization* . . . but all their authority, as to the manner of their proceeding, from the Legislation." In pronouncing this assumption, Iredell made no reference to the fact that specific language in the Constitution apparently gave the Congress extensive authority over the lower courts' jurisdiction and the Supreme Court's appellate jurisdiction. In contrast, there was no such language relevant to the Supreme Court's original jurisdiction. Iredell's refusal to take notice of the obvious in this instance is in glaring contrast to his careful parsing of the relevant constitutional language in the *Ravara* case. No other Justice at the time, before, or since has shared Iredell's bold assertion of Congressional power over the Supreme Court's original jurisdiction.[15]

Following the logical dictates of his analysis, Iredell then turned to the relevant statutory provisions. He began by arguing that section 14 of the Judiciary Act (now known as the All Writs Act) made no provision for the writs or judicial orders necessary to implement the Court's jurisdiction in an action against a state. In response, Justice Blair plausibly argued that the All Writs Act spoke only to remedial writs that might be used to enforce a judgment against the state. These writs would not be necessary if the state voluntarily complied with the judgment or if the judgment was in favor of the state.[16]

The All Writs Act was, in any event, peripheral to Iredell's basic argument that the Court could not exercise its original jurisdiction without an implementing act of Congress. The main obstacle to Iredell's analysis was section 13 of the Judiciary Act, which clearly provided that the Supreme Court "shall have exclusive jurisdiction of all [suits] where a state is a party, except between a state . . . and citizens of other states, or aliens, in which latter case it shàll have original but not exclusive jurisdiction." Iredell cleverly read this provision for a concurrent jurisdiction as a limit to the Supreme Court's jurisdiction that preserved the states' traditional sovereign immunity. According to Iredell, the concurrent jurisdiction provision had the effect of equating the Supreme Courts' jurisdiction with state court jurisdiction. Following this reading, a Supreme Court jurisdiction broader than the state courts' jurisdiction would not be concurrent and therefore would not be authorized by the Act. He then demonstrated in great detail that under the common law there was no right to sue the state for breach of contract.[17]

---

15. 2 U.S. (2 Dall.) at 432 (emphasis original). For Ravara, see chapter 5 at 139–41 and chapter 8 at 222–25.

16. *Compare* 2 U.S. (2 Dall.) at 433–50 (Iredell, J.) *with id.* at 450–53 (Blair, J.).

17. *See* 2 U.S. (2 Dall.) at 445–50.

The key to Iredell's analysis was his notion that the provision for concurrent jurisdiction was intended as a limitation to the Supreme Court's
authority. He adamantly insisted that his reading was "unquestionably
... the clear intention of the act," but in reality his interpretation was
perverse. Without the concurrent jurisdiction provision, a state would
have been banned from authorizing suit against itself in its own courts.
Therefore the self-evident purpose of the provision was simply to permit
a concurrent state court jurisdiction—not to limit the Supreme Court's
jurisdiction. Moreover, Iredell fully understood this permissive purpose;
he had written in the circuit court that the provision "ought to be construed as implying a permission for such jurisdiction to continue as before in the state courts."[18]

Although Iredell would have determined the case on perverse read-
ings of the Constitution and the Judiciary Act, all the other Justices believed that the case turned directly upon the Constitution. Justices Blair
and Cushing delivered capable but unimaginative opinions that emphasized the Constitution's text. Chief Justice Jay and Justice Wilson took
great pains to write far more elaborate opinions.

In the late twentieth century, Wilson's opinion seems largely irrelevant
and replete with "furbelows of learning, a great deal of which was dis-
pensable." Instead of addressing the policy and text of the Constitution,
he spent page after page discussing general theory and utterly obscure
history. William R. Davie's contemporary analysis seems to foreshadow
this modern reading. Davie was a capable and firm supporter of state
sovereign immunity who warmly endorsed his good friend Iredell's dissenting opinion. Davie privately described Wilson's opinion as "more like
an epic poem than a Judge's argument." But even this vehement critic
begrudgingly conceded that "notwithstanding the tawdry ornament and
poetical imagery with which it is loaded and bedizened, it may still be
very 'profound.' "[19]

If one of Wilson's most adamant contemporary critics admitted that
his opinion might be "very profound," there must be more to the opinion
than meets the twentieth-century eye. That additional element is a natural-law orientation. Wilson simply was not a legal positivist. He was
strongly inclined to believe that laws came from and were legitimized by
human reason and the command of God. Any principle of statutory,
common, or constitutional law that lacked a natural-law justification was,

---

18. *Compare* 2 U.S. (2 Dall.) at 436–37 *with* Iredell, Circuit Court Opinion, *quoted in*
this chapter at 189.

19. *See* GOEBEL 731 ("furbelows"); William R. Davie to James Iredell (June 12, 1793),
excerpted in 2 IREDELL CORRESPONDENCE 382–83.

in his mind, therefore arbitrary, suspect, and possibly illegitimate. Wilson fully understood — to use his words — that *Chisholm* was "a case of uncommon magnitude."[20] He sought therefore to deliver the strongest opinion possible, and in the late eighteenth century, a case of uncommon magnitude demanded resort to natural-law reasoning. If human reason and the command of God indicated that the states should be suable, and if the words of the Constitution pointed to the same conclusion, then the strongest possible case had been made.

Wilson said as much in his introductory remarks. "I shall," he stated, "examine the important question before us, by the Constitution of the United States, and the legitimate result of that valuable instrument."[21] He did not seek the result of that valuable instrument; he sought the *legitimate* result. He sought not only to establish that the states were suable under the Constitution but also to establish by resort to natural-law principles that the Constitution had ordained a "legitimate result."

As a natural lawyer, Wilson turned first to "the principles of general jurisprudence" because natural law was based upon general principles. He appropriately and sincerely began his substantive analysis of general principles by invoking God's perfect wisdom. "MAN, fearfully and wonderfully made, is the workmanship of his all perfect CREATOR: A *State;* useful and valuable as the contrivance is, is the *inferior* contrivance of *man;* and from his *native* dignity derives all its *acquired* importance."[22] This key passage was not a rhetorical flourish; it was an appeal to ultimate authority. Man, which is to say the people, was closer to God than the state was, and therefore the people were superior to the state.

Wilson proceeded to establish other pertinent principles of general jurisprudence. For example, fundamental fairness has always been a touchstone of natural law. "A dishonest State [that] wilfully refuses to discharge" a contract is "like a dishonest merchant." Therefore, "upon general principles of right," both should be required "to answer the fair demands of its creditor."[23]

Wilson concluded the first section of his opinion with a powerful attack on the theoretical underpinning of the state's claim to sovereign immunity. He saw the state's claim as an attempt to wrest sovereignty from the people and give it to the state. He traced this notion to the feudal system that had overtaken Europe and been arbitrarily imposed on England by "the conqueror." According to Wilson, the feudal system vested the king

---

20. 2 U.S. (2 Dall.) at 453.
21. *Id.*
22. *Id.* at 453, 455 (emphasis original).
23. *Id.* at 456.

"with jurisdiction over others, [and] it excluded all others from jurisdiction over him." By the eighteenth century, Blackstone and other Englishmen had transformed this feudal system into a false principle that "all human law must be prescribed by a [human] *superior.*" Wilson emphatically rejected this protopositivism. "Another principle," he said, "very different in its nature and operations, forms, in my judgment, the basis of sound and genuine jurisprudence; laws derived from the pure source of equality and justice must be founded on the CONSENT of those, whose obedience they require." This idea that laws are derived from "equality and justice" rather than the command of the state epitomizes the difference between natural law and legal positivism.[24]

In the second part of his opinion, Wilson turned from legal theory to legal history. In a wide-ranging survey, he adduced relevant historical precedent from Socrates' Greece, a suit by the son of Christopher Columbus against King Ferdinand of Spain, traditions in the medieval province of Aragon, English practice before and after William the Conqueror, and the words of Frederick the Great of Prussia. All of these historical precedents recognized the right of an individual to sue his state. Wilson did not offer this survey to elucidate the background and meaning of the Constitution but rather almost certainly saw this array of historical precedent as an aid to inducing principles of natural law. Less than two years earlier, he had explained in his *Lectures on Law* that "In every period of his existence, the law, which the divine wisdom has approved for man, will be fitted, to the contemporary degree." From this perspective Wilson could present his historical precedents as divinely ordained examples of the proper application of natural-law principles.[25]

After this survey of historical precedent, Wilson turned to "the Constitution of the *United States,* and the legitimate result of that valuable instrument." An important purpose of his elaboration of general principles and historical precedent was to establish that sovereignty resided in the people, not the state. The "inference, which necessarily results, is, that the Constitution ordained and established by *those* people; and, still closely to apply the case, in particular by the people of *Georgia, could* vest jurisdiction or judicial power over those States and over the State of *Georgia* in particular."[26]

When Wilson finally addressed the precise question of whether the Constitution actually vested the Court with jurisdiction to try an action

---

24. *Id.* at 458 (emphasis original).

25. 2 U.S. (2 Dall.) at 459–61; James Wilson, *Lectures on Law,* in 1 THE WORKS OF JAMES WILSON 353–54 (R. McCloskey ed., 1967).

26. 2 U.S. (2 Dall.) at 461, 464 (emphasis original).

against the state for breach of contract, his analysis was anticlimactic. In comparison to the lengthy elaboration of general principles and historical precedents that dominated most of his opinion, the final portion of it seems cursory, uninspired, and even pedestrian. But from a natural-law perspective, this latter portion was relatively unimportant. Wilson had established by resort to the command of God and human reason that states were suable. It was thus almost inconceivable that the Constitution's reference to suing the states did not incorporate this independent and preexisting principle of natural law.

Although Wilson's opinion was a tour de force in natural-law reasoning, it was disquietingly similar to his brilliant opinion on the Continental Congress's authority to charter a national bank. In both situations, his brilliance was marshaled in support of his personal financial interest. Wilson knew that his opinion in *Chisholm* was determinative of the Court's jurisdiction over the Indiana Company's claim that was before the Court in *Hollingsworth v. Virginia*. Moreover, Wilson had become a shareholder of the Indiana Company in 1781, and according to the original complaint in *Hollingsworth*, he was still a shareholder. He therefore had a direct and significant financial interest in the Court's jurisdiction to provide a remedy against a state.[27]

Judged by twentieth-century standards of judicial conduct, Wilson's failure to recuse himself in *Chisholm* is unjustifiable. Eighteenth-century attorneys and judges apparently took a different view of the matter. According to Blackstone, "judges or justices cannot be challenged [for partiality]. For the law will not suppose a possibility of bias or favour in a judge, who is already sworn to administer impartial justice, and whose authority greatly depends upon that presumption and idea." Moreover, the issue in *Chisholm* was legal rather than factual in nature, and under the predominant theory of the judicial process, Wilson may have viewed his opinion as virtually a ministerial explication of the Constitution's positive language coupled with preexisting natural-law principles. Wilson's membership in the Indiana Company was a matter of public record, and the Court's decision in *Chisholm* was controversial. If Wilson's conduct was as flagrantly improper as it seems from the vantage point of two hundred years later, the absence of any contemporary condemnation in private correspondence or the public press is strange.[28]

---

27. Bill in Equity in Hollingsworth v. Virginia, *excerpted in* 5 DHSC 299–316. *See also* this chapter at 190.
28. 3 BLACKSTONE 361. *But see* 5 MATTHEW BACON, A NEW ABRIDGMENT OF THE LAW, Trial § (L)3, at 244 (1778); Process and Compensation Act of 1792, ch. 36, § 11 (1792), 1 stat. 275, 278–79.

Chief Justice Jay essentially agreed with Wilson that the sovereignty of the people and their ratification of the Constitution made the Constitution superior to any form of sovereignty that the states might claim. The state governments were thus subject to the will of the people as expressed in the Constitution. Moreover, like Cushing, Blair, and Wilson, the Chief Justice concluded that the Constitution's express reference to federal jurisdiction over suits involving states rendered Georgia subject to suit by a citizen of another state.[29]

Justice Iredell had avoided the constitutional issue through his ipse dixit on plenary Congressional power over the Supreme Court's original jurisdiction. He almost certainly, however, was aware of his colleagues' contrary views and took the unusual step of giving an advisory opinion on the constitutional issue. He evidently believed that the constitutional provision for suits between a state and citizens of another state was implicitly limited to suits in which a state appeared as a plaintiff and possibly to suits in which the common law clearly recognized a citizen's right to sue a state. He believed therefore that "every word in the Constitution may have its full effect without involving this consequence, and nothing but express words, or an insurmountable implication (neither of which I consider, can be found in this case) would authorize the deduction of so high a power." Iredell simply did not believe that the people had actually spoken to the issue of state sovereign immunity.[30]

Some modern scholars with an eye toward the proper scope of state sovereign immunity in the late twentieth century have suggested that Iredell believed that sovereign immunity would not protect the states from suit on a claim arising directly under federal law.[31] These scholars emphasize the fact that the Supreme Court's jurisdiction in *Chisholm* was based upon the state's being a party to the litigation rather than upon the presence of a federal question in the case. This modern twist to Iredell's opinion is unwarranted revisionism. Iredell specifically said that "nothing but express words, or an insurmountable implication . . . would authorize the deduction of so high a power." If the Constitution's express reference to suits in which states were a party was not sufficient, it is difficult to believe that the more general

29. 2 U.S. (2 Dall.) at 472–73.

30. *Id.* at 450.

31. *See* Akhil Amar, *Of Federalism and Sovereignty,* 96 YALE L. REV. 1425, 1472–73, 1482 (1987); John Nowak, *The Scope of Congressional Power to Create Causes of Action Against State Governments and the History of the Eleventh and Fourteenth Amendments,* 75 COLUM. L. REV. 1413, 1432–33 (1975). *See also* Fletcher, *A Historical Interpretation of the Eleventh Amendment: A Narrow Construction of an Affirmative Grant of Jurisdiction Rather Than a Prohibition Against Jurisdiction,* 35 STAN. L. REV. 1033, 1058, 1063 (1983).

constitutional language extending jurisdiction to suits arising under federal law would have met Iredell's test.

THE ELEVENTH AMENDMENT

Although Iredell's opinion in *Chisholm* was deeply flawed, he proved to be accurate in his visceral political judgment that the states should not be subject to suit for monetary damages. The day after the Court announced its decision, Theodore Sedgwick, a leading Federalist from Massachusetts, proposed a constitutional amendment in the House of Representatives to overturn the Court's decision. Sedgwick's proposal was

> That no state shall be liable to be made a party defendant, in any of the judicial courts, established, or which shall be established under the authority of the United States, at the suit of any person or persons whether a citizen or citizens, or a foreigner or foreigners, of any body politic or corporate, whether within or without the United States.

The second Congress, however, never voted on Sedgwick's proposal.[32]

The next day, Senator Caleb Strong, another Massachusetts Federalist, drafted a different proposal that was submitted in the Senate. This second proposal is in Strong's handwriting and is almost identical to the proposal that was approved the next year by the third Congress and subsequently ratified by the states as the Eleventh Amendment. The third Congress's proposal was endorsed "Mr. Strong's motion" and was also in Strong's handwriting. Thus Caleb Strong may be considered to be the father of the Eleventh Amendment, and his initial proposal was the Amendment's first draft. Strong wrote,

> The Judicial Power of the United States shall not extend to any Suits in Law or Equity commenced or prosecuted *by any foreign State or by any Individual or Individuals whether Citizens or Foreigners*, against any one of the United States by Citizens of another State, or by Citizens or Subjects of any foreign State.

The underscored language in this draft are words that Strong deleted.[33]

Strong's deletions indicate that his initial idea was that the "Judicial Power of the United States shall not extend to any Suits in Law or Equity

---

32. Philadelphia Gazette of United States, Feb. 20, 1793, *reprinted in* 5 DHSC 605–06.

33. For Strong's proposal in the Second Congress, *see* 5 DHSC 607–08. *See also* 3 Annals 651–52 (printing Strong's proposal without mention of his deletions). For Strong's subsequent proposal in the Third Congress, *see* 5 DHSC 613–14. *See also* 4 Annals 25 (printing Strong's subsequent proposal without mention of its provenance).

commenced or prosecuted *by any foreign State or by any Individual or Individuals whether Citizens or Foreigners,* against any one of the United States." He apparently decided against this version and deleted the underscored words. He then added a new description of parties that "commenced or prosecuted" suits and submitted the following proposal to the Senate: "The Judicial Power of the United States shall not extend to any Suits in Law or Equity commenced or prosecuted against any one of the United States by Citizens of another State, or by Citizens or Subjects of any foreign State." This proposal—like Sedgwick's the day before—never came to a vote in the second Congress.[34]

The Congress's failure to take immediate action on these proposed amendments should not be viewed as evidence of political opposition. Apparently a member from "the southward thought [the proposals] so popular in Congress, that he ventured to tack with the bill one less so . . . to exclude all holders in the bank [of the United States] from a seat in Congress." There was reason to believe that almost a fifth of the members held bank stock. This parliamentary maneuver therefore "raised such a clamor among the stock jobbers that nothing was done."[35]

Congress did not reconvene until December, and in the interim the states' sovereign immunity became an issue of public controversy throughout the nation. Hotheads in the lower house of the Georgia legislature approved a bill "providing that any federal marshall or other person who executed any process in [*Chisholm*] should be declared guilty of felony and should suffer death 'without benefit of clergy,' by being hanged." The upper house of the Georgia legislature, however, apparently did not concur in this extreme measure.[36]

Many other state legislatures voiced their firm disapproval of *Chisholm* and called for a constitutional amendment to overturn the decision. The Virginia legislature, undoubtedly motivated by the Indiana Company litigation, passed a resolution condemning the decision and reaffirming the states' sovereign immunity. Connecticut was not a defendant in specific litigation in federal court, but the state had been threatened with suit. In October, the Connecticut General Assembly requested the state's senators and representatives to procure an amendment to the Constitution to overrule *Chisholm*. This resolve was in response to a circular letter

---

34. *See* 5 DHSC 607–08.

35. Mercy Warren to George Warren (Oct. 16, 1793), *excerpted in* 5 DHSC 444–45; Thomas Jefferson, Notes on Stockholders in Congress (Mar. 23, 1793), *reprinted in* 25 JEFFERSON PAPERS 432–35. For the amendment, *see* 3 ANNALS 663.

36. *See* JACOBS 55–57.

that Connecticut had received from Massachusetts. A joint session of the New Hampshire legislature passed a similar resolution.[37]

Massachusetts, like Virginia, was the defendant in a major lawsuit. In *Vassall v. Massachusetts*, the state was sued a few months after *Chisholm* by an individual who claimed that his property had been confiscated in violation of the Treaty of Paris. *Chisholm* had obvious implications for Vassall's claim, and Fisher Ames reported that "the entire active force of the state politics [was] hostile to [*Chisholm*]." The Massachusetts General Court therefore "instructed" its senators and "requested" its representatives to

> adopt the most speedy and effectual measures in their power, to obtain such amendments in the Constitution of the United States as will remove any clause or article of the said Constitution which can be construed to imply or justify a decision that a State is compellable to answer in any suit by an individual or individuals in any Court of the United States.

Caleb Strong was undoubtedly thinking of this formal instruction when he returned to the Senate from Massachusetts in December 1793.[38]

In apparent compliance with his state's instruction, Strong resubmitted his constitutional amendment to the third Congress. His new proposal, which was endorsed "Mr. Strong's motion," was virtually identical to his prior proposal that had been tabled: "The Judicial Power of the United States shall not *be construed to* extend to any Suit in Law or Equity, commenced or prosecuted against one of the United States by Citizens of another State or by Citizens or Subjects of any foreign State." The only possibly significant changes to his prior proposal were the new underscored words "be construed to." Advocates occasionally suggested in the 1790s that the purpose of these words was to indicate that "the amend-

---

37. The Virginia Resolution is *reprinted in* 5 DHSC 338–39. In 1791 the Treasurer of Connecticut refused payment to a William Maxwell on some five hundred fifty pounds in Connecticut bills of credit. Mr. Maxwell, who was a citizen of New York, then threatened to sue the state in the Supreme Court if his claim was not treated "with fairness." Letter from Pierpont Edwards to Governor Samuel Huntington (Nov. 3, 1791) (DLC). (Edwards, who was the U.S. Attorney for Connecticut, was serving as Maxwell's private attorney.). The state legislature responded by enacting private legislation to settle the claim. 7 RECORDS OF THE STATE OF CONNECTICUT 364–65, 509. For the Connecticut and New Hampshire Resolutions, *see* 5 DHSC 609 & 618–19.
38. Vassall v. Massachusetts (filed in the U.S. Supreme Court in August term 1793), *discussed in* 5 DHSC 352–449. Fisher Ames to Alexander Hamilton (Aug. 31, 1793), *excerpted in* 5 DHSC 415. For the Massachusetts Resolution, *see* 5 DHSC 440–41.

ment . . . does not import an alteration of the Constitution, but an authoritative declaration of its true construction."[39]

Two efforts were made in the Senate to amend Strong's proposal. Albert Gallatin of Pennsylvania sought to authorize the adjudication of cases like *Vassall v. Massachusetts* by excluding "cases arising under treaties made under the authority of the United States" from the proposed prohibition. Another senator—perhaps Rutherfurd of New Jersey—sought an even broader exclusion that would have prevented the Eleventh Amendment from operating retroactively upon causes of action arising before the amendment's ratification. Both changes were rejected, and the Senate then approved Strong's proposal by an overwhelming majority of 23 to 2. The two nays were Gallatin and Rutherfurd.[40]

In the House of Representatives an effort was made to change Strong's proposal by limiting the prohibition to suits in which the defendant "State shall have previously made provision in their own Courts, whereby such suit may be prosecuted to effect." This change was easily defeated by a vote of 77 to 8, and Strong's proposal was then approved by a similar vote of 81 to 9. Zephaniah Swift, a Federalist from Connecticut, wrote a friend that the Eleventh Amendment passed the House "with little debate or opposition."[41]

Some have suggested that the Eleventh Amendment was almost a partisan anti-Federalist measure and that the Federalists eventually accepted the measure with reluctance. According to this theory, in 1793 the Federalists were initially enthusiastic about *Chisholm's* expansive view of federal judicial power, but their enthusiasm was gone by 1794, when the Congress overwhelmingly approved the Eleventh Amendment. During this intervening period, a number of states had called for a constitutional convention, and the war scare of 1794 had commenced. Therefore—again according to the theory—the Federalists begrudgingly voted for the Amendment to forestall a constitutional convention and to avoid appearing to be pro-British when war with Britain was being contemplated.

---

39. *See* this chapter at 197. Respublica v. Cobbet, 3 U.S. (3 Dall.) 467, 472 (Pa. 1798). *See also* United States v. Peters, 3 U.S. (3 Dall.) 121, 127 (1795). *But see* Respublica v. Cobbet, 3 U.S. (3 Dall.) 467, 475 (Pa. 1798) (M'Kean, C. J.: "When the judicial law was passed, the opinion prevailed that States might be sued, which by this amendment is settled otherwise.").

40. *See* 4 ANNALS 30–31.

41. *See* 4 ANNALS 476–78; Zephaniah Swift to David Daggett (Mar. 5, 1794), *excerpted in* 5 DHSC 624.

This theory of begrudging support lends historical legitimacy to narrow interpretations of the Amendment.[42]

The theory, however, is seriously undermined by the Amendment's legislative history. At least the Federalists in Congress do not seem to have experienced a change of heart about *Chisholm*. Within two days after the decision was announced, Caleb Strong and Theodore Sedgwick, who epitomized New England Federalism, proposed constitutional amendments to restore the states' sovereign immunity. Their proposals were "popular in Congress" and were obviously conceived well before either the states called for a constitutional convention or the subsequent British war scare. Nor does it appear that Strong and Sedgwick were influenced by litigation against their home state of Massachusetts. Both of these staunch Federalists proposed their amendments in the spring, months before *Vassal v. Massachusetts* was filed in the Supreme Court. Moreover, if the Eleventh Amendment was an anti-Federalist proposal that eventually gained only begrudging support from the Federalists, it is strange that the tiny group in the Senate who unsuccessfully sought to preserve the Federal government's power to enforce treaties against the states was led by Senator Gallatin, who was a leading anti-Federalist.[43]

The most plausible explanation of the Amendment's provenance is that it was bipartisan or nonpartisan. Zephania Swift, who was also an adamant Federalist and who was present when the Amendment was considered in the House, wrote in private that its passage did not "seem to be owing to the exertion of any party unfriendly to [the Federalist] Government."[44] Given the sponsorship of Sedgwick and Strong, the opposition of Gallatin, Swift's understanding that there was little significant opposition and no partisan opposition, and the overwhelming House and Senate votes, the Eleventh Amendment cannot possibly have been an anti-Federalist measure that received only begrudging Federalist support.

After the amendment was approved by the House and the Senate, it was transmitted to the states. Under the Constitution, the amendment could not become effective until it was ratified by three-fourths of the

---

42. *See* John Nowak, *The Scope of Congressional Power to Create Causes of Action Against State Governments and the History of the Eleventh and Fourteenth Amendments*, 75 Colum. L. Rev. 1413 (1975); John Gibbons, *The Eleventh Amendment and State Sovereign Immunity: A Reinterpretation*, 83 Colum L. Rev. 1889 (1983); Calvin Massey, *State Sovereignty and the Tenth and Eleventh Amendments*, 56 U. Chi. L. Rev. 61 (1989); Lawrence Marshall, *Fighting the Words of the Eleventh Amendment*, 102 Harv. L. Rev. 1342 (1989).

43. *See* Mercy Warren letter in this chapter note 35; 1 DHSC 492 (Supreme Court Docket for Vassall).

44. *See* Zephania Swift letter in this chapter note 41.

state legislatures. This majority was accomplished by February 1795, less than a year later and only two years after *Chisholm* was decided. Notwithstanding colorable arguments to the contrary, the Court subsequently held that the amendment was to be applied retrospectively as well as prospectively.[45]

THE SCOPE OF THE ELEVENTH AMENDMENT

To modern eyes, the Eleventh Amendment has puzzling lacunae. On its face, the amendment does not apply to admiralty litigation, suits by a foreign state, or suits in which a state is sued by one of its own citizens. Yet in cases decided long after the amendment was ratified, the Supreme Court concluded that states enjoy a sovereign immunity that bars each of these categories of litigation from the federal courts.[46] Whether Americans in the late eighteenth century would have reached the same conclusion is difficult to determine, because the surviving evidence is sparse. Nevertheless, some historically plausible judgments are possible.

The impetus behind the adoption of the Eleventh Amendment was in part a theoretical concern for the dignity of the individual states. This mere theoretical concern, however, probably would not have sufficed to overturn *Chisholm*. At least this was Chief Justice Marshall's later judgment.[47] The states had pragmatic concerns about three categories of actual ongoing litigation: suits arising under the Treaty of Paris, suits involving land disputes, and ordinary suits for breach of contract. Any historically plausible explanation of the scope of the state's sovereign immunity must take these specific concerns into account.

The states' concern about suits arising under the Treaty of Paris should not be confused with the ongoing and related problems of British creditors who were seeking to recover debts owed to them by private citizens. These latter British creditors' suits were filed against private debtors—not states—and were governed in significant part by Article IV of the Treaty of Paris. As Justice Chase noted in *Ware v. Hylton*, Article IV "only speaks of the *original debtor*, and says nothing about a recovery from any of the States." In contrast, a state's sovereign immunity was directly involved in cases like *Vassall v. Massachusetts*, in which a loyalist directly challenged the validity of the state's confiscation of his property. These

---

45. *See* Jacobs 67; Hollingsworth v. Virginia, 3 U.S. (3 Dall.) 378 (1978).
46. *See* Hans v. Louisiana, 134 U.S. 1 (1890); Ex parte New York, No. 1, 256 U.S. 490 (1921); Principality of Monaco v. Mississippi, 292 U.S. 313 (1934).
47. *See* Cohens v. Virginia, 19 U.S. 264, 406 (1821).

cases were governed by Article VI of the Treaty of Paris, which forbade "future Confiscations" of loyalists' properties.[48]

The second type of controversy that the states did not want to see litigated in federal court involved major land disputes like *Hollingsworth v. Virginia*. The Constitution, as construed in *Chisholm*, opened the Supreme Court to this kind of suit for damages. Finally, the states were concerned about their general liability for breach of contract. *Chisholm* epitomized cases involving contracts in which a state had purchased goods or services from a private party on a promise to pay that had not been satisfied to the sellers' expectations. The states were also concerned about their liability on straight loans and on bills of credit that were used as money and had been emitted before the Constitution was ratified.[49]

SUITS BY FOREIGN STATES

Because none of these three specific areas of state concern were obviously implicated by the federal courts' jurisdiction over a suit brought by a foreign state, the Eleventh Amendment's silence on this narrow head of jurisdiction is not surprising. The Eleventh Amendment clearly did not bar foreign states from federal court, and this omission was the result of a conscious drafting decision. Senator Strong, who drafted the Amendment and was the measure's moving proponent, was a capable lawyer with a sophisticated understanding of the federal judicial system. He had been a delegate to the Constitutional Convention and in the first Congress was one of Ellsworth's two principal allies in drafting the Judiciary Act. When Strong began drafting the Eleventh Amendment, he specifically considered and rejected language that would have included foreign states' claims within the Amendment's prohibition.[50]

Years later, Chief Justice Marshall explained that the Eleventh Amendment was adopted primarily to protect the states from their creditors. He then noted that

> there was not much reason to fear that foreign or sister States would be creditors to any considerable amount, and there was reason to retain the jurisdiction of the Court in those cases, because it

---

48. 3 U.S. (3 Dall.) at 245 (emphasis original); Treaty of Paris art. IV, VI (1783), *reprinted in* 2 TREATIES (Miller) 155.

49. For a discussion of bills of credit, *see* Craig v. Missouri, 29 U.S. (4 Peters) 410, 431–32 (1830). In Chisholm, Chief Justice Jay indicated that the court's decision would be a windfall for holders of bills of credit, and therefore he suggested that states might not be suable on bills of credit 2 U.S. (2 Dall.) at 479.

50. *See* this chapter at 197.

might be essential to the preservation of peace. The amendment, therefore, extended to suits commenced or prosecuted by individuals, but not to those brought by States.[51]

This analysis of competing considerations is consistent with Senator Strong's decision to delete suits by foreign states from his amendment's prohibitions. His purposeful exclusion of suits commenced by a foreign state was also consistent with the broad instructions that he subsequently received from the Massachusetts legislature. The Massachusetts resolution applied only to suits by individuals.

Chief Justice Marshall's explanation that suits by foreign states implicated important national interests but were not a significant threat to state finances is borne out by the early Supreme Court's experience with litigation between a foreign state and a state. Only one such case was filed in the Supreme Court in the eighteenth century, and it was sui generis. *Cutting v. South Carolina* involved a frigate that South Carolina chartered from the Prince of Luxembourg during the Revolution. After the ship was captured, South Carolina submitted the issue of its liability to arbitration and agreed to reimburse the Prince for the vessel's loss. Subsequently the Prince died, and there was a question of whether his estate or the French government was entitled to the money owed by South Carolina. To resolve this problem, the administrator of the Prince's estate sued South Carolina in the Supreme Court. The eventual disposition of this strange case is unclear. In any event, the case should not be treated as a suit against a state. The plaintiff's attorney explained that because South Carolina had admitted its liability, the suit was commenced "principally . . . for the purpose of having it decided to whom the money could be paid with safety by the State." In other words, *Cutting* was an action in the nature of an interpleader in which South Carolina was functionally—if not procedurally—a mere stakeholder.[52]

SUITS IN ADMIRALTY

In contrast to the conscious omission of suits by foreign states from the Eleventh Amendment, the omission of admiralty litigation was probably coincidental. An admiralty suit involving a violation of the Treaty of Paris

---

51. Cohens v. Virginia, 19 U.S. 264, 406–7 (1821).

52. *See* Marcus & Wexler 81–83; 5 DHSC 450–95. *See also* Alexander Dallas to Governor of South Carolina (Mar. 1797) (agreeing to treat the case as an interpleader), *reprinted in* 5 DHSC 489–90; Timothy Pickering to Henry De Saussure (June 25, 1796) (Timothy Pickering Papers, MHi); Timothy Pickering to Thomas Parker (Nov. 21, 1797) (Timothy Pickering Papers, MHi).

is difficult to conceive, and admiralty jurisdiction over a land dispute is downright impossible. The admiralty cases that would have most clearly implicated the states' actual fiscal concerns as opposed to theoretical dignitary concerns would have been suits for breaches of maritime contracts. Such a suit is conceivable. For example, South Carolina's initial liability in *Cutting v. South Carolina* was based upon a contractual obligation under a charter party. This type of commercial dispute, however, was not typical of eighteenth-century admiralty litigation.

A state is simply not a plausible defendant in the paradigmatic public law categories of eighteenth-century admiralty litigation. Under what circumstances would a privateer or naval officer ask a federal court to adjudicate the lawfulness of a capture taken from one of the United States? Similarly, a state was unlikely to appear as a defendant in either a criminal prosecution or a revenue collection case. Even in the case of private admiralty litigation, the state is not an obvious defendant in the paradigmatic suit for seamen's wages. Given this eighteenth-century understanding of admiralty litigation, Americans of the Founding Generation probably had no thought one way or another regarding the states' sovereign immunity in admiralty.[53]

ENFORCEMENT OF FEDERAL RIGHTS

The most interesting conundrum created by the Eleventh Amendment's peculiar wording is the extent to which a state might be sued in federal court by one of its own citizens to enforce a federal right. Because there is no diversity of citizenship between the plaintiff and the defendant in such suits, the Constitution's provision for diversity jurisdiction is, by definition, inapplicable. Several modern scholars have argued that a citizen may sue his or her own state under the separate constitutional provision extending federal jurisdiction to cases arising under federal law.[54] Their modern explanation is based upon the assumption that the Eleventh Amendment was drafted solely to strip the federal courts of jurisdiction based solely upon the parties' diversity of citizenship. This kind of party-based jurisdiction may or may not involve the direct enforcement of a federal right or interest. In contrast, the courts' federal

---

53. *See* Casto, *Admiralty;* James Madison, Report on the Virginia Resolutions (Jan 7, 1800) (state may not be a criminal defendant), *reprinted in* 17 MADISON PAPERS 303, 330.

54. *See generally* William Fletcher, *The Diversity Explanation of the Eleventh Amendment: A Reply to Critics*, 56 U. CHI. L. REV. 1261 (1989); William Marshall, *The Diversity Theory of the Eleventh Amendment: A Critical Evaluation*, 102 HARV. L. REV. 1372 (1989).

question jurisdiction over cases arising under federal law involves, by definition, the direct enforcement of a federal right or interest. The modern, diversity explanation was written with a conscious eye to the proper scope of state sovereign immunity in the late twentieth century, and therefore its historical accuracy is inherently suspect—which is not to say inevitably incorrect.

The principal problem with the modern diversity explanation of the Eleventh Amendment is that it is not subject to reasonably conclusive proof. The surviving records of public and private discourse in the Founding Era contain no clear evidence that anyone ever knowingly endorsed or knowingly rejected the diversity explanation of the Eleventh Amendment. This absence of evidence suggests that the diversity explanation may be an anachronistic figment of the modern imagination. Perhaps no one ever endorsed the explanation because no one ever thought of it, and perhaps no one ever rejected it for the same reason. The absence of evidence, however, might be due to the fact that the issue of state liability on a claim arising under federal law was never squarely raised in the 1790s. Perhaps Americans of the Founding Generation believed that the federal courts could adjudicate claims against the states arising under federal law but did not want to address this sensitive issue unless it was absolutely necessary. Given the pragmatic inclination of virtually all of the Founding Generation, this alternative explanation of the absence of evidence cannot be dismissed out of hand as implausible.

One way to test the diversity explanation is to look at it through the eyes of Caleb Strong, who drafted the Amendment. Strong was a capable and sophisticated attorney, a staunch Federalist, and a respected politician. The language of his amendment is at least consistent with the diversity explanation. His choice of words was clearly tailored to the Constitution's provision for diversity jurisdiction and clearly did not bar federal question jurisdiction. At least his language did not bar federal question claims by a citizen against his or her own state.

The diversity explanation is further strengthened if the wording of Strong's proposal is compared with that of the proposal that Sedgwick introduced in the House of Representatives. In sharp contrast to Strong's Amendment, Sedgwick's proposal clearly would have barred all individual plaintiffs' suits against states without regard to whether the claim was based upon a federal right. This apparent difference between the two proposals that were drafted within a day of each other cannot be ignored, but certainly the difference cannot be explained on the basis of politics. Strong and Sedgwick were both staunch members of the Massachusetts Federalist establishment.

The similarities between Strong's and Sedgwick's politics suggest a plausible explanation of their apparently different proposals. Both men were almost certainly seeking to achieve precisely the same immediate result. Sedgwick proposed a stand-alone amendment that by its own terms would have completely barred all suits against states by individuals. Strong's proposal accomplished the same result if it is read in conjunction with the Judiciary Act that he had helped to craft.

Strong knew that the Judiciary Act did not authorize federal-question suits against the states in the inferior courts because the Act did not vest those lower courts with what we call today general federal-question jurisdiction. Today some might argue that the district courts' admiralty jurisdiction could extend to suits against states, but to apply this insight to the eighteenth century is probably anachronistic. If the Judiciary Act did not authorize the inferior courts to try a suit against a state, only one federal court was left—the Supreme Court. But under both the Constitution and the Judiciary Act, the Supreme Court's trial jurisdiction over suits by an individual against a state was absolutely limited to party-based jurisdiction. The Supreme Court's federal-question jurisdiction was constitutionally limited to appeals that were effectively preempted by the lower courts' lack of original federal-question jurisdiction. Strong's amendment precisely and completely eliminated the comparatively narrow scope of the Supreme Court's original party-based jurisdiction over suits filed by individuals against states. The practical effect of his proposal was therefore the same as Sedgwick's. When the Judiciary Act is taken into account, both proposals barred all suits in federal court against states by individuals regardless of whether or not a suit involved the enforcement of federal rights.

The idea that Sedgwick's and Strong's superficially different proposals were intended to effect identical constrictions of federal jurisdiction is consistent with Massachusetts's subsequent response to the controversy caused by *Vassall v. Massachusetts*. The Massachusetts legislature desired a comprehensive, stand-alone amendment similar to the one that Sedgwick had already proposed. The legislature's instruction to Strong was even more stringent than Sedgwick's original proposal. Strong and Sedgwick were old friends and political allies and undoubtedly consulted with each other. Notwithstanding their legislature's directive, they apparently settled on Strong's proposal. When the third Congress commenced its work, Strong resubmitted his original proposal with a slight change, and nothing further was heard of Sedgwick's rhetorically more comprehensive measure.[55]

---

55. *Compare* Sedgewick's Proposal *discussed* this chapter at 197 with the Massachusetts Resolution *discussed* this chapter at 199; *see* RICHARD WELCH, THEODORE SEDGWICK, FEDERALIST: A POLITICAL PORTRAIT 219 n.33 (1965).

Although Strong's proposal was not superficially as broad as the Massachusetts Resolution, the possibility that he disregarded his home state legislature's desires seems remote. He had been elected to the Senate by the Massachusetts legislature and was later elected governor of his state. Far from opposing his home state's political establishment, he was part and parcel of it.[56]

Further evidence of the intendment of Strong's language is found in the House of Representatives vote on the Eleventh Amendment. Massachusetts, Connecticut, New Hampshire, and Virginia had each passed resolutions urging their delegates to frame an amendment that would bar from the federal courts all suits against states by individuals. Together, these four states sent more than forty representatives and senators to the first session of the third Congress. If these men thought the Eleventh Amendment was inconsistent with the broad directives from their states, the inconsistency surely would have been challenged. But Strong's proposal passed both the House and the Senate by majorities of 90 percent or better and with little debate or opposition. Moreover, only two of the representatives from Massachusetts, Connecticut, New Hampshire, and Virginia voted against the measure. In the Senate, none of the four states' senators voted against the measure. Similarly, the legislatures of all four states quickly ratified the Amendment with no significant opposition.[57]

Notwithstanding these inferences, the possibility remains that Senator Strong was trying to have his cake and eat it too. His Amendment, coupled with the Judiciary Act, clearly barred both diversity and federal-question litigation from the federal courts. At the same time, the Amendment did not expressly bar a future Congress from vesting the courts with federal-question jurisdiction over suits against the states. Whether he or anyone else had this clever stratagem in mind must be left to pure conjecture.

Senator Gallatin's unsuccessful motion to change Strong's proposal seems pertinent. Whatever Gallatin's general attitudes may have been toward sovereign immunity, he clearly believed that a federal forum should be available in cases like *Vassal v. Massachusetts,* in which a foreigner sued to enforce Article VI of the Treaty of Paris. He therefore proposed to except "cases arising under treaties" from the Amendment's prohibition. His proposal, however, was resoundingly defeated.

---

56. *See Caleb Strong,* 18 DICTIONARY OF AMERICAN BIOGRAPHY 144–46 (D. Malone ed., 1936).
57. *See* 4 ANNALS 30–31, 476–78.

The Senate's firm rejection of Gallatin's motion seems inconsistent with the modern notion that the Eleventh Amendment was directed at party-based jurisdiction but was intended to be neutral in respect of cases arising under federal law. A plausible reading of this episode is that Gallatin believed Strong's amendment was directed at cases arising under treaties of the United States, because he tried to except such cases from the Amendment's operation. Similarly, if the Senate majority believed that the Amendment would not apply to cases arising under federal law, why was Gallatin's motion rejected?

Defenders of the diversity explanation have taken a formalistic view of the Gallatin motion.[58] They stubbornly maintain (albeit without any positive evidence) that the Eleventh Amendment was intended solely as a limit to party-based jurisdiction and was to have no impact on federal-question jurisdiction. If this assumption is true, then Gallatin's motion had nothing to do with jurisdiction based directly upon a case's having arisen under federal law. Instead, Gallatin intended merely to preserve the Supreme Court's party-based jurisdiction in cases involving treaty violations. Similarly, the Senate's rejection of Gallatin's motion was meant to limit the Constitution's party-based jurisdiction in treaty cases but to leave unaffected the Constitution's separate provision for jurisdiction arising under federal law.

We will never know whether members of the Founding Generation actually thought in such formal and highly theoretical categories. This kind of formalism seems inconsistent with their generally pragmatic inclinations. The Senate obviously intended to foreclose foreigners from using party-based jurisdiction as a basis for enforcing their federal treaty rights against states. Whether the Senate simultaneously intended to preserve the constitutional possibility that precisely the same parties might litigate exactly the same rights under the Constitution's "arising under" jurisdiction is much less likely. Surely the substantive treaty right was more important than the technical basis for the federal courts' jurisdiction.

In all likelihood, the framers and ratifiers of the Eleventh Amendment were simply trying to solve the immediate problems created by the *Chisholm* case. They sought to foreclose all citizens and foreigners from recovering damages against the states, and one of the types of litigation that they specifically sought to bar was suits to enforce federal treaty rights. By carefully meshing the Eleventh Amendment with the existing

---

58. *See* John Gibbons, *The Eleventh Amendment and State Sovereign Immunity: A Reinterpretation*, 83 Colum. L. Rev. 1889, 1936 (1983); Fletcher, *The Diversity Explanation of the Eleventh Amendment: A Reply to Critics*, 56 U. Chi. L. Rev. 1261, 1287 (1989).

Judiciary Act, Senator Strong accomplished this immediate objective. He did not extend the language of his Amendment to the Constitution's provision for jurisdiction arising under federal law, because the Judiciary Act clearly did not authorize such suits.

Perhaps there was no intent one way or another for the Eleventh Amendment to limit jurisdiction arising under federal law. If so, a state's amenability to suit in a case arising under federal law would have been determined by reference to the Constitution as originally ratified. The resolution of this issue would have been troubling to the Justices of the Jay and Ellsworth Courts. The constitutional grant of original trial jurisdiction to the Supreme Court was not written in terms of cases arising under federal law. Therefore, such a case would have to be tried in an inferior federal court pursuant to a positive congressional grant of federal-question jurisdiction. In other words, a judicial declaration that such a grant violated the states' sovereign immunity under the Constitution would have involved the Court's judicial review of Congress's legislative decision to vest the inferior courts with jurisdiction.

Iredell presumably believed that the Constitution did not expressly, or by insurmountable implication, authorize federal-question jurisdiction over suits against states, so he probably would have ruled such legislation unconstitutional. But the question of Congressional authority to vest the federal courts with a federal-question jurisdiction over suits against states would have been more difficult for the other Justices. The Eleventh Amendment made it clear that states could not be sued in federal court under a party-based jurisdiction, but it did not expressly speak to federal-question jurisdiction. During the ratification process, capable individuals had taken both sides of the sovereign immunity issue, and the Constitution's language did not clearly resolve the issue one way or the other. The Justices who were in the majority in *Chisholm* seemed inclined to believe that the Constitution permitted the states to be sued in federal court, and therefore they were likely to have believed that the issue was at least unclear. Under the prevailing explanation and justification of judicial review, the Justices would have been reluctant to overrule the Congress's decision without clearer constitutional guidance.[59]

This conjecture about the early Court's likely reaction to congressional legislation vesting the federal courts with federal-question jurisdiction

---

59. For Iredell, *see* this chapter at 196. For the ratification process, *see* William Fletcher, *A Historical Interpretation of the Eleventh Amendment: A Narrow Construction of an Affirmative Grant of Jurisdiction Rather Than a Prohibition Against Jurisdiction*, 35 STAN. L. REV. 1003, 1047–52 (1983). For the prevailing explanation of judicial review, *see* chapter 8 at 214–27.

over suits against states is severely limited by a stubborn historical fact. The Congress never enacted such legislation, and the Senate's firm rejection of Gallatin's motion strongly suggests that there was no political support for such legislation.

THE FEDERALISTS AND THE ELEVENTH AMENDMENT

The widespread support of the Eleventh Amendment indicates a need for caution in assuming that the Federalists were ardent nationalists bent upon a general consolidation of power in the federal government. At the beginning of the nineteenth century, a thoughtful opponent of the Federalists wrote that "the two great objects of *federalism*, as it is called here, is to draw away as much as possible from the state governments to the general government, and of that to draw as much as possible to the Executive."[60] This does not mean, however, that the Federalists were precociously striving to create a national government as powerful and centralized as the one we have today. The extent of the Federalists' desire for a strong central government is best understood in the context of eighteenth-century ideas on the appropriate allocation of power between the federal and state governments, not twentieth-century ideas.

The Eleventh Amendment clearly limited the national government's power and yet was drafted by a staunch Federalist and fully supported by the Federalists in Congress, who voted for it in overwhelming numbers. No state was more Federalist than Connecticut, and after *Chisholm* was decided, the Connecticut General Assembly passed a resolution urging a constitutional amendment giving the states an extensive immunity from suit in federal court. A member of the state's Standing Order reported that "there is a great unanimity of sentiment [in favor of an amendment]; it will be a happy circumstance if irritating measures which are not immediately necessary can be avoided." A few months later, Connecticut's Federalist representatives in the Congress viewed the amendment's quick passage with "satisfaction" and thought it "most prudent." The Connecticut legislature then approved the amendment "by almost a unanimous vote."[61]

The Federalists' general approval of the Eleventh Amendment indicates a measured attitude toward the cession of power to the federal gov-

---

60. Abraham Baldwin to Joel Barlow (Mar. 26, 1800) (emphasis original, CtY).
61. Chauncey Goodrich to Oliver Wolcott Jr. (Oct. 30, 1793), *excerpted in* 5 DHSC 609–10; James Hillhouse to Samuel Huntington (Mar. 5, 1794), *excerpted in* 5 DHSC 623; Zephania Swift to David Daggett (Mar. 5, 1794), *excerpted in* 5 DHSC 624; Silvester Gilbert to Samuel Peters (Sept. 1, 1796), *excerpted in* 5 DHSC 628.

ernment. The power necessary to accomplish important national objectives was to be ceded. In contrast, powers that were not immediately necessary—powers like the federal courts' jurisdiction over private suits against states—were willingly withheld. Though the Federalist Justices in *Chisholm* were not this pragmatic, they probably felt constrained by the apparent plain meaning of the Judiciary Act and the Constitution.

8

THE COURT
AND THE CONSTITUTION

In the late twentieth century, the Supreme Court's most prominent function is to construe and give effect to the Constitution's limits to government activities, but this role was not as significant in the Court's first decade. Though the Justices occasionally resorted to constitutional interpretation, their primary objective was to bolster and consolidate the new federal government. In this role they engaged in the vigorous, high-profile enforcement of federal criminal law and spent a significant amount of time on international law issues. The Treaty of Paris and the French alliance had to be construed, and the law of nations applicable in prize cases had to be identified and applied. Although the Constitution was relevant in many of these cases, the primary rules of decision were subconstitutional.

One reason that the Constitution played a comparatively secondary role stems from the fundamental concept that the Constitution serves primarily as a limitation to governmental powers. As Oliver Ellsworth stated at the Connecticut ratification convention,

> This Constitution defines the extent of the powers of the general government. If the general legislature should at any time overleap their limits, the judicial department is a constitutional check. If the United States go beyond their powers, if they make a law which the Constitution does not authorize, it is void; and the judicial power, the national judges, who to secure their impartiality are to be made independent, will declare it to be void.[1]

There was therefore no need to resort to the Constitution except in situations in which the government might have exceeded its proper limits.

In the first decade, a confluence of political coincidences unique to the

---

1. Oliver Ellsworth, Speech of Jan. 7, 1788, *reprinted in* 3 DHRC 547, 553.

nation's history effectively preempted the possibility of the Court's being embroiled in many constitutional cases. From the Court's perspective, Ellsworth's idea that the Court served as a "constitutional check" to the government was not really significant unless the Justices believed that the government had actually overleaped its limits. But the likelihood of a significant disagreement between the Court and the government in the 1790s was remote. All the Justices were conservative Federalists who were appointed by two Federalist Presidents. Moreover, the Federalists had at least working control of the Senate and frequently the House of Representatives throughout most of the decade. This control was not always sufficient to insure the enactment of legislation, but it was enough to prevent the enactment of legislation inconsistent with Federalist policy. Given this control, there was no chance of a serious disagreement between the political branches and the bench. Nevertheless, the Court and the Justices on circuit did address a number of significant constitutional issues in its first decade.

JUDICIAL REVIEW OF FEDERAL ACTIONS

On rare occasions such as the Washington Administration's 1793 request for an advisory opinion, the Supreme Court is called upon to test its own official conduct against the limits of the Constitution. Most constitutional issues that come before the Court, however, involve the review of actions taken by another branch of government. If the Court in these latter cases determines that the action is unconstitutional, the Court, exercising its power of judicial review, declares the action void and refuses to give it any effect. This power gives the Court authority to override the considered judgment of a coordinate branch of government and has always been politically controversial.

In the late twentieth century, the Supreme Court's power of judicial review over coordinate branches of the federal government—especially Congress—no longer seems inevitable. This ultimate power is mentioned nowhere in the Constitution, and it is radically inconsistent with the unwritten English constitution, which vested Parliament with ultimate authority to enforce constitutional principles. Likewise, the power is at first glance inconsistent with the theory of government prevalent in the late eighteenth century, which saw the representative legislative branch as the ultimate guarantor of constitutional government.

Perhaps the power of judicial review does not seem inevitable from the hindsight of the twentieth century because the passage of two hundred years has made it difficult to comprehend political institutions and society the way the Founders did. From the time the Constitution was drafted and throughout the Chief Justiceships of Jay and Ellsworth, few people denied that American courts operating under a written constitution had an implicit power of judicial review. To the contrary, numerous individuals at the Constitutional Convention and in the ratification process expressly stated their assumption that the Supreme Court would exercise a power of judicial review. After the Constitution was ratified and the first Congress was convened, Congressmen continued to assume that "if we [decide an issue of constitutional law] improperly the judiciary will revise our decision."[2]

The Court under Chief Justice Jay was certain of its authority to declare an act of Congress unconstitutional. When the carriage tax case was argued in the circuit court for Virginia in 1795, John Wickham, counsel for the government, offered to address the issue of judicial review, but Justice Wilson apparently said no. Wickham later related that the bench informed him that the question whether a federal court could declare an act of Congress to be unconstitutional had "come before each of the judges in their different circuits, and they had all concurred in opinion." It was therefore, he said, "improper as well as unnecessary for me to argue the question." When Wilson foreclosed argument in the carriage tax case, he may have been thinking of Justice Paterson's opinion delivered the previous month in *Vanhorne's Lessee v. Dorrance*. In addition, he undoubtedly had in mind the Invalid Pensioner opinions in which all of the other Justices had agreed that Congress's attempt to impose nonjudicial duties on the circuit courts was unconstitutional and therefore void.[3]

THE SOVEREIGNTY OF THE PEOPLE

In one of the Invalid Pensioner opinions, Justices Wilson and Blair explained that a written Constitution is a legislative act of the people and therefore took precedence over any act of the Congress. Acting in this supreme legislative capacity, the people had ordained that " 'This constitution' is 'the supreme law of the land' " and that "all judicial officers of

---

2. 11 DOCUMENTARY HISTORY OF THE FIRST FEDERAL CONGRESS OF THE UNITED STATES OF AMERICA: DEBATES IN THE HOUSE OF REPRESENTATIVES 884 (Charlene Bickford et al. ed. 1992). For other statements by members of Congress, *see* Maeva Marcus, *Judicial Review in the Early Republic, in* LAUNCHING THE "EXTENDED REPUBLIC": THE FEDERALIST ERA (R. Hoffman ed., publication forthcoming by the University Press of Virginia). For discussions of judicial review at the Constitutional Convention and in the ratification process, *see* chapter 1 at 19–22. For an elaboration of the present chapter's analysis of judicial review in the early Republic, *see* Casto, *Iredell.*

3. JOHN WICKHAM, THE SUBSTANCE OF AN ARGUMENT IN THE CASE OF THE CARRIAGE DUTIES, DELIVERED BEFORE THE CIRCUIT COURT OF THE UNITED STATES, IN VIRGINIA, MAY TERM, 1795, at 15 (1795); Vanhorne's Lessee v. Dorrance, 2 U.S. (2 Dall.) 304 (C.C.D. Pa. 1795). For the Invalid Pensioners opinions, *see* chapter 6 at 175–78.

the United States are bound by oath, or affirmation, to support [it.]" The Justices' unstated conclusion was that they were obliged to follow the people's will and to refuse to enforce any congressional acts contrary to the Constitution.[4]

Although Wilson and Blair presented little more than a cursory outline of their analysis, Justices Iredell and Paterson have left more detailed explanations of judicial review in otherwise unrelated analyses of state constitutional law. In *Vanhornes' Lessee v. Dorrance,* Justice Paterson affirmed the federal courts' power to review the constitutionality of a Pennsylvania statute under the Pennsylvania Constitution. Similarly, some four years before joining the Court, Iredell forcefully argued as a private attorney that North Carolina courts had an implied power of judicial review under the North Carolina constitution. In 1785 the North Carolina legislature passed a statute denying a jury trial to individuals who sought to regain land confiscated during the Revolution. The next year Iredell argued to the state superior court that the statute violated the state constitution's guaranty of trial by jury. Subsequently he published an extensive essay on the issue. In 1787 he reargued the case and persuaded the court to declare the statute unconstitutional. Although Iredell first presented his ideas as an advocate, he subsequently reiterated his beliefs at length in private correspondence with a capable fellow attorney who questioned the propriety of the North Carolina court's exercise of judicial review. After Iredell joined the Supreme Court, he frequently stated that the federal courts had the same power of judicial review under the federal Constitution.[5]

Justice Iredell's explanation and justification merit special attention. Although he developed his ideas in 1787–88 without the assistance of any preexisting analysis of judicial review, his explanation accurately foreshadowed virtually all subsequent judicial discussions of the issue in the early Republic.[6] But his analysis is more than representative. No Justice of the Supreme Court—including Chief Justice Marshall—has ever

---

4. James Wilson, John Blair, and Richard Peters to George Washington (Apr. 18, 1792), *reprinted in* 1 ASP, Miscellaneous 51 and 2 U.S. (2 Dall.) at 411 n. For an elaboration of Wilson's views, *see* James Wilson, *Lectures on Law* (1791), *reprinted in* 1 THE WORKS OF JAMES WILSON 69, 326–31 (Robert McCloskey ed., 1967).

5. *See* Bayard v. Singleton, 1 Martin 42 (N.C. 1787). Iredell's early views are expressed in *An Elector* (Aug. 17, 1786), *reprinted in* 2 IREDELL CORRESPONDENCE 145–49; James Iredell to Richard Spaight (Aug. 12, 1787), *reprinted in id.* 168–70. For subsequent statements by Iredell, *see* this chapter at 222–25 & 229–30.

6. *See* Nelson, *Changing Conceptions of Judicial Review: The Evolution of Constitutional Theory in the States, 1790–1860,* 120 U. PA. L. REV. 1166 (1972). *See also* SYLVIA SNOWISS, JUDICIAL REVIEW AND THE LAW OF THE CONSTITUTION (1990).

written more comprehensive and sophisticated analyses of the issue. Finally, Iredell's explanation and justification of judicial review virtually dictated the fundamental rule of judicial interpretation that the early Justices used in gauging the constitutionality of acts of Congress.

Iredell believed, as all subsequent American attorneys have, that a written constitution is a fundamental law superior to mere legislation. The Constitution was logically fundamental in that it created and limited the legislature. More importantly, he explained that constitutional law is fundamental because it comes directly from the people.

> The people have chosen to be governed under such and such principles. They have not chosen to be governed, or promised to submit upon any other; and the Assembly have no more right to obedience on other Terms, than any different power on earth has a right to govern us; for we have as much agreed to be governed by the Turkish Divan as by our own General Assembly, otherwise than by the express Terms prescribed.

He viewed the Constitution as a "real, original contract between the people and the future Government."[7]

In forming their Constitution or original contract, the people were perfectly familiar with the idea of vesting the legislature with absolute, unreviewable powers. Iredell reminded his readers that this was the model of the unwritten English constitution and that they "had severely smarted under its effect."[8] In America, written constitutions were adopted as express limitations to the English theory and practice of legislative omnipotence. This distinction between written and unwritten constitutions was not simply a matter of form. In the case of an unwritten constitution, the people's approval had to be inferred from longstanding custom and acceptance. In contrast, the process of reducing a constitutional proposal to writing and obtaining its approval by the people's representatives in the ratifying conventions clearly established the constitution's legitimacy. Unlike inferences drawn from custom, the express limitations of a written constitution had a direct and obvious sovereign provenance.

In making the case for judicial review, Iredell had to confront John Locke's idea that the legislative branch is supreme and that the proper

---

7. *An Elector* (Aug. 17, 1786), *reprinted in* 2 IREDELL CORRESPONDENCE 145, 146; James Iredell to Richard Spaight (Aug. 12, 1787), *reprinted in id.* 172. This idea was not unique to Iredell. *See* WOOD chapter 7.

8. *An Elector* (Aug. 17, 1786), *reprinted in* 2 IREDELL CORRESPONDENCE 146.

remedy for legislative abuse is for the people to dissolve the government. Iredell understood "the great argument . . . that though the Assembly have not a *right* to violate the constitution, yet if they *in fact* do so, the only remedy is, either by a humble petition that the law may be repealed, or a universal resistance of the people." He condemned the principle of resistance as a "dreadful expedient" and a "calamitous contingency." Moreover, universal resistance would be feasible only in the face of *"universal [legislative] oppression"* and therefore would not effectively protect minority rights. The humble remedy of petition excited his "indignation," and he rejected it out of hand as contrary to the sovereign relationship between the people and the legislature. "[T]he remedy by petition implies a supposition, that the electors hold their rights by the *favor of their representatives.*"[9]

Nor did he "conceive the remedy by a new election to be of [significant] consequence." Refusing to reelect errant legislators was simply a peaceful form of universal resistance and therefore "would only secure the views of a majority." In Iredell's opinion, "every citizen . . . should have a surer pledge of his constitutional rights than the wisdom and activity of any occasional majority of his fellow-citizens, who, if their own rights are in fact unmolested, may care very little for his."[10]

Although Iredell thus saw the judiciary as a protector of minority rights under the Constitution, he was well aware that many of his fellow Americans distrusted the judiciary. He therefore felt constrained to note several structural checks to judicial abuse. In the first place, the judges were limited by the nature of the judicial process. Iredell emphatically denied "that the judges are appointed arbiters, and to determine as it were upon any application, whether the Assembly have or have not violated the Constitution; but when an act is necessarily brought in judgment before them, they must, unavoidably, determine one way or another." This idea is readily recognizable as a nascent version of the case or controversy requirement that has come to play a prominent role under the Constitution.[11]

In addition, Iredell addressed some other factors that would control judicial abuse. No public official, he stated, wants "to make himself *odious* to the people by giving unnecessary and wanton offence." Moreover, under the North Carolina constitution—as was not the case under the sub-

---

9. *Id.* 147 (emphasis original); JOHN LOCKE, THE SECOND TREATISE OF GOVERNMENT chapters 13 and 19.

10. James Iredell to Richard Spaight (Aug. 122, 1787), *reprinted in* 2 IREDELL CORRESPONDENCE 175.

11. *Id.* 173. *See* WOOD 301–5.

sequent federal Constitution—the judges' salaries were subject to legislative reduction. Iredell believed that this limited legislative control would likely "prevent a wanton abuse of [judicial] power." Nevertheless, he believed that legislative control over salaries was on balance undesirable. Foreshadowing the federal Constitution's establishment of a more absolute judicial independence, he cautioned that North Carolina's legislative control over judicial salaries "may in some instances produce an actual bias the other way, which, in my humble opinion, is the great danger to be apprehended." Finally, Iredell offered a pragmatic—even cynical—argument: in any event, "if the judges should be disposed to abuse their power . . . they have means of doing so" by merely misconstruing the meaning of legislative acts. *"[T]hose acts may be wilfully misconstrued, as well as the constitution."*[12]

Notwithstanding these restraints upon judicial abuse, Iredell admitted that the power of judicial review "is indeed alarming," because under the North Carolina constitution there was no court of appeals to review the state's primary trial court. "I don't think," concluded Iredell, "any country can be safe without some Court of Appeals that has no original jurisdiction at all, since men are commonly careful enough to correct the errors of others, though seldom sufficiently watchful of their own, especially if they have no check upon them." This improvement, which was much to be desired, was more or less obtained under the federal Constitution.[13]

In the twentieth century, the rise of legal positivism has seriously attenuated the persuasiveness of Iredell's analysis. Today virtually all American lawyers believe that law is the expression of government policy. In addition, today's lawyers believe that judges are themselves lawmakers and that the judicial resolution of a particular case is largely an outcome of the judges' understanding of appropriate governmental policy. From this new philosophical viewpoint, the issue of judicial review entails a clash between the Congress's and the judiciary's conflicting views of appropriate constitutional policy. Certainly there is nothing in the Constitution that warrants an arbitrary preferment of judicial policy judgments to legislative judgments. The doctrine of judicial review is therefore more subject to theoretical objection than it was two hundred years ago.

---

12. James Iredell to Richard Spaight (Aug. 12, 1787), *reprinted in* 2 IREDELL CORRESPONDENCE 177 (emphasis original); *An Elector* (Aug. 17, 1786), *reprinted in* 2 IREDELL CORRESPONDENCE 148–49 (emphasis original).
13. James Iredell to Richard Spaight (Aug. 12, 1787), *reprinted in* 2 IREDELL CORRESPONDENCE 176.

But this late-twentieth-century analysis would not have bothered Iredell. In his mind, judicial review did not involve a clash between Congress and the judiciary but rather one between the Congress and the sovereign will of the people, with the judiciary serving as a ministerial tool for implementing the people's sovereign and constitutional judgment. From this eighteenth-century viewpoint, the proper resolution of the conflict was self-evident.

Iredell was, however, a sophisticated attorney who fully understood that judges were capable of misconstruing the Constitution and in effect supplanting the will of the people with their own judicial will. He divided this problem of judicial misconstruction into two general categories. The judges might willfully and knowingly reject the Constitution's clear meaning, or they might be forced to construe an ambiguous constitutional provision that had no clear meaning. In either case, a declaration that a statute was unconstitutional could not be founded on the people's sovereignty.

Iredell was troubled by the possibility of abuse and adduced several factors that would constrain abuse. He also believed that "[t]his kind of objection, if applicable at all, will reach all judicial power whatever." Moreover, *"when once you established the necessary existence of any power, the argument as to abuse ceases to destroy its validity."* Iredell was simply unwilling to renounce judicial review because an occasional aberrant judge might willfully abuse the power.[14]

In the twentieth century, the most troubling aspect of judicial power involves unclear cases in which judges give an admittedly ambiguous constitutional provision a good-faith judicial construction. The exercise of judicial review in such a case could not be described as the ministerial implementation of the people's sovereign and constitutional will, and consistent with his theory, Iredell renounced judicial review in such cases. "In all doubtful cases, to be sure," he wrote, "the [legislative] Act [under review] ought to be supported; it should be unconstitutional beyond dispute before it is pronounced such."[15]

JUSTICE CHASE'S DOUBTS

Throughout the Court's initial decade of operation, the only Justices who might possibly have had doubts about the propriety of judicial review were Justice Chase and the nonentity Alfred Moore. When Iredell successfully argued the case of *Bayard v. Singleton* to the North Carolina

---

14. *Id.* 173 (emphasis original).

15. *Id.* 175.

court, Moore represented the other side and may, in his capacity as an advocate, have argued against judicial review. If Moore had qualms about the propriety of judicial review, the famous case of *Marbury v. Madison* presented an opportunity for him to air his doubts. But Moore was absent from the Court when *Marbury* was argued and decided. In contrast to Moore, Justice Chase frequently demonstrated considerable legal talent while serving on the Court, and Chase was initially noncommittal toward the doctrine of judicial review.[16]

At the time that Justice Wilson stated during argument before the circuit court on the constitutionality of the carriage tax that all the Justices had concurred in the propriety of judicial review, Justice Chase was not a member of the Court. Two years later, when the *Hylton* case reached the Court, Chase had no qualms about holding that the carriage tax was constitutional. He clearly stated, however, that he was withholding his opinion on the fundamental issue of judicial review. "As I do not think the tax on carriages is a *direct* tax, it is unnecessary *at this time*," he said, "for me to determine, whether this court, *constitutionally* possesses the power to declare an act of Congress *void*, on the ground of its being made contrary to and in violation of, the Constitution." Two years later he stated that he had yet to decide the issue.[17]

Whether Chase actually entertained any serious doubts on the subject is unclear. If he did, he had resolved his doubts by 1800, when he unequivocally embraced the power of judicial review in a grand jury charge. Chase based his conclusion on the same analysis that Iredell had presented with great detail in North Carolina more than ten years earlier and that Justice Paterson had reiterated on circuit in *Vanhorne's Lessee v. Dorrance*. Rather than present his own analysis, Chase merely cited a specific passage from *Vanhorne's Lessee* in which Paterson had stated,

> The Constitution is the work or will of the People themselves, in their original, sovereign, and unlimited capacity. Law is the work or will of the Legislature in their derivative and subordinate capacity. . . . The Constitution fixes limits to the exercise of legislative authority, and prescribes the orbit within which it must move. . . . Whatever may be the case of other countries [Great Britain, for example], yet in this there can be no doubt, that every act of the Legislature, repugnant to the Constitution, is absolutely void.

---

16. For Moore, *see* 1 Martin 42, 48 (N.C. 1787); Leon Friedman, *Alfred Moore, in* FRIEDMAN & ISRAEL 269, 277.

17. Hylton v. United States, 3 U.S. (3 Dall.) 171, 175 (1796) (emphasis original); Calder v. Bull, 3 U.S. (3 Dall.) 387, 392 (1798).

This rationale is the same that numerous state judges adopted in the 1790s and that Chief Justice Marshall advanced in 1803 when he delivered his opinion in *Marbury v. Madison*.[18]

INTERPRETING THE CONSTITUTION

"Unconstitutional Beyond Dispute"

Throughout the 1790s Justice Iredell and his fellow Justices frequently reiterated the idea that the power of judicial review should be exercised only when the statute in question was "unconstitutional beyond dispute," but they did not perceive this limitation as an absolute mechanical rule. The most interesting discussion of the relationship between judicial review and constitutional interpretation took place in response to a preliminary motion by the defense to dismiss the criminal prosecution in *United States v. Ravara*.[19] This litigation took place in the circuit court for Pennsylvania before a distinguished panel consisting of Justices Wilson and Iredell and Judge Peters. Iredell would have declared the pertinent act of Congress unconstitutional and dismissed the prosecution, but Wilson and Peters disagreed with him, and the case proceeded forward.

The *Ravara* case is an example of the uneven quality of Alexander Dallas's *Reports*. Three different versions of Iredell's opinion and two versions of Wilson's opinion have survived. Iredell prepared a typically comprehensive written opinion that he delivered personally in court. In addition, two years later, he wrote a memorandum recording, as best as he could recollect, his opinion and Wilson's conflicting opinion. Finally, Dallas, who served in the case as defense counsel, published a brief report of the conflicting opinions. Although Dallas's report is written in the first person as if Iredell were speaking, the report is in reality Dallas's two-sentence summary of Iredell's detailed opinion. Similarly, Iredell's subsequent recollection of Wilson's and Peters's majority opinion is more

---

18. Vanhorne's Lessee v. Dorrance, 2 U.S. (2 Dall.) 304, 308 (C.C.D. Pa. 1795) (Paterson, J.), *referred to in* Justice Chase, Charge to the Pennsylvania Grand Jury (Apr. 12, 1800), *reprinted in* 3 DHRC 408, 412, For state judges' views of judicial review, *see* Nelson article cited *supra* note 6. For reiterations of Chase's belief in judicial review, *see* United States v. Callender, Wharton's State Trials 688, 715–18 (C.C.D. Va. 1800); Samuel Chase to John Marshall (Apr. 24, 1802), *reprinted in* 6 MARSHALL PAPERS 109, 112–13.

19. 2 U.S. (2 Dall.) 297 (C.C. D. Pa. 1793), *discussed* in chapter 5 at 139–41.

detailed and significantly more nuanced than Dallas's cursory report of their opinion.[20]

The defense motion was highly technical and hardly worth considering but for the disagreement it sparked between Wilson and Iredell. The Constitution provides that "*In all cases affecting* ambassadors, other public Ministers, and *Consuls,* and those in which the state shall be a party, *the Supreme Court shall have original jurisdiction* [that is, trial jurisdiction]. In all the other cases before mentioned the Supreme Court shall have appellate jurisdiction."[21] Mr. Ravara's counsel argued that this provision vesting the Supreme Court with original jurisdiction over all cases affecting consuls was exclusive and that Ravara therefore could not be tried in the Circuit Court.

Justice Wilson and Judge Peters rejected this assertion of exclusive jurisdiction. They believed that the case was within the circuit court's general criminal jurisdiction under the Judiciary Act. Two years later, Iredell wrote:

> I think the principal reasons assigned by Judge Wilson and Judge Peters were that [the prosecution was within the general] Act of Congress . . . that tho' an Act of Congress plainly contrary to the Constitution was void, yet no such construction should be given in a doubtful case; and that in this case, the Constitution, tho' it said "the Supreme Court should have *original* jurisdiction," yet not having said it should be also *exclusive,* it was not necessary to give such an interpretation to it. I think these were substantially the reasons.[22]

In other words, Wilson and Peters concluded that the Congress had established a concurrent trial jurisdiction in both the circuit courts and the Supreme Court and that the Constitution did not clearly prohibit this concurrent vesting of original jurisdiction. *Ravara* was a perfect case in which to invoke the idea that the power of judicial review should not be exercised in a doubtful case, and the majority expressly invoked this general principle.

---

20. *See generally* Joyce, *The Rise of the Supreme Court Reporter,* 83 Mich. L. Rev. 1291, 1294–1306 (1985). For the three versions of Iredell's opinions, *see* United States v. Ravara, 2 U.S. (2 Dall.) 297, 298–99 (C.C. Pa. 1793); Iredell, Manuscript Opinion in Ravara (Charles E. Johnson Papers, Nc-Ar); Iredell, Recollection of the Opinions in Ravara (McDougall Papers, NHi) (mislabeled "Memoranda by John Jay").

21. U.S. Const. art. III, § 2 (emphasis added).

22. Iredell, Recollection (emphasis original), *cited in supra* note 20.

The opinion of Wilson and Peters in *Ravara* was well reasoned, and it was to be adopted ninety years later by the Supreme Court. Nevertheless, Iredell was not convinced. He had a powerful counteranalysis that—like the best legal arguments—combined the text of the applicable written laws with cogent public policy. Iredell reasoned that the Constitution specifically vested the Supreme Court with original jurisdiction over cases involving foreign diplomats or in which a state is a party "on account of [these cases'] superior importance to the peace & welfare of the Union." He believed that the majority's idea of concurrent jurisdiction was insufficiently protective of the nation's peace and welfare because the choice between trial in the Supreme or circuit court was, as a practical matter, left to the prosecution rather than the defendant diplomat.[23]

Even worse, Iredell pointed out that the plain meaning of the Constitution seemed to bar the Supreme Court from exercising an appellate jurisdiction in cases within its original jurisdiction. Iredell's analysis of the Supreme Court's appellate jurisdiction was essentially textual. He noted that the Constitution divided the Supreme Court's jurisdiction into two separate categories of trial and appellate authority. The Court's original jurisdiction included cases affecting consuls, and "in all other cases" the Court had an appellate jurisdiction. To Iredell, the obvious meaning of the phrase "in all other cases" was to exclude the original jurisdiction cases from the Court's appellate jurisdiction. In Iredell's mind, this lack of Supreme Court appellate jurisdiction over consul cases virtually precluded Wilson's idea of a concurrent trial jurisdiction in both the Supreme Court and the inferior circuit court. Obviously the framers of the Constitution believed that these cases were extremely important to the national peace and welfare. He reasoned therefore

> that as the Supreme Court was thought proper to be selected as the court of express original jurisdiction, an [express] appellate jurisdiction in such cases would likewise have been given to it, if those who framed the constitution had themselves considered a concurrent authority of this nature could under their own constitution have been vested in any other court.[24]

When Iredell recollected the case two years later, he displayed a little more concern about the overturning of an express legislative judgment. After presenting his textual analysis, he suggested that "no one could

23. *See* Bors v. Preston, 111 U.S. 252 (1884). *See also* Ames v. Kansas, 111 U.S. 449 (1884). Iredell, Manuscript Opinion, *cited in supra* note 20.
24. Iredell, Manuscript Opinion, *cited in supra* note 20.

imagine that Congress, tho' they might in the hurry of business inadvert-
ently make a provision inconsistent with the Constitution, deliberately
meant to transgress it." In this context, he reiterated an idea that he had
only mentioned in his original opinion. Perhaps the Congress had not
consciously intended to vest the circuit courts with a concurrent power
over criminal prosecutions against consuls because "the act of Congress
had not given express Jurisdiction to the circuit court in this instance."
Under this analysis there was no real conflict between the Constitution
and the Judiciary Act.[25]

In contrast to the majority opinion in *Ravara,* the requirement that an
act must be unconstitutional beyond dispute did not play a prominent
role in the Justices' opinions in *Hylton v. United States.* Justice Chase concluded his opinion with an affirmation that he would exercise the power
of judicial review only *"in a very clear case,"* but he and the other Justices
devoted their opinions to the substantive question of whether the carriage tax was constitutional. Given the importance of the power to tax,
the split decision in the circuit court, and the widespread opposition
to the tax, a Supreme Court decision suggesting that the tax's constitutionality was unclear would have been a political catastrophe. The
government's appeal was significantly motivated by a desire to obtain a
Supreme Court decision firmly supporting the tax. The Justices may
therefore have gone straight to the merits of the case in order to validate
the tax and provide judicial support to the government's efforts to raise
revenues.[26]

Four years later, in the last term of Court before John Marshall became
Chief Justice, the Justices again had occasion to resort to the fundamental principle that the Court should overturn only clearly unconstitutional
statutes. In *Cooper v. Telfair* a former resident of Georgia sued a Georgia
citizen to recover a debt originally incurred in 1774. The plaintiff, Mr.
Cooper, had sided with the King during the Revolution and fled the
state. In 1782 the Georgia legislature passed a bill of attainder listing
Cooper by name, declaring that he was guilty of treason, and confiscat-
ing all debts owed to him. In Cooper's subsequent civil action to recover
the debt, he argued that the bill of attainder was unconstitutional under
the Georgia constitution. The federal Constitution specifically prohibited state bills of attainder, but Cooper's counsel did not rely upon the
federal Constitution. His counsel probably believed that the federal Con-

---

25. Iredell, Recollection, *cited in supra* note 20.
26. Hylton v. United States, 3 U.S. (3 Dall.) 171, 175 (1796) (emphasis original),
discussed in chapter 4 at 101–05.

stitution should not be applied to a bill of attainder enacted before the Constitution was ratified.[27]

Although bills of attainder were generally held in disfavor, they were not specifically forbidden by the Georgia constitution. The plaintiff's attorneys therefore had to be inventive. They argued that the bill of attainder passed by the Georgia legislature was actually a judicial act because it constituted a conviction for treason. Thus the bill violated the Georgia constitution's separation of powers clause and another more specific clause requiring "treason against the state, to be tried ['by jury'] in the county where the crime was committed." This respectable argument was rejected in the circuit court by Chief Justice Ellsworth and the district judge.[28]

The Supreme Court decided the case while Ellsworth was in Europe, and the Justices delivered their opinions seriatim. Apparently the specific activities found by the legislature to be treasonous had been committed outside the state and therefore did not come within the literal scope of the state constitution's treason clause. Justice Washington said that if the offense had been committed within the state, he would have ruled the bill unconstitutional because Cooper was not tried by jury in the county where the crime was committed. He was not, however, willing to rely upon the Georgia constitution's vague clause on the separation of powers. In Washington's view, the "presumption, indeed, must always be in favor of the validity of laws, if the contrary is not clearly demonstrated."[29]

Justice Paterson was of much the same mind. He wrote,

> The constitutions of several of the other states of the Union, contain the same general principles and restrictions; but it never was imagined, that they applied to a case like the present; and to authorize this court to pronounce any law void, it must be a clear and unequivocal breach of the constitution, not a doubtful and argumentative implication.

The separation of powers argument was too vague.[30]

Justice Chase was also leery of the separation of powers argument. "The general principles," he wrote, "contained in the constitution are

---

27. 4 U.S. (4 Dall.) 14 (1800). For the federal Constitution, *see* U.S. Const. art. I, § 10.

28. *See* Opinion of Chief Justice Ellsworth in Cowper v. Telfair, unreported (C.C.D. Ga. 1799), *reprinted in* Casto, *Iredell.*

29. 4 U.S. (4 Dall.) at 18.

30. *Id.* at 19.

not to be regarded as rules to fetter and control; but as matter merely declaratory and directory." The reporter, Alexander Dallas, also indicates that Chase drew a distinction between the constitutionality of state legislation enacted before rather than after the federal Constitution was ratified. Dallas's summary of Chase's opinion is garbled, but apparently Chase was addressing the question of whether the legislation was contrary to the federal Constitution. He believed it was not.[31]

In theory *Cooper* and *Ravara* were two different types of cases. One involved the use of judicial review to give effect to the federal Constitution, while the other involved a state constitution. But the Justices do not seem to have treated this difference as significant. In both situations they stated that legislation should be declared unconstitutional only when it appeared unconstitutional beyond dispute. In both situations, this fundamental principle of interpretation guarded against the judicial creation of constitutional rights and limitations that the people in their sovereign capacity as constitution makers had not intended.[32]

Calder v. Bull

According to the fundamental interpretive corollary of judicial review, only legislation that was unconstitutional beyond doubt should be declared void. This corollary, however, did not provide any guidance for determining in a given case whether particular legislation was or was not unconstitutional beyond doubt. The actual interpretation of the Constitution required resort to additional principles. A good example is *Hylton v. United States,* in which the Court was greatly influenced by a perceived underlying constitutional purpose to vest the federal government with an effective authority to raise revenues. Guided by this nontextual purpose, the Court gave a very narrow construction to the Constitution's direct-tax clause to facilitate the government's ability to raise revenues. Another principle of interpretation is embodied by Justice Iredell's resort in *Ravara* to the plain grammatical meaning of the Constitution's allocation of original and appellate jurisdiction to the Supreme Court.[33]

These and additional interpretive techniques are found in *Calder v. Bull,* an otherwise insignificant Connecticut case involving a dispute over a will. In *Calder* a state probate court initially refused to recognize the validity of the will in question. Apparently the losing side failed to file an

---

31. *Id.* at 19.
32. *See* Casto, *Iredell.*
33. For Hylton, *see* chapter 4 at 101–05; For Ravara, *see* chapter 5 at 139–41 and this chapter at 222–25.

appeal within the time specified by state law and petitioned the state legislature for relief. An act was then passed granting a new probate hearing, and at the second hearing the probate court held that the will was valid after all. The case was then appealed through the state courts to the United States Supreme Court. In the Supreme Court, the state act granting a new hearing was challenged as contrary to the federal constitutional provision that "no State shall . . . pass any . . . ex post facto Law."[34]

Because of illness, Chief Justice Ellsworth did not hear the arguments in *Calder* and therefore did not participate in the decision. Although Justice Paterson initially had some doubts, he and the other associate Justices eventually agreed that the Constitution had not been violated and delivered their opinions seriatim. The report of Justice Cushing's opinion is brief and casts little light on the interpretive process. But the opinions of Chase, Paterson, and Iredell provide some valuable insights.[35]

Chase began by noting that the ex post facto clause literally forbade the states to enact laws after the fact. But this literal reading gives no indication of "*what fact; of what nature,* or *kind;* and by *whom* done."[36] Therefore the words of the Constitution taken in their general sense provided no significant guidance to the clause's meaning. Chase, however, along with Paterson and Iredell, was able to flesh out the clause's meaning.

After his attempt to give a literal meaning to the clause, Chase turned to the context of the clause within the Constitution's other provisions. In addition to the ex post facto clause, the Constitution forbade the states to "make anything but gold and silver coin a Tender in Payment of Debts [or to pass any] Law impairing the Obligation of Contracts." Chase reasoned that these provisions would have been unnecessary if the ex post facto clause was a general prohibition against any state law that might retroactively impair any preexisting personal right. Therefore, in order to avoid a redundancy, he was inclined to infer that the ex post facto clause was not intended to protect private or personal rights that one citizen might have against another.[37]

Justice Paterson drew the same inference. "Where is the necessity or use," he wrote, of the specific provision against impairing contractual obligations,

> if a law impairing the obligation of contracts, be comprehended

---

34. Calder v. Bull, 3 U.S. (3 Dall.) 386 (1798).

35. *See* Casto, *Iredell.*

36. Calder v. Bull, 3 U.S. (3 Dall.) at 390 (emphasis original).

37. *Id.* at 390.

within the terms *ex post facto law?* It is obvious from the specification of contracts in the last member of the clause, that the framers of the Constitution, did not understand or use the words in the sense contended for on the part of the Plaintiffs in error.

This parsing of the precise words of the Constitution is similar to the textual analysis that Justice Iredell urged without success in the *Ravara* case. In an earlier essay, Paterson wrote that "the constitution of the United States is reduced to written certainty and exactitude; and, therefore, all we have to do is to open our eyes and read."[38]

Whether Paterson and Chase would have been willing to base their opinions entirely upon an inference drawn from the Framers' diction is unclear. Perhaps their bare inference would have sufficed in a case like *Calder,* in which the result was to sustain rather than overturn the statute in question. But Paterson and Chase had another interpretive strategy that supplemented and supported their inference. They each noted that although the constitutional language in question had no readily identifiable general meaning, it had a well-known technical meaning. Chase emphasized that the "expressions 'ex post facto laws,' are *technical,* they had been in use long before the Revolution, and had acquired an appropriate meaning, by *Legislators, Lawyers,* and *Authors.*" Paterson agreed. Specifically, the expression "ex post facto law" had come to be limited to laws that imposed a retroactive criminal punishment. Both men relied upon Blackstone's *Commentaries* to establish this technical meaning. Similarly, both pointed to various state constitutional provisions in which the phrase was clearly used in the narrow technical sense that spoke to retroactive criminal laws but not retroactive civil laws.[39]

Justice Iredell also delivered an opinion, but his analysis lacked his characteristic comprehensiveness. Because he had "not had an opportunity to reduce [his] opinion to writing," he limited himself to the statement of some "general principles." After reviewing the philosophical basis for judicial review, he turned to the ex post facto clause. Implicitly adopting a well-established common-law method of construing written or positive laws, he first considered the mischief or harm that the ex post facto clause was designed to remedy. "The history of every country in *Europe,*" he said, "will furnish flagrant instances" of the tyrannical imposition of retroactive criminal penalties. "The temptation to such abuses

---

38. *Id.* at 397; William Paterson, *On the U.S. Constitution & Other Forms of Govt.* (ca. 1794–1795) (William Paterson Papers, NjR).

39. Calder v. Bull, 3 U.S. (3 Dall.) at 391 (Chase, J.) (emphasis original); *id.* at 396 (Paterson, J.).

of power is unfortunately too alluring for human virtue; and, therefore, the framers of the *American* Constitutions have wisely denied to the respective Legislatures, Federal and well as State, the possession of the power itself."[40]

Iredell went on to note that the "policy, the reason and humanity of the prohibition" should not be extended to civil cases because "private rights must yield to public exigencies." For example, "Highways are run through private grounds. Fortifications, Light-houses, and other public edifices, are necessarily sometimes built upon the soil owned by individuals." Justice Chase had voiced a similar thought in his opinion when he noted that the expansion of the ex post facto clause beyond the criminal realm would "greatly restrict the power of the federal and state legislatures; and the consequences of such a *construction* may not be foreseen."[41]

This excursion into public policy is inconsistent with the then regnant model of the judicial process. Perhaps Iredell and Chase were responding to a portion of Justice Paterson's opinion in which Paterson stated a "strong aversion" to all "retrospective laws in general."[42] When viewed in this light, Iredell's and Chase's discussion of policy could be seen as a defense of the wisdom of the Constitution rather than constitutional interpretation. In any event, the Justices' resort to public policy was in the context of a decision to validate rather than invalidate a legislative act.

Framers' Intent

Although the early Supreme Court Justices used a variety of interpretive strategies in seeking the Constitution's meaning, one approach is noticeably absent from their opinions. In the late twentieth century, legal arguments about the Constitution's meaning are frequently based, at least in part, upon the records of debate in the Constitutional Convention. The legitimacy of this particular form of analysis is based upon a simple and powerful idea. If a clause was intended by the Framers to establish a particular constitutional principle and the clause has not been amended, it should be enforced some two hundred years later as it was

---

40. *Id.* at 399 (emphasis original). For a more elaborate discussion by Justice Iredell on the constitutional meaning of ex post facto, *see* Minge v. Gilmour, 17 F. Cas. 440, 444 (C.C.D. N.C. 1798) (No. 9631).

41. 3 U.S. (3 Dall.) at 399 (Iredell, J.); *id.* at 393 (Chase, J.) (emphasis original).

42. *Id.* at 397. Earlier that summer Iredell noted in another case that when Calder first came to the Court, a "majority of the judges appeared to be convinced" that the ex post facto should be given its traditional technical meaning, "but upon the doubt of one of them, the case was not decided." Minge v. Gilmour, 17 F. Cas. 440 (C.C.D. N.C. 1978). Apparently Justice Paterson was the one who was initially doubtful.

originally intended. This straightforward mode of analysis is impossible, however, without persuasive evidence that establishes the original intent with reasonable certainty. Modern original-intent arguments therefore commonly rely upon the records of debate at the Constitutional Convention. Those records, however, were not published in the eighteenth century. Moreover, early Supreme Court Justices who had direct knowledge of the proceedings in Philadelphia almost never used this form of analysis.

In *Calder*, both Paterson and Chase specifically referred to "the framers of the Constitution," but they may have used this phrase primarily as a literary device. In each instance Paterson and Chase stated that other specific clauses protecting against the retrospective abridgment of private property or contract rights indicated that the ex post facto clause was not intended by "the framers" as a general bar to all retrospective laws. In this context, the reference to the framers' intent added nothing to the structural argument.[43]

Although Paterson did not use framers'-intent arguments, others of his generation factored the Constitutional Convention's deliberations into their constitutional analyses. For example, in his first State of the Union Address, President Washington recommended that Congress consider "the institution of a national university." When the House subsequently took up this recommendation, Roger Sherman argued that the creation of a national university was beyond the Congress's constitutional powers. Sherman noted that "a proposition to vest Congress with power to establish a National University was made in the General Convention, but it was negatived. It was thought sufficient that this power should be exercised by the States in their separate capacity." No further action was taken on the President's recommendation.[44]

Six years later, President Washington refused a formal request by the House of Representatives for executive papers related to the Jay Treaty. In explaining and justifying his refusal, the President reminded the House that he had "been a member of the General Convention and [knew] the principles on which the Constitution was formed." He explained, among other things, that

proofs . . . may be found in the journals of the General Convention, which I have deposited in the office of the Department of State. In

---

43. Calder v. Bull, 3 U.S. (3 Dall.) at 397 (Paterson, J.); *id.* at 394 (Chase, J.). *See also* Casto, *Iredell.*

44. George Washington, First Annual Address (Jan. 8, 1790), *reprinted in* RICHARDSON 57–59; 2 ANNALS 1551 (Mr. Sherman).

those journals it will appear that a proposition was made "that no treaty should be binding on the United States which was not ratified by a law [that is, concurred in by the House]," and that the proposition was explicitly rejected.

Because the House had no constitutional role in the process of making treaties, the President refused to provide the requested papers.[45]

Although Washington, Sherman, and others clearly thought resort to framers' intent was a legitimate mode of constitutional interpretation, other capable individuals—most notably, James Madison—emphatically argued to the contrary.[46] The most plausible explanation of this jumbled historical record is that the Founding Generation was not guided by a consensus on the abstract issue of whether resort to framers' intent was legitimate. Instead they seem to have viewed framers' intent as a plausible argument to which there was a plausible counterargument. This pragmatic explanation, however, does not explain the almost total absence of framers'-intent analyses in the Supreme Court's opinions. The early Justices were pragmatic men. Why did they not use a framers'-intent analysis when it supported their decisions?

Perhaps the answer lies in the theoretical underpinning of the doctrine of judicial review, whose fundamental premise was the ultimate sovereignty of the people. The framers in Philadelphia merely drafted a document that was subsequently approved by the people's representatives in the ratification conventions. The Constitution's legitimacy derived from the ratification process, not the drafting process. Therefore, to the extent that the Court construed the Constitution by reference to secret Convention proceedings unknown to the people, the Court's construction lacked the imprimatur of the people's fundamental authority.

James Madison advanced this very argument in the House debates over the call for the Jay Papers. The extent to which this argument was persuasive to his fellow representatives is unclear. Debate in the early Congresses indicates that the members were quite eclectic in their interpretation of the Consitution and more freewheeling than the Court. Madison's argument, however, would have been especially powerful in the context of judicial review. One of the problems with judicial review was that, as a general proposition, Congress is clearly more representative of the people's will than is the Court. As Justice Chase noted in one of his discussions of judicial review, "It should be remembered, that the

---

45. *See* chapter 4 at 97–98; George Washington, Message to the House of Representatives (Mar. 30, 1796), *reprinted in* Richardson 186–88.
46. *See* 5 Annals 775–781, *discussed in* this chapter at 235.

members of Congress are chosen *mediately*, and *immediately* by *the people*, in the manner, and for the period *they themselves* prescribed, and it is their fault if they do not elect men of *abilities*, and *integrity*." In contrast, federal judges are appointed for life; they are not subject to reelection. Under the doctrine of judicial review, the Court could overturn the legislative decisions of the people's representatives only when it was ministerially enforcing the people's constitutional judgment. Therefore, in exercising this ministerial power, the Court could not legitimately resort to information that had not informed the people's judgment. At least that is the clear implication of the generally accepted justification for judicial review.[47]

This relationship between the theoretical underpinning of judicial review and the propriety of resorting to framers' intent would not be relevant in situations in which the Court was not reviewing the constitutionality of legislation, but the Ellsworth and Jay Courts almost never construed the Constitution except in cases involving the constitutionality of legislation. The sole exception was the Justices' refusal to answer the questions asked by President Washington at the height of the Neutrality Crisis of 1793.[48] In that context, the Court was not asked to override the decision of the people's legislative representatives; nor was it asked to override a firm demand from the President. The Justices' apparent resort to framers' intent therefore did not raise the serious problem that a similar reliance in the context of judicial review would have.

Although this idea about the relationship between judicial review and framers' intent logically follows the accepted justification for judicial review and is consistent with the Justices' various opinions, the idea can be neither proven nor disproven. Unfortunately, there do not seem to be surviving documents that clearly indicate whether the Justices ever viewed resort to framers' intent in this light. Moreover, even if the idea is historically accurate, the Justices probably would have considered it more as a pragmatic consideration than an absolute limitation.

Whether the Justices would actually have resorted to the Convention's proceedings in a close case is difficult to determine. Being pragmatic, in a close case they would probably have used a framers'-intent argument to bolster a decision that particular legislation was constitutional. In such a case they would be affirming rather than rejecting the judgment of the people's elected representatives. *Calder* was not such a case because

---

47. *Id.*; Justice Chase, Charge to the Pennsylvania Grand Jury (Apr. 12, 1800) (emphasis original), *reprinted in* 3 DHSC 408, 411. *Accord*, Currie's Administrators v. Mut. Assurance Soc., 14 Va. (4 Hen. & M.) 315, 347 (1809) (Roane, J.).
48. *See* chapter 4 at 75–82.

Calder was not close. As the Justices amply demonstrated, everyone knew that the phrase "ex post facto" had a specific technical meaning limited to criminal sanctions.

In contrast, the Justices probably would not have resorted to the Convention's proceedings as a determinative basis for declaring an act of Congress unconstitutional. If the conflict between the Constitution and the legislation were unclear, the fundamental premise of judicial review would not permit the Court to declare the act unconstitutional. In such a case, resort to framers' intent would not significantly alter the fact that the Court was exercising the power of judicial review in a manner not provided for by the sovereign people. On the other hand, if an act of Congress were clearly unconstitutional, there would be no need to resort to the framers' intent. Nevertheless, in a clear case the Justices might have referred to the Convention's proceedings as window dressing for their opinion.

Ratifiers' Intent

In contrast to the framers' intent, the Supreme Court frequently used arguments ultimately founded on the ratifiers' intent. In fact, under the prevailing constitutional theory, any mode of interpretation that was not based upon the ratifiers' intent was suspect. The Constitution was not an agreement among the various states but rather came from the people and became effective upon being approved or ratified by the state ratifying conventions. These bodies represented the people and operated independently from the state governments, at least in theory.[49] Because the Constitution's validity was based upon its status as the direct expression of the people's sovereign will, the people's intent evidenced by the ratification process was a valid consideration in any issue of constitutional interpretation.

Except for the apparent reliance upon framers' intent in the 1793 refusal to provide an advisory opinion, all of the early Supreme Court's approaches to constitutional interpretation can be viewed as quests for the ratifiers'intent, which is essentially to say the people's intent. At first glance this statement seems inconsistent with the language of the Justices' opinions in which they occasionally referred to the framers' intent. In all likelihood, however, this occasional usage does not represent a conscious endorsement of resort to framers' intent as opposed to ratifiers' intent. The Justices' diction was probably based upon an unexamined as-

---

49. *See, e.g.,* FEDERALIST No. 40. *See generally* WOOD at 532–36.

sumption of unity between the intent of the framers who drafted the Constitution and the people who ratified it. In *Calder,* Justice Iredell said that "the people of the *United States* [had] framed the Federal Constitution." If the Justices meant to import ideas into the Constitution that had not been approved by the people, they were flatly rejecting the accepted constitutional theory that sovereignty resided in the people.[50]

The Justices themselves never had occasion to address the difference between framers' and ratifiers' intent, but James Madison did in the congressional debates over the House's request for papers related to the Jay Treaty. During the debate, the Federalists argued that the House had no right to the papers because the Constitution vested the Senate with exclusive authority over matters related to treaties. In support of this general argument, William Vans Murray sprang an immensely clever debater's trick. With great irony and almost unctuous flattery, he asked James Madison to tell the House what the Convention had decided on the issue of the House's authority over treaties. Madison's friend and ally Albert Gallatin initially responded to Murray's ploy, but after President Washington relied on the Convention's proceedings in his refusal to provide the requested papers, Madison felt obliged to address the issue of framers' intent.

Madison began with a brilliant and detailed analysis of the difficulty of determining after the fact the collective intent of a deliberative body. He concluded by denying the legitimacy of referring to the framers' intent even if the intent could be ascertained. The Constitution recommended by the Convention, he said, was "nothing more than the draft of a plan; nothing but a dead letter." This draft was merely a proposal "until life and validity were breathed into it by the voice of the people speaking through the several State Conventions." Therefore the sense of the Philadelphia Convention "could never be regarded as the oracular guide in expounding the Constitution." Madison consistently cleaved to this analysis for the rest of his life.[51]

The principal strength of Madison's argument was that it was firmly grounded in accepted constitutional theory. If the Justices' occasional references to framers' intent are read as literal and exclusive references to the Convention's proceedings, the Justices were using an analysis at

---

50. *See, e.g.,* Hylton v. United States, 3 U.S. (3 Dall.) 171, 173 (1796) (Chase, J.); *id.* 176, 177, 178 (Paterson, J.); United States v. Ravara, Manuscript Opinion (C.C.D. Pa. 1793) (Iredell, J.), *quoted supra* this chapter at 224; Calder v. Bull, 3 U.S. (3 Dall.) 386, 399 (1798).

51. 5 ANNALS 775–76. *See* Charles Lofgren, *The Original Understanding of Original Intent?,* 5 CONST. COMM. 77 (1988).

odds with the prevalent constitutional theory. This seems unlikely. A more plausible explanation is that the Justices assumed without analysis that the framers' intent was the same as the ratifiers' intent, or perhaps their occasional usage was simply a literary device. The explanation is consistent with all the cases in which the Justices used the phrase "framers' intent."

In *Hylton v. United States*, Justices Chase and Paterson emphasized that one of the primary purposes of the Constitution was to vest the new government with an effective power to raise revenues. They concluded therefore that the Constitution's direct-tax limitation should be construed narrowly. This purpose, however, is not obvious from the wording of the Constitution. Undoubtedly Chase and Paterson personally believed that the government needed an effective power to raise revenues, and Paterson had tried to create a government with such an effective power when he was a delegate to the Philadelphia Convention. But neither Chase nor Paterson individually nor the delegates to the Convention collectively were the embodiment of the people's sovereign will. Paterson's and Chase's interpretive approach to *Hylton* was, however, legitimate because during the ratification process the Constitution was explained and justified as being necessary to provide effective national authority to raise revenue.[52]

Supraconstitutional Principles

In the twentieth century, some have argued that the early Supreme Court was guided in part by supraconstitutional principles when it reviewed the constitutionality of statutes.[53] To the extent that the Justices may have resorted to supraconstitutional principles as clues to the people's sovereign will as expressed in the Constitution, they were acting consistently with principles of constitutional law that were accepted at the time. But a radical vision of resort to supraconstitutional principles is possible. Under this radical vision, the Justices saw supraconstitutional principles as a source of independent judicial power that could be exercised without the imprimatur of the people's sovereign will. This latter vision is anachronistic and essentially without supporting evidence.

52. *See* chapter 4 at 101–05. For discussions during the ratification process on the need for revenue, *see, e.g.*, Oliver Ellsworth, Speech of Jan. 7, 1788, *reprinted in* 3 DHRC 548–54; FEDERALIST No. 30 (A. Hamilton).
53. *See, e.g.*, Suzanna Sherry, *The Founders' Unwritten Constitution*, 54 U. CHI. L. REV. 1127 (1987); Suzanna Sherry, *Natural Law in the States*, 61 U. CIN. L. REV. 171 (1992). *See also* WOOD 291–305, 453–63.

This anachronistic reading of the early Justices' understanding is based primarily upon prefatory remarks by Justice Chase in *Calder v. Bull*. Before Chase commenced his exploration of the meaning of the Constitution's ex post facto clause, he affirmed,

> There are certain *vital principles* in our *free Republican governments*, which will determine and over-rule an *apparent and flagrant* abuse of *legislative* power; as to authorize *manifest injustice by positive law;* or to take away that security for *personal liberty*, or *private property*, for the protection whereof the government was established. ... It is against all reason and justice, for a people to entrust a Legislature with SUCH powers; and, therefore, it cannot be presumed that they have done it. ... To maintain that our Federal, or State, Legislature possesses *such powers*, if they had not been *expressly* restrained; would, in my opinion, be a *political heresy*, altogether inadmissible in our *free republican governments*.

If these words are read in isolation, they certainly suggest the existence of a body of *"vital principles ... which will ... over-rule ... manifest injustice."* Moreover, these *"vital principles"* are applicable even though they may not be *"expressly"* enumerated in the Constitution.[54]

Notwithstanding Justice Chase's prefatory remarks, he did not there or anywhere else intend to espouse a freewheeling judicial authority to correct manifest legislative injustices without regard to the express words of the Constitution. In the first place, Chase's understanding of the origin of laws was unusual for the eighteenth century. He emphatically rejected the notion that rights and presumably laws might exist in nature and independent of government.[55] Therefore, the *"vital* principles" to which he referred had no standing as law until they were adopted by an appropriate human lawmaking institution. All modern legal thinkers accept that the twentieth-century Supreme Court makes constitutional law, but no one in the eighteenth century—not even Chase—believed this. Chase and all of his contemporaries believed that constitutional law came from the people, not from judges.

Consistent with this vision of the people's sovereignty, Chase as a judge could overrule a legislative act only if he believed it was contrary to the

---

54. 3 U.S. (3 Dall.) at 388–89 (emphasis original). For a critical discussion of historical evidence supporting the theory of supraconstitutional principles, *see* Helen Michael, *The Role of Natural Law in Early American Constitutionalism: Did the Founders Contemplate Judicial Enforcement of "Unwritten" Individual Rights?*, 69 N.C. L. Rev. 421 (1991).

55. *See* chapter 5 at 145.

people's will embodied in the Constitution. He was willing to consider vital principles not expressly stated in the Constitution to the extent that these principles had been embraced by the people, but this willingness would have been narrow in the case of judicial review of legislation. The simple fact was that he believed the structure of government made the legislature superior to the judiciary in judging the people's will. There-fore, as he emphatically concluded in *Calder*, "I will not decide *any law to be void, but in a very clear case*."[56]

In addition to Justice Chase's remarks in *Calder*, the Ninth Amend-ment's provision that "The enumeration in the Constitution of certain rights shall not be construed to deny or disparage others retained by the people" suggests the existence of rights outside the Consitution. There are, however, serious doubts whether the Amendment's reference to "rights" meant constitutional-type rights as that term has come to be un-derstood in the late twentieth century. In addition, even if the Amend-ment was originally intended to affirm the existence of unenumerated rights, that does not mean that the Amendment was intended to em-power the judiciary to overturn legislation. In most cases, the existence and scope of these unenumerated rights would have been unclear and subject to debate. Therefore, a court could not claim to be functioning as the ministerial agent of the people, and judicial review would be inap-propriate. In the eighteenth century, the legislature rather than the ju-diciary would have been the proper governmental institution for vindicating these unenumerated rights.[57]

Although the generally accepted rationale for judicial review severely undercut direct judicial resort to natural-law principles, the judges of the Founding Generation did not and could not ignore natural law. They were natural lawyers themselves and undoubtedly assumed that state and federal written Constitutions were based upon and embodied natu-ral-law principles. Certainly the notion that the people might approve a Constitution that violated natural law would have been anathema; thus natural-law principles might be consulted in seeking the meaning of the Constitutions that the people had approved. Similarly, natural-law prin-ciples might be used to construe a statute on the theory that the legisla-ture could not have intended a result contrary to natural law. These interpretive strategies assumed that in legislating Constitutions and stat-

---

56. 3 U.S. (3 Dall.) at 395. *Accord,* Hylton v. United States, 3 U.S. (3 Dall.) 171, 175 (1796) (Chase, J.). For Congress's structural superiority, *see* this chapter at 232–33.
57. *See* Casto, *Iredell*.

utes, the people and the legislature were informed by natural-law principles.[58]

Finally, the judges of the Founding Era might in a clear case have been willing to declare a statute void on the basis of natural-law principles for which there was no positive sanction in the applicable written Constitution. The basis for their opinion, however, would have to have been the undisputed existence of a natural-law principle that was clearly embraced by the people. These tight restrictions impose the equivalent of a shock-the-conscience test in which the benchmark is the people's collective conscience rather than the judge's individual conscience. The safeguard of the electoral process, however, virtually guarantees that a legislature would not enact legislation contrary to vital principles clearly embraced by the sovereign people. It therefore comes as no surprise that neither Justice Chase nor any of his fellow federal judges ever declared a law void for violation of supraconstitutional principles not expressly stated in the Constitution.

CONGRESSIONAL POWER TO RESTRICT JURISDICTION

Although the doctrine of judicial review vested the courts with immense potential power, the Constitution provided political checks to this power. In addition to the appointment and impeachment processes, a significant political check was Congress's authority to control the courts' original and appellate jurisdiction. The Constitution was consciously drafted to vest Congress with this authority, and the Founding Generation fully understood the political possibilities inherent in it.[59] In the first Congress, Oliver Ellsworth's agreement to sweeping limits to the federal courts' jurisdiction had greatly facilitated the Judiciary Act's passage. He agreed to limit the Supreme Court's appellate jurisdiction over state courts to the comparatively narrow range of legal issues that were controlled by positive federal law. More significantly, the inferior courts' trial

---

58. *See* Casto, *Iredell.*

59. *See* chapter 1 at 12–15 and chapter 2 at 36–36 & 41–47. In recent years some have argued that the Constitution was not originally intended to vest the Congress with extensive authority over the aggregate jurisdiction of the Supreme Court and inferior courts. *See, e.g.*, Robert Clinton, *A Mandatory View of Federal Court Jurisdiction: A Guided Quest for the Original Understanding of Article III*, 132 U. Pa. L. Rev. 741 (1984). For a sophisticated version of this argument, *see* Akhil Amar, *The Two-Tiered Structure of the Judiciary Act of 1789*, 138 U. Pa. L. Rev. 1499 (1990). These arguments, however, have been crafted by lawyers with a conscious eye toward modern issues and have virtually no historical basis. *See* Casto, *Congress*; 26 B.C. L. Rev. 1101 (1985); Casto, *Orthodox*.

jurisdiction was consciously manipulated to keep a great deal of British creditor litigation out of the federal courts. This limitation of the courts' trial jurisdiction was motivated in part by neutral concerns for fairness, but everyone knew that consigning the British creditors to state trial courts would have the practical effect of partially nullifying Article IV of the Treaty of Paris.

As a result of the Judiciary Act's limitations in favor of local debtors, the country's ongoing noncompliance with the Treaty of Paris continued throughout the 1790s and required extensive negotiations between Great Britain and the United States.[60] Nevertheless, no one seriously challenged the fundamental principle of Congressional control over federal jurisdiction. To the contrary, this legislative authority was reaffirmed with little controversy.

In 1790 the House of Representatives asked Attorney General Randolph to study the Judiciary Act and make recommendations for its amendment. When Randolph complied with the House's request at the end of the year, influential members of Congress pronounced the report dead on arrival, and nothing ever came of it.[61] Nevertheless the report provides some valuable insights into Randolph's thinking, and Randolph was, after all, a capable and knowledgeable lawyer who had been an influential participant in the framing and ratification of the Constitution.

Randolph proposed, among other things, an amount in controversy limitation that would have completely barred the federal courts from hearing any claim below an unspecified figure. The only exceptions from this general exclusion were admiralty and revenue cases and cases that the Constitution allocated for trial under the Supreme Court's original jurisdiction. Randolph believed that the Constitution authorized his proposal because, as he explained, "The supreme court, though inherent in the Constitution, was to receive its first motion from Congress; the inferior courts must have slept forever, without the pleasure of Congress. Can the sphere of authority over value be more enlarged?"[62] Thus Ran-

---

60. *See* The Jay Treaty (1794), *reprinted in* 2 Treaties (Miller) 245–74; Convention Regarding Articles 6 and 7 of the Jay Treaty and Article 4 of the Definitive Treaty of Peace (1802), *reprinted in id.* 488–91.

61. *See* Theodore Sedwick to Ephraim Williams (Jan. 13, 1791), *reprinted in* 4 DHSC 549; Caleb Strong to David Sewall (Jan. 17, 1791), *excerpted in* 4 DHSC 550. *See generally* Wythe Holt, *"Federal Courts as the Asylum to Federal Interests:" Randolph's Report, The Benson Amendment, and the "Original Understanding" of the Federal Judiciary,* 36 Buff. L. Rev. 341 (1988); 4 DHSC 122–67.

62. Randolph, *Report on the Judiciary,* 4 DHSC 128, 162 n6.

dolph believed that Congress had quite extensive authority over the federal courts' jurisdiction.

The limits of Randolph's analysis were tested a year and a half later when he appeared as the plaintiff's counsel in *Chisholm v. Georgia*. In his capacity as an advocate, Randolph argued that the Constitution vested the Supreme Court with original jurisdiction and that the Judiciary Act merely "recognized" this preexisting jurisdiction. Justice Iredell was not persuaded. He "conceive[d], that all the Courts of the *United States* must receive, not merely their *organization* as to the number of Judges of which they are to consist; but all their authority, as to the manner of their proceeding, from the Legislation only."[63]

We do not know whether Randolph ever tried to reconcile the plenary power analysis in his report with his argument in *Chisholm*. In fact, his report recommended a diminution of the Supreme Court's appellate jurisdiction but would have left the Court's original jurisdiction intact. He might therefore have reconciled his apparently contradictory positions by reference to the Constitution's exceptions and regulations clause, which expressly gives Congress authority over the Court's appellate jurisdiction but is not applicable to the Court's original jurisdiction.

In 1796 the Court addressed the issue of Congressional power over its appellate jurisdiction in the otherwise insignificant case of *Wiscart v. Dauchy*. The case involved a circuit court decision that the defendant, Mr. Wiscart, had fraudulently transferred his property to another person as part of a scheme to defraud his creditors. On appeal, Wiscart asked the Court to set aside the factual determination that the property transfer was fraudulent. In the Supreme Court, the principal issue was whether the Court had appellate jurisdiction to review findings of fact. Chief Justice Ellsworth, speaking for a majority, concluded that the Court lacked jurisdiction, and Justice Wilson delivered a dissenting opinion.[64]

Most of Wilson's and Ellsworth's opinions were devoted to capable but tedious interpretations of the Judiciary Act. Ellsworth argued that the Act limited the Court's appellate jurisdiction to writs of error, which could be used to review conclusions of law but not findings of fact. Wilson argued that in cases of equity and admiralty jurisdiction, the Act provided for the broader civil-law concept of an "appeal" that encompassed both facts and the law. In retrospect, Ellsworth had the better argument, and a majority of the Court agreed.

---

63. *See* chapter 7 at 188–97.
64. 3 U.S. (3 Dall.) 321 (1796).

By way of introduction, Ellsworth noted that under the Constitution, the Court's appellate jurisdiction was subject to "such exceptions, and under such regulations, as the Congress shall make." He continued,

> Here then, is the ground, and the only ground, on which we can sustain an appeal. If Congress has provided no rule to regulate our proceedings, we cannot exercise an appellate jurisdiction; and if the rule is provided, we cannot depart from it. The question, therefore, on the constitutional point of an appellate jurisdiction, is simply, whether Congress has established any rule for regulating its exercise?

Ellsworth obviously viewed the Constitution as vesting the Congress with plenary power over the Supreme Court's appellate jurisdiction: "If Congress has provided no rule to regulate our proceedings, we cannot exercise an appellate jurisdiction."[65]

This view of plenary congressional power over federal jurisdiction is reminiscent of Justice Iredell's extreme analysis in *Chisholm v. Georgia*, and Attorney General Lee assumed that *Wiscart* went this far. But Ellsworth expressly linked his analysis to the exceptions and regulations clause that gave Congress authority to legislate exceptions and regulations regarding the Supreme Court's appellate jurisdiction. In contrast, *Chisholm* had involved the Supreme Court's original or trial jurisdiction, and therefore Ellsworth's analysis would have been inappropriate in that earlier case. Moreover, in one of his *Landholder* essays advocating ratification of the Constitution, Ellsworth had indicated that Congress might not have plenary power over the Supreme Court's original jurisdiction.[66]

Ellsworth's analysis of plenary power in *Wiscart* had a slight technical flaw. The Judiciary Act literally was not written in terms of exceptions and regulations to the Court's jurisdiction; it purported instead to vest the Supreme Court with a limited jurisdiction. In his dissenting opinion, Justice Wilson pointed out that the Constitution created the Supreme Court and vested it with appellate jurisdiction "both as to law and fact." He continued, "The Legislature might, indeed, have made exceptions, and introduced regulations [under the exceptions and regulations clause]; but it has not done so."[67] Although Wilson's reading of Article III is more faithful to the Constitution's phrasing, he placed little emphasis upon this literal but highly technical reading.

---

65. *Id.* at 327.
66. 3 Op. Att'y Gen. 71 (1797); *Landholder VI, reprinted in* 3 DHRC 487, 490.
67. 3 U.S. (3 Dall.) at 326.

Even under Wilson's reading, the Congress had at least some authority to legislate exceptions to the Court's appellate jurisdiction. Therefore the Judiciary Act's provision for appeals by writs of error could be read as creating a negative inference that appellate review of facts are excluded. Nine years later, Chief Justice Marshall construed legislation granting the Supreme Court appellate jurisdiction as creating just such a negative inference.[68]

The most interesting aspect of Wilson's dissent in *Wiscart* is a brief, un-elaborated idea buried in the middle of his opinion. Although he believed that Congress had authorized appellate review of facts, he casually noted without explanation, "Even, indeed, if a positive restriction [excluding appellate review of facts] existed by law, it would, in my judgment, be superseded by the superior authority of the constitutional provision."[69] Exactly what he meant by this statement—aside from implicitly reaffirming the Court's power of judicial review—is not known. A plausible explanation is that the purpose of the Congressional power to exclude the Supreme Court's appellate review of facts (as opposed to issues of law) was to authorize Congress to protect jury verdicts. Given this purpose, the exceptions and regulations clause might be read as not authorizing a restriction of the appellate review of facts in equity and admiralty cases in which juries were not used. This possible explanation would narrow the exceptions and regulations clause in respect to the appellate review of facts but would not be pertinent to the Judiciary Act's extensive limitations on the Supreme Court's appellate review of state courts' determinations of legal issues as opposed to factual issues.

Three years after *Wiscart*, the Congress's control over federal jurisdiction was once more before the Supreme Court. In *Turner v. The Bank of North America,* the Court addressed a Congressional limitation not to its own jurisdiction but to the circuit courts' jurisdiction.[70] *Turner* was a suit on a promissory note given by a North Carolina citizen to Biddle & Company. After the North Carolina citizen died, Turner, who was the administrator of his estate and was also a citizen of North Carolina, refused to pay the note, and a suit on the note was filed in the federal circuit court of North Carolina. At some point either before or after the default on the note but before an action was filed in federal court, Biddle & Company sold the note to the Bank of North America, which was clearly a citizen of Pennsylvania. Because the suit was between a Pennsylvania citizen and a

---

68. United States v. More, 7 U.S. (3 Cranch) 159, 173 (1805).
69. 3 U.S. (3 Dall.) at 325.
70. 4 U.S. (4 Dall.) 8 (1799).

North Carolina citizen, the constitutional provision extending federal jurisdiction to controversies "between citizens of different states" was applicable. Turner, however, contended that the case should be dismissed on the basis of a provision of the Judiciary Act that narrowed the diversity of citizenship jurisdiction authorized by the Constitution.

When the Judiciary Act was framed, there was a fear that holders of promissory notes might attempt to manufacture diversity of citizenship by simply assigning the notes to aliens or citizens of other states. The Act therefore provided that no federal court "shall have cognizance of any suit to recover the contents of any promissory note . . . in favor of an assignee, unless a suit might have been prosecuted in such Court [by the original payee of the note]." Under this limiting language, the plaintiff Bank had to establish diversity of citizenship not between itself and the defendant but between Biddle & Company and the defendant. If this limit were enforced, the case would have to be dismissed, because, for purposes of the litigation, Biddle & Company would be treated as a North Carolina citizen.[71]

During oral argument, the Bank's counsel argued that "the judicial power, is the grant of the constitution; and congress can no more limit, than enlarge, the constitutional grant." Chief Justice Ellsworth was not impressed. He had been a delegate to the Constitutional Convention and understood the compromise on inferior federal courts that had been brokered by Madison and Wilson. Indeed, during the ratification process he had explained in one of his *Landholder* essays that "nothing hinders but . . . that all the cases . . . may in the first instance be had in the state courts and those trials be *final* except in cases of great magnitude." In *Turner,* he incredulously asked the Bank's counsel, "How far is it meant to carry this argument? Will it be affirmed, that in every case, to which the judicial power of the *United States* extends, the federal Courts may exercise a jurisdiction, without the intervention of the legislature, to distribute, and regulate, the power?" In his subsequent opinion for the Court, Ellsworth implicitly rejected the Bank's argument without comment.[72]

Justice Chase was more direct than Ellsworth. During the oral argument, he bluntly stated that "the political truth is, that the disposal of the judicial power, (except in a few specified instances) belongs to congress. If congress has given the power to this Court, we possess it, not other-

---

71. Judiciary Act § 11. The objection to manufacturing federal jurisdiction by assignments was raised in the Virginia Ratification debates. *See* 3 ELLIOTT at 526 (George Mason).

72. 4 U.S. (4 Dall.) at 10 (emphasis original); *Landholder VI, reprinted in* 3 DHRC 487, 490.

wise: and if congress has not given the power to us, or to any other Court, it still remains at the legislative disposal." Chase went on to suggest that Congress's allocation of judicial power to the courts was properly based upon considerations of expediency.[73]

The *Turner* case recognized a congressional power over the inferior courts' jurisdiction that had no apparent limits. Clearly Congress could have opted to create no inferior courts whatsoever. As Attorney General Randolph pointed out, "the inferior courts must have slept forever without the pleasure of Congress."[74] This option was the essence of the Madisonian Compromise, as a result of which the constitutional language authorized only "such inferior courts as the Congress may from time to time ordain and establish" was added to the Constitution.

The authority to establish no inferior courts whatsoever presumably included a lesser authority to establish inferior courts vested with only a portion of the full range of jurisdiction authorized by the Constitution. Attorney General Randolph clearly endorsed this idea of selective vesting in his report, and the first Congress's Judiciary Act presupposed the propriety of selective vesting. An objection to selective vesting of jurisdiction was the precise issue that was raised and emphatically rejected in *Turner.*

Congressional power over the Supreme Court's jurisdiction is a different matter, because the Madisonian Compromise dealt solely with the lower courts. In *Chisholm,* Justice Iredell contended that Congress had a plenary power over the Supreme Court's original and appellate jurisdiction, but the more plausible analysis was implicit in Randolph's report and explicit in *Wiscart* and *Turner.* The textual basis for congressional power over the Supreme Court was the constitutional provision that authorized Congress to make exceptions and regulations to the Court's appellate jurisdiction but which had no application to the Court's original jurisdiction. In *Wiscart,* Ellsworth expressly based his constitutional analysis on this provision. In *Turner,* Chase's statement that "in a few specific instances" Congress lacked authority to limit the Court's jurisdiction was probably a reference to the Court's original jurisdiction.[75]

In affirming the Congress's virtually plenary power over the federal courts' jurisdiction, the Court was fully aware that Congress might use its power to accomplish indirectly results that could not be accomplished directly. In the late twentieth century, theorists have devoted considerable

---

73. 4 U.S. (4 Dall.) at 10.
74. *See* this chapter at 240.
75. *Accord,* Ellsworth's *Landholder VI, discussed* this chapter at 244.

thought to the conundrum of whether Congress may in effect overrule a judicially declared principle of constitutional law by depriving the federal courts of jurisdiction to hear any case in which the principle is applicable. For example, bills have occasionally been introduced in the Congress to deny both the federal trial courts and the Supreme Court jurisdiction over any case involving issues of abortion or school prayer.[76] This strategy was never used in the 1790s, however. *Chisholm v. Georgia* was the only constitutional decision that might have stimulated a statute stripping the Court of jurisdiction, but *Chisholm* involved the Supreme Court's original jurisdiction. The Congress's authority was therefore dubious at best.

Although the early Congress never tried to use its power over jurisdiction to change or avert the federal courts' enforcement of the Constitution, Congress's treatment of British creditors was in many ways analogous to the modern conundrum. The British creditor cases clearly implicated important issues of national supremacy and national security. Moreover, the substantive rule at issue was Article IV of the Treaty of Paris. Like the Constitution, the Treaty of Paris could not be altered by Congress. As Chief Justice Ellsworth explained, "a treaty cannot be repealed or annulled by statute, because it is a compact with a foreign power, and one party to a compact cannot dissolve it, without the consent of the other."[77] Nevertheless, the first Congress used its plenary power over the federal courts' jurisdiction to bar a large majority of British creditors' claims from the federal trial courts and relegate them to the state trial courts. This legislative decision was undoubtedly made on the assumption that federal trial courts were more likely to enforce the Treaty than state courts were.

---

76. *See* HART & WECHSLER at 377–79.

77. Oliver Ellsworth to Jonathan Trumbull (Mar. 13, 1796), *in* George Washington Papers (Microfilm ed., Series 4, Reel 108), *discussed in* chapter 4 at 97–98. Today this issue is viewed as more complicated than Ellsworth's words suggest it was in his time. *See* LOUIS HENKIN, FOREIGN AFFAIRS AND THE CONSTITUTION 157–67 (1972).

9

AN ASSESSMENT

Society in the late twentieth century—particularly political society—
is usually viewed primarily in terms of conflicts of values and interests.
From this viewpoint, the Supreme Court's greatness resides in its ability
to resolve conflicts and impose its judgments upon others—particularly
upon other governmental units. Accordingly, the modern paradigms
of great Supreme Court decisions are *Marbury v. Madison* and *Brown v.
Board of Education.* In the first case, Federalist Justices whose coalition
was out of power tweaked the nose of the dominant coalition led by
Thomas Jefferson and reaffirmed the Court's authority to use the power
of judicial review to overturn political branch decisions. In the latter case,
the Court struck boldly at a national disgrace when the political branches
were morally paralyzed. In each of these cases, the Court was in conflict
with powerful societal forces and firmly reiterated its constitutional role
as a shield against abuses of governmental power. These were great cases
because the Court was opposing governmental policy rather than supporting it.

The abiding theme of the early Supreme Court, however, was precisely to the contrary. The Court sought to support the political branches
of the new federal government, not to oppose them. In correspondence
with his initial appointees to the Court, President Washington stressed
that the Court was "the Key-stone of our political fabric" and "the Chief
Pillar upon which our national Government must rest."[1] The President
and his nominees fully understood that the new government was an experiment that might fail and that judicial opposition to the government
would have been disastrous.

In addition to seeking individuals who would support the new government, the President sought men whose public reputation would enhance

---

1. *See* 1 DHSC 11, 21–22, 29, 35, 51, 58.

the government's political legitimacy. Chief Justice Jay exemplified this concern for public reputation. His credentials were political rather than professional. Jay had virtually no prior judicial experience, but he was widely respected for his extensive national service and sound judgment in the realm of foreign affairs. Although Jay's service on the Court was brief and his only major opinion was in the *Chisholm* case, his appointment was a success because his presence assured the nation that the Court would be led by a man of sound judgment.

Chief Justice Ellsworth had significant prior judicial experience, but his appointment was in the same vein as Jay's. At the time of his appointment, Ellsworth was essentially a legislator. From 1789 to 1796, he served as the de facto leader of the Senate and earned a reputation as a tough, hardworking legislator who was sincere and fair-minded. A fellow Connecticut lawyer who respected him wrote that Ellsworth's service in the Senate had "accustomed [him] to view things as a politician, rather than a lawyer." In the wake of the Rutledge fiasco, President Washington needed a Chief Justice with solid Federalist credentials and an equally solid reputation for sound judgment. Ellsworth fit the bill. Even at the height of the controversy over the Sedition Act, Ellsworth's harshest critics conceded that portions of his grand jury charge reaffirming the legitimacy of common-law crimes did him "the utmost honor as a judge, and as a man."[2]

Needless to say, Chief Justices Jay and Ellsworth firmly supported the new government. For example, both provided the President with private advisory opinions. Jay concluded his first grand jury charge by strongly affirming "the Duty and Interest . . . of all good Citizens . . . to support the laws and the Government." Similarly, Ellsworth stated in his first charge, "The national laws give to the whole, harmony of interest, and unity of design. They are the means by which it pleases heaven to make of weak and discordant parts, one great people." The importance of this theme of harmony is emphasized in a religious tract that Ellsworth participated in writing shortly after leaving the Court. "The design of all government," explained the tract, "is to make every one feel the relation in which he stands to the community, and to compel him to conduct as

---

2. Letter to David Daggett (Apr. 20, 1798) (CtY). For Ellsworth's critics, *see* chapter 5 at 151.

becomes that relationship." In light of this conviction, judicial opposition
to the new government would have been an anathema.[3]

In theory, the desire for harmony might have led to conflict if the political branches of the federal government had pursued policies that the
Justices deemed improper. In practice, however, there was a unique harmony of interest between the early Supreme Court and the political
branches that was never to be repeated in the next two hundred years.
Throughout the 1790s Federalists headed the executive branch at all
times, and all the Justices were Federalists. In fact, all but two of the Justices were appointed by the same president. Similarly, throughout the
decade, the Federalists always had at least a working control of the Senate and frequently a similar control of the House. This control may not
always have been sufficient to insure the enactment of Federalist legislation, but it was always enough to block legislation that the Federalists
deemed unwise. Therefore, with the apparent exception of the Invalid
Pension problem, the Justices never found themselves in serious political
conflict with the political branches, and they could dutifully accept and
support the Federalist government's policies without a qualm. Thus a
unique political happenstance virtually guaranteed that the Justices
would never find themselves in serious conflict with the political
branches of the federal government.

Over the last two centuries, many capable individuals have served on
the Supreme Court, and some of them have been great Justices. But today the early Supreme Court is usually dismissed as a mediocre collection of reasonably competent lawyers. When asked what they think of the
early Court, most people with an interest in the law and legal history respond that they do not think about the early Court. This indifference
informs a survey of law school deans and professors of law, history, and
political science who believed that the Justices before John Marshall were
just average.[4] None, they believed, were "great" or "near great," and
none were "failures." Ten were "average," and two were "below average."
This judgment of mediocrity is probably due to the direct conflict between the modern judicial paradigm of conflict and the early Court's
paradigm of support.

---

3. John Jay, Charge to the New York Grand Jury (Apr. 12, 1790), *reprinted in* 2
DHSC 15, 30; Oliver Ellsworth, Charge to the Georgia Grand Jury (Apr. 25, 1796),
reprinted in 3 DHSC 119–20; MISSIONARY SOCIETY OF CONNECTICUT, A SUMMARY OF
CHRISTIAN DOCTRINE AND PRACTICE 54 (1804). For Ellsworth's membership on the
drafting committee, *see* Second Book of Records of the Trustees of the Missionary
Society of Connecticut 25 (1802–1822) (CtHUCC).

4. HENRY J. ABRAHAM, JUSTICES AND PRESIDENTS App. A-D, at 412–27 (3d ed., 1992).

The modern blurring of the early Justices into an anonymous collection of undistinguished and indistinguishable journeymen belies the clear gradations of talent within the early Court. Among the associate Justices, Paterson and Iredell stood head and shoulders above their fellows. In particular, Iredell was a lawyer's lawyer whose work was distinguished by comprehensive analysis and exhaustive attention to detail. As pure legal thinkers, Iredell and Paterson could easily have held their own on any of the Courts in the succeeding two centuries. These two men, however, had more of a gift for careful analysis than for original thought. In contrast, Wilson and Chase clearly had the ability to transcend analysis and see new ways of looking at problems. These latter two Justices could have been the intellectual stars and leaders of the early Court, but they never reached their potential. Wilson's personal finances were on the verge of collapse as early as 1793 and totally collapsed in 1797. These difficulties undoubtedly distracted him from his judicial duties. As for Chase, his obnoxious, undisciplined, and narcissistic personality obscured his brilliance and precluded any possible leadership role for him on the Court.

If the paradigm of support is used to judge the early Justices' collective service, the Court is entitled to high marks. With the minor exception of the sporadic grumbling over circuit riding, the Justices bent to the wheels of government with enthusiasm and success. The federal government could not operate without adequate revenues, and one of the primary reasons for creating the federal courts was to assure the effective enforcement of revenue laws. In *Hylton v. United States,* the Court enhanced the government's flexibility to tax by narrowly construing the Constitution's limitation on direct taxes.[5] Then in *La Vengeance,* the Court effectively removed juries from the enforcement of the nation's principal revenue laws by ignoring traditional limits of admiralty jurisdiction.[6]

In cases more directly relating to foreign policy and national security, the Court was equally supportive. In *Glass v. The Sloop Betsy,* the Court—without comment or explanation—emphatically rejected settled prize law in order to assist the Washington Administration in steering a neutral course in the European war between France and Great Britain.[7] Six years later, when the country was involved in an undeclared naval war with France, the Court dealt in *Bas v. Tingy* with the thorny issue of armed conflicts that fall short of all-out war. Although the Constitution could be

---

5. *See* chapter 4 at 101–05.
6. *See* chapter 4 at 105–09.
7. *See* chapter 4 at 82–87.

read as requiring a formal declaration of war as a prerequisite for the United States to initiate armed conflict with another country, the Court settled on a far more flexible construction.[8]

The Justices were also quick to cooperate in using criminal proceedings to support the new government. When they delivered grand jury charges, they served as "Republican Schoolmasters" for the better instruction of the nation in the wisdom and morality of the Washington and Adams Administrations. They also used grand jury proceedings as a forum for the delivery of formal advisory opinions on pressing legal issues of the day.

In the secret Senate debates of 1789, Oliver Ellsworth had warned "that there will be Attacks on the General Government that will go to the Very Vitals of it," and the Justices were enthusiastic in their use of federal criminal law against individuals who violated written and unwritten federal criminal laws. To say that the Justices were enthusiastic is not, however, to say that they overleapt the bounds of propriety to achieve improper political goals. With the notable exception of Samuel Chase, they were reasonably judicious in their conduct of trials with political implications. At least as Albert Gallatin's judgment of Justice Paterson's conduct in the Whiskey Rebellion trials suggests, their actions comported with late-eighteenth-century standards of judicial conduct.[9]

In addition to taking an active role in the indictment and trial of criminal defendants, the Justices (again with the notable exception of Samuel Chase) filled the lacunae in the federal criminal code by expounding a federal common law of crimes. Although this doctrine eventually became entangled with the political controversy over congressional legislative authority, the idea of common-law crimes was by no means innovative. The comparatively narrow concept relating to violations of the law of nations and the more general doctrine of common-law misdemeanors were well established, and according to natural-law theory, these branches of the law already existed and were fully applicable. The Justices simply decided that the federal courts rather than the state courts should try violations of preexisting law insofar as the criminal activities involved direct attacks on the federal government.

In retrospect, the Justices' administration of criminal law seems unduly political, but the Justices themselves undoubtedly believed that their conduct was quite proper. The era's predominant natural-law theory encouraged individuals to assume that for each legal problem

---

8. *See* chapter 4 at 120–24.
9. *See* chapter 5 at 163–65.

there was a single correct solution dictated by God and human reason. At the same time, the early Court was remarkably homogeneous. Therefore the Justices could plausibly have mistaken their shared political values for natural verities. This kind of unspoken and unexamined assumption would make it very easy for them to believe that they were acting quite properly—even apolitically—in seeking to impose their political values upon the nation.

Occasionally the Justices found themselves in direct opposition to the other branches of the federal government or to state governments. For example, in *Ware v. Hylton* and *Chisholm v. Georgia,* the Court overrode clear state interests. And in the Correspondence of the Justices and the Invalid Pensioner opinions, the Justices said no to the President and the Congress. There is, however, less than meets the eye in these confrontations. *Chisholm* and *Ware* involved not so much confrontations between the Court and the states as the Court's mediation of direct conflicts between state interests and the fairly clear mandate of positive federal laws. In *Ware,* the Court simply gave effect to the obvious intendment of the Constitution's Supremacy Clause and the Treaty of Paris.[10] In *Chisholm,* the statutory and constitutional language giving the Supreme Court jurisdiction over a suit between a state and the citizen of another state was almost as clear.[11] When the Congress and the states gave the back of their hand to *Chisholm* by amending the Constitution, the Court did not quibble over technicalities like whether the amendment should be applied retroactively; it immediately acquiesced.

In their Invalid Pensioner opinions the Justices managed to oppose and support congressional policy simultaneously.[12] They decided that the Act's claim procedure was unconstitutional. At the same time, however, they came up with a wildly improbable interpretation of the Act that authorized them to assess claims as commissioners. They were equally pragmatic when they formally refused to provide President Washington with an advisory opinion on neutrality and the French Alliance.[13] They knew that the President's cabinet was fully capable of answering the questions that had been posed, and they may not have wanted to get in the middle of the dispute between Jefferson and Hamilton on some of the more technical questions. Moreover, the Justices knew that the more important questions were being answered in their grand jury charges. They also may have planned an accelerated review of

---

10. *See* chapter 4 at 98–101.
11. *See* chapter 7.
12. *See* chapter 6 at 175–78.
13. *See* chapter 4 at 75–82 and chapter 6 at 180–83.

cases like *Findlay v. The William* and *Glass v. The Sloop Betsy* that were being filed in the district courts.[14]

Chief Justices Jay and Ellsworth believed that "a strong, energetic federal government is necessary for the United States,"[15] and the abiding principle of the Supreme Court's first decade was to enhance the new government's strength and energy. The Justices—with the occasional exception of Chase—generally were pragmatic in their resolution of the specific issues that came before them. They seldom felt bound by absolute general principles. This is not to say that they were unprincipled. Their actions were principled, but their principles were substantive rather than metaphysical. The Justices sought to assist in the establishment of an energetic national government that could effectively defend itself from attacks by foreign and domestic foes, and they were successful in these efforts.

---

14. *See* chapter 4 at 82–87.
15. 2 ELLIOT 282 (Jay). For Ellsworth, *see* chapter 2 at 48–49.

TABLE OF CASES

Adams v. Kellogg, Kirby 438 (Conn. 1786), 152

Ames v. Kansas, 111 U.S. 449 (1884), 224

Bas v. Tingy, 4 U.S. (4 Dall.) 37 (1800), 111, 120–24, 250–51

Bayard v. Singleton, 1 Martin 42 (N.C. 1787), 216, 220–21

Bingham v. Cabbot, 3 U.S. (3 Dall.) 19 (1795), 111

Bors v. Preston, 111 U.S. 252 (1884), 224

Brown v. Board of Education, 347 U.S. 483 (1954), 247

Brown v. Van Braam, 3 U.S. (3 Dall.) 344 (1797), 111

Calder v. Bull, 3 U.S. (3 Dall.) 386 (1798), 111, 187–88, 221, 227–30, 231, 233–34, 237–38

The Catherine, DECREE ON THE ADMIRALTY SIDE OF THE DISTRICT COURT OF NEW YORK (Evans no. 26,915: 1794) (D. N.Y. Jan. 28, 1794), 84

Chisholm v. Georgia, 2 U.S. (2 Dall.) 419 (1793), 55, 63–64, 111, 188–97, 198–202, 202–03, 210, 211–12, 241, 242, 245, 246, 252

Clark v. Russel, 3 U.S. (3 Dall.) 415 (1799), 111

Cohens v. Virginia, 19 U.S. (6 Wheat.) 264 (1821), 202, 203–04

Cooper v. Telfair, 4 U.S. (4 Dall.) 14 (1800), 225–27

Craig v. Missouri, 29 U.S. (4 Peters) 410 (1830), 203

Cutting v. South Carolina, unreported (U.S. filed 1795), 204

Dunlop v. Ball, 6 U.S. (2 Cranch) 180 (1804), 9

Fairfax's Devisee v. Hunter's Lessee, 11 U.S. (7 Cranch) 603 (1813), 186

Farquhar v. Georgia, Manuscript Opinion, James Iredell Papers, Duke University (C.C.D. Ga. 1791), 188–89, 192

Fenemore v. United States, 3 U.S. (3 Dall.) 357 (1797), 111

Findlay v. The William, 9 F. Cas. 57 (D. Pa. 1793) (No. 4790), 82–83, 253

The Flying-Fish. See *Little v. Barreme*

Folger v. Lecuyer, Boston Centinel, Jan. 4, 1794 (D. Mass. Dec. 6, 1793), 84

255

Fowler v. Lindsey, 3 U.S. (3 Dall.) 411 (1799), 111

Fries, Case of. See *United States v. Fries*

Georgia v. Brailsford, 2 U.S. (2 Dall.) 415 (1793), 111

Glass v. The Sloop Betsy, Maryland Journal and Baltimore Advertiser, Oct. 31, 1793 (D. Md. Aug. 16, 1793), *aff'd.*, unreported (C.C.D. Md. Nov. 7, 1793), *rev'd.*, 3 U.S. (3 Dall.) 6 (1794), 81, 83–87, 109, 112–13, 115, 250, 253

Grayson v. Virginia, 3 U.S. (3 Dall.) 320 (1796), 190

Hamilton v. Eaton, 11 F. Cas. 336 (C.C.D.N.C. 1796) (No. 5980), 100

Hans. v. Louisiana, 134 U.S.1 (1890), 202

Hayburn's Case, 2 U.S. (2 Dall.) 409 (1792), 55, 177

Henfield's Case. See *United States v. Henfield*

Hollingsworth v. Virginia, 3 U.S. (3 Dall.) 378 (1798), 190, 195, 202, 203

Hylton v. United States, 3 U.S. (3 Dall.) 171 (1796), 101–05, 111, 185

Little v. Barreme, 6 U.S. (2 Cranch) 170 (1804), 124

Marbury v. Madison, 5 U.S. (1 Cranch) 137 (1803), 122, 247

Martin v. Hunter's Lessee, 14 U.S. (1 Wheat.) 304 (1816), 186–87

Miller v. Miller, 2 U.S. (2 Dall.) 1 (Fed. Ct. App. 1781), 86

Moodie v. The Ship Phoebe Anne, 3 U.S. (3 Dall.) 319 (1796), 23, 114

Moodie v. The Ship Alfred, 3 U.S. (3 Dall.) 307 (1795), 113–14

Moxon v. The Fanny, 17 F. Cas. 942 (D. Pa. 1793) (No. 9895), 83

Olney v. Arnold, 3 U.S. (3 Dall.) 308 (1796), 184

Olney v. Dexter, unreported (U.S. 1796), 184

Ex Parte New York, No. 1, 256 U.S. 490 (1921), 202

Osborn v. Bank of the United States, 22 U.S. (9 Wheat.) 738 (1824), 36, 42

Principality of Monaco v. Mississippi, 292 U.S. 313 (1934), 202

Respublica v. De Longchamps, 1 U.S. (1 Dall.) 111 (Pa. 1784), 131–32, 137, 141, 160

Rose v. Himely, 8 U.S. (4 Cranch.) 241 (1808), 86

Sims Lessee v. Irvine, 3 U.S. (3 Dall.) 425 (1799), 111

Swift v. Tyson, 41 U.S. (16 Pet.) 1 (1842), 162–63

Talbot v. Jansen, 3 U.S. (3 Dall.) 133 (1795), 111, 113

Triquet v. Bath, 97 Eng. Rep. 936, 3 Burr. 1480 (K.B. 1764), 132–33, 137, 140, 141, 160, 161

Turner v. The Bank of North America, 4 U.S. (4 Dall.) 8 (1799), 111, 243–45

United States v. Callender, 25 F. Cas. 239 (C.C.D. Va. 1800) (No. 14,709), 166–69, 172, 222

United States v. Cooper, 25 F. Cas. 631 (C.C.D. Pa. 1800) (No. 14, 865), 166

United States v. Fries, 9 F. Cas. 826 (C.C.D. Pa. 1799) (No. 5126), *retried*, 9 F. Cas. 924 (C.C.D. Pa. 1800) (No. 5127), 169–71, 172

United States v. Greenleaf, unreported (C.C.D. N.Y. 1797), 137

United States v. Henfield, 11 F. Cas. 1099 (C.C.D. Pa. 1793) (No. 6360), 82, 130–39, 141, 143, 144, 154, 155, 160

United States v. Hopkins, unreported (C.C.D. N.Y. April 13–14, 1790), 130

United States v. Hudson & Goodwin, 11 U.S. (7 Cranch) 32 (1812), 162

United States v. Judge of the District Court of the United States for the District Court of Virginia, unreported (U.S. 1796), 107

United States v. La Vengeance, 3 U.S. (3 Dall.) 297 (1796), 105–10, 112, 185, 250

United States v. Mitchell, Wharton's State Trials 176 (C.C.D. Pa. 1795), 164

United States v. More, 7 U.S. (3 Cranch) 159 (1805), 243

United States v. Peters, 3 U.S. (3 Dall.) 121 (1795), 86

United States v. Ravara, 2 U.S. (2 Dall.) 297 (C.C.D. Pa. 1793), 139–41, 191, 222–25, 227, 235

United States v. Rivers, Dunlop and Claypoole's American Daily Advertiser, Dec. 11, 1793 (C.C.D. Ga. 1793), 135

United States v. The Schooner Betsy, 8 U.S. (4 Cranch) 443 (1808), 108

United States v. Smith, 27 F. Cas. 1147 (C.C.D. Mass. 179[7]) (No. 16,223), 161

United States v. Vigol, Wharton's State Trials 175 (C.C.D. Pa. 1795), 163–64

United States v. Williams, 29 F. Cas. 1330 (C.C.D. Conn. 1799) (No. 17, 708), 152–55

United States v. Worrall, 28 F. Cas. 774 (C.C.D. Pa. 1798) (No. 16,766), 141–47, 148, 154, 157, 160, 161, 251

United States v. Yale Todd, 54 U.S. (13 How.) 52 (1794), 177–78

Vanhorne's Lessee v. Dorrance, 2 U.S. (2 Dall.) 304 (C.C.D. Pa. 1795), 215, 216, 221–22

Van Stophorst v. Maryland, 2 U.S. (2 Dall.) 401 (1791), 190

Vassall v. Massachusetts, unreported (U.S. filed 1793), 199, 200, 201, 202, 207, 208

Ware v. Hylton, 3 U.S. (3 Dall.) 199 (1796), 98–101, 186, 187, 202, 252

Western Insurgents, Trial of, Wharton's State Trials 102 (C.C.D. Pa. 1795), 105, 154–55, 163–65, 251

Wiscart v. Dauchy, 3 U.S. (3 Dall.) 321 (1796), 241–43, 245

Wilford v. Grant, Kirby 114 (Conn. 1786), 152, 153

Index

Adams, John: Appoints Chief Justice Ellsworth to dual office, 119; Comments on failure of Rutledge nomination, 94; Pardons John Fries, 171; Quasi-War with France, 118–19. *See also* Chase, Samuel; Supreme Court Nominations

Adams, Thomas: On *Bas v. Tingy*, 121, 122; On Supreme Court nominations, 67

Admiralty Jurisdiction: Crimes, 39, 130, 163; Eleventh amendment, 202, 204–05; French prize courts, 77–78, 81, 86, 115; Importance of, 7, 40; Judiciary Act of 1789, 32, 38–41; Jury trials, 106–09; Restitution of prizes, 82–87, 112–14, 250, 252; Revenue collection, 39, 44, 105–09, 250; Sale of prizes, 87, 115–17; Salvage of prizes, 120–24; U.S. Constitution, 7, 9. *See also* Washington, George

Advisory Opinions, 25, 178–83, 248; Given, 71–72, 74–75, 97–98, 116–17, 141, 149, 178, 179, 180–81, 248; Given on criminal matters, 74–75, 141, 149, 178–79; Not given, 77–82. *See also* Natural Law

The Alfred (ship), 113–14

Algerian corsairs. *See* Barbary Powers

Alienage Jurisdiction. *See* U.S. Courts' Subject Matter Jurisdiction

Alien Tort Claims. *See* U.S. Courts' Subject Matter Jurisdiction

All Writs Act, 191

The Amity (ship), 115 n.109

Amount in Controversy. *See* U.S. Courts' Subject Matter Jurisdiction

"Arising under" jurisdiction. *See* U.S. Courts' Subject Matter Jurisdiction

Articles of Confederation, 8, 48–49

"Auxiliary Precautions." *See* Madison, James

Baldwin, Abraham: On Ellsworth, 28, 93 n.55; On federalism, 211

Barbary Powers, 88

Bayard, James, 157

The Betsy (ship), 83–87

The Betsy (schooner), 108 n.94

Blackstone's *Commentaries*, 21, 34–35, 107, 142, 158, 159, 195

Bills of Credit, 203

Blair, John (Associate Justice): Biography of, 58–59; Judicial review, 215–16; Opinions by 177, 191; Grand Jury Charge by, 164 n.87; Resigns, 96

Bradford, William (U.S. Attorney General), 102, 105; Opinions by, 137 nn.27–28

British Debt Cases. *See* U.S. Courts' Subject Matter Jurisdiction; Treaty of Paris

Brutus, 20–22
Burr, Aaron, 89–90
Butler, Pierce, 11, 48, 53

Callender, James, 166–69
Carriage Tax, 101–05
The Catherine (ship), 84 n.31
Chase, Samuel (Associate Justice):
  Assessment of, 97, 250; Attacks
  Jefferson, 165–66; Biography of,
  69–70, 96–97; Electioneering for
  President Adams, 165; Federal
  common law crimes, 144–47, 157,
  251; Grand jury charges by, 129,
  145, 165–66, 222 n.18, 232–33;
  Impeachment, 172; Judicial review,
  220–22, 225, 226–27, 237–39;
  Natural law, 145, 157, 237–39;
  Obnoxious behavior, 97, 171–72,
  250, 251; Opinions by, 100, 104,
  106, 108, 121–22, 123, 144–47,
  167–69, 170, 178, 225, 226–27,
  228, 229, 230, 231, 235, 236,
  244–45
Chisholm, Alexander, 188
Circuit Riding, 45, 55, 250
Constitution. *See* U.S. Constitution;
  U.S. Constitution, Convention of
  1787; U.S. Constitution,
  Interpretation
Constitutional Convention of 1787.
  See U.S. Constitution, Convention
  of 1787
Convention of 1800. *See* Treaty of
  Mortefontaine
Convention of 1802, 101
Cooper, Thomas, 166
Coxe, John, 135 n.24
Coxe, Tenche, 141, 143
Criminal Laws. *See* Federal Criminal
  Laws
Cushing, William (Associate Justice):
  Biography of, 59, 124–25;
  Opinions by, 175–77, 192, 228;
  Comments on need for Crime Bill,

130; Friend of Ellsworth, 112;
  Declines Chief Justiceship, 95

Dallas, Alexander, 142–44, 146. *See
  also* Dallas's Reports
Dallas's Reports, 107–08, 146, 222–
  23, 227
Davie, William R., 119, 192
Declaration of Independence, 2, 153
De Longchamps, Chevalier, 7–8;
  Related legal issues, 43, 132, 137,
  141, 160
Duane, James (U.S. District Judge),
  130; Opinions by, 84, 175, 176–77,
  180
Duponceau, Peter: Advocate, 86,
  106–08, 113, 135, 140; Opinions
  by, 113, 135 n.24, 138–39, 140
Eleventh Amendment: Enforcement
  of federal rights, 205–11; Framing
  and ratification, 197–202, 211–12;
  Suits by foreign states, 203–04;
  Suits in admiralty, 204–05. *See also*
  Sovereign Immunity
Ellsworth, Oliver (Chief Justice):
  Alleged mental infirmity, 93;
  Assessment of, 27–28, 248–249,
  253; Biography of, 27–28, 95–96;
  Chief Justice Rutledge, 92;
  Drafting Judiciary Act of 1789,
  27–38, 41–51, 52–53, 184–85, 187,
  226, 239, 251; Drafting Process Act
  of 1789, 51; Dual office holding,
  119, 173, 181; Ex-officio duties,
  174, 181; Federal common law
  crimes, 149, 150–52, 160–61;
  Framing Constitution, 12–16, 18,
  23; Grand jury charges by, 150–52;
  Initially opposes federal courts,
  12–13; Interstitial federal common
  law, 154–55; Judicial review, 19,
  213; Majority opinions, 110–12;
  Mission to France, 93, 118–19, 124;
  Opinions by, 33, 37, 97–98, 100,
  107–08, 109, 114, 115–16, 149,

152–53, 178–79, 182–83; 241–42, 244–46; Ratifying Constitution, 19, 48–49, 213, 236 n.52, 242, 244–45; Rebukes Justice Chase, 171–72; Resigns, 124
Erie Doctrine. *See* Federal Common Law
Ex post facto clause. *See* U.S. Constitution

Fairfax, Lord, 186
Fauchet, Jean, 139
Farquhar, Robert, 188
Federal Common Law: In civil cases, 162–63; In criminal cases, *see* Federal Criminal Law
Federal Criminal Law: Common law crimes, 129–63, 251; Maritime crimes, 39, 130, 163; Political uses of, 159–60, 163–72, 251–52; Predominantly administered by Circuit Courts, 45, 126; Sedition Act, 147–50, 165–71; Statutory crimes, 163–71; Used to protect government, 7–8, 43, 48, 49, 53, 126–29, 251. *See also* Advisory Opinions; Judiciary Act of 1789; U.S. Supreme Court
The Flad Oyen (ship): 41 n.25, 86 n.37
Florida, 43, 136–37
Framer's Intent. *See* U.S. Constitution, Interpretation
France, 2, 73–74. *See also* Admiralty Jurisdiction, French prize courts; Admiralty Jurisdiction, Restitution of prizes; Admiralty Jurisdiction, Sale of prizes; Admiralty Jurisdiction, Salvage of prizes; Genêt, Edmond; Neutrality Crisis of 1793; Quasi-War; Treaty of Alliance; Treaty of Mortefontaine, XYZ Affair
The Fanny (ship), 83 n.29
The François Le Lion (ship). *See The Leo*
Fries, John, 169–71.

Fries Rebellion, 105, 169.

Gallatin, Albert, 164–65, 200, 208–09, 211, 235
The Ganges (ship), 120–21
Genêt, Edmond: Launches privateering campaign, 76–78; Seeks criminal prosecution against Chief Justice Jay and Senator King, 137–39
Gerry, Elbridge, 223
Gorham, Nathaniel, 14, 23
Grand Jury Charges, 126–29, 163–64, 172, 251; Used as advisory opinions, 75, 81, 128, 131, 150–52, 178, 251. *See also* Federal Criminal Law; Individual Justices, Grand jury charges by
Grayson, William, 48
Great Britain, 2, 72–74. *See also* Admiralty Jurisdiction, French prize courts; Admiralty Jurisdiction, Importance of; Admiralty Jurisdiction, Restitution of Prizes; Admiralty Jurisdiction, Sale of Prizes; Barbary Powers; Convention of 1802; Jay Treaty; Neutrality Crisis of 1793; Nootka Sound Crisis; Sierra Leone, Raid on; Treaty of Paris; U.S. Courts' Subject Matter Jurisdiction, British Debt Cases
Griffin, Cyrus (U.S. District Judge), 102

Hamilton, Alexander: 74, 81–82, 93, 102, 125; Drafting Constitution, 6; Ratifying Constitution, 5–6, 17, 18–19, 21–22
Harrison, Robert H.: Biography of, 61, 68; Declines appointment as associate justice, 61
Harper, Robert Goodloe, 148 n.57, 155 n.72
Hawkins's *Pleas of the Crown*, 142

Henfield, Gideon, 82, 130–34, 155
Henry, Patrick, 58, 68; Considered for nomination to Supreme Court, 69; Declines Chief Justiceship, 95; Declines diplomatic post, 119.
Holt, Wythe, 27 n.1, 30, 52
Huntington, Samuel, 50

Ingersoll, Jared: Advocate, 135; Opinion by, 135 n.24
Interim Appointment Clause. See U.S. Constitution
"Intrigue and cabal," 16–17
Invalid Pensioners Act, 175–78
Iredell, James (Associate Justice): Assessment of, 250; Biography of, 61–62, 67–68; British debt cases, 99–100, 101; Chief Justice Rutledge, 92–93; Circuit riding, 55; Death, 120; Federal Common law crimes, 131, 133; 136; Grand jury charges by, 127, 131, 133, 136; Invalid Pensioners Act, 176–77; Judicial Review, 216–20, 222–25, 229–30; Newspaper essay by, 179 n.16; Opinions by, 99–100, 104, 169, 175 n.6, 176–77, 182, 188–89, 190–92, 196–97, 222–25, 227, 229–30, 235 n.50; States' sovereign immunity, 190–92
Izard, Ralph, 54, 90 n.48

Jay, John (Chief Justice): Assessment of, 248, 253; Biography of, 56–57; Declines reappointment 124; Dual office holding, 89–90, 181–82; Ex-officio duties, 174; Grand jury charges by, 1–2, 75–76, 127–28, 131, 173–74, 180, 248; Opinions by, 71–72, 74–75, 79–80, 175, 176, 176–77, 178, 178–79, 180, 182–83, 188, 196; Resigns, 90. See also Genêt, Edmond; Jay Treaty
Jay Treaty: 87–90, 101 n. 75, 135n 24, 152; Opposition to, 90–91,

97–98, 231. See also Treaty of Alliance
Jefferson Thomas: Federal common law crimes, 129, 131n 13, 135, 137, 162; Impeachment of Justice Chase, 129, 172; Relations with Britain and France, 74, 77, 87–88; Seeks advisory opinion, 78, 81–82. See also Chase, Samuel
Johnson, Thomas (Associate Justice), 62–63, 175 n.6, 177
Johnson, William Samuel, 65
Judicial Appointments. See U.S. Supreme Court Nomination Process
Judicial Compensation. See U.S. Supreme Court
Judicial Review: Discussions of, in ratification process, 19–22; Consensus on propriety of, 19–22, 215, 220–22, 243; Review of nonlegislative actions, 233; Review of state legislation, 187–88, 227; Theoretical justification of, 214–20, 232–33, 234, 237–38; "Unconstitutional Beyond Dispute," requirement of, 210, 222–27, 234, 238, 239. See also U.S. Constitution, Interpretation
Judiciary Act of 1789: Admiralty jurisdiction, 38–41; Conflicts with state courts avoided, 33–36, 50, 184–87; Ellsworth's committee, 27–29; Lower courts' jurisdiction, 41–47; Principal drafters, 27, 28; Supreme Court jurisdiction, 33–38; Trial by jury, 29–30, 37, 45–46, 107, 108; See also Madison, James; U.S. Courts' Subject Matter Jurisdiction; U.S. Supreme Court
Jury, Trial by: 106–09, 134, 167–69, 243; Distrust of, 11, 45–46, 101, 108–09, 168–69. See also Judiciary Act of 1789

King, Rufus. *See* Genêt, Edmond

Law, Richard, 50
Lee, Arthur, 68–69
Lee, Charles (U.S. Attorney General): 106–07, 108; Opinions by, 136–37, 242
Lee, Richard Henry, 28–30, 47–48
Legal Positivism, 2, 157, 192. *See also* Natural Law
The Leo (ship): 115–16
The Little Democrat (ship; initially *The Little Sarah*), 77–78
The Little Sarah (ship). *See The Little Democrat*
Livingston, Edward, 98
Livingston, Brockholst, 139
Locke, John, 217–18
Lowell (U.S. District Judge), 83–84

Madison, James: Attacks Sedition Act and federal common law crimes, 150, 156–57, 168; "Auxiliary Precautions" against abuse, 9, 11–12, 17, 18, 25; Constitutional interpretation, 232, 235; Drafting the Constitution, 9, 11–12, 17, 18, 25; Fails to oppose Judiciary Act of 1789, 50–51; Ratifying the Constitution, 4; Relations with Britain, 88. *See also* Madisonian Compromise
Madisonian Compromise, 12, 14, 15, 29, 43, 47
Majority Opinions. *See* U.S. Supreme Court
Mansfield, Lord, 132, 133, 137, 140, 141, 160
Marbois Affair. *See* De Longchamps, Chevalier
Marshall, John (Chief Justice): Becomes fourth Chief Justice, 125; Chiefly leadership, 111; Declines nomination as Associate Justice, 118; Federal common law, 153,

155; Opinions by, 36, 42, 122, 124, 202, 243, 247
Martin, Luther, 23, 24
Mason, George, 17, 29, 244 n.72
Mitchell, John, 163–64
Moodie, Benjamin: British vice consul in Charleston, 86, 112, 114, 115 n.109
Moore, Alfred (Associate Justice): Biography of, 120, 220–21; Assessment, 122, 220; Opinions and grand jury charges by, 122
Morris, Governeur, 17
Mortefontaine, Treaty of. *See* Treaty of Mortefontaine
Moultrie, William, 76
Murray, William Vans: Comments on Ellsworth, 96; Debate over Jay Treaty papers, 235; Minister to The Hague and France, 118

Natural Law: Contrasted to Legal Positivism, 2, 34, 157, 158; 192, 194; Importance of 2; Influence upon advisory opinions, 183; Influence upon *Chisholm v. Georgia*, 192–95; Influence upon Common Law Crimes, 136, 145, 146, 151–52, 157–58, 160, 251; Influence upon concepts of judicial bias, 195, 251–52; Influence upon constitutional interpretation, 236–39; Influence upon Judiciary Act of 1789, 34–36. *See also* Chase, Samuel; Legal Positivism.
Neutrality Crisis of 1793: 73–87, 128, 173, 178–79, 181. *See also* Genêt, Edmond
Neutrality Proclamation. *See* Proclamation of Neutrality
New Jersey or Paterson Plan. *See* U.S. Constitution, Convention of 1787
Nomination process, *See* U.S. Supreme Court Nomination Process

"Necessary and proper" Clause, *See* U.S. Constitution

Nicholas, Wilson Cary, 149–50

Nootka Sound Crisis, 71–22, 80, 178

Otis, Harrison, 148–49

Paca, William (U.S. District Judge), 83, 84n 31, 85n 35

Paterson, William (Associate Justice): Assessment of, 52, 164–65, 250, 251; Biography of, 64–65; Comments on relations with France, 118; Drafting the Constitution, 12–14; Drafting the Judiciary Act of 1789, 28, 32, 45, 49, 52, 53, 109; Grand jury charges by, 128, 163–64; Newspaper essays by, 179; Not nominated to be Chief Justice, 125; Opinions by, 99, 103–04, 121, 123, 136, 152, 216, 221, 226, 228–29, 230, 231, 236; Petit jury charge by, 164

Paterson or New Jersey Plan. *See* U.S. Constitution, Convention of 1787.

The Peggy (ship), 122 n.128

Peters, Richard (U.S. District Judge): Assessment of, 82, 164–65; Comments on Justice Chase, 147, 169–70; Opinions by, 82–83; 85, 146–47, 175 n.6, 177 n.11, 222–23

Petition in Error. *See* U.S. Supreme Court, Writ of error

The Phoebe Anne (ship), 114

Pickering, Timothy: Comments on Rutledge appointment, 91; Receives advisory opinion from Chief Justice Ellsworth on Sedition Act, 149, 179; Seeks advisory opinion from Chief Justice Ellsworth on sale of prizes, 116–17

Pickney, Charles: Submits plan at Constitutional Convention, 6–8; Declines U.S. Supreme Court nomination, 67

Portugal, 88

Potts, Richard, 63

Process Act of 1789. *See* Ellsworth, Oliver

Proclamation of Neutrality, 74–75, 131

Prizes. *See* Admiralty Jurisdiction

Privateers. *See* Admiralty Jurisdiction

Quasi-War: 118, 120–24

Randolph, Edmund (U.S. Attorney General): Advises President, 63, 64; Advocate, 189; Drafting Constitution, 6, 13, 14, 15, 16 n.26; Drafting Judiciary Act of 1789, 42–43; Drafting Neutrality Proclamation, 75; Federal common law crimes, 130–31, 135, 137–38; Opinions by 87, 130–31, 137–38; Report on Judiciary, 25, 43 n.28, 240–41

Ratifiers' Intent. *See* U.S. Constitution, Interpretation

Ravara, Joseph, 139–41

Rawle, William (U.S. Attorney), 132, 140, 143–44, 160

Read, Jacob, 93–94

Read, William, 90–91

Report on the Judiciary. *See* Randolph, Edmund

Revenue Collection. *See* U.S. Courts' Subject Matter Jurisdiction

The Roehampton (ship): 84 n.31

Rutherfurd, John, 200

Rutledge, Edward, 67

Rutledge, John (Chief Justice): Appointed Associate Justice, 54; Appointed Chief Justice, 91–92; Attacks Jay Treaty, 90–91; Attempted suicide, 95; Biography of, 57–58; Drafting Constitution, 10–12, 16; Resigns Associate Justiceship, 62; Resigns Chief

Justiceship, 95; Senate refuses to
confirm, 90–95

Sedition Act of 1798. *See* Federal
Criminal Law
Sedgwick, Theodore, 93; Drafting
Eleventh Amendment, 197, 201,
206–07
Separation of Powers. *See* U.S.
Constitution
Sergeant, Jonathan Dickinson, 135
Seriatim Opinions. *See* U.S. Supreme
Court
Sierra Leone, 137 n.27
Sherman, Roger: Drafting
Constitution, 11; Opinion by, 33,
37; Uses framers' intent, 231
Sinking Fund Commission, 174, 178
Sitgreaves, John (U.S. District Judge):
175 n.6, 182
Sovereign Immunity: *Chisholm* case,
188–97; Ratification of original
constitution, 210
Spain, 2, 43, 72, 162. *See also* Florida;
Nootka Sound Crisis
States. *See* Judicial Review; Sovereign
Immunity; U.S. Supreme Court
Story, Joseph (Associate Justice): 157,
186–87
Strong, Caleb: Drafting Eleventh
Amendment, 197–98, 199, 200,
201, 203, 206–08; Drafting
Judiciary Act of 1789, 28, 37n 20
Subject Matter Jurisdiction. *See* U.S.
Courts' Subject Matter Jurisdiction
Supremacy Clause. *See* U.S.
Constitution
Supreme Court. *See* U.S. Supreme
Court; U.S. Supreme Court
Nomination Process
Swift Doctrine. *See* Federal Common
Law
Swift, Zephaniah, On common law
crimes, 141–42; On Eleventh
Amendment, 200, 201, 211

Taylor, John, 89, 167
Tazewell, Henry, 94–95
Thomas, Joseph, 138–39
Tingy (Captain of *Ganges*), 120–21
Treaty Making Process, 97–98, 231–
32, 235, 246
Treaty of Alliance (with France), 73;
Impact of Jay Treaty upon, 115;
Rights of privateers, 75–82, 84, 87,
113–14, 115
Treaty of Mortefontaine, 124
Treaty of Paris: American obligations
under Article IV, 8–9, 30–31, 42,
43, 44, 46–47, 50, 52–53, 72,
98–101, 202–03, 246, 252;
American obligations under Article
VI, 199, 202–03, 208; Articles IV
and VI distinguished, 202–03;
British obligations under Article
VII, 9 72–73
Trial by Jury. *See* Jury, Trial by

U.S. Circuit Courts, 45–46. *See also*
Circuit Riding; U.S. Courts' Subject
Matter Jurisdiction
U.S. Constitution: Contract clause,
228–29; Ex post facto clause, 228–
30; Interim appointment clause,
91–92; Necessary and proper
cause, 148–49; Separation of
powers, 23–25, 79–80, 89–90, 119,
173–74, 181–83, 226; Supremacy
clause, 100, 187, 252; Tax clauses,
101–05, 236, 250; War powers, 100,
123–24, 250–51. *See also* Eleventh
Amendment; Federal Common
Law, Common law crimes; Judicial
Review; Madisonian Compromise;
U.S. Courts' Subject Matter
Jurisdiction; U.S. Supreme Court
Nomination Process
U.S. Constitution, Convention of
1787: Federal courts' subject matter
jurisdiction, 5–15; Judicial
appointments, 16–18; Judicial

U.S. Constitution, Convention of
1787 (continued)
tenure and compensation, 18–19;
Nonjudicial duties, 23–25; Paterson
Plan, 7, 13–14; Virginia Plan, 6–7,
9–10, 23; *See also* Judicial Review;
Madisonian Compromise; U.S.
Constitution, Interpretation
U.S. Constitution, Interpretation:
20–22, 227–30; Framers' intent,
230–34; 235–36; Judicial and
legislative interpretation contrasted,
231–34; Ratifiers' intent, 234–36;
Supraconstititional or natural law
principles, 236–39. *See also* Judicial
Review
U.S. Courts' Subject Matter
Jurisdiction: Alienage Jurisdiction,
7, 8, 45–47; Alien Tort Claims,
43–44; Amount in controversy,
46–47; Attempts to constrict,
10–14, 41–53, 243–49; British debt
cases: 8–9, 30–31, 33–34, 42, 44,
46–47, 50, 52–53, 72–73, 98–101,
246, 252; Compromises in the
Judiciary Act of 1789, 29–53;
Congressional control over, 12, 14,
15, 239–41, 243–46; Criminal
cases, 32, 44–45, 48, 49, 53;
Defined, 5–6; Diversity jurisdiction,
9, 45–47; Federal question or
"arising under" jurisdiction, 36,
42–45, 135–36, 143–44, 205–11;
International law cases, 7–9, 30–31,
213; Revenue Collection, 44,
48–49, 101–04, 108–09, 250; U.S.
Constitution, 5–15. *See also*
Admiralty Jurisdiction; Sovereign
Immunity; U.S. Supreme Court
U.S. District Courts, 44–45. *See also*
Admiralty Jurisdiction; U.S. Courts'
Subject Matter Jurisdiction
U.S. Mint, 174, 181
U.S. Supreme Court: Advisory
opinions, 75–82; Appellate
jurisdiction, 33–38, 45;

Compensation, 18–19, 98; Early
inactivity, 54–55; Jurisdiction,
congressional control over, 15,
33–38, 239–43, 245–46; Majority
and seriation opinions, 110–11;
Original or trial jurisdiction, 38,
188, 189–90, 199, 204, 223–25;
Review of state courts, 33–36, 50,
64, 184–88; Writ of error, 32 n.20.
See also Judiciary Act of 1789;
Judicial Review; U.S. Constitution,
Convention of 1787; U.S. Courts'
Subject Matter Jurisdiction; U.S.
Supreme Court Nomination
Process
U.S. Supreme Court Nomination
Process: Drafting the Constitution,
16–18; President Adams' criteria,
66, 117–18, 120, 124–25; President
Washington's criteria, 55–56,
63–64, 65–70, 97, 247–48;
Ratifying the Constitution, 17–18;
Role of Senate, 18, 54, 91–95. *See
also* Individual Justices, Biography
of; "Intrigue and cabal"; Rutledge,
John

Vans Murray, William. *See* Murray,
William Vans
La Vengeance (ship), 105–09
Vigol, Phillip, 163–64
Virginia Plan. *See* U.S. Constitution,
Convention of 1787

Walton, George, 94
War Powers. *See* U.S. Constitution
Warren, Earl (Chief Justice), 111
Washington, Bushrod (Associate
Justice): Biography of, 117–18;
Opinions by, 121–22, 226
Washington, George: Appoints Chief
Justice Jay to dual office, 87–90;
Comments on Arthur Lee, 68;
Comments on Patrick Henry, 69;
Comments on Samuel Chase, 70;
Comments on violations of

Treaty of Paris, 9; Leads army against Whiskey Rebellion, 163; Proposes national university, 231; Refuses request for Jay papers, 98, 231–32; Requests prize legislation, 84; Resorts to framers' intent, 231–32; Seeks advisory opinion from Chief Justice Jay, 71–72; Seeks advisory opinion from U.S. Supreme Court, 75–82; *See also* Supreme Court Nominations, Nootka Sound Crisis

Whiskey Rebellion, 163; Related legal issues, 105, 154–55, 163–65, 251

Wickham, John, 215

The William (ship), 82–83

Williams, Isaac, 152, 155

Williams, Otho, 39

Wilson, James: (Associate Justice): Biography of, 54, 60–61, 66; Assessment of, 60–61, 250; *Chisholm* case and natural law, 192–95; Conflicts of interest, 60–61, 195; Death, 117; Federal common law crimes, 131–32; Financial problems, 117, 250; Framing the Constitution, 12, 80; Grand jury charges by, 81, 131; Invalid Pensioners Act, 177; Judicial review, 215–16, 223–24, 243; *Lectures on Law*, 194, 216 n.4; Need for prize courts, 40–41; Opinions by, 102, 103–04, 175 n.6, 192–95, 215–16, 222–24, 241, 242–43; Petit jury charge by, 134–35

Wingate, Paine, 28

Wirt, William (U.S. Attorney General), Opinion by, 140 n.36

Writ of Error. *See* U.S. Supreme Court, Writ of error

Wolcott, Oliver, 50 Wolcott, Jr., Oliver, 31 n. 10, 91, 92

Worrall, Robert, 141–47

XYZ Affair, 148, 169

www.ingramcontent.com/pod-product-compliance
Lightning Source LLC
Chambersburg PA
CBHW020510270326
41926CB00008B/815